THE FABER BOOK OF SOCCER

by the same author

THE VISIT
A POETRY CHRONICLE
THE LITTLE MAGAZINES
ROBERT LOWELL: A BIOGRAPHY
FIFTY POEMS
IN SEARCH OF J. D. SALINGER
WRITERS IN HOLLYWOOD

The Faber Book of
SOCCER

Edited by

IAN HAMILTON

faber and faber

LONDON · BOSTON

First published in 1992
by Faber and Faber Limited
3 Queen Square London WC1N 3AU

Phototypeset by Intype, London
Printed in Great Britain by Clays Ltd, St Ives plc

© Ian Hamilton, 1992

Ian Hamilton is hereby identified as the
author of this work in accordance with Section 77
of the Copyright, Designs and Patents Act 1988.

A CIP record for this book
is available from the British Library

ISBN 0–571–14402–0

2 4 6 8 10 9 7 5 3 1

Contents

Introduction	1
Obituary: Death of the Right Honourable Game Football ANON.	5
The New Football Mania CHARLES EDWARDES	6
The Art of Captaincy JOHN DEVEY	12
Riot in Glasgow ANON.	15
Much More Terrible Than Guns ARNOLD BENNETT	21
The Last Defender VLADIMIR NABOKOV	23
The First Cup Final at Wembley, 1923 ANON.	24
The Off-sider DON DAVIES	28
Chapman's Arsenal DON DAVIES	30
Saturday in Bruddersford J. B. PRIESTLEY	35
The Sporting Spirit GEORGE ORWELL	37
Faith in Genius: Tom Lawton JOHN ARLOTT	40
Blackpool v. Bolton Wanderers: The Cup Final, 1953 PAUL GARDNER	43
Stanley Matthews JOHN ARLOTT	49
Stanley Matthews ALAN ROSS	54
The Fall of Willie Woodburn HUGH MCILVANNEY	56
The Match of the Century – I GEOFFREY GREEN	65
The Match of the Century – II ANON.	68
Inside Forwards FRANK NORMAN	75
Sunday Soccer JOHN MOYNIHAN	76
The Munich Disaster, 1958 GEOFFREY GREEN	86
What I Owe to Football ALBERT CAMUS	91
Danny Blanchflower BRIAN GLANVILLE	93
The George Eastham Case GEOFFREY NICHOLSON	111
Cock-a-Double-Do A. J. AYER	119
Bobby Charlton ARTHUR HOPCRAFT	122
Denis Law JOHN RAFFERTY	132
Turf Moor, and Other Fields of Dreams BLAKE MORRISON	134
Away HAROLD PINTER	144
The Soccer Conspiracy Case ARTHUR HOPCRAFT	146
The World Cup Final, 1966 HUGH MCILVANNEY	152

Mr Sugden BARRY HINES   157
George Best GEOFFREY GREEN   172
Even the Scots Had Tears in Their Eyes:
    The World Cup, 1970 HUGH MCILVANNEY   176
The Brazilians, 1970 HANS KELLER   181
Goalies FRANK KEATING   185
How We Taught the Turks the Meaning of Worship:
    Leeds in Turkey COLIN WELLAND   188
Three Managers BARRY NORMAN   191
Stuck In GORDON WILLIAMS   198
Pretty Bubbles SEBASTIAN FAULKS   211
A Present for the Wife: Tottenham in France HUNTER DAVIES   215
A Player's Diary EAMON DUNPHY   233
Jock Stein: A Hero Worshipped by His People
    HUGH MCILVANNEY   252
A Particularly Violent Day JAY ALLAN   257
'The White Nigger' DAVE HILL   270
The Long March from Vicarage Road: Watford in China
    MARTIN AMIS   278
Side by Side JAMES KELMAN   286
Liverpool v. Wimbledon: The Cup Final, 1988 DAVE HILL   292
Fanzines PHIL SHAW   295
World Cup 1990: A Diary KARL MILLER   312
Taking the City BILL BUFORD   317
Match of the Day MARTIN AMIS   328
The Same Old Thing PETE DAVIES   329
Acknowledgements   335

Introduction

In my local library there are as many books about bridge, coarse fishing and badminton as there are about association football. Soccer is notoriously a sport without much of a literature: unlike cricket or rugby, it has few links with higher education. The soccer-intellectual tends to treat soccer as an off-duty self-indulgence, like old movies or detective novels – it's a strictly trivial pursuit. And old soccer players rarely transfer with distinction to the press-box: for cricket's Mike Brearley we get David Sadler, of the *Sun*.

The small stock of soccer books at my library consists of coaching manuals, bumper compendia, club histories and 'as-told-to' star autobiographies – the run of these put together in a rudimentary prose aimed at the average tabloid punter. Indeed, most of their ghost-authors are in reality down-market sports-page hacks. The books themselves are short, heavily illustrated and generously margined and are not often sponsored by a mainstream publisher. 'Thinking' books about soccer, it is said, have no market because soccer fans don't think.

But soccer fans *do* think, and all the recent signs are that lots of them are getting fed up with the yob label. As Phil Shaw describes in his *Whose Game is it, Anyway?*, the hundreds of club 'fanzines' that have cropped up during the last decade are evidence of a new will to articulate that goes well beyond the terrace chant. So far, in most of these small publications, the language is more like a Vinny Jones late tackle than a John Barnes pirouette, but we don't need to be educationists to know why this is so. What's heartening about the fanzine movement is that it manifests energy in search of eloquence – and the character of that energy is not just impudent or grumpy. At its best, it really does seem to want to make imaginative sense of all those weird Saturday sensations.

As an anthologist, my aim is similar and I would like to have found in the fanzines material that was good enough to collect, that had more than local or potential merit. In ten or twenty years, who knows what some other anthologist might find? I have included one or two fan's-eye pieces where the content and the credible 'feel' of the thing seem to me to outweigh considerations of literary finesse, but actually I think I am of the wrong generation to sup too whole-heartedly of 'youth culture', however much I might sympathize with bits of it.

This book of soccer does have a documentary aspect – as perceived by someone in his early fifties. I have tried to make it cover British soccer's main historical ups and downs, with a slight leaning towards those that I've grown old with. I have included 'great matches', 'great players', 'great disasters', and I have moved chronologically forward from ribald material dating from the cigarette-card era to up-to-the-minute controversies about the sweeper system. I have also tried to depict some of the behind-the-scenes life of the game. Soccer fans, I know from conversation, are avid for inside dope and yet are strangely cut off from the secret workings of the clubs they follow. Most supporters' pub debate is stiff with rumour and counter-rumour, but you rarely hear much that sounds authoritative. Ex-players now and then tell all, but they do it in halting tabloid-speak. Their real habit is to stick together and stay mum – especially if they want to 'stay in the game' now that their 'careers' are over. The mere fan hardly ever gets down that dressing-room tunnel. In consequence, investigative-style reporters like Hunter Davies and Arthur Hopcraft are now thought of as 'classic' soccer authors (they are formally enshrined as such in a series put out by the excellent Sportspages publishing company), and when a real player like Eamon Dunphy opens up his pretty articulate diary for us, we are almost whimperingly grateful. The great soccer documentary has yet to be written, and we have heard enough (too much) from social anthropologists about 'the state of our national game'. What we really want is what all spectators want – more access.

Most good soccer writing of the past has been done by spectators, fans at heart: some of them, like John Arlott and Hugh McIlvanney, with a rare gift for celebratory rhetoric; others, like Brian Glanville and Geoffrey Green, able to season their sound reporting with a hint that they have once or twice enjoyed a peek behind the veil. These men have written about soccer for a living, hastily and against crazy deadlines, and it is greatly to their credit that several of the million or so words they have phoned through over the years do stand up to more than just nostalgic scrutiny.

Sports writing is mostly done by fantasists, by would-be practitioners, by 'could-have-beens'. John Moynihan, writing from bitter-sweet experience, is very good on this subject, and so too are Blake Morrison and Sebastian Faulks, and the few pieces of worthwhile soccer fiction I have been able to locate are similarly fuelled.

My own 'could-have-been' story takes several small-hours to relate, and I can't any longer remember how much of it is true. I can detect, though, as I look through the final contents of this book, an outline of my own fan-autopsy: early on, Glasgow Rangers and Scotland, an exile's passion sustained by my Scottish aunt's weekly mailings of the *Sunday Post*. I kept a Rangers scrapbook and dressed my Subbuteo men in blue but I'd only ever been to Ibrox twice. How was it that, pre-girls, the only time I ever got *that* dry in the mouth was when I heard the chap on the radio say, 'Scottish League, Division One'? It didn't last. After seeing the Spurs 'double' side of 1961 thrash Rangers at White Hart Lane, I discovered that I had corruptly switched my loyalty to Tottenham and – well, not to England, exactly, but to that handful of players that Spurs seem so good at getting hold of: players who are *too good* to fit happily into the England 'set-up': Greaves, Hoddle and now Gascoigne.

These, I confess it, are my hang-ups and, in compiling this panoramic football-fest, I swear that I have done my best to keep them under some sort of control. All the same, it will be pointed out, I'm sure, that I am readier to pay homage to Bertie Chapman than to Bertie Mee. Well, maybe so, but even impartiality has limits, does it not? On this at least, I'd guess, most soccer fans are likely to agree.

Anthologies usually owe something to their predecessors and I would like to make grateful mention of *The Footballer's Fireside Book* (1963), compiled by Terence Delaney, and *The Footballer's Companion* (1962), edited by Brian Glanville. My thanks also to David Barber of the Football Association Library.

Ian Hamilton
London, 1991

3

Obituary:
Death of the Right Honourable Game Football
ANON.

It becomes our painful duty to record the death of the Right Honourable Game Football, which melancholy event took place in the Court of Queen's Bench on Wednesday, Nov. 14th, 1860. The deceased Gentleman was, we are informed, a native of Ashbourn, Derbyshire, at which place he was born in the Year of Grace, 217, and was consequently in the 1643rd year of his age. For some months the patriotic Old Man had been suffering from injuries sustained in his native town, so far back as Shrovetide in last year; he was at once removed (by appeal) to London, where he lingered in suspense till the law of death put its icy hand upon him, and claimed as another trophy to magisterial interference one who had long lived in the hearts of the people. His untimely end has cast a gloom over the place, where the amusement he afforded the inhabitants will not soon be forgotten.

We cannot allow a calamity like the one we have detailed to pass over without giving publicity to circumstances proving so fatal in their results. It appears that the Honourable Game Football has long celebrated his birth in the most rational and peaceful manner, the tradesmen closing their shops, and the entire population turning out to take part in his festivity. The old custom was carried on from generation to generation, until it so happened that 'certain of the powers that be' determined that this harmless old custom should be done away with, and they accordingly issued a formal Notice that they intended riding *iron shod* over the town on Shrove Tuesday and Ash Wednesday, and any person causing any annoyance or interfering in any way with their authority would be dealt with according to *their* law. As the eventful day approached, great was the anxiety manifested as to whether these Distributors of Justice and Friends of Liberty would carry out their threat. Not long, however, were Mr. Football and his friends kept in suspense; sixty persons were more or less injured through their reckless determination, and the Right Honourable Gentleman, whose name we adore, received those fatal wounds from which he never recovered. Professional aid was at once obtained, a celebrated Practitioner recommended immediate removal to another district, giving the opinion that if the instructions laid down were strictly adhered to, the unfortunate victim would ultimately recover; but those who knew him best saw that his end was fast approaching. He died honoured and in peace.

The funeral was public, though without ostentation, and the expenses (£200) were subscribed by his surrounding friends. We understand that the Honourable Gentleman is succeeded by an only Son, a young man of Herculean strength, who inherits the valour of his Father, and his coming of age will be celebrated by Playing at the Old Game next Shrovetide.

The following epitaph will be found on the Hon. Mr. Football's Tombstone:

> May Liberty meet with success,
> May Prudence protect her from evil;
> But may tyrants and tyranny tine[1] in the mist
> And wander their way to the Devil.

[This was a handbill issued after a legal case brought to put a stop to the ancient street football game in Ashbourne, Derbyshire. The players lost the case, carried it to the Court of Queen's Bench, and lost again.]

Court Circular, 1860

The New Football Mania
CHARLES EDWARDES

The new football is a far more effectual arouser of the unregenerate passions of mankind than either a political gathering or a race meeting. No doubt at Epsom or Newmarket it is vexatious in the extreme when the favourite loses five times in succession in one afternoon. But the British public controls itself fairly well under these trying circumstances. At a modern football match between, let us say, two League

1. Kindle.

6

teams, it is a distinct point that the players are human beings, with sensibilities much on a par with the sensibilities of the spectators. These latter are well aware of the fact. And it is by playing loudly upon their sensibilities that the spectators endeavour to incite their darlings to strain every nerve to win. However, the gain of one side is the loss of the other. You are jubilant, while your neighbour uses language not to be found in grammars for the use of schools. It all depends upon the measure of civilization in your locality whether there is or is not a good deal of fighting after the match. Of drinking it may be taken for granted that there is abundance. In all our large towns, and most of the small ones, north of Birmingham to the Tweed, from September to April, Saturday is consecrated to football. Saturday evenings are devoted to football symposia, and the newspapers issue special editions one after the other, with from three to four columns of reports and gossip about the results of the day's games and the players.

There is no mistake about it: the exercise is a passion nowadays and not merely a recreation. It is much on a par with the bull fight in Spain or the ballet in France. A spirit of adamantine intention pervades it. No matter what the weather, a League fixture must be fulfilled. And no matter what the weather, there will always be found a number of spectators enthusiastic enough to be present at the game. Thrice during the last season, the writer witnessed matches in violent snowstorms; and on one of these occasions, with snow and slush ankle deep on the ground, the downfall was so severe that a layer of more than an inch of snow accumulated on the shoulders and hats of the enthusiasts, who were packed so closely together that they could not move to disencumber themselves. You would have thought they were all possessed of some sovereign preventive of the many diseases that proceed from simple catarrh. Yet, of course, such was not the case. Probably more than one of them was fast asleep in his grave ere the match of the ensuing Saturday.

It is something else as well as a passion. It is a profession. This of itself would be enough to explain the very remarkable energy of modern football. In other professions, if a man is bent on pre-eminence, with its various rewards of lucre and public estimation, he must strive hard to attain it. I will not add that he must not be too scrupulous about the means he employs for his purpose, though this is a common belief. Nor is it different in football. It depends upon

7

the vigour, craft, and strength of the player whether he is worth 2*l*., 3*l*., or 4*l*. a week during eight months of the year. To the old-fashioned votary of amateur football this will seem a very lamentable state of affairs. Yet it is not thought so in the North, though in the far North (Scotland) professionalism as it now exists in England is still under taboo. Nor do the players themselves consider that they are degraded by their vocation of making sport for the British Saturday afternoon. Indeed, no. It is quite otherwise. In their respective neighbourhoods they are the objects of the popular adoration. They go to the wars in saloon carriages. Their supporters attend them to the railway station to wish them 'God speed,' and later in the evening meet them on their return, and either cheer them with affectionate heartiness, or condole with them and solace them with as much beer as their principles (that is, their trainer) will allow them to accommodate. They are better known than the local members of Parliament. Their photographs are in several shops, individually and grouped. The newspaper gives woodcuts of them and brief appreciative biographical sketches. Even in their workaday dress they cannot move in their native streets without receiving ovations enough to turn the head of a Prime Minister. But their honest heads are not easily turned. They go their way and survive their banquets of hebdomadal applause and flattery with a stolidity that argues them well-knit mentally and of excellent tough digestions.

They are marketable goods and they are not ashamed. Why, it may be asked, need they be ashamed of it? Every man has his price, we are told by a great authority. Nor can the fell innuendo which attended this saying when it was uttered be applied to the modern professional football player. Whatever he may not be, he is bound to be thorough. The Club Committee who have bought him will stand no shilly-shallying, no trimming about the ball in merely dilettante fashion. As for the spectators, they would come within a hair's-breadth of assassinating him if they got an inkling that he was playing them false. Modern football may not be an immaculate form of 'sport,' but, in spite of one or two rumours, it seems irreproachably 'straight'.

If it be an advantage to see ourselves as others see us, the accomplished professional football player will not be expected to resent being catalogued and described on the agent's list much as if he were a bull of highly reputable lineage. It is the agent's aim to minister to the young man's self-esteem. Not directly, of course. He

8

may not be very sound of wind, or he may have a small varicose vein, but the agent will not be bound to mention these slight defects any more than the auctioneer, who sells a fine piece of Dresden china, is compelled to whisper his suspicion that it sounds a bit cracked somewhere.

The football agent numbers his clients and advertises them. This is how he portrays them:

Nos. 154 and 155. – Goalkeepers, two champions, second to none in England; the name of either is a sufficient record; both are respectable, steady young men. One is 6 feet high, 13 stone weight, 23 years of age, and smart as a bee; fears nothing; is a regular stone wall against a charge, and a most consistent and earnest player. The other is a League player in one of the very best teams, and his superior cannot be found; he has played in nearly all the principal matches of his club during the present and last seasons. Both these men have decided to change . . . Terms 3*l*. per week and 40*l*. bonus each.

Again:

No. 163. – Right or left full back. This is one of the most likely youngsters I have ever booked. He gives reference to a well-known pressman, who has repeatedly seen him play, and knows what he can do, and has a high opinion of his abilities and future prospects. Just note – height, 5 feet 11 inches; weight, 12 stone; age, 20. There's a young giant for you . . . this is a colt worth training.

The above may suffice. Considering the hundreds of good teams of football which are, nowadays, throughout the land, there seems really a lucrative opening for the smart mediator between players and committees. The business is, however, in its babyhood as yet. Some think the wages of professional players, though to gentlemen in other professions already they do not seem much amiss, will rise much higher than they are at present. It really is to be hoped they will not, or else football matches will be as expensive a pleasure as an international 'box'. But if they do, it will be a great temptation for the sons of middle- and upper-class families to try the career. Existing professionals do not describe themselves as gentlemen. When we find paid teams of the most promising graduates of our Universities touring the land like the trained players of the lower classes, then professional football may claim to be at its zenith. But we are not at present within a calculable distance of such proceedings.

It is quite odd to see how strongly the people in League districts are smitten by the football fever. Many old people and women are so caught by it that they would not, on any ordinary account, miss a local match. They may be seen, too, wedged in the crowd of youths and young men who patronize the excursion trains to fields of combat 50 or 100 miles from home. There must be a special Providence for them, or else they become extraordinarily hardened by exposure. I know a blind man who is regularly conducted to the football field, and works himself up into as hot a state of eagerness as his neighbours.

This poor gentleman follows the game with his ears. To some of the rest of the spectators in certain parts of the country it would be a positive convenience if they could, on the other hand, during the match, suspend their faculty of hearing, as well as their sense of smell. The multitude flock to the field in their workaday dirt, and with their workaday adjectives very loose on their tongues. In Lancashire and the Black Country it is really surprising what a number of emphatic and even mysterious expletives may be heard on these Saturday afternoons. Some of them are, however, remarkably unpleasant and not fit for a lady's ears, even to the remotest echo.

The players themselves may be supposed largely deaf to the shouts and even abuse which they excite. They are not wholly so; but they have a knack of discriminating between the flippant and the earnest. Their supporters often forget themselves in the ferocity of their cries. 'Down him!' 'Sit on his chest!' 'Knock their ribs in!' are invitations often addressed to them, and in no playful mode be it understood.

But, as a rule, they keep their tempers wonderfully well. They know that the referee has extensive powers to punish any deeds done on the field 'of malice prepense', and modern football legislation is a very real thing indeed. A player who is suspended for intentional rough play is wounded in the pocket, and he feels it.

It is ludicrous to see how boys of a very tender age get possessed of a frenzy at some of these matches. Their cries to the players are not a whit less turbulent than those of their elders, though they do not carry so far; and certain of them forget themselves in a way that would bring upon them the high displeasure of their nurses at home. At Bolton, last October, a youngster was observed to burst into tears because the referee gave a decision against the home team. It was at Bolton, too, that a worthy town councillor, who chanced to die during the football season, was, at his dying request, carried to the grave by four of the team. Like many other of the Lancashire manufacturing towns, Bolton is not at all a pretty place. But it has a talent for football, and a particularly 'soft' field, which in wet weather almost engulfs players who are not used to it.

It is hard to prophesy about the future development of the game. Already professional football is in full swing for eight months out of the twelve. Nor is this enough for some people. They grumble loudly when the milder, yet equally national, game of cricket asserts itself. Cricket is slighted as tame and flat compared to football. The interest is too attenuated. Better a furious thrill for an hour or so than the protracted gentle pleasure of the bats and stumps.

This, however, seems unreasonable. During the dog days one does not require furious thrills. They are a deal too inflammatory.

There are plenty of Timons abroad who regard the existing football mania among the people as a very bad symptom. 'It's ruining the country. The young men talk of nothing else. Their intellect all goes into football. They can't do their work properly for thinking of it. Never saw such a state of affairs in my life. The lower middle and the working classes may be divided into two sets: Fabians and Foot-ballers, and, 'pon my word, it's difficult to say which is the greater nuisance to the other members of society.' These words from one antipathetic to excitement in any form may not carry much force, but they are typical.

At present, however, the tide is with the game: every September proves it. Our mob politicians have a very fine catch-word in the phrase 'A free breakfast table and football gratis', if they like to use it in our provincial manufacturing towns. The Government audacious enough to promise serious consideration to such a programme would meet with an astonishing amount of support.

Who knows? The incidents of civilization may repeat themselves in this particular, as in so many others.

from The Nineteenth Century, October 1892

The Art of Captaincy
JOHN DEVEY

[John Devey captained Aston Villa against West Bromwich Albion in the last Cup Final played at Kennington Oval, on 12 March 1892.]

The captain should be the mouthpiece of the team; it is necessary for the welfare of the players and of the club generally that he should be their mouthpiece, for, after all, the interests of players and committee are identical. The captain should be proud of his men; and the men should be proud of their captain. They should look up to him. It is not necessary that the captain should be chosen merely because he is a hard worker, and yet that is in the case of many clubs the basis of selection. It is important that the captain should be able to set an example to his men in this respect, but it may happen that he is not physically fitted to outshine all his rivals in respect of hard work. A man may be a great captain and yet lack the power to rank as the greatest worker. You play a captain for the manifestation of his brain power; it is conceivable that a man may be invaluable as a captain when he is no longer the most sprightly member of the eleven.

You want the office of captain to be invested with a certain sense of dignity. The captain should be the brainiest man in the eleven; he should be looked up to by both management and players alike.

A captain should never be dictatorial; he should strive to obtain a community of interest among the players under his charge. It is not a bad thing for a captain to go to a man and say, 'Now, you use me as your tool. We should all be tools to one another; all should be tools in turn. Every time you have the ball and cannot get away with it, I am there to help you out of a difficulty; use me as your tool. If I have the ball, you be my tool.'

An indifferent captain is better than several captains on the field. Nothing is more disastrous than a conflict of authority. The captain should be in sole control; and no one should venture to usurp his prerogative. I believe in a captain consulting his players. You may agree with their conclusions or not, but I believe in soliciting their opinions. If your ideas are strengthened as the result of an interchange of opinion, well and good; if the result is in the opposite direction, then no harm has been done. It may be that things have been presented to you in quite a different light to that in which you had previously viewed them. At the same time, it is gratifying to all the men to know that their opinion has been asked. It is a nice feeling for the youngest man in the team to think, 'He appreciates my opinion, although I am the youngest player on the side.' He feels flattered, and will play better football if he thinks his skipper is interested in him than he would if he held the idea that he was regarded as a mere cypher in the team.

We want to look deep down into football; there is too much surface watching done. If we look right into the science of football – and it is a more wonderful science than most people think – we can detect deep schemes. The spectators may not see them – nay, they cannot see them. The captain has to watch the game most critically. He sees, perhaps, at a certain time that his opponents have the run of the ball. He has to bring every ounce of intelligence to bear upon the process of staving off the daring and impetuous attacks which are being made upon his position. He has to counteract those attacks, and it often happens that if he does so diplomatically he converts his side from one which is being overrun into a winning team. Just when the tide is flowing against his side, he grasps the situation, and then we see an example of defensive combination. The inside-forwards silently fall back and help the halves, but the two outside men and the centre are ever ready to dash off and, maybe, find a weak place in the opposing defence. They do not waste their energies; they conserve them, but they keep the other defenders playing all the time while the hostile forwards are working at twice the pace that a vanguard normally does. But the defence is so systematic that the whirlwind attack gradually dies away, and then the side which has been content to remain on the defensive gradually raises the siege, and it becomes their turn to attack. The game is won, but few of the crowd can do full justice to the tactics which made victory probable.

I can recall many occasions in the seasons when Aston Villa won the League championship when diplomacy won us games in which our opponents were excessively dangerous. We would be occupied in resisting impetuous attacks when suddenly one of our men would get off; in would come a flying centre, the ball would come to John

Campbell, he would send in one of his brilliant shots, and the whole position would be changed. We seldom received the credit for this to which we were entitled; it was not realized that we were following a carefully thought-out plan of campaign; sometimes we were told that we had scored 'a lucky goal'. There is more method in some of these lucky goals than some of the critics realize. You have all watched games in which one side has manifested infinitely more devil for a given period than they have shown in any other portion of the match. It is the captain's duty to watch the play of his opponents during that period, and if he can cope with it he will have broken the backbone of that team. Indifferent captaincy at such a time would probably mean a lost game; and yet the position of captain is one which many would treat lightly!

By the exercise of discretion the captain may train his men to promptly interpret the word he may utter, or any action he may go through in the form of signalling. When danger threatens, a motion of the arm may send back both inside-forwards to strengthen the half-back line, and the casual onlooker marvels at the manoeuvre. It is the science of the game, and a captain who has studied football from all its offensive and defensive bearings is able to take advantage which the moment may suggest. But first-class players do what is required naturally; it is part of their football education to watch how the game is going.

It is not essential that all the instruction should come from the captain; indeed, it is far better that the men, following the advice of their skipper, should institute a system whereby exchange of thought can be readily understood. Secret signalling in this sense is invaluable, and it has seldom been carried into effect with more striking result than in the case of the famous Preston North End eleven which carried the country by storm in consequence of the unison with which they worked.

Another important function which devolves upon the captain is the correction of any misapprehension which may exist as the outcome of injudicious criticism from the crowd. The tendency of spectators is to judge a player by exactly what catches the eye. A captain who knows what's what should lay himself out to correct disparagement from the onlookers by offering personal encouragement to the player concerned.

A captain should make a point of encouraging the players on every possible occasion. He should try, too, to study the individual temperaments of all the men under his care. It is here that the complexity of a captain's work lies. He has ten players to deal with, and there may be ten altogether different temperaments among them. There is the hot-headed player; he is an easy man to manage, because you get at the bottom of him at once. Then you have the sulky player; he is a very different individual to deal with; you never get at the bottom of him. Still, an encouraging word is not often wasted, even on the sulkiest of players. Football brings out a man's characteristics very pronouncedly. If you see a man sticking closely to the ball and never giving his colleagues a chance, you may rely upon it that that man is a selfish man off the field. If, on the other hand, you come across a player who is ready to do anything for you, and delights in making openings for you, you may depend upon it that he is good-tempered and unselfish.

But whatever a man is, you have to so shape your conduct as to get the best out of him. After all, we are ruled by our temperaments. Sometimes a man can master his temperament, but oftentimes it is too strong for him.

from *The Book of Football*, 1906

Riot in Glasgow
ANON.

Glasgow, which holds the record for football disasters, was on Saturday afternoon and evening the scene of a riot which will take rank as one of the most disgraceful blots disfiguring the annals of the game. The finalists in the competition for the Scottish Cup are the Celtic and Rangers, Glasgow clubs which on 10 April drew with two goals each. The replay took place yesterday on the ground of the Queen's Park at Hampden, Mount Florida, and again the teams drew, on this occasion with one goal each. At the close of the game the spectators incensed at the decision not to play an extra half-hour, and thus resolve the destiny of the Cup, broke all bounds, and a riot ensued, in which the police and the mob came into prolonged conflict, with the most serious consequences. The scene is described as resembling that of a battlefield; and after the long-drawn mêlée, the horrors of which were heightened by the action of the crowd in setting fire to all the combustible material on which they could lay their hands, it was found that no fewer than sixty people were on the official list of casualties, suffering from injuries, in some cases of a dangerous nature. This list does not include many who were attended on the field without being sent to the Infirmary or dealt with officially. The number of the unknown injured is computed at a figure equal to that of those known, which brings the final casualty list to considerably over a hundred.

Saturday afternoon was beautifully fine, and a crowd of spectators estimated at between 60,000 and 70,000 persons was attracted to Hampden Park, which occupies a romantic site on the outskirts of the city, generally included by antiquaries as part of the historic battlefield of Langside. The rivalry between the teams is of the keenest nature, and the crowd, as is usual on such occasions, was divided into two camps whose excitement rose to the highest pitch when, at the close of the play of an hour and a half's duration, the teams were level. It seems to have been generally understood that in the event of a draw on this occasion the contest would be fought to a finish with an extra half-hour's play. In the official police report it is stated that after the referee had blown his whistle announcing the finish, the members of the Celtic team remained on the field, thus heightening the prevailing impression. The members of the Rangers team quitted the pitch, however, and their example was followed shortly afterwards by their opponents. Strong in their preconceived belief, the majority of the spectators retained their positions for some time, although many thousands took their departure.

Meantime the Football Association had decided that the game would not be renewed, and an intimation to this effect was made. Keen dissatisfaction prevailed among the crowd, and protests were heard on many hands, culminating in threats and an outbreak of disorder among the more rowdy elements. The first overt action which resulted in the lamentable scene of the day was the invasion of the playing pitch by a number of the dissatisfied onlookers, their evident intention being to proceed to the dressing-rooms, whither the players had retired. A considerable force of police were, of course, on the ground, and they naturally endeavoured to keep the crowd in order, and to induce them to leave the field peacefully. What actually first led to a collision between the police and the civilians is at present matter of the most conflicting opinion. Soon, however, the mob were venting their rage on the police force, who were subjected to a fusillade of stones, bottles, brickbats, and every conceivable missile of which the roughs could become possessed. Overwhelmed and swept aside by superior numbers, the police rallied, and endeavoured to cope with their assailants. To this end they were forced to use their batons, and shortly they were engaged in a hand to hand conflict. The gravity of the situation became apparent when a number of the policemen were seen to have sustained such injuries that they were rendered prostrate, and had to be carried off the field.

It would be impossible adequately to describe the many cruel incidents which went to make up a riot now proceeding in almost every quarter of the field. Stricken men fell with blood streaming from their wounds, and the rage and tumult became more intense. Many of the police were beaten and injured in the most brutal and callous fashion, and the force as a whole were the chief sufferers of the day. It was generally remarked that those of the crowd most active in the disturbance were composed of the most degraded section of the community, the self-respecting portion having as far as possible retired when the character of the fray became apparent. Thousands, however, who would gladly have quitted the scene, now found it impossible to leave, since those outside were massed at the exits, and outlet was a matter of great difficulty. Maddened by excitement, and relying on their overwhelming numbers, the rioters now proceeded to the extremest limits. The goalposts were attacked and uprooted, the nets torn to pieces, and the woodwork round the enclosure broken down to be used as weapons against the police. Acting with commendable patience and restraint, the police force, who were shortly reinforced by the arrival of reserves from almost every district in the city, persevered in their attempt to clear the ground. A number of mounted men were found to be of great assistance; but the mob took a malicious delight in surrounding the horsemen, and endeavouring to force them to dismount.

They beat man and horse most unmercifully, and in some cases the man was pulled to the ground. Not only had the police to persist in their own work of overcoming the mob, but they had to protect and rescue each other. Where a solitary policeman was trapped he was dealt with in the most outrageous manner, and it is little wonder that rumour had it that several of them had been killed.

The objective of the rioters, as has been indicated, was evidently the dressing-boxes of the players, but the police force were successful in repelling the attack. It was soon obvious, however, that new outlets for the prevalent passion had been found. Quantities of the broken barricading were collected, piled in a heap, and ignited. Quite a number of the crowd were in possession of bottles containing whisky, and they were actually seen to pour the fluid on the broken timber in order to aid its quicker ignition. Soon a huge bonfire was in progress, fed by fuel brought from every possible quarter. Attention was next directed to the pay boxes at the north-west entrance, and they were also soon a mass of flame. It was found necessary to summon the Fire Brigade, who arrived on the scene shortly after six o'clock. The defenceless firemen were on their arrival maltreated in similar fashion to the police, and at least one of them, John Kennedy, of the Queen's Park Division, was seriously injured. He is suffering from a number of broken ribs. When the firemen attempted to set to work their hose-pipes were seized and thrown into the flames. Others, which were brought into position, were cut and hacked at with knives. Stones, bottles, and the other available missiles were hurled at the firemen, who of course were quite unable to defend themselves. Ultimately they succeeded in extinguishing the fire, but not before very considerable damage was done.

When all the reserves had been hurried up from the district police offices, there would be about 200 constables on the field, including about sixteen horsemen. The difficulty was to drive the crowds up the slopes surrounding the pitch, and the method adopted was to force them out of the ground in batches. But long before comparative order had been restored, the casualty list had reached appalling proportions. A number of medical men who happened to be present set themselves devotedly to the work of attending to the injured. These gentlemen included two doctors, Jamieson, father and son, and Dr. D. M'Ardle, of Stothill Hospital. Later they were reinforced by assistance from the Victoria Infirmary, which is situated in the neighbourhood. Ambulance waggons were summoned, and, after being temporarily attended to, the sufferers were conveyed to the Victoria Infirmary. One of the injured was attended at the Royal Infirmary, which is several miles distant. The spectacle presented in the football pavilion and neighbourhood, where the medical work was proceeding, resembled nothing so much as what one would picture occurring in the heat of a battle. Numbers of men were being brought in in an unconscious condition, suffering from wounds in the fight and, in some instances, from the crushing which occasionally took place.

It would be about ten minutes past five o'clock when the football match finished, and an idea of the prolonged character of the riot will be gained when it is stated that order was not restored until half-past seven. Gradually the police effected a clearance of the pitch and its environs, but not before the field had been reduced to a wreck. At one time a section of the crowd tore up and down the field with a road roller, cutting the ground badly, and committing every damage in their power. With the exception of the pavilion and the Press box, all the other erections were damaged or wrecked by fire or assault. The police stationed outside the barricading had their hands as full as those inside. When the unruly roughs were ultimately ejected from the field they remained in great crowds outside, and continued the fusillade of brickbats. Not a piece of glass escaped which could be reached by stones, and the crowd exhibited a delight in wreaking their revenge on the persons of the police and firemen and in the destruction of the property of the club. Fortunately they were unaware that the Football Association officials were occupants at the moment of rooms in Somerville Place, on the opposite side of the street from the main entrance to the park. These gentlemen had in their possession drawings to the amount of £1,400, and were also guarding the Scottish Cup, which would have been awarded to the victor of the game. It may be mentioned that among the spectators of the day was Captain Gilman, prospective Unionist candidate for East Renfrewshire. His duty would have been to hand the Cup to the successful team, had the game not been drawn.

Among the minor incidents of the day was the exhibition of the craze for souvenirs. The cross-bar of one of the goalposts was carried from the field into Somerville Road in front of the burning pay-boxes, and a crowd of men and boys hacked at it with pocket-knives and pocketed the chips. Among the *débris* littering the ground were a number of policemen's helmets, which had been lost in the day's struggle. These were also the objective of the souvenir-hunter, being cut into strips and carried away.

Needless to say the district was in a condition of seething excitement during the course of the unfortunate affair. The windows in Somerville Drive, which overlook the ground, were crowded with people, who followed the progress of the events with nervous dismay. Thousands of those who had attended the match left as it was concluding, and were totally unaware of what subsequently occurred. Many, however, who would otherwise have proceeded home with the utmost dispatch hung about the vicinity to watch the spectacle. Not till the evening journals issued their late editions was the city apprised of the riot. The news created an interest comparable only to that aroused by the occurrence of the great Ibrox Park disaster, at which hundreds of people were injured and over twenty killed. The magnitude of Saturday's mêlée was exaggerated by rumour, and it was confidently asserted that several of the injured had succumbed. Fortunately there has been in no case a fatal result, and such an eventuality is not anticipated. Only five of the injured are detained in Victoria Infirmary, although the case of the fireman Kennedy is probably as serious as any.

Curious to relate, only one man was arrested in the course of the outbreak. He has been lodged in the Queen's Park Office, and will be brought up today on a charge of assaulting a policeman and a soldier. It is stated that a plain-clothes constable obtained the assistance of the soldier to effect the arrest. The police were, of course, practically powerless in the matter of apprehensions. Instances are recorded of rioters being taken into custody, but so savagely were the police handled that they were forced to let go their quarry.

All day yesterday crowds of people flocked to Mount Florida to view the scene. Overnight there were posted on the ground thirty constables in case of the eventuality of the return of the mob. A force of police still guarded the ground yesterday, and the public were rigidly excluded from it. Early in the morning the services of a number of joiners had been requisitioned, and the barricading and shattered gates set to rights as much as possible. Notwithstanding their exertions, however, the place presented a sorry sight. All the woodwork at the Somerville Drive entrances had been burned away or remains charred, and what is left is a mass of torn, twisted or bent galvanized iron. The enclosure itself is a litter of stones and broken bottles and scarred patches where the fire has been at work. All the public lamps in the vicinity have been smashed. Only the roughest estimate can be obtained of the amount which will be required to set the place to rights, but £800 is considered a moderate figure. Interesting questions as to liability must arise. It may be confidently expected that many different claims will be lodged.

The question of a replay of the game will be discussed at a meeting of the Football Association to be held in Glasgow this evening.

The Scotsman, 1909

Much More Terrible Than Guns
ARNOLD BENNETT

We went on the Grand Stand, which was packed with men whose eyes were fixed, with an unconscious but intense effort, on a common object. Among the men were a few women in furs and wraps, equally absorbed. Nobody took any notice of us as we insinuated our way up a rickety flight of wooden stairs, but when by misadventure we grazed a human being the elbow of that being shoved itself automatically and fiercely outwards, to repel. I had an impression of hats, caps, and woolly overcoats stretched in long parallel lines, and of grimy raw planks everywhere presenting possibly dangerous splinters, save where use had worn them into smooth shininess. Then gradually I became aware of the vast field, which was more brown than green. Around the field was a wide border of infinitesimal hats and pale faces, rising in tiers, and beyond this border fences, hoardings, chimneys, furnaces, gasometers, telegraph-poles, houses, and dead trees. And here and there, perched in strange perilous places, even high up towards the sombre sky, were more human beings clinging. On the field itself, at one end of it, were a scattered handful of doll-like figures, motionless; some had white bodies, others red; and three were in black; all were so small and far off that they seemed to be mere unimportant casual incidents in whatever recondite affair it was that was proceeding. Then a whistle shrieked, and all these figures began simultaneously to move, and then I saw a ball in the air. An obscure, uneasy murmuring rose from the immense multitude like an invisible but audible vapour. The next instant the vapour had condensed into a sudden shout. Now I saw the ball rolling solitary in the middle of the field, and a single red doll racing towards it; at one end was a confused

21

group of red and white, and at the other two white dolls, rather lonely in the expanse. The single red doll overtook the ball and scudded along with it at his twinkling toes. A great voice behind me bellowed with an incredible volume of sound:

'Now, Jos!'

And another voice, further away, bellowed:

'Now, Jos!'

And still more distantly the grim warning shot forth from the crowd:

'Now, Jos! Now, Jos!'

The nearer of the white dolls, as the red one approached, sprang forward. I could see a leg. And the ball was flying back in a magnificent curve into the skies; it passed out of my sight, and then I heard a bump on the slates of the roof of the grandstand, and it fell among the crowd in the stand-enclosure. But almost before the flight of the ball had commenced, a terrific roar of relief had rolled formidably round the field, and out of that roar, like rockets out of thick smoke, burst acutely ecstatic cries of adoration:

'Bravo, Jos!'

'Good old Jos!'

The leg had evidently been Jos's leg. The nearer of these two white dolls must be Jos, darling of 15,000 frenzied people.

Stirling punched a neighbour in the side to attract his attention.

'What's the score?' he demanded of the neighbour, who scowled and then grinned.

'Two – one – agen – uz!' The other growled. 'It'll take our b—s all their time to draw. They're playing a man short.'

'Accident?'

'No! Referee ordered him off for rough play.'

Several spectators began to explain, passionately, furiously, that the referee's action was utterly bereft of common sense and justice; and I gathered that a less gentlemanly crowd would undoubtedly have lynched the referee. The explanations died down, and everybody except me resumed his fierce watch on the field.

I was recalled from the exercise of a vague curiosity upon the set, anxious faces around me by a crashing whooping cheer which in volume and sincerity of joy surpassed all noises in my experience. This massive cheer reverberated round the field like the echoes of a battleship's broadside in a fjord. But it was human, and therefore much more terrible than guns. I instinctively thought: 'If such are the symptoms of pleasure, what must be the symptoms of pain or disappointment?' Simultaneously with the expulsion of the unique noise the expression of the faces changed. Eyes sparkled; teeth became prominent in enormous, uncontrolled smiles. Ferocious satisfaction had to find vent in ferocious gestures, wreaked either upon dead wood or upon the living tissues of fellow-creatures. The gentle, mannerly sound of hand-clapping was a kind of light froth on the surface of the billowy sea of heartfelt applause. The host of the 15,000 might have just had their lives saved, or their children snatched from destruction and their wives from dishonour; they might have been preserved from bankruptcy, starvation, prison, torture; they might have been rewarding with their impassioned worship a band of national heroes. But it was not so. All that had happened was that the ball had rolled into the net of the Manchester Rovers' goal. Knype had drawn level.

from *The Matador of the Five Towns*, 1912

The Last Defender
VLADIMIR NABOKOV

Of the games I played at Cambridge, soccer has remained a windswept clearing in the middle of a rather muddled period. I was crazy about goal keeping. In Russia and the Latin countries, that gallant art had been always surrounded with a halo of singular glamour. Aloof, solitary, impassive, the crack goalie is followed in the streets by entranced small boys. He vies with the matador and the flying ace as an object of thrilled adulation. His sweater, his peaked cap, his kneeguards, the gloves protruding from the hip pocket of his shorts, set him apart from the rest of the team. He is the lone eagle, the man of mystery, the last defender. Photographers, reverently bending one knee, snap him in the act of making a spectacular dive across the goal mouth to deflect with his fingertips a low, lightning-like shot, and the stadium roars in approval as he remains for a moment or two lying full length where he fell, his goal still intact.

But in England, at least in the England of my youth, the national dread of showing off and a too grim preoccupation with solid teamwork were not conducive to the development of the goalie's eccentric art.

23

This at least was the explanation I dug up for not being oversuccessful on the playing fields of Cambridge. Oh, to be sure, I had my bright, bracing days – the good smell of turf, that famous inter-Varsity forward, dribbling closer and closer to me with the new tawny ball at his twinkling toe, then the stinging shot, the lucky save, its protracted tingle . . . But there were other, more memorable, more esoteric days, under dismal skies, with the goal area a mass of black mud, the ball as greasy as a plum pudding, and my head racked with neuralgia after a sleepless night of verse-making. I would fumble badly – and retrieve the ball from the net. Mercifully the game would swing to the opposite end of the sodden field. A weak, weary drizzle would start, hesitate, and go on again. With an almost cooing tenderness in their subdued croaking, dilapidated rooks would be flapping about a leafless elm. Mists would gather. Now the game would be a vague bobbing of heads near the remote goal of St John's or Christ, or whatever college we were playing. The far, blurred sounds, a cry, a whistle, the thud of a kick, all that was perfectly unimportant and had no connection with me. I was less the keeper of a soccer goal than the keeper of a secret. As with folded arms I leant my back against the left goalpost, I enjoyed the luxury of closing my eyes, and thus I would listen to my heart knocking and feel the blind drizzle on my face and hear, in the distance, the broken sounds of the game, and think of myself as of a fabulous exotic being in an English footballer's disguise, composing verse in a tongue nobody understood about a remote country nobody knew. Small wonder I was not very popular with my team-mates.

from *Speak, Memory*, 1966

The First Cup Final at Wembley, 1923
ANON.

BOLTON WANDERERS 2 WEST HAM UNITED 0

The Bolton Wanderers beat West Ham United in the Cup Final at the Wembley Stadium on Saturday by two goals to none.

This bald statement represents the result of the football side of a matter which has been discussed from many points of view for months.

The fact that the Wembley Stadium has been advertised as the greatest of its kind had much to do with the enormous crowd which came from all sorts and conditions of places to see the first Cup Final to be played there. The claims made for the Stadium were not in the slightest degree extravagant. It was built to hold 125,000 people in comfort and to give to each and every one of that huge total a fair view of the football ground and track. The Stadium can hold even more than that number, and yet give to all the spectators a fair view, but no building and ground could accommodate 300,000 people, and at least that number must have turned up on Saturday at Wembley.

The reasons for the mammoth congregation were many. The opening of the Stadium for the first Cup Final might become – as in fact it has become – an historic occasion. There was the fact that a London club were in the Final Tie; the day was perfect; and, by the irony of fate, the superb organization of the many police. The Bolton Wanderers were leading at the time by one goal to none, having scored in the first two minutes; but, five minutes before the second interruption, West Ham United had nearly equalized, Watson missing a chance which he would have taken with absolute certainty on an ordinary occasion.

Taken merely as an Association Football match, the play at Wembley on Saturday was rather disappointing. No doubt, the long wait and the doubt as to the possibility of the game being finished, even if begun, had an effect on players already keyed up to a high state of tension. To win a Cup-tie medal is preferred, by quite a many, to winning an international cap. West Ham United had not only been preparing to win the Cup, they had also, if possible, to force their way into the League Championship next season. The double event has proved beyond their powers, but they certainly deserve promotion on the season's play. They were a good side for the first ten minutes of the great final, but, afterwards, they were never convincing. When the sun was against them in the first half both the backs and the half-backs kicked too high and too hard. In the second half, when the sun was shining in the faces of the Bolton Wanderers' defence, the high kicking, followed by a rush, with all the forwards in something like a line, might have proved extremely good tactics. The Bolton Wanderers' backs and half-backs, however, seldom had to use their heads for safety in the second half. The game was started at a great pace, and the Bolton Wanderers scored after just two minutes' play. Nuttall dribbled up the field, half drew a man, and passed perfectly to Jack. Jack took the ball along slowly and feinted to pass out to Butler; when the pass looked as good as made, he dribbled inside to the left, went through the West Ham United defence at a great pace and scored from close in with a hard high shot into the right-hand corner of the net. Hufton could strike only at the direction in which he hoped the ball would take, and he cannot be blamed for letting the ball pass him. Three minutes later came the great chance for West Ham United to equalize. Pym, misjudging a perfectly taken corner by Ruffell, came out of goal and missed the ball. The ball came to Watson, who had an open goal yawning only a few yards in front of him. How he managed to kick the ball over the cross-bar instead of into the net one cannot imagine; if a player tried to do it, the odds against him would be generous. Watson, however, did fail to score.

West Ham United were every bit as good as their opponents until the second stoppage of play occurred. Even when the match was continued the crowd were actually on the touch-line and sometimes over it. The West Ham United outsides never showed confidence near to the crowd; one was reminded constantly of the speech of the Maltese Cat on the subject of crowding in Rudyard Kipling's wonderful polo story, called after the great pony.[1] Now Vizard seemed to enjoy the human wall which marked or obliterated the touch-line. On an ordinary day Bishop might have held him; in the circumstances his mentality was at fault, for which he is scarcely to blame. Richards made one brilliant dribble and break through for West Ham United and Pym fumbled a clever shot, though he eventually cleared comfortably. A little later a beautiful centre by Vizard was headed just wide by J. R. Smith. Bolton Wanderers continued to attack, and J. R. Smith scored from a clever centre from Butler. J. R. Smith was ruled offside, although he appeared to be well behind the ball when it was kicked. The Press Stand, however, is some distance in mere yards from the field of play, and the angle was not easy to judge. Until half-time Bolton Wanderers were always the more dangerous combination, and, but for the magnificent game which Henderson played at right full-back, they would probably have scored again on at least one occasion.

The teams did not leave the field at half-time – if they had done so, the match would not have been finished on Saturday – but crossed

1. 'The Maltese Cat'; see Rudyard Kipling, *Selected Stories*, ed. Andrew Rutherford, Penguin, 1987, p. 271.

over and resumed play after a five-minutes' interval. West Ham United began the second half well, and Watson had a good chance from a centre of Kay's, the centre-half having worked out on to the wing with a clever individual effort. Watson, however, misjudged the flight and direction of the ball and did not start for it in time. Pym saved two shots quietly and confidently and then came the movement that settled the result of the match. Vizard niggled the ball down the wing, very close to the touch-line. Suddenly he kicked and ran, passed Bishop and centred right across the goal mouth. J. R. Smith got to the ball and shot immediately. The ball hit the inside of the cross-bar and bounced out again into play. It was, however, a goal and the referee had not the slightest hesitation in ruling it as such. Even before this goal was scored a rivulet of spectators were leaving the ground; now this rivulet swelled to a steady stream. The match, to all intents and purposes, was over.

Bolton Wanderers, on the day's play, were always the better side after the first ten minutes. They did not realize the hopes of the big contingent of their supporters, whose Saga, after the second goal was scored, 'One, Two, Three, Four, Five,' was repeated mechanically and at brief intervals until the finish. Seddon, the Bolton Wanderers centre-half-back, carried off the honours of the match. He called the tune to his side, and generously they piped. All of them could be picked out for good work, at times for brilliant work; but the other ten would be the first ten to award merit where merit was due, and would fasten on Seddon as the ultimate winner of the F.A. Cup.

At the finish of the match the King presented the Cup to J. Smith, the captain of the Bolton Wanderers, and the medals to the different players. He drove away amidst a scene of heartfelt enthusiasm.

| Bolton Wanderers: | Pym; Howarth, Finney; Rowley, Seddon, Jennings; Butler, Jack, Smith (J. R.), Smith (Joseph) (captain), Vizard. |
| West Ham United: | Hufton; Henderson, Young; Bishop, Kay (captain), Tresadern; Richards, Brown, Watson, Moore, Ruffell. |

The Times, 1923

The Off-sider
DON DAVIES

William McCracken was an Irish International right-back and a storm centre of his generation. He was a specialist in off-side tactics and as such was the cause of more demonstrations of hostility and resentment than any other player before or since. He had the same demoniac qualities as Spofforth,[1] the same ability to get on players' nerves, and his sardonic smile as he went about his disruptive task could rouse passions to fever-heat. Being an Irishman, he naturally took a deep delight in that most of his playing time was spent in twisting the tails of British players. Being an artist he played sixteen times for Ireland and nigh on twenty seasons in one of the most illustrious club sides of all time, Newcastle United of the early 1900s. As a zealous student of Association football as well as one of its foremost practitioners he applied all the resources of a keen mind to the problems of defensive strategy with such success in off-side moves that in his day he could reduce the cleverest forward line to a rabble of hesitant and bewildered units.

That McCracken, though widely respected as an individual and always feared as a player, was not exactly a universal favourite is understandable. Who but a snake charmer would fall in love with a serpent? It was his province as a setter of off-side traps of unwonted slickness and cunning to jolt his contemporaries out of their conventional ruts and make them substitute adaptability and resource to rule of thumb; to force them to realize that the only antidote to subtlety and deceit was even greater subtlety and deceit. In short, he made them think, and that has never been a popular mission. Crowds flocked to watch him, composed mainly of angry and prejudiced men, and few there were who had the patience to acknowledge the beauty of McCracken's technique in the abstract. All they saw was a player whose phenomenal mastery over a defensive mood could repeatedly disrupt and arrest a game, the smooth rhythmic ebb and flow of which

1. Frederick Robert Spofforth (1853–1926), Australian cricketer; known as 'The Demon', he took 14 English wickets for 90 runs in the 'Ashes' test at the Oval in 1882.

was its greatest charm; matches in which McCracken appeared usually degenerated into dull repetitions of tiresome infringements and stoppages. Tempers frayed and angry scenes developed. On one occasion at Hyde Road McCracken teased and tormented the Manchester City forward line to such purpose that the crowd felt obliged to intervene.

Where McCracken outstripped all his rivals was in his ability to judge his opponent's intentions correctly and to time his counterstrokes effectively. Until he retired no one arose who could match his superiority in that. It followed that in all the furious disputes in the 1920s (and there were many), concerning the desirability or otherwise of changing the off-side law,[2] a step which seemed inevitable as the only means of freeing forwards from the shackles which defences were increasingly putting upon them, McCracken's name was cited and remains so to this day as that of the arch-criminal. But even McCracken could not play for ever and by the early 1920s his appearances were growing rarer; Caspar's work was done, or very nearly. Before the door closed finally on his career and he hung up his boots for the last time there could be heard, like the roll of revolutionary drums, the unceasing clamour for revision growing stronger and stronger, until in 1925 even the great W. I. Bassett lent his name to the popular cry for reform.

At a meeting in London on 15th June, 1925, the F.A. adopted by the necessary two-thirds majority the 'Two-for-Three Scheme' as it was called. Thus the old law which had stood untouched since 1866 (except for its limitations to one half of the field in 1907) was scrapped, mainly, as men thought, through the perverse genius of an Irishman who loved to meddle in British affairs. Not for the first time in our island story was a decision made which seemed to penalize those who used their brains in order to make things easier for those who either could not or would not use theirs. Off-side traps, even as perfected by McCracken, could still be sprung by forwards who had the wit to hold the ball and dribble well ahead of their colleagues before making their passes. But that was a new idea and [as] has been well said, 'there is nothing so painful to human nature as the pain of a new idea,' particularly when, as in this instance, it involved the abandonment of conventional rule-of-thumb methods and the substitution of creative thought.

2. Before 1925, the rule was that an attacker would be 'onside' if *three* defenders (including the goalkeeper) were between him and the goal.

By the middle of the 1925–6 season, the first under the new rule, it appeared as though the earthly paradise had indeed arrived, for all, that is, except the poor goalkeepers. Forwards everywhere kicked over the traces, and scoring became fantastic. Seven league matches alone produced a crop of sixty-four goals in one afternoon! But amid general rejoicing, when Sunderland, for example, were averaging five goals per match, and centre forwards like David Halliday were running amok, a certain Yorkshire club, Hull City, was seen to be oddly stubborn in its refusal to conform to the prevailing fashion of giving away goals like largesse; on the contrary, it was making scoring so difficult that in the first five matches of the season not a single goal had been scored against it. Chilly doubts again assailed observers. Not McCracken again, surely! But facts were facts and soon the alarming rumour spread, later confirmed by eye-witnesses, that the enterprising coach, critic and tactical adviser to the Hull City Football Club was none other than our old friend the Irish Mephistopheles, William McCracken, as ever a peerless defender in his own day, still adding cubits to his stature as the game's arch-obstructionist. Thoughtful men peered into the future with alarm and misgiving. The ghost was still walking.

from Jack Cox, Don Davies – 'An Old International', 1963

Chapman's Arsenal
DON DAVIES

On the 15th June 1925 in London the Football Association formally adopted the new off-side rule passed by the F.I.F.A. in Paris two days before. On the same day Mr Herbert Chapman signed his first contract for manager of Woolwich Arsenal F.C. Two events which few connected at the time but which were to react strongly on each other and profoundly influence the development of British soccer in the next twenty-five years. Herbert Chapman sat down to organize football much as a business magnate settles down to organize profits. In his view, every device used by the industrialist to speed up the production of goods could be used equally well to speed up the production of goals.

Specialization? The Arsenal team became a household word as a group of specialists whose tasks were outlined for them with a clarity never before envisaged. Functionalism? Was there ever a team where the players were more strikingly suited to the parts they had to play? Up-to-date machinery? Champman left no stone unturned to get the best football machine brains could devise or money could buy. Salesmanship? None knew better than Chapman how to market his ideas, whether to his directors, who were cozened by his ready tongue, to his players, who had faith in his keen tactical insight, or to his competitors, who were only too willing to follow the lead of a manager who appeared able to harness success to his very chariot wheels. Publicity? There never was a manager either before or since who could use publicity more skilfully, or guide it more surely for his own ends.

Within three months of taking up his new post Chapman had the country buzzing with excitement and controversy over his fanciful deal with Sunderland for Charles Buchan's transfer, £2,000 down and an additional £100 to be paid to the Sunderland club for every goal scored by Buchan during his first season with his new club! What did this portend? An innocent essay in payment by results, a fresh approach to incentives, or some dark web of financial jiggery-pokery? The public at large seemed inclined to accept this imaginative stroke at its face value, but those in high places felt there was a catch somewhere and placed a ban on all such future transactions, but not before Chapman had got what he wanted, an inside forward of real genius to lead his attack, and a wealth of nation-wide publicity. To him the purely financial aspect was a minor consideration. Chapman teased and cajoled the London Underground Railway Company into changing the name of the station nearest the new stadium at Highbury from 'Gillespie Road' to 'Arsenal', thus enabling him to use the railway as an advertising medium as well as a transport convenience for the swelling crowds. One can imagine the reaction of the public at large. 'Must be a wonderful club this. Got a station of its own now. Never been known before.' By these and similar devices Chapman kept the Arsenal club constantly in the public eye.

If ever it could be said that the hour produced the man, that surely was true of 1925 when Chapman began his stewardship at Highbury. The immediate effect of the new off-side rule had been to throw British football into the melting pot. All the existing notions of strategy

31

and tactics had to be scrapped. Age-old dispositions in the field had to be reconsidered; attacking centre half-backs, once the fiery hotspurs of any tussle, were now out-worn conventions. The old concept of five forwards moving up-field in line abreast with three half-backs in close support, a manoeuvre of unforgettable beauty as carried out by teams like Aston Villa or Newcastle United of the Golden Age of football, had to be discarded ruthlessly. Ca'canny, that paralysing curse of industry, was creeping into our football fields; defences henceforth must stay curiously at home separated from their own forward lines by wide stretches of no-man's land, across which new lines of communication had to be charted. A new monster, a veritable headache for centre forwards, was slowly evolving, the 'stopper' centre half-back or third full-back. A new orientation was being given the duties of wing-halves; these galley slaves no longer shadow their wing-men but must guard the route to goal in mid-field, and keep up a constant shuttle service between a withdrawn defence and a remote attack. They were in fact key men and were to need speed, resource, ball control and an iron stamina equal to that of the most accomplished forward if they were to attempt to fulfil their manifold tasks.

Behind these must operate two full-backs big enough to resist the heaviest challenge, fast enough to overtake opposing wing-men, yet mobile enough to be always at hand when the need arose for mutual cover. The tempo of the game as a whole had quickened considerably and the speed of thought required to meet the changing contingencies had quickened also. It goes without saying that in this period of revolutionary change the acute mind of Herbert Chapman was in its element. No one foresaw more clearly than he did the glittering prizes that awaited the first manager who could evolve from the seething fermentation of new ideas some definite strategic plan. Because of the notoriety of 'Policeman' Roberts as the most successful, at any rate, of the first stopper centre half-backs, Chapman is often wrongfully credited with inventing this effective device. Actually the idea was tried out by Newcastle United at Villa Park as early as September 1925, and there is reason to believe that Andrew Cunningham of Glasgow Rangers was advocating its adoption even before that. But where Chapman scored was that he was the first to realize that it was not enough to pay lip-service to the new practice by making positional changes with existing playing staffs. To extract the maximum benefit from the new tactical arrangements it was essential that every single player in the team should be a specialist of his own field. Backs must be tall, fast and powerfully built, like Male and Hapgood, with the stopper centre half-backs all topping the lot; wing-halves, too, like Crayston, must be physically well-endowed unless, like Copping, they had the bite in their tackling, which made up for lack of inches. Wingmen must be flyers and deadly shots, as 'Joe' Hulme and Bastin; centre forwards must be bustlers or battering rams with the shoulders of a Lambert or Drake; inside forwards, astute and cunning, and adept at veiling impending moves. Was ever a pair more happily blended, yet more strikingly contrasted, than James and Jack? That such men were ferreted out, and, once found, were induced to throw in their lot with Arsenal, was a tribute at once to the discernment, tact and bargaining power of this Metternich among football managers. His willingness to spend with a bold prodigality also helped.

Other aspiring managers before Herbert Chapman, and since, have tried short cuts to success by spending lavishly on brilliant individualists, only to find that personal vanities, petty rivalries and unreasoning jealousies have ruled out that one indispensable requisite of team success, internal harmony. It is the measure of Chapman's mastery of the art of handling men that his glittering assortment of richly endowed but widely diverse footballers from Wales and Scotland, Lancashire and Yorkshire, from the Home Counties and the Western Region, all blended together and played for years with the close-knit unity and the dedicated sense of a special mission that marked Cromwell's Ironsides. It was inevitable, too, that a team so essentially the product of one mind should have a marked personality of its own; it drew crowds like a magnet. Football lovers everywhere flocked to see these cool exponents of the new strategy, experts so sure of the strength and skill of their superb defence that they deliberately and ever so artfully fell back on the defensive, and positively invited attack for fully 80 per cent of every match in which they played. Years went by before opponents rumbled that this falling back was voluntary and not compelled, that it was a vital part of an overall plan to lure opponents further and further away from the close protection of their own goal, since, as Chapman calculated, the further Arsenal's opponent could be lured down-field the more scope there was for Hulme's tear-away speed and Bastin's opportunism.

How often on provincial grounds has one seen the redoubtable Arsenal apparently scrape home by a solitary winning goal after spend-

33

ing four-fifths of the game seemingly fighting with backs to the wall? With what a nicely simulated air of alert watchfulness and dogged determination would Arsenal defy the headlong attempt of the 'Johnnie Raws' to storm their bastions until the time was ripe and the situation apt for the crucial counter-attack! Then would come the long ball driven to the remote right wing and with a capacious swerve on it to elude the opposing back. Followed a flash of Hulme's heels, a swift low cross to the opposite wing and there would be the ice-cool Bastin leisurely picking his spot. In the 1932–3 season Arsenal scored 118 goals and of these Hulme (20) and Bastin (33) claimed 53 from the wings. This James–Hulme–Bastin cross-field manoeuvre was one of the boldest and deadliest match-winning moves of its time, and owed as much to the restraint with which it was used as to the skill and cunning with which it was executed.

It has fallen to few managers to leave as great an imprint on the football of his time as Chapman. In the nine years between signing a contract as manager and his sudden death in 1934, Arsenal won four First Division championships and figured in three F.A. Cup Finals, an impressive record for a club which had not before tasted such sweets. Small wonder that legends grew up round the personality of this smiling, urbane, far-seeing Yorkshireman, who appeared to have the Midas touch in everything he did. His contemporaries fell over themselves in their eagerness to follow his example, which did not disturb him in the least, for he knew that without the unique specialists whom he had so shrewdly cornered in advance, his tactical plan would prove a snare and a delusion. Chapman knew that players of exceptional talent are always in short supply; how many of his rivals were likely to find another winger as fast as Hulme, another master of feint and swerve to compare with Jack, another schemer as subtle as James, hiding his quick brain beneath a purposely assumed cloak of slovenliness and leaving his partner, Bastin, to fend for himself on the wing? Bastin, yes, was Kipling's footballer 'the cat that walked by himself and all places were alike to him'; without such types his rivals would find themselves clamped down under a system far too burdensome for them, pinning their faith on the system and not on the peculiar gifts of the players who had to make it work. So Chapman could afford to sit back and watch their struggles with quiet amusement; like the skipper of the *Mary Gloucester*, he had sufficient confi-

34

dence in his own ability and inventiveness to keep well ahead of his challengers:

> They copied all they could follow, but they couldn't copy
>   my mind,
> And I left them sweating and stealing a year and a half behind!

Chapman's nine years at Highbury passed quickly in a swirl of creative activity, for he was never so happy as when experimenting with something new. But not all his brainwaves were received cordially. He must have been a thorn in the flesh to some who had to adjudicate on the merits of novel ideas (as they were then) such as floodlit football, forty-five-minute clocks, goal judges, numbered jerseys, white balls, rubber pitches, limits to transfer fees, schemes to do away with the relegation bogey and so on. There seemed no end to the fellow's interfering ways and inventiveness! Why couldn't he let well alone? Time has shown how many of Chapman's suggestions, spurned at first, have since been incorporated into our national winter game; the absurdities of yesterday have become the commonplace of today. When death struck him down Chapman was striving to repeat his other field triumphs and coax Arsenal along to three First Division championships in a row. Two of these had already been safely garnered and the players who followed him to his grave saw to it that the third was duly gathered in. Only thus could they fittingly acknowledge the immense debt of gratitude which they owed to their lost leader, a man whose vision, enterprise and originality had given them the widest scope for their talents and had led them triumphantly from obscurity to fame.

from Jack Cox, Don Davies – 'An Old International', 1963

Saturday in Bruddersford
J. B. PRIESTLEY

Something very queer is happening in that narrow thoroughfare to the west of the town. It is called the Manchester Road because it actually leads you to that city, though in order to get there you will have to climb to the windy roof of England and spend an hour or two with the curlews. What is so queer about it now is that the road itself cannot be seen at all. A grey-green tide flows sluggishly down its length. It is a tide of cloth caps.

These caps have just left the ground of the Bruddersford United Association Football Club. Thirty-five thousand men and boys have seen what most of them call 't'United' play Bolton Wanderers. Many of them should never have been there at all. It would not be difficult to prove by statistics and those mournful little budgets (How a Man May Live – or rather, avoid death – on Thirty-five Shillings a Week) that seem to attract some minds, that these fellows could not afford the entrance fee. When some mills are only working half the week and others not at all, a shilling is a respectable sum of money. It would puzzle an economist to discover where all these shillings came from. But if he lived in Bruddersford, though he might still wonder where they came from, he would certainly understand why they were produced. To say that these men paid their shillings to watch twenty-two hirelings kick a ball is merely to say that a violin is wood and catgut, that *Hamlet* is so much paper and ink. For a shilling the Bruddersford United A.F.C. offered you Conflict and Art; it turned you into a critic, happy in your judgment of fine points, ready in a second to estimate the worth of a well-judged pass, a run down the touch line, a lightning shot, a clearance kick by back or goalkeeper; it turned you into a partisan, holding your breath when the ball came sailing into your own goalmouth, ecstatic when your forwards raced away towards the opposite goal, elated, downcast, bitter, triumphant by turns at the fortunes of your side, watching a ball shape Iliads and Odysseys for you; and what is more, it turned you into a member of a new community, all brothers together for an hour and a half, for not only had you escaped from the clanking machinery of this lesser life, from work, wages, rent, doles, sick pay, insurance cards, nagging wives, ailing children, bad bosses, idle workmen, but you had escaped with most of your mates and your neighbours, with half the town, and there you were, cheering together, thumping one another on the shoulders, swopping judgments like lords of the earth, having pushed your way through a turnstile into another and altogether more splendid kind of life, hurtling with Conflict and yet passionate and beautiful in its Art. Moreover, it offered you more than a shilling's-worth of material for talk during the rest of the week, a man who had missed the last home match of 't'United' had to enter social life on tiptoe in Bruddersford.

from *The Good Companions*, 1928

The Sporting Spirit
GEORGE ORWELL

Now that the brief visit of the Dynamo football team[1] has come to an end, it is possible to say publicly what many thinking people were saying privately before the Dynamos ever arrived. That is, that sport is an unfailing cause of ill-will, and that if such a visit as this had any effect at all on Anglo-Soviet relations, it could only be to make them slightly worse than before.

Even the newspapers have been unable to conceal the fact that at least two of the four matches played led to much bad feeling. At the Arsenal match, I am told by someone who was there, a British and a Russian player came to blows and the crowd booed the referee. The Glasgow match, someone else informs me, was simply a free-for-all from the start. And then there was the controversy, typical of our nationalistic age, about the composition of the Arsenal team. Was it really an all-England team, as claimed by the Russians, or merely a league team, as claimed by the British? And did the Dynamos end their tour abruptly in order to avoid playing an all-England team? As usual, everyone answers these questions according to his political predilections. Not quite everyone, however. I noted with interest, as an instance of the vicious passions that football provokes, that the sporting correspondent of the russophile *News Chronicle* took the anti-Russian line and maintained that Arsenal was not an all-England team. No doubt the controversy will continue to echo for years in the footnotes of history books. Meanwhile the result of the Dynamos' tour, in so far as it has had any result, will have been to create fresh animosity on both sides.

And how could it be otherwise? I am always amazed when I hear people saying that sport creates goodwill between the nations, and

1. The Moscow Dynamos, a Russian football team, toured Britain in the autumn of 1945 playing against leading British clubs.

that if only the common peoples of the world could meet one another at football or cricket, they would have no inclination to meet on the battlefield. Even if one didn't know from concrete examples (the 1936 Olympic Games, for instance) that international sporting contests lead to orgies of hatred, one could deduce it from general principles.

Nearly all the sports practised nowadays are competitive. You play to win, and the game has little meaning unless you do your utmost to win. On the village green, where you pick up sides and no feeling of local patriotism is involved, it is possible to play simply for the fun and exercise: but as soon as the question of prestige arises, as soon as you feel that you and some larger unit will be disgraced if you lose, the most savage combative instincts are aroused. Anyone who has played even in a school football match knows this. At the international level sport is frankly mimic warfare. But the significant thing is not the behaviour of the players but the attitude of the spectators: and, behind the spectators, of the nations who work themselves into furies over these absurd contests, and seriously believe – at any rate for short periods – that running, jumping and kicking a ball are tests of national virtue.

Even a leisurely game like cricket, demanding grace rather than strength, can cause much ill-will, as we saw in the controversy over body-line bowling and over the rough tactics of the Australian team that visited England in 1921. Football, a game in which everyone gets hurt and every nation has its own style of play which seems unfair to foreigners, is far worse. Worst of all is boxing. One of the most horrible sights in the world is a fight between white and coloured boxers before a mixed audience. But a boxing audience is always disgusting, and the behaviour of the women, in particular, is such that the army, I believe, does not allow them to attend its contests. At any rate two or three years ago, when Home Guards and regular troops were holding a boxing tournament, I was placed on guard at the door of the hall, with orders to keep the women out.

In England, the obsession with sport is bad enough, but even fiercer passions are aroused in young countries where games playing and nationalism are both recent developments. In countries like India or Burma, it is necessary at football matches to have strong cordons of police to keep the crowd from invading the field. In Burma, I have seen the supporters of one side break through the police and disable the goalkeeper of the opposing side at a critical moment. The first big football match that was played in Spain about fifteen years ago led to an uncontrollable riot. As soon as strong feelings of rivalry are aroused, the notion of playing the game according to the rules always vanishes. People want to see one side on top and the other side humiliated, and they forget that victory gained through cheating or through the intervention of the crowd is meaningless. Even when the spectators don't intervene physically they try to influence the game by cheering their own side and 'rattling' opposing players with boos and insults. Serious sport has nothing to do with fair play. It is bound up with hatred, jealousy, boastfulness, disregard of all rules and sadistic pleasure in witnessing violence: in other words it is war minus the shooting.

Instead of blah-blahing about the clean, healthy rivalry of the football field and the great part played by the Olympic Games in bringing the nations together, it is more useful to inquire how and why this modern cult of sport arose. Most of the games we now play are of ancient origin, but sport does not seem to have been taken very seriously between Roman times and the nineteenth century. Even in the English public schools the games cult did not start till the later part of the last century. Dr Arnold, generally regarded as the founder of the modern public school, looked on games as simply a waste of time. Then, chiefly in England and the United States, games were built up into a heavily-financed activity, capable of attracting vast crowds and rousing savage passions, and the infection spread from country to country. It is the most violently combative sports, football and boxing, that have spread the widest. There cannot be much doubt that the whole thing is bound up with the rise of nationalism – that is, with the lunatic modern habit of identifying oneself with large power units and seeing everything in terms of competitive prestige. Also, organized games are more likely to flourish in urban communities where the average human being lives a sedentary or at least a confined life, and does not get much opportunity for creative labour. In a rustic community a boy or young man works off a good deal of his surplus energy by walking, swimming, snowballing, climbing trees, riding horses, and by various sports involving cruelty to animals, such as fishing, cock-fighting and ferreting for rats. In a big town one must indulge in group activities if one wants an outlet for one's physical strength or for one's sadistic impulses. Games are taken seriously in London and New York, and they were taken seriously in Rome and Byzantium: in the Middle Ages they were played, and probably played with much physical brutality, but they were not mixed up with politics nor a cause of group hatreds.

If you wanted to add to the vast fund of ill-will existing in the world at this moment, you could hardly do it better than by a series of football matches between Jews and Arabs, Germans and Czechs, Indians and British, Russians and Poles, and Italians and Jugoslavs, each match to be watched by a mixed audience of 100,000 spectators. I do not, of course, suggest that sport is one of the main causes of international rivalry; big-scale sport is itself, I think, merely another effect of the causes that have produced nationalism. Still, you do make things worse by sending forth a team of eleven men, labelled as national champions, to do battle against some rival team, and allowing it to be felt on all sides that whichever nation is defeated will 'lose face'.

I hope, therefore, that we shan't follow up the visit of the Dynamos by sending a British team to the USSR. If we must do so, then let us send a second-rate team which is sure to be beaten and cannot be claimed to represent Britain as a whole. There are quite enough real causes of trouble already, and we need not add to them by encouraging young men to kick each other on the shins amid the roars of infuriated spectators.

from *Tribune*, 14 December 1945

Faith in Genius: Tom Lawton
JOHN ARLOTT

Saturday the 26th January 1952 was a cold, grim day in London. Arsenal and Chelsea were both playing interesting fixtures at home, but old memories drew me to Shepherd's Bush where, on a frost-bound pitch covered by a thin layer of snow, Queen's Park Rangers were playing Notts County. It was not, by normal standards, an attractive match. The local team were having a bad spell, as clubs unable to pay large transfer fees are always likely to have while they are waiting for their young players to develop.

At centre-forward for Notts County, however, was Tommy Lawton – formerly of Burnley, Everton and Chelsea – now some three seasons past his day as England's centre-forward, but, with England still strikingly failing to find his successor, still a nostagically regretted figure of the game, and the hub of some great footballing memories. Genius, in any field, is always rewarding to watch and, of the thousands of good, and scores of outstanding footballers that the last twenty years of the game have shown us, a bare dozen may be said to have had utter genius for the game and to fit the adjective 'great'. Lawton is one of those few, or had been when I saw him last. That game, I recalled on my way to that match, had been an international, his last.

Should I, I wondered, even at the last minute, turn away, go to another match, even to a theatre? Should I be disappointed: was it fair to smear the memory of greatness by watching the same man being less than himself? I have faith in genius: I went in.

Lawton was not, it seemed, disposed to break his neck on the hard surface. Some less-than-accurate passes came somewhere near him but he barely noticed them. He was never one to tear his heart out in chasing kicks he could not catch, and I have sometimes suspected that he regarded some of the football played round him with impatience. Football was, I am sure, such a natural process with him that he was irritated by the errors of others: it was, perhaps, that he could not conceive of a footballer being unable to think the right thing or unable technically to perform it.

There is, I reflected, a time in the thirties when the body, to protect its bones as they become more brittle, rebels against the attempts of the brain to drive it into danger. A shot fired at the Queen's Park Rangers' goal cannoned out: Lawton was waiting for it, as precisely placed as if he had been told in advance what was to happen: almost lazily, and with utter certainty, he placed it firmly into the net and turned away unmoved.

There was, perhaps, no need to be the great Lawton? On such a surface, was it, for him, necessary only to wait for the mistakes which would give him goals? There were, indeed, some touches of the great Lawton one remembered. He was being marked by Spence, formerly a good Portsmouth reserve to those two fine centre-halves, Flewin and Froggatt. Spence is a young player, fit, well made, tall, strong in the tackle, with height in the climb, a reliable header of the ball and, in general, a calm and sound defender. Several times Spence, covering Lawton closely, went up for a ball, and Lawton, when he challenged, would let Spence begin his leap and then, starting later, go higher and win the duel, to tap the ball smartly from that smoothly greased head to the feet of a colleague. He strolled on those heavily muscled legs into the right positions and, once there, performed deftly and with ridiculous ease the movements necessary to turn or assist the ball to the point where a fellow forward might most effectively use it.

The second half began. Two or three good balls from Lawton's head created opportunities which were not used. There was a brilliant run by Frank Broome – who seems to lose little of his legendary speed with years – which suddenly lit up the afternoon. It may also have put Lawton on his mettle. Crookes, his outside-left, made ground down the wing, moved inside and pushed the ball hard and square towards Lawton just outside the Rangers' penalty area. Lawton swung his body as if to move across to the right with the ball. The opposing defenders, to a man, moved the same way and, suddenly, while they were still moving, like some diagram of counter-stresses come to life, Lawton was moving in the opposite direction. Seeming to dig his feet into that false surface like a man climbing up shale, he had taken the ball and, his previous move no more than a feint, he was going to the left. He went round the end man of the group – a half-back who was striving desperately to stop going the wrong way – and hammered the ball with his left foot, waist-high and wide of the goalkeeper, to produce a flying save good enough to cause one to wonder which of the applause was for Lawton and which for the goalkeeper.

Only five minutes later, a long low ball down the middle found Lawton with Spence, the right-half and right-back all within 10 feet of him and between him and the goal. There was no stud-hold on the icy ground. Lawton took the ball and, half-trudging, half-strolling, he walked round each of the defenders, one after the other: not one of them managed to touch him or the ball. Pushing it round the third of them, he half-looked at the goal and lazily swung his right leg. The ball went straight into the far corner of the net, hard against the iron support no more than a foot from the ground. Lawton turned round without excitement and walked back to the centre.

Towards the end of the game, a free kick to Notts County on their left wing and just inside their opponents' half was taken by the left-half. He lofted it high into a goal-mouth packed with players. Lawton went up and, with that fantastic power he always seemed to have of being able to hover at the peak of his climb, appeared to assess the situation below him and, hitting the ball smartly with his forehead, directed it accurately to the feet of Crookes who had only to kick it into the net from 2 yards' range.

On possibly ten occasions during that match – which Notts County won by 3–1 – Lawton, without appearing to exert himself, played in such a way as no other centre-forward in England, indeed in Britain or, for all I know, in the world, could have excelled: let us be accurate, not one of them could have equalled it.

Notts County will be in London again within a few weeks: on that occasion I shall have no doubt whatever on my way to watch Lawton.

from *Concerning Soccer*, 1952

Blackpool v. Bolton Wanderers: The Cup Final, 1953
PAUL GARDNER

Thinking there might be a heavy fog, or an accident, or perhaps a strike – well, so many things can upset railway timetables – I got up at 5 a.m. to catch a train hours earlier than I really needed, with the result that I arrived in London around nine o'clock, leaving me some five hours to dispose of before I had to be at the stadium.

This was 1953, and in those days London on Cup Final day was like a town under benevolent siege. There always seemed to be at least one northern team represented (that year it was Blackpool and Bolton, both from the north) and the supporters flowed in in boisterous little knots, drifting about the streets trying somehow to make a dent in the apathy of the big city. In the narrow streets that used to surround Euston station these working-class fans – they could have been Priestley's Bruddersfordians – were instantly at home, absorbed without trouble into the cheap boardinghouses and the sleazy little cafés, where their broad Lancashire accents badgered the waitresses endlessly, 'Gie us anoother coop o' tea, lass,' and they talked about soccer. Not intelligently, but with the blind partisanship that had caused them to come all those miles to this heathen city, and to deck themselves out with huge rosettes and scarves and hats and even whole suits in their club colours.

'It's Stan's year, lads, it's Stan's year, I bloody know it. I bloody told you so when we beat 'uddersfield, I bloody knew it then, and I'll tell you now, bloody Bolton aren't gonna stop him. Who've they bloody got? Banks? He's a big ox, Stan'll make 'im look bloody daft, he'll wish he'd stayed home with the missus . . . how about anoother coop here, lass?' Solid agreement from all his Blackpool mates. They had a London newspaper in which one of the writers had picked Bolton – 'What the bloody 'ell does 'e know about it?' – the very idea, a London writer daring to give opinions about northern teams.

I sat for a while, a middle-class interloper, listening to them tear Bolton apart until it hardly seemed worthwhile playing the game. As it happened, I agreed with them. I had no ties to either team, but I wanted Blackpool to win. Just because of Stan.

I had first seen Stanley Matthews play maybe ten years earlier, and had never missed an opportunity to see him again. He had shown me, as he must have shown tens of thousands of others, just how superb a game soccer could be. Any game with Stan in it was likely to be a magical occasion. His nickname, said the papers, was The Wizard of the Dribble. In the papers, maybe, but never on the terraces. There it was always just plain Stan. 'Come on, Stan, show 'im, Stan.' And Stan, stooping, balding, his face a blank but always slightly drawn – the only thing about him that suggested anything approaching effort – would show them.

At his feet, the ball was at home, comfortably nestling in absolute security, caressed with soft little touches as Stan shuffled his bowed legs toward yet another hapless fullback. Watch the ball, not the man is considered the defender's golden rule, and you would see them with a mesmerized, almost frightened, concentration on the ball as Stan approached. But how could you not watch a man whose seductive body movements seemed to telegraph his every move? Surely no one could lean that far to his left, unless he were actually going to take a step in that direction? And so the fullback would move, had to move, and all was lost. In one smooth burst Stan would straighten up and sail away to his right, leaving the fullback staring at nothing but air, or falling on to his back as he tried to turn while off-balance.

Then the roar for Matthews as he headed for the goal line, the ball always just that calculated distance ahead of him where he could get to it but an opponent could not. Matthews was not a speedster, but I doubt whether anyone has ever been faster over those first few yards after he had beaten his man. There was never any hope of the fullback, even if he was still on his feet, catching Matthews. Usually, another defender would come running across to cover, but this was just what Stan wanted. A player coming in at full speed to tackle a moving Matthews had the most impossible of tasks. He had to get to the ball at once, and as his foot came in, Stan would pull the ball back and cut inside, or he would push it forward, what looked like just a few tantalizing inches beyond the outstretched tackler's foot, which he would step over as though it didn't exist, and complete his enchanted path to the goal line.

There the ball would be pulled sharply back and sent arching into the penalty area where it would arrive like some gently falling bomb, always out of reach of the goalkeeper, always within reach of the attacking forwards surging in to meet it.

Inevitably, the torment of having to face Matthews invited rough tactics, and Stan was kicked and fouled more than most. The resilient, wiry body bore it all, and the stoic, rather sad face remained as blank as ever. He never had to be cautioned by a referee, and to my knowledge he never retaliated, in a thirty-three-year-long career.

What I and most of England – except Bolton – wanted to see was Stan being presented with a Cup Winner's medal, just about the only honour in the game that he had never won. This was Matthews's third final in six years; twice before, in 1948 and 1951, Blackpool had been beaten and Matthews had walked off the field a loser. Now he was thirty-eight years old and this must surely be his last chance.

The Blackpool fans had it all worked out; it would be 3–1 Blackpool when the final whistle went, and I left them happily plotting Bolton's downfall amid the empty teacups and the greasy plates. Pick another café and you'd have found the same Lancashire accents, wearing black and white, and telling you that Blackpool could put 100 bloody Matthewses on the field if they liked, it was goals that counted, and 'our Nat', Nat Lofthouse, scores goals, laddie – how many goals has Stan scored lately? And there was a lot of truth in that, too.

I walked into the West End, a different world this, of large smart stores, one where the little groups of fans stood out as foreign elements and defiantly made all the more noise because of it. By one o'clock I was impatient. 'You are advised to take up your position by not later than 2:30 p.m.,' said my ticket, which left me ninety minutes to make a twenty-minute Underground journey. But you never knew, there

45

might be a delay of some sort, an accident. By 1:30 I was at Wembley Stadium, proffering my ticket at the turnstile, holding my breath in case it was rejected as counterfeit (I had no reason to think it was, I had obtained it in the most respectable way, but you never knew . . .).

My seat, I decided, was not a good one, too far to one end, giving an excellent view of one goal but a long-range look at the other. The stadium was already a third full, maybe 30,000 people gathered, mostly behind the two goals. Between them the famous Wembley turf, rich, green and glowing like a massive emerald carpet. A treacherous carpet, though, one that did strange things to players' legs. There always seemed to be cramps and pulled muscles and twisted knees at a Wembley final.

Community singing came next. Led by a military band standing in the middle of the field, we sang popular songs and music-hall numbers until, with the stadium almost full and only fifteen minutes left, we were ready for sterner stuff, *Land of Hope and Glory*, and then the traditional *Abide with Me*, a solid working-class hymn sung with a fervour it would never command in any chapel. There is no real ending to *Abide with Me* at Wembley; the last note slides into a sustained cheer as banners wave and rattles rattle, a cheer that turns suddenly to an amorphous deafening roar of relief and expectation from 100,000 throats as the two teams walk sedately side by side on to the field.

More frustrating preliminaries. The new Queen Elizabeth, crowned earlier that same year, came on to the field to meet the teams – 'As if she bloody cares, one lot's the same as t'other to her,' said a Blackpool neighbour as the pinnacle of Britain's aristocracy and the nobility of its working classes met for a fleeting moment.

Then . . . a whistle, and an ever-changing mosaic of orange shirts and white shirts on the green, all commanded by the movements of a small light-brown ball. Within two minutes, tragedy for Blackpool. Our Nat got the ball some 20 yards out and shot, an unimpressive effort that looked almost like a miskick. The ball spun across in front of the Blackpool goalkeeper, Farm, who went for it much too late . . . and went in.

While the Bolton fans rejoiced, poor Farm stood in dejected agony, engulfed by the noise his error had caused. Wembley nerves, I thought, something everyone knew about, but something you didn't talk about for fear of inviting the worst. At least there was plenty of time left for Blackpool to reply. But within minutes the powerful Lofthouse was streaming through again, and this time his shot was hit perfectly, a searing drive that had the crowd yelling 'Goal!' the instant it left his foot. Again, Farm hardly moved as the ball rocketed past him, only to crash against the goal post with a solid smack that seemed to echo around the stadium in a moment of quiet as Blackpol's fans were mutely waiting the worst and Bolton's were drawing breath for the final triumphant yell. Blackpool were reprieved with their head on the block, but Farm looked anything but happy. 'Go easy on 'im, Nat, the poor bugger's shell-shocked!' crowed a Bolton voice.

Then it was Blackpool's turn to roar. Down at the other end, where I couldn't really see what was going on, Stan Mortensen ('the other Stan' on the Blackpool team) got the ball in the net. A mistake by the Bolton goalie, they said, so at least the Wembley nerves were striking impartially. But before half-time Farm had let through another shot he should have saved, and Bolton went to the locker rooms leading 2–1, having looked much the better team.

Matthews? He had done little, but then the same could be said of all the other Blackpool forwards. I hoped for better things in the second half, when we would be attacking the goal in front of me. Soon after the restart, Wembley's major jinx struck. Bell, the Bolton left halfback, was injured. In those days there was no such thing as substitution so Bell, barely able to run, was left on the field as a limping passenger in the rather optimistic hope that he might prove a slight nuisance to the Blackpool defenders. Within ten minutes he had done the impossible, leaping high to meet a centre from the right to head Bolton's third goal. Even now, playing against only ten fit men, Blackpool were floundering. They were getting more of the ball, certainly, but their attacks were half-hearted affairs, quickly snuffed by the Bolton defence.

With some twenty minutes left and their team apparently home and dry, the Bolton fans were in full voice, shouting cheerfully, 'Coom on the ten men!', yelling derisively every time a Blackpool attack broke down.

But it was not the noise of the crowd that was to decide the game that afternoon. It was to be the genius of Stanley Matthews. The pressure on the Bolton defence mounted and always the ball was finding its way to Stan's feet, out on the right wing. I could see him cutting and corkscrewing his way through the left flank of the Bolton defence, stopping, accelerating, twisting to avoid desperate tackles, and now it was the Blackpool fans who roared, grasping feverishly at the hope that Stan was destined to get his medal after all, that he *must* bring off the miracle.

Another incredible Matthews run, going past defender after defender, an early centre beautifully judged to lure the goalkeeper out, and in the race for the ball it was Stan Mortensen who got there first to score. Bolton 3 Blackpool 2 – one more goal (and it would be Blackpool's, for Bolton were in deep trouble, burned out as an attacking force) would send the game into overtime. But how many minutes were left? 'Plenty of time, lad, plenty,' said my Blackpool neighbour, but the minutes ticked away and despite all the Matthews magic, the trail of dazed defenders he was leaving after him every time he got the ball and the terrible tangles he was causing in the Bolton ranks, the crucial goal would not come.

I calculated there couldn't have been more than a minute or two left when Mudie, the Blackpool inside left, was brought down directly in front of goal, some 20 yards out. Back came every Bolton player into his own penalty area to defend against the free kick. A wall of white shirts blocked off one side of the goal while goalie Hanson, crouching and rubbing his hands together, guarded the other half. Mortensen, one of the hardest kickers of a dead ball I have ever seen, aimed his shot at the top corner furthest away from Hanson. Either he had spotted a gap in that human wall, or he gambled that someone would move out of the way of his ferocious drive.

Whichever, his shot flashed into the top of the goal, straight and unstoppable. All Hanson could do was to turn and watch as the ball bulged the netting and fell to the grass inside the goal. We were all on our feet now, Wembley Stadium nothing but noise as the late afternoon sun seemed to pick out the orange Blackpool shirts with a suggestively triumphant glow.

Time didn't matter now; the game would go into overtime and Blackpool, running riot against a demoralized Bolton, would be the winner. There was less than a minute to go and the ball had found its way back to Matthews, lurking out on the wing, just inside the Bolton half. With the ease of a skater, Matthews was away on another flexuous run, inside one defender, then past the fullback, racing for the goal line. Barrass, the Bolton centre-half – and a good one – was drawn out of the middle to cope with the danger. The fatal error.

Cutting in, Matthews ran the ball straight at Barrass until, just when it seemed the two must collide, there was that diabolical pivot, that almost ninety-degree turn on the run. The move did not get Matthews past Barrass, but that wasn't the idea; all Stan wanted now, having drawn Barrass out to the edge of the penalty area, was room to get the ball into the middle, and he created the space he needed with that one masterful swerve.

Matthews's centre was the final perfect touch. Did he look up to see where he was putting it, or was it just a sixth sense, a soccer sense, that told him what to do? All I saw was the ball flashing low across the face of the Bolton goal, and I remember thinking, maybe saying, 'Christ, no, Stan,' certain that it must be intercepted by a Bolton defender. But Barrass, the key man, was out of position and the ball ran through, untouched, until Perry, the Blackpool left winger, met it at the far post and hit it, firm and low, into the goal.

With under a minute left, Blackpool were sure winners and from the roar even the Bolton fans must have been cheering, not for the goal, but for the man who had turned the game around, who had treated us all to one of soccer's greatest games. The roar was for Stan Matthews.

from *The Simplest Game*, 1976

Stanley Matthews
JOHN ARLOTT

He has been photographed in every possible pose and setting, he has been interviewed, presentations have been made to him, public meetings have been held about him, posters have been plastered through the Potteries – and we have seen him play at outside-right, a footballing experience we shall never forget. But, when a future generation which never saw him asks itself, or us, just how good he was – and why – we may find that we have committed little to print which tells the essential facts. Thus it may be that our grandchildren will look at the photograph of this quiet, short, slight man and say: 'Ah, yes, Matthews; he was probably quite good, but not so good as you say, not so good as our modern players.' Let us then, briefly, consider this footballer under three headings – his character in so far as if effects his approach to football, his purpose as a player, and his method. We shall then find that his football is not a mystery but a series of facets each of which has been painstakingly perfected.

First of all, in his approach to the game, he is the answer to the manager's prayer. Conscious that he is a great player, he will do almost anything to maintain or improve his standard, and he is always thinking to that end. It is doubtful if any footballer of our time is fitter than Matthews, for he realizes that the relative degrees of fitness of two players in opposition may, in a single moment, decide a match by inches. This fitness means that, ply Matthews with ball after ball, and each will find him cool, balanced, breathing easily, capable of his best. The man marking him may become flustered, panting, but not Matthews. He does not drink or smoke – partly because neither interests him, but even more because it might detract by a fraction from his performance. He nurses his fitness, too; notice his completely relaxed stillness in the field, only his alert eyes moving when he is not directly concerned with the play.

His father, Jack Matthews, the Fighting Barber from Hanley, was a boxer with a reputation as a battler. He brought his sons from their beds at six in the morning to do deep-breathing exercises, to lift barbells and to use a chest-expander. If these exercises did not give Stanley Matthews a huge physique – for he is narrow-chested and has a slight stoop – it taught him to train, and to value the general physical well-being which fitness generates. So, too, did the 2 miles each way – in the morning, before and after lunch and again in the evening – which his father made him walk between their house and the Stoke City ground, when, in 1930, fifteen-year-old Stanley Matthews, ex-schoolboy international winger, began to work on the ground staff of the local club. To this day, Matthews trains, of his own volition, far harder than a trainer *asks* any player to do. He is quite single-minded in his determination to be a great footballer. Once, when he recovered from an injury, the Stoke City management were reluctant to change a winning team and asked Matthews to play in the reserves. He asked for a transfer. He recognized the wisdom of not changing a successful eleven. But, as he saw it, that winning combination might go on winning while he lost some of the 'edge' on his play and, above all, some of his confidence in the 'stiffs'. Granted an interview with the director, he was firm but reasonable. He regained his place and withdrew his transfer request. The second time it happened, he stood out for his transfer and, on 10 May 1947, Blackpool bought the finest footballer of our age for £11,500, as a fit, loyal, gifted player, his main ambition still to be a success in his career: twenty years of big football have not changed his original aim.

Both in the broad sense and in detail, Stanley Matthews has *worked out* his football. Since football is a team game, he realizes – as some narrower-minded players have failed to do – that the greatest individual success is gained by effective work in the team's interest. He consciously works towards his team's success by two methods – by psychological attack on the confidence of the opposing side and, simultaneously, by actually playing the ball to the end of making goals. Thus, if he breaks the confidence of the left-back opposing him, or if he immobilizes two players deputed to mark him, he has done his share towards defeating his opponents completely apart from what he does with the ball.

His actual playing method has been described as 'wizardry' – and left at that too often for the demand of the future: 'What manner of footballer was Matthews?' Much of this lack of description, of course, derives from the fact that the spectacle of a Matthews dribble is so stirring as to demand a positive effort of will to concentrate on technical detail. Let us, however, examine his playing method – noticing, as we go, to what an extent his clear and eminently practical thinking enables him to make use of facts so simple that many people ignore them. He is, by nature, and training, fast on his feet: he was a successful sprinter as a schoolboy. He has made himself faster still, merely by observing that a man in plimsolls runs faster than a man in boots and, hence, that a man in football boots lighter than those his opponent is wearing might gain a vital foot in 20 yards. Therefore, Matthews designed for himself – and also marketed, for he is not in football or business for charity – a pair of football boots half a pound lighter then the normal type. Already they have become a commercial success. These boots, size 6½ for his neat, well-kept size-8 feet, he wears unpadded for perfect 'feel' of the ball.

Given this background of pace and fitness, and with detailed care even to such details of his equipment as constantly renewed bootlaces, let us watch Matthews at work. In his early days he was a frequent shooter at goal, but he soon recognized that the angle from which a winger is usually forced to shoot gives him every opportunity of putting in a shot which, as he says, may look good to the crowd but is no trouble to the goalkeeper. Thus, he now concentrates on disorganizing the opposing defence and then making a precise pass to the better-situated inside-forwards who can head or shoot at goal from square-on. It is here that the significant difference is to be observed between Matthews and Finney of Preston, for so long his rival for his place in the England side and public esteem. Often as spectacular and effective as Matthews in beating opponents, Finney demonstrably lacks Matthews's keen appreciation of the moment at which to 'loose' the ball to a better-placed colleague. On this vital count Matthews shows himself the greater.

Like all real footballers, he is a fine player *without* the ball. Few wingers of our time, and certainly none so habitually closely marked as Matthews, have managed to give themselves so much room in which to receive and initially control the ball. In order to get the ball, he will often go back well into his own half or even, when his side is on the defensive, move across to the inside-left position. Then, the opposing full-back has either to leave Matthews unmarked, or, by following him, throw the entire defence out of position. This is deliberately conceived strategy on Matthews's part. Often, too, even before he receives the ball, a body swerve, little more than a shrug, will send a defender the wrong way, away from him, as if to check a move at which Matthews, with intent to deceive, has only hinted. The same difficulty arises when he is in possession of the ball. The defender marking him *must* play the ball: to watch Matthews's body, with its feints and swerves, is to be sent in every direction but the one Matthews proposes to take. In the same way, it is almost useless to try to shoulder-charge him for he has so many different running paces and such close and controlled variation of them that it is virtually impossible to keep step with him or even level with him from stride to stride.

Much of Matthews's so-called dribbling is not dribbling at all. Particularly this is so when he backs away from a man, seeming to take the ball with him; in fact, he has merely allowed the ball, as it comes to him, to continue its course while he backs with it, not actually touching it, but passing his feet over or across the ball and drawing the defender with him. When he does dribble, he possesses the rare gift of compelling decisive action. He will take the ball up to the defender and, either force him to tackle and then beat the tackling foot, or take the ball quickly on. Here, too, he exhibits a rare gift which tennis players, in particular, will recognize. When one is in constant practice at tennis, one becomes so adjusted to the flight of the ball that it is possible to take the eye off the ball for a second in order to notice the opponent's position. Matthews, I suspect, is in such sympathetic touch with the football at his feet that he does not need to concentrate on it to the degree that most dribblers do, but can take his eye off it to observe the reaction of his opponent. Once the opponent commits himself to a tackle with a particular foot, which he does as soon as he takes balance on the other, Matthews is away, past the anchored, non-tackling foot.

In dribbling, he much prefers to use his right foot because, as the natural foot, it grants him that last degree of accuracy to which he always aspires. On the other hand, if you tackled him twenty times consecutively to the right, he would go twenty times to the left. With his continual tap-tapping on the ball, he keeps it closer than any other dribbler of such speed; his body over the ball, his control utterly perfect. It is this minute precision, absent from the spectacular loose dribbling of so many famous players, which characterizes Matthews's ball play. Thus he will control the ball, comfortably, bare inches from an opponent on the touchline. He has been described as over-elaborate; in fact, he will always go directly for goal when he can, going backwards or on the inside of a full-back only often enough to leave doubt in the defender's mind. One of his favourite dribbles is to start to go away to the right of the full-back, and then check as if to suggest the usual dribbling gambit of going the other way, only to move off again to the right with that immense burst of speed which derives from his intensive short-spring training methods and with which, even now, in his thirties, he can pull away from almost any defender in the game. He is still fast enough, too, to push the ball to one side of a defender and go the other way round him. 'When I have got the ball,' he says, 'I have the advantage; I know what I am going to do, the full-back does not.'

When a fellow-forward is in a good position, Matthews will pass to him at once, but when he goes on, he will often work his way in along the goal-line, not for the sake of elaboration but because it disorganizes the opposing defence, because it allows of the shorter pass – always more accurate and less likely to be intercepted – and, above all, because it guarantees against the offside decision so often caused by the winger's forward pass. Very rarely indeed does he merely 'cross' the ball, hitting it into the goalmouth in general, as most wingers do; a centre from Matthews is a *pass* to a specific position. Again, with a balanced sense of the worth of the simple argument, his corners are never the fashionable inswinger kicked with the left foot, but the straightforward right-foot cross which carries the ball away from the reaching hands of the goalkeeper to where his fellow-forwards have an even chance in the 'climb' with the defenders.

At Blackpool there is a cheer on the rare occasion – about once in two or three matches – when Matthews heads the ball. He is simply not interested in heading; he prefers to play football with his feet, where complete control may be achieved. There would be still more surprise if he were to show anger or if he indulged even the mildest foul: he recognizes, with his usual good sense, that control of temper is as vital as control of ball or body.

It was in 1932 that Stanley Matthews first played for Stoke City's first team. Over the twenty years since then, he has been increasingly closely marked, his play has become better known, more widely examined and discussed by those whose business it is to stop him. Now, perhaps, he is growing old, as footballers go. Every great player has his 'off' days – only the mediocre can be completely consistent. Yet, Matthews out of form for one match is news – 'Is he finished?' Under the increasing burden of marking, defensive strategy, age and criticism, to be – as Matthews is – still the greatest of them all, is to be great indeed.

from *Concerning Soccer*, 1952

Stanley Matthews
ALAN ROSS

Not often *con brio*, but *andante, andante*,
    horseless, though jockey-like and jaunty,
Straddling the touchline, live margin
    not out of the game, nor quite in,
Made by him green and magnetic, stroller

Indifferent as a cat dissembling, rolling
A little as on deck, till the mouse, the ball,
       slides palely to him,
And shyly almost, with deprecatory cough, he is off.

Head of a Perugino, with faint flare
Of the nostrils, as though Lipizzaner-like
       he sniffed at the air,
Finding it good beneath him, he draws
Defenders towards him, the ball a bait
They refuse like a poisoned chocolate,
       retreating, till he slows his gait
To a walk, inviting the tackle, inciting it.

Till, unrefusable, dangling the ball at the instep,
He is charged – and stiffening so slowly
It is barely perceptible, he executes with a squirm
Of the hips, a twist more suggestive than apparent,
       that lazily disdainful move *toreros* term
              a Veronica – it's enough.
Only emptiness following him, pursuing some scent
Of his own, he weaves in towards,
       not away from, fresh tacklers,
Who, turning about to gain time, are by him
       harried, pursued not pursuers.

Now gathers speed, nursing the ball as he cruises,
Eyes judging distance, noting the gaps, the spaces
Vital for colleagues to move to, slowing a trace,
As from Vivaldi to Dibdin, pausing,
       and leisurely, leisurely, swings
To the left upright his centre, on hips
His hands, observing the goalkeeper spring,
       heads rising vainly to the ball's curve
Just as it's plucked from them; and dispassionately
Back to his mark he trots, whistling through closed lips.

Trim as a yacht, with similar lightness
       - of keel, of reaction to surface – with salt air
Tanned, this incomparable player, in decline fair
       to look at, nor in decline either,

Improving like wine with age, has come far –
    born to one, a barber, who boxed,
Not with such filial magnificence, but well.
'The greatest of all time', *meraviglioso* Matthews –
    Stoke City, Blackpool and England.
Expressionless enchanter, weaving as on strings
Conceptual patterns to a private music, heard
Only by him, to whose slowly emerging theme
He rehearses steps, soloist in compulsions of a dream.

from *To Whom It May Concern*, 1958

The Fall of Willie Woodburn
HUGH MCILVANNEY

The photograph on the fading page of the newspaper files might date from the thirties. It shows two men stepping from the bare doorway of a Glasgow office building. Three strides in front is the older of the two, his thin face grim under a hat with a large crown and a floppy brim. He is wearing a baggy double-breasted suit. The trousers of the younger man are outlandishly wide, his jacket is open, exposing a striped club tie. He has his coat swung casually over his left shoulder, in the manner of someone who has taken a walk on the prom and found the sun warmer than he had expected. But his face, too, is drawn, his eyes cast down towards the large toecaps of his shoes.

The date of the scene fossilized in the back numbers of the national press is September 14, 1954, and the man with the coat is Willie Woodburn. Far from taking a carefree walk, he is making a humiliating and irrevocable exit from football, the game that has been his life since he was a schoolboy, in which he has won many honours and the reputation of being one of the two or three greatest centre-halves Britain has ever produced. The late summer sun is shining on the shabby buildings in Carlton Place, Glasgow, but Woodburn carries with him the permanent chill of the most sensational sentence ever passed by the Referee Committee of the Scottish Football Association. Meeting in secret to consider the latest in a series of violent misde-

56

meanours by Woodburn, the six members of the Committee had voted to suspend Woodburn *sine die*, without limit. At the time the impression created was that their decision was unanimous but subsequently it emerged that three of the judges had been disposed to apply a limit to the punishment, to fix a definite date for the condemned man's return to the game. In the end it was left to the chairman, Mr John Robbie of Aberdeen, to gave a casting vote and he declared the punishment *sine die*. The same calamity had overtaken other players but never before had one of such distinction been involved.

Woodburn was thirty-four, so clearly his best years were behind him, but he had always been in exceptional physical condition. Even now, on the brink of fifty, tall and straight with a waist trim enough to shame men twenty years younger, he emanates a physical vitality that persuades those who meet him that he could still strip and do a job for Rangers or Scotland. We know it is an illusion but it is almost as compelling as that which accompanies Jack Dempsey in boxing. Dempsey is well into his seventies but he is an eternally contemporary figure and when he takes his magnetic, virile presence into the training camp of a modern champion many who see him find themselves possessed by the ludicrous conviction that if he took off his street clothes, put on the gloves and went into the ring, he would be no worse than even money to come out on top. In football terms, there is something of the same magic about Woodburn.

In 1954 there was nothing illusory about the belief that he was fit to go on playing for several seasons. The older man in that newspaper picture had no doubts. Scot Symon had just been appointed manager of Rangers when the Woodburn crisis developed. Writing of the implications of the disaster ten years afterwards, Symon indicated a depth of concern that was not obscured by the occasional intrusion of melodrama in his prose. 'When the door of the Referee Committee Room opened at last and Willie came out, one look at his face was enough to tell me the verdict. "That's it all finished," he shrugged. His words carried their own meaning. My feelings were immediate and instant. For Willie. For Rangers. I felt as if "The Castle" which once perched so proudly on top of the Ibrox grandstand, had come tumbling to the ground around my ears.

'When I had taken over the managership of Rangers a few weeks before I was well aware that it was a big job – with equally big

57

problems. Age had caught up with several star players. The team was in a period of transition and a lot of rebuilding would have to be done. But there was one great consolation. There was still that masterful, dominating personality at centre-half who would be the sheet anchor of my new team . . . Willie was a football manager's ideal centre-half. I could entrust all thoughts of defensive play to him. Willie knew exactly what had to be done on the field. I reckoned that he had another two or three seasons as a Scotland and Rangers player left . . . Looking back, Woodburn's suspension threw me out of gear more than the loss of any other player who has been under my control.'

Of course, Symon had known that Woodburn's punishment would be stiff. The seriousness of the latest offence and the record of previous convictions made that inevitable. Though the manager–player relationship had scarcely begun, Symon had known Woodburn for a long time and he had witnessed at close quarters the accumulation of the big man's troubles. He was a spectator in the enclosure at Parkhead in 1938 when Woodburn, as a precocious nineteen-year-old, played in his first Rangers–Celtic match against one of the most formidable sides ever to wear the green and white hoops: Kennoway; Hogg, Morrison; Geatons, Lyon, Paterson; Delaney, McDonald, Crum, Divers, Murphy. In that game Symon saw evidence of the impetuosity that was to grow so much later into a menace that would destroy Woodburn's career. With the score 1–1, Jimmy Delaney challenged Rangers goalkeeper Jerry Dawson and Woodburn moved in to shoulder the winger out of the way. Willie Lyon gave Celtic the lead from the penalty and soon afterwards Lyon came upfield again to score with a free-kick awarded for a foul by Woodburn on Malcolm McDonald at the edge of the area. The encouragement of those goals set Celtic going and they slaughtered Rangers 6–2. Symon, swaying in the crowded enclosure, had his own troubles (in the crush he missed a step and aggravated an ankle injury) but he had time to sympathize with the young defender whose blunders had made the day a personal disaster. Rangers at that time were, of course, managed by the legendary autocrat Bill Struth and he was the last man to ignore such lapses. However, Struth's strictures and homilies were comparatively restrained. 'You're far too impetuous,' he told Woodburn. 'The man who never made a mistake never made anything. But most of the centre-half's work is in the penalty area and you can't afford to make mistakes there. You've still got this juvenile habit of holding the ball and inviting trouble. All we expect of you here is that you clear your lines. Leave the wing-halves to play football.'

Woodburn found himself able to absorb only a diluted version of that advice. Though his game developed a striking economy, and he always sought to play with a classic simplicity, he remained very much a footballing centre-half. Sadly, he also remained a physically impulsive one and the problem grew as he got older. In August, 1948, he was ordered off after a violent exchange with Davie Mathie, the Motherwell centre-forward, and subsequently was suspended for fourteen days. On March 7, 1953, he was sent off for a foul on Billy McPhail of Clyde and was banned for twenty-one days. September 26, 1953, saw him ordered off in the Rangers–Stirling Albion match and that time he was suspended for six weeks and it was made clear that 'a very serious view would be taken of any subsequent offence.' Strangely, Stirling Albion were again the opposition when the ultimate catastrophe came on August 28, 1954. Woodburn's capacity for becoming enraged during matches with such undistinguished opposition may be seen as confirmation of the obvious truth that his massive aberrations had little to do with an external context of events and were basically a manifestation of an internal problem, of the chemistry of his own personality. That is perhaps a facile interpretation, because there is no doubt that the pressures applied by the mere fact of being a Rangers player (a unique complication that will be considered in more detail later) are immensely relevant in any discussion of what happened to Woodburn.

It is questionable if many people, even among those who feel that they have a vivid recollection of Woodburn's removal from the game, can remember the man who was involved with him in the final sordid episode at Ibrox Park, the victim who, unintentionally, was the instrument of Woodburn's destruction as a footballer. He was Alec Paterson, the Stirling inside-left, a young man whose career before and after that brief, unfortunate period in the limelight was respectably obscure. The frightening simplicity of what happened on the field at Ibrox, the hideous suddenness of it and the sickening discrepancy between the trivial origins of the incident and the permanence of its implications – all this is conveyed in the cold, abbreviated account that emerged from the Referee Committee. 'When the game was almost finished Paterson, lying on the ground, caught Woodburn round the legs. As Paterson rose, Woodburn went towards him and struck him with his fist. When Woodburn was called he explained that he felt a jab of pain on his knee and lost his temper.' Woodburn's appearance before the Committee lasted exactly four minutes.

Naturally enough, there were few men in Scottish football who believed that the S.F.A. would adhere to the stunning terms of their judgment. Certainly Glasgow Rangers and their banished star were convinced that the Association would relent. Indeed, it was that confident expectation of a reprieve that prevented Woodburn from figuring in a remarkable court case, a challenge to football authority that would have been a highly controversial forerunner of George Eastham's successful action against Newcastle United [see page 111]. Woodburn had the ammunition to cause a furore in the courts but for several reasons – all of which can be seen in retrospect to have been inadequate – he decided against using it.

The man who armed him was John Cameron Q.C., now Lord Cameron, a Court of Session Judge. At the instruction of the Scottish Players' Union, Woodburn had sought an opinion from Cameron, probably the most impressive Scottish advocate of the day, and when it came it was explosive material. For thirty months after his suspension, Woodburn recalled later, the document lay in his desk 'like a smouldering fuse'. The opinion made it clear that if he went to law there was a real chance of having the verdict of the Referee Committee overturned. Cameron pointed out that the powers of suspending a player possessed by the S.F.A. were nowhere clearly defined and that the *sine die* suspension really meant an indefinite and compulsory deprivation of the right to work or receive the reward. 'This is a very substantial power indeed,' wrote Cameron, 'and in my opinion not to be lightly inferred unless such a construction is in accordance with the natural meaning of the language used.' In considering Article 122 of the S.F.A. Cameron found the last sentence significant because it provided that a suspended player should be eligible to resume on the date on which his suspension expired. 'This is positively expressed,' insisted Cameron, 'and gives a right to the suspended player, a right to resume playing (and consequently earning money) from a prescribed and therefore presumably ascertainable date.' In any action the essence of Woodburn's argument would have been the fact that he had been suspended *sine die*, without definite date.

Cameron suggested that after a season the S.F.A. had no right to maintain the suspension, on the grounds that Woodburn's registration lasted only until April 30 and that jurisdiction to suspend should only be exercisable in the case of registered players. He felt a *sine die* suspension was not warranted by the Articles of the S.F.A. In addition, he believed that the procedure followed at the hearings might have been such as to prevent the offender's case from being fairly presented or considered. Cameron concluded: 'I have only to add that I think the detailed circumstances of the hearing and occasion of the final suspension should be investigated in detail and also the circumstances of the ineffective appeal.'

Woodburn's reasons for declining to use these powerful words in a fight to get back into the game will appear peculiarly flimsy, even fatuous, to outsiders, but their influence must be related to his background and personal loyalties. For instance, he was heavily swayed by the comments of John Wilson, the elderly Glasgow bailie who was then chairman of Rangers. When he was shown the legal opinion and asked for his advice Bailie Wilson said: 'Don't take it as far as the courts. Rangers are behind you and we don't want to take it into court.' The desire to avoid that course if at all possible was shared by Woodburn. 'I had been a Rangers player for seventeen years and the club had been generous to me,' he wrote afterwards. 'The last thing I wanted to do was to bring it into open conflict with the S.F.A. and clearly if I had gone ahead Rangers would have been on my side. There was also the thought that if I won my fight against the S.F.A. and came back into football by means of a court order, things could be most awkward for me. I'd be a player apart, one who had challenged authority and won. Even if right was on my side I knew there would be people who would resent it . . . But most of all I was sure that after a reasonable period the ban would be lifted. I knew my offence merited a stiff punishment but when the sentence was pronounced words failed me completely. Later I thought of all the things I would have liked to have told the Referee Committee when asked if I had anything to say. I was still certain that after six months or even at the end of the 1954–55 season I would be cleared. I had given good service to Scotland. I was thirty-four and it was obvious that I didn't have many years left in football. The stigma of *sine die* was punishment enough. I had good grounds for believing that the S.F.A. might relent after a few months. There was the top legislator who had obviously heard that I was considering legal action. He phoned me with an urgent plea: "Don't do it, Willie. Things will work out for the good, you'll see."

'I was left with only one channel to get back into the game, to appeal to the S.F.A. – and even my appeals were rationed to one every six months.' When the second appeal was thrown out Woodburn's lawyers again pressed him to take his case into court but again he refused. 'I know one thing,' he says now. 'If I was faced with the same decision today I wouldn't hesitate for a moment to carry my fight for justice to the limit.'

Eighteen months after the suspension the door was opened slightly when the S.F.A. ruled that Woodburn could come back into football – as anything except a player. Understandably, he saw that meagre concession as the equivalent of handing sweets to a child and warning him that he must not eat any. For him, re-entering the game meant pulling on a pair of boots. But the total lifting of the ban was not approved until April 23, 1957, and by then it was too late. The inactivity had lasted just too long. Woodburn, in the midst of his appealing and protesting and hoping, had become an ex-player. There was, he insists, substantial consolation in the knowledge that a great deal of public sympathy was on his side. Throughout the fight, players, fans and many officials had gone out of their way to express their support. On the morning after he was cleared he had two pleasant surprises. The first was a letter. It was a benefit cheque from Rangers, £750 they had been unable to pay him while he was under suspension. An hour later the doorbell rang again and Woodburn found a telegram boy carrying a message from his old rival, Gordon Smith, the great winger. The telegram said: 'Hope to be playing against you soon.' Smith's brilliant career, which had reached wonderful heights with Hibernian, was to span exciting seasons with Hearts and Dundee but he was not to be opposed by the formidable defensive skills of Woodburn again.

Altogether Woodburn was capped five times against England, four times against Wales, four times against Ireland, three times against France, twice against Belgium, twice against Austria and once against Portugal, Denmark and America. His international record, which also included seven appearances in inter-League matches, must be seen in the light of the extreme eccentricity that traditionally afflicts Scottish selectors. In most other countries Woodburn would have been an immovable feature of the national team. The Scots, typically, felt entitled to lift or leave his great talent. However few of those who played with him or against him had any doubts about his worth.

None had a better opportunity to judge him on and off the field than Willie Waddell, who shared so much of his Rangers and Scotland careers. Waddell, a determined, engagingly forthright man, whose achievements as a manager with Kilmarnock brought five-figure offers from England before he chose to be a full-time journalist, is unequivocal: 'Willie Woodburn impressed me more as a footballer and a man than anyone else I have ever met in the game. As a centre-half he had everything. That is said about a lot of players but with him it was literally true. The thing that always struck me most about him was that he had no weak side. It didn't matter whether the ball was coming at him from the left or the right, in the air or on the ground, he took it with the same perfect timing, the same tremendous authority. Only the really great defenders can do that. The fact is that you couldn't think of a quality you would want in a man in that position that Woodburn didn't have – unless, of course, you included a balanced temperament. Willie would admit – well, he'd have no option, would he? – that he had deficiencies in that respect. But it would be absolutely ridiculous to think of him as a maliciously violent man. You couldn't meet a more generous, likeable man. Tell me how many people in the game really disliked him.

'Some of the wild men in football come from rough backgrounds where they had to fight or be trampled underfoot. But Willie comes from a marvellous family, quite well-off and terrifically respectable. They were always a very united family, very close, just as Willie is with his wife and three daughters. He was brought up to behave like a gentleman and if he didn't always manage it on the field there were very special reasons for that. He was always a fierce competitor, a real professional who considered it his job to go out there and give everything he had. But I think that basic determination was distorted by the mystique of Rangers. There is no doubt that in our time the very act of pulling that blue jersey over your head did something to you. All the talk about tradition, about the privilege and responsibility that went with being a Rangers player, definitely had its effect. Obviously, a lot of it was nonsense, a mixture of myths and exaggerations that put things completely out of perspective, but it got through to us as players. The atmosphere of Ibrox, the attitude of everyone connected with the club, made you feel that it was your duty to shatter all opposition, to prove that there was only one Rangers. I remember we had a fellow playing with us called Eddie Rutherford. Eddie was the nicest character you could meet, the nicest man in the team. He was always smiling. But when we lost I used to hate him. "Look at that wee bastard," I used to say. "He's still smiling." It was crazy, I suppose, but that's how we felt and I think Woodburn felt it more than any of us. I am sure that obsession with winning for Rangers had a lot to do with his troubles.'

Woodburn's nickname among his team mates was Big Ben, which might be interpreted as a tribute to his size and total reliability. In fact, he earned the name in Lisbon in the late forties after Rangers had trounced Benfica. At the celebration afterwards Woodburn insisted on raising his glass every few minutes and bellowing 'Viva Benfica.' He went on doing it well into the next day and Waddell and a few others felt his performance had to be permanently commemorated. Waddell was unlikely to forget that trip in any case. He was immediately attracted to the hostess on the plane going out and she was soon his wife. 'The last time we met Woodburn he picked up the wife and nearly broke half-a-dozen ribs,' Waddell told me. 'She said, "That man's mad." I said, "Well, you've known him long enough now." He can be wild. Yet when I was best man at his wedding I had to hold his hand all through the ceremony.'

Sheer vitality, an immense physical vigour that is constantly threatening to spill over into horseplay, is one of the first characteristics one notices in Woodburn. After a few drinks at a party he is liable to deliver some friendly shoulder charges or lift someone off his feet just for fun. The only occasions when I have seen his good nature clouded with resentment have all been associated with football. Apart from owning a garage and being a partner in the family building business, he does journalistic work and when he is in the Press box he plays every ball, kicking the boards in front of his legs, leaping from his seat as a player strains for a header. At the end of a recent under-23 international in which the England team gave Scotland some harsh treatment, he strode along behind the rows of English reporters, saying in a loud, challenging voice: 'Hammer-throwers, bloody hammer-throwers.'

Fortunately, no one was unwise enough to question the judgement. I agree with Willie Waddell's assessment of Woodburn's generosity

of nature and I, too, like him a great deal. But there is a deep reservoir
of violence in the man and anyone who opens the sluice gates had
better be a strong swimmer. There is no point in wailing over that
explosive temper. It is part of him. We should be grateful that before
it did its ultimate damage we had a good long look at one of the
greatest centre-halves who ever kicked a ball.

from John Arlott (ed.), Soccer: The Great Ones, 1968

The Match of the Century – I
GEOFFREY GREEN

ENGLAND 3 HUNGARY 6

Yesterday by 4 o'clock on a grey winter's afternoon within the bowl
of Wembley Stadium the inevitable had happened. To those who had
seen the shadows of recent years creeping closer and closer there was
perhaps no real surprise. England at last were beaten by the foreign
invader on solid English soil. And it was to a great side from Hungary,
the Olympic champions, that the final honour fell. They have won a
most precious prize by their rich, overflowing, and to English patriots
unbelievable victory of six goals to three over an England side that
was cut to ribbons for most of an astonishing afternoon. Here, indeed,
did we attend, all 100,000 of us, the twilight of the gods.

There is no sense in writing that England were a poor side. Everything in the world is comparative. Taken within the framework of
British football they were acceptable. This same combination – with
the addition of the absent Finney – could probably win against Scotland at Hampden Park next April. But here, on Wembley's velvet
turf, they found themselves strangers in a strange world, a world of
flitting red spirits, for such did the Hungarians seem as they moved
at devastating pace with superb skill and powerful finish in their cherry
bright shirts.

One has talked about the new conception of football as developed
by the continentals and South Americans. Always the main criticism
against the style has been its lack of a final punch near goal. One has
thought at times, too, that perhaps the perfection of football was to
be found somewhere between the hard-hitting, open British method

and this other more subtle, probing infiltration. Yesterday the Hungarians, with perfect team work, demonstrated this midway point to perfection. Theirs was a mixture of exquisite short passing and the long English game. The whole of it was knit by exact ball control and mounted by a speed of movement and surprise of thought that had an English team ground into Wembley's pitch a long way from the end. The Hungarians, in fact, moved the ball swiftly along the ground with delicate flicks, or used the long pass in the air. And the point was that they used these variations as they wished, changing the point of attack at remarkable speed. To round it off – this was the real point – they shot with the accuracy and speed of archers. It was Agincourt in reverse.

One has always said that the day continental football learned to shoot would be the moment British football would have to wake up. That moment has come at last. In truth, it has been around the corner for some time, but there can no longer be any doubt. England's sad end on the national stage now proclaims it to the skies. Outpaced and outmanœuvred by this intelligent exposition of football, England never were truly in the match. There were odd moments certainly when a fitful hope spurted up, such as when Sewell put us level at one-all at the quarter hour and later during a brave rally that took England to half-time 2–4 down. Yet these were merely the stirrings of a patriot who clung jealously to the past. The cold voice of reason always pressed home the truth. Indeed from the very first minute the writing loomed large on Wembley's steep and tight-packed banks. Within sixty seconds Hungary took the lead when a quick central thrust by Bozsik, Zakarias and Hidegkuti left the centre-forward to sell a perfect dummy and lash home, right foot, a swift rising shot to the top corner of Merrick's net. The ball was white and gleaming. It could have been a dove of peace. Rather it was a bird of ill-omen, for from that moment the Hungarians shot ten times to every once of England.

Just before England drew level a sharp move of fascinating beauty, both in conception and execution, between Czibor and Puskas was finished off by Hidegkuti. But the Dutch referee gave the centre-forward offside, which perhaps was charitable as things ended. Yet the English reply when it did come also arrived excitingly, for Johnston, intercepting in his own penalty area, ran forward to send Mortensen through. A quick pass to the left next set Sewell free and that was one-all as a low left-foot shot beat Grosics. But hope was quickly stilled. Within twenty-eight minutes Hungary led 4–1. However disturbing it might have been, it was breathtaking. At the twentieth minute, for instance, Puskas sent Czibor racing down the left and from Kocsis's flick Hidegkuti put Hungary ahead again at close range, the ball hitting Eckersley as he tried a desperate interception. Almost at once Kocsis sent the fast-moving Czibor, who entered the attack time after time down the right flank, past Eckersley. A diagonal ground pass was pulled back by Puskas, evading a tackle in an inside-right position – sheer juggling this – and finished off with a fizzling left-foot shot inside the near post: 1–3.

Minutes later a free kick by the progressive Bozsik was diverted by Puskas' heel past the diving Merrick, and England, 4–1 down with the half-hour not yet struck, were an army in retreat and disorder. Certainly some flagging courage was whipped in that rally up to half-time by Matthews and Mortensen, both of whom played their hearts out, crowded as they were, but though it brought a goal it could no more turn back the tide of elusive red shirts than if a fly had settled on the centre circle. After an acrobatic save by Grosics to a great header by Robb it was Mortensen, dashing away from a throw-in, losing then recovering the ball and calling up some of his dynamic past, who now set Wembley roaring as he sped through like a whippet to shoot England's second goal. But 2–4 down at half-time clearly demanded a miracle in the space left after some of the desperate escapes at Merrick's end that had gone hand in hand with the telling Hungarian thrusts and overall authority.

Within ten minutes of the interval the past was dead and buried forever. A great rising shot by Bozsik as the ball was caressed back to him on the edge of the penalty area after Merrick had turned Czibor's header on to the post made it 5–2, and moments later Hidegkuti brought his personal contribution to three within a perfect performance as he volleyed home Hungary's sixth goal from a lob by Puskas. It was too much. Though Ramsey said the last word of all for England with a penalty kick when Mortensen was brought down half an hour from the end, the crucial lines had been written and declaimed long since by Hungary in the sunshine of the early afternoon. Ten minutes before the end Grosics, with an injured arm, surrendered his charge to Geller, his substitute, but by now a Hungarian goalkeeper was but a formal requirement.

So was history made. England were beaten at all points, on the ground, in the air, and tactically. Hidegkuti, a centre-forward who played deep in the rear supplying the mid-field to probing and brilliant inside-forwards and fast wingers, not only left Johnston a lonely detached figure on the edge of England's penalty area but also scored three goals completely to beat the English defensive retreat. But Johnston was not to blame; the whole side was unhinged. The speed, cunning and shooting power of the Hungarian forwards provided a spectacle not to be forgotten. Long passes out of defence to five forwards who showed football dressed in new colours was something not seen before in this country. We have our Matthews and our Finney certainly, but they are alone. Taylor and Sewell, hard as they and the whole side now fought to the last drop, were by comparison mere workers with scarcely a shot between them at the side of progressive, dangerous artists who seemed able to adjust themselves at will to any demand. When extreme skill was needed, it was there. When some fire and bite entered the battle after half-time, it made no difference.

English football can be proud of its past. But it must awake to a new future.

England: Merrick; Ramsey, Eckersley; Wright, Johnston, Dickinson; Matthews, Taylor, Mortensen, Sewell, Robb.
Hungary: Grosics; Buzanszky, Lantos; Bozsik, Lorant, Zakarias; Budai, Kocsis, Hidegkuti, Puskas, Czibor.

from *The Times*, 1953

The Match of the Century – II
ANON.

A HUNGARIAN ACCOUNT

25 November was an ordinary sort of day in London. Early in the morning a dense fog still enveloped the trees of Hyde Park, but when around nine o'clock the Hungarian players began to assemble in the hall of the Cumberland Hotel, the porter said by way of encouragement: 'The fog will have cleared up completely by the time the game starts. As a matter of fact a bit of sunshine is expected.' The boys were

gratified to hear this weather forecast, for on the previous evening a heavy rainfall had drenched the London streets and there were some whose nerves were so ruffled by the bad weather that they had hardly slept a wink during the night.

The greatest event in the hours just before a game is the tactical conference. The ponderings of long months, daring plans and novel ideas that are the fruits of many sleepless nights were given expression in the words of Gusztav Sebes at this tactical conference. 'England are great opponents but they can be defeated,' were his first words at the conference. He did not say much, so as not to tire the players. 'You, Nandi Hidegkuti, will begin playing as an advanced centre-forward. This will confuse the English, who think that you will with-draw immediately. After the first minutes you will really play as a withdrawn centre-forward, but you will constantly change your pos-ition.' Then he explained in detail the tasks of the two wing-forwards: 'Budai and Czibor, your jobs won't be easy. You will have to play the entire length of the field and frequently you will have to meet the two English outside-forwards when they attack into the Hungarian penalty area.' Then the leader of the Hungarian team turns to Bozsik: 'You are a key man. The English will pay less attention to you than to our forwards. Make every effort to break through the gaps and shoot for goal, but defence is an important part of your task.' And Bozsik, the soft-spoken, modest sportsman, nodded his head in approval: 'That's how it will be, Uncle Guszti.'

At 12.45, two policemen with motor-cycles arrived to escort the bus to the Wembley Stadium. Once at the stadium, there was still an hour before the game. On other occasions they would have used this time to inspect the field and get acquainted with the spectators. But this time it was different. Everybody hurried to the dressing-room, and, without speaking, quietly began to change. When the English managers invited them to take a little walk out on the field Jozsef Zakarias remarked with grim humour: 'Who's interested in seeing the operating theatre before the operation?' Everyone was greatly pleased by the appearance in the dressing-room of Gyula Hegyi, chairman of the National Committee for Physical Training and Sport, who was on his way to Chile with the Hungarian pentathlon team for the modern pentathlon world championship, and interrupted his journey to see the game.

The stands were already filled to capacity. The crowd was listening

69

to the music of the Royal Air Force band, or looking over their official programmes. Finally the referee's whistle was heard. The members of both teams marched out on to the field . . .

What will happen in London? Who will be the winner? Will the English be able to preserve their record of no home defeats?

In Hungary, in the factories, co-operative farms and shops, the schools, the trams and restaurants, the England–Hungary match was the main topic of conversation. Everybody talked about the London weather, the ball, the dimensions of the field, about Puskas and the blond Wright, about Grosics and the reckless Merrick, about Bozsik and the lightning-swift Sewell, and about Lorant and the lion-hearted Mortensen with as much learning as the oldest football fans. Young and old, little boys and grandfathers, little girls and grandmothers – who have probably never seen a football match in their lives – were all in the greatest excitement over the England–Hungary game.

The people of the entire country sent the Hungarian national team off on their journey with great confidence and affection and it is no exaggeration to say that on the day of the great match the entire country awaited the news from London with keen interest and excitement. The electrical shops did hurried business in the loaning of loudspeakers, amplifiers and radios. In the windows of department stores, restaurants and shops notices were displayed: 'We are broadcasting the match of the century.' All over Budapest electricians busily installed loudspeakers. People besieged the offices of the newspapers. 'How is the weather in London?' 'Have any of the boys been injured?' 'It is true that there is a dense fog in London?'

Around three o'clock in the afternoon people were to be seen hurrying about. They were rushing to get home, or to a place where the match was being broadcast. By a quarter past three Budapest seemed to be deserted; only at a few places were there to be seen crowds where people had gathered around loudspeakers. The cinemas were showing films to almost empty houses; in the trams the crowding stopped during this otherwise busy hour and there were no passengers on the buses either. In many of the factories, at the request of the workers, the shift was begun earlier than usual.

The 25th. The time in London is 2.17 p.m. and Hidegkuti launches the ball on its ninety-minute course. It is worthwhile reviewing the happenings of the first forty seconds.

Hidegkuti plays the ball to Kocsis, who rolls it back to Bozsik, who is 3 to 4 yards behind him. Bozsik passes steeply to Budai on the outside-right, but the English left half-back saves in front of the Hungarian forward by taking the ball over the side line. Budai takes the throw-in, but because of a foot fault the referee gives the English a throw-in. Zakarias seizes the English throw-in, takes one or two steps with the ball then plays it to Bozsik. The right half-back slips it with lightning speed to Hidegkuti. There are three English players in front of Hidegkuti but the centre-forward carries the ball past the withdrawing English defence and lets loose a powerful shot from the penalty area. Goal!!! The white English ball is in the net.

There is paralysed silence in the stands. The English spectators can't believe their eyes. One or two seconds go by before the Hungarian players, too, wake up to what has happened. But then everybody rushes over to Hidegkuti. They hug and kiss the 'old man' as his team-mates affectionately call him. One up for Hungary!

There is no time for irritation over Hidegkuti's disallowed goal, but after three wonderful passes by the English players the equalizing goal is scored. But what happens afterwards has hardly if ever been recorded before in the annals of football. The spectators are plunged into amazement after amazement. The Hungarian players carry out the tactical instructions to the letter. The forwards constantly change positions. Not infrequently it happens that the forward line is as follows: Czibor, Puskas, Budai, Hidegkuti, Kocsis.

Then comes the twenty-fifth minute: the most beautiful goal of the 'Match of the Century', perhaps of the century. The ball hugs the ground from five or six players' feet finally to get to Czibor, who has withdrawn to the right outside position. Czibor 'serves' the ball to Puskas, who is in the inside-right position, and the latter takes the ball past Wright and from the side of the goal where the goalkeeper is standing sends it into the left corner with tremendous force. The spectators applaud the wonderful goal for a long time.

There is nothing surprising about the fact that the Hungarian team play frequently moves the sportsmanlike English spectators to applause. But it certainly makes one think when the most noted experts of international football, who usually maintain their calmness and self-possession during the exciting moments of many a fine game, now also come under the spell of the match. Each one gives expression to his enthusiasm, according to his individual temperament, when the fourth, the fifth and finally the sixth Hungarian ball crashes into Merrick's net.

Along the inside border of the high grandstand the yellow arc-lights so typical of London are turned on. A real London fog descends on the playing field when the match comes to an end. And just as after the final at the Olympic Games, now, too, the victorious Hungarian team stand in the middle of the field before the camera lenses of the English photographers, drenched, tired, but infinitely happy.

Many would think that after such a great triumph the walls of the Hungarian dressing-room would be almost flying apart from joy. But this isn't the way it is. The players are boundlessly happy but they are still under the influence of the great physical and mental exertion. They struggled through the ninety minutes not only with their feet but also with their hearts and brains. It is understandable that after the great excitement they rest quietly, without speaking, on the little benches. However, they soon find their tongues. But by this time every Hungarian footballer has about ten English newspaper reporters about him. They fire questions at them rapidly.

'How did you feel during the great match?'

'What are your thoughts now after your great victory?'

The players in the English dressing-room are quiet, but they are not depressed in spirit. 'Any selected team would have been beaten by this Hungarian team on this afternoon,' says Ramsey, the famous right-back. 'They not only have the most technique but are also the most sportsmanlike eleven we have ever encountered' – this from Matthews, the best English player. 'The most sportsmanlike eleven.' This is praise indeed from the lips of an English footballer.

It is evening, the evening of the great match. The strains of a song can be heard from the adjoining dressing-room: the Hungarian footballers are singing.

Three o'clock. Practically the whole of Hungary was sitting beside the radio. And hardly a minute of the broadcast was heard, when boundless joy in Budapest, and in the other towns and villages, welcomed the first Hungarian goal. They thought of a novel method in the mines: the scores were marked up on the sides of the 'cages' descending into the pits, to keep the miners informed on the course of the match. And after every fresh Hungarian goal enthusiastic hurrahs were heard: strangers and friends alike hugged each other and perhaps the shouts of joy resounded all the way to the Wembley

Stadium. The victory 6–3 was greeted with tremendous joy throughout the whole country. In the streets of towns and villages everyone told everyone else about the sensational result, old and young spoke of the brilliant success, the wonderful stand of the Hungarian sportsmen, with an enthusiasm never witnessed before. Far into the night everyone was still revelling in wild joy, the face of the nation was that of New Year's Eve . . .

Soon after the victory – not long after the radio broadcast – special editions of newspapers appeared on the streets and passers-by snatched up the first on-the-spot reports like hot cakes. And in the first moments of the joy over the victory, old football fans and new recruits, workers and peasants, students, apprentices and the great camp of sportsmen composed telegrams of greetings to send to London. No fewer than 8,000 wires were sent that day from Hungary to the victors.

In the days after the victory the country was still under its spell. Everybody spoke with gratitude and love of those superb footballers who won this victory, who after so many shining Hungarian sporting victories once again proved the high level of the sports movement in the Hungarian People's Democracy. And this triumph was all the more precious because the Hungarian selected team achieved it over opponents who are famous all over the world for their mastery, perseverance and ability.

Perhaps never in its history has the little frontier railway station in Hegyeshalom been as active as on the night of 2 and 3 December. Not only did the local residents stay up all night but many people of the surrounding region and even Budapest came to be the first to shake hands with the London victors. And truly this wonderful moment, when the train bearing the footballers pulled into Hegyeshalom and the Hungarian national anthem was played, made everyone forget every bit of fatigue. 'Puskas! Bozsik! Kocsis!' The names are shouted as the players appeared at the windows of the train. Their families, sporting friends and strangers hurried to the train that they may be able to speak to them as soon as possible. The train started on its way to Budapest. All along the way waves of enthusiasm met the boys. In Gyor, Komarom, Tatabanya and wherever the train stopped, showers of flowers, gifts and recognition for their performance met the footballers. Everywhere the fans wanted to delay the train.

73

On the train, the match was the chief topic of conversation. The coaches and the leaders of the sports associations listened with great attention to the most minute details of the London match. Lorant described how the English players marked Puskas and how he was still able to shoot two goals. Zakarias praised the sportsmanlike English spectators who applauded the Hungarian goals just as much as those scored by the English players ... Coach Gyula Mandi recalled how wonderfully the players adhered to instructions and how much the forwards moved about and even helped in the rear when necessary. There would have been much more to talk about, but the train was already in the outskirts of Budapest. And when it rolled into the glass-roofed building of the East Railway Terminus, the next few minutes were memorable. Tens of thousands of the capital's population greeted the players with boundless affection.

The delegates of the Hungarian Working People's Party, the Government, the mass organizations, the factories and large groups of Young Pioneers greeted the heroes who had proved the high quality of Hungarian football, the strength and maturity of Hungarian sport, before the whole world. The enthusiasm increased when, in the name of the players, Ferenc Puskas, team captain, expressed thanks for the great affection shown them.

'We thank the Party, the Government and our people for making it possible for us to prepare undisturbed for the greatest sporting task of our lives. We ask you to place your faith in us in the future too, and we promise you that by applying all our knowledge we shall endeavour heart and soul to solve the great tasks of the future.'

And a few days later in the Parliament building ... In the reception room of the Presidential Council, under the brilliance of the photo-floodlamps, Grosics, Buzanszky, Lantos, Lorant, Bozsik, Zakarias, Budai, Kocsis, Hidegkuti, Puskas, Czibor, and Geller, and the team officials Gusztav Sebes, Pal Titkos and Gyula Mandi, one after the other received State decorations. The sportsmen, veterans of many tough battles, were deeply moved, gazing with moist eyes at the glittering Orders of Merit, which expressed the finest recognition of their country and the millions of its people.

from the Hungarian News and Information Service, 1953

Inside Forwards
FRANK NORMAN

Every year they have what they call the cup finale this as you may imagian is a game of football, but in the nick this is almost unreconiseable as such, the reason being it is so bent that it could be anything from water polo to a wrestling match. This high light in the sporting year is always held on a Saterday afternoon and on this particular Saterday afternoon it always rains but this does not dampen the high spirits of the chaps, and the barons and book makers did a very brisk trade.

The most important thing to the book-makers was to get which ever side had the most snout on it, to go bent, this was'nt all that hard to do as all they had to do was put a bit of snout about in the direction of the goal keeper and may be the left back, and one or two of the others and there you are he'd have them straitend before you can say knife.

The only thing about this was the punters used to go poty and some very strong language would change hands and in some cases the out come may take the shape of a punch on the end of the hooter for the punter or maybe the baron and the book-make will sudenly develope a pain in the head caused by half a house brick wraped up in a sock.

The kick off is at half past two and they get a proper reffery from the outside, I should think that when he has finished his ninty minutes reffereing for ever, but every year this same reffery turns up, I think they must pay him danger money or something.

Also some of the locale gentry turn up to see the game, they are the same people who are members of the visiting commity, when the match is over one of them presents the cup to the winning team and makes a little speech every year, in which he thanks the rcf for giveing up his time to come, and he also says that he has never seen a finer game of football in his life. After he has made his speech he asks the captain of the winning team to come and get the cup, so the captain limps painfully forward shakes hands with the geezer and takes the cup. The cup is inscribed with the words:

It is also pretty much knocked about but no one worries about this all that much, as all they are interested in is colecting their snout.

Of corse I would be telling a lie if I said that every one who played football was bent, but the ones that dont go bent dont count; at all.

from Bang to Rights, 1958

Sunday Soccer
JOHN MOYNIHAN

It goes without saying these days that the pastures of Hyde Park opposite Knightsbridge Barracks are littered with games involving actors, writers, poets, painters, doctors, lawyers, architects, publishers, accountants, journalists, spies, con men, script writers, rancid layabouts, hostile Jews, cantankerous Catholics, dirty Protestants, Italian waiters, greasy Irishmen, turgid Greeks . . . and so on.

Our mass enthusiasm for the job is emphasized by the adroit manner in which we waggle our protruding arses as we run forward in search of the ball, by the way in which our voices rise in anger: 'You bastard. Keep your elbows down.'

Some of us look very spruce in new exotic strip with Vidal Sassoonish haircuts, medallions, diamond-trimmed jockstraps and gold teeth. Our wives and mistresses stand on the touch line, toeing the earth like exotic mares, fluffy and uncritical and longing for this madness to end. The sides in question have strange-sounding names like Chelsea Casuals, Battersea Park, Coffin Casuals, TV Scriptwriters, Cecil Gee, Soho, Primrose. We hate to lose.

Standing in Hyde Park with the sky a glorious dirty sheet of ambling black, with the rain lashing down and mud up to the ankles so that the goalkeepers have the appearance of Early Man, it is not hard to loosen a tear into the glass-tinted acres around the centre circle and say: 'Hey, hey, I was around when all this started and there were a handful of us and we didn't wear shorts because we were afraid to show our knees.' It was 1956, and Sunday soccer wasn't fashionable and actors grew fat by staying in bed until lunchtime, chipping the white froth off their tongues while waiting for the lunchtime kettle to whistle for Nescafé. This was long ago when men like Sean Connery did not hurry off to football grounds on a Sunday afternoon and join in a game far below the dreams of James Bond. When we began it was a hard grinding road in which we were faced with almost every conceivable disaster and every conceivable humiliation. The beginnings were slow.

When I was finally let out of the army, in which I had only been quietly eliminated from further soccer progress after letting in thirteen goals before half-time against the Royal Horse Artillery at Aldershot, the actual chance of playing the game seemed to have finally passed me by.

There seemed no opportunity of playing the game in London. The whole network was a closed circle; a postman could play for Mount Pleasant, a printer for Reuters, a porter for Covent Garden, but for professional people I have mentioned there wasn't a game to be had and anyway the volunteers were few. Soccer was still considered the property of the working classes and should be played by them because they were the only people with talent to play it; a worthy notion.

So we grew fat and sat in pubs on Sunday mornings and talked about the game we had seen at Stamford Bridge or White Hart Lane the afternoon before. To gain exercise I wrote infuriated letters to football critics complaining of their treatment of Chelsea Football Club. Alan Ross of the *Observer* wrote back to me on one occasion: 'I know from experience that it is hard to see a team about which one feels strongly with sober eyes, but I cannot really believe you can find anything in Chelsea play to give you pleasure.'

The Royal Borough of Chelsea at that time was on the eve of a social change, which was to rip out its Bohemian guts and transform it into a headquarters for the clever-clever, the zany-fashionable. It was in the Queen's Elm in the Fulham Road where I first heard that I was to be included in a team which would be playing in Hyde Park the following Sunday. In the side were a number of curios from Finch's, the Queen's Elm and the Markham Arms.

The Queen's Elm was still basically a headquarters for artists rather than footballers and actors, at that time, including John Minton, Lucien Freud, Ruskin Spear, Robert Colquhoun, Robert MacBryde, Francis Bacon, George Barker, the poet, wearing a rustic goalkeeper's cap: a rumbustious moody centre. On the bar stool sat the late *Daily*

Express journalist, John Macadam, who was one of the few customers there who really knew the game. He was a marvellous wit and his wingy moustache bobbed up and down as he told funny stories about goalkeepers. When I told him I was actually playing football, he said: 'You'd better kick off with a rush.'

I looked forward eagerly to that game, cutting down on the lobster and gulls' eggs at Claridge's, offered nightly in mounds by the mothers of debutantes who wanted this roving gossip-columnist to put their names in the paper. It was a case of getting vaguely fit and the regime was ordered.

It was a regime which was not adhered to. David Stone, the novelist, who recently died, gave a memorable party in Edith Grove in which the house received excessive mutilations. The police arrived and were promptly almost disembowelled by a carnivorous painter who showed great dexterity in knocking off their helmets. As they dragged him off in a state of exhaustion with blood spurting out of his nostrils, I asked David, who had chosen our side, if he was selected for our team. 'No,' said David, 'but I've got a Hungarian.' This was a touch of genius because the Hungarian was called Sandor and had played for a class team in Budapest; a refugee who had recently escaped during the 1956 revolution.

The next night we trailed into Finch's for a drink and met the Hungarian, a somewhat frail, pale-faced refugee, who was reeling and muttering: 'I want a woman.' I visualized him joining the SW3 mob who were forming into a clique called the Chelsea Set.

Whatever they say to the contrary, this over-glamorized set lived through days and nights of aimless boredom gatecrashing parties and hanging against the bar of Finch's and the Markham Arms, waiting and waiting for the next party, the next man or the next girl. It was easy to get into and less easy to get out. This was usually done through the resources of genuine talent.

This was what fashion-designer Mary Quant had, and she actually profited from the whole mystique, making money in quantities with her King's Road shop and 'super' designs. And Samantha Eggar, with windswept, robin-redbreast-coloured hair, became a Hollywood star. Others drifted back to where they had come from, to wither in the cosiness of their ancestral homes married to pimply girls, who had decided it was time to brush their teeth.

But some of it was hilarious if you didn't let it hold you down, and some of the girls were beautiful. It was in this atmosphere that Sandor, David and I drank that evening in Finch's and Sandor let out the odd belch.

Sex, of course, was a predominant problem at that hour of night, but most available crumpet had flown and Sandor had to moon over his drinks. We felt if we didn't find him a woman he wouldn't play for us against the other mob.

The other mob was a side of Cambridge people I didn't personally know at that time. They had in fact been playing a number of weeks, a sturdy bunch of lads including a thin, handsome young Scot called Karl Miller, who had just come down from Cambridge, now literary editor of the *New Statesman*, Tony White, then an Old Vic actor of distinction, now an author, and Neil Ascherson, the Bonn correspondent of the *Observer*, and Jonathan Miller, who went on 'Beyond the Fringe'.

On that first morning, during the Suez crisis, six of them and one intrepid girl went out into the park, in a sense to work off feelings of antipathy towards Eden. Six out of forty had accepted.

David eventually dragged Sandor off home, the muscular Magyar uttering mild obscenities below his breath as he tiptoed down the Fulham Road with the grace of a mating ostrich.

The next morning I woke up red-rimmed in my basement flat, with rock-n-roll cackling in my ears. 'You're playing football this morning,' said my flatmate, who had made tea for his actress girlfriend, unleashing mild squeaky snores from the next room. 'Poor bastard. What do you want to play football for?' 'Because of this,' I said, pointing to my belly. 'And besides I love the game. Got an Alka-Seltzer?'

I put on my duffle-coat over a pair of rugby shorts drifting below my knees and a T-shirt with moth holes on my chest and made off for the park, my football boots, Army surplus, tucked in a suitcase full of Spanish sand.

A cold, misty morning in February. As I crossed the park in the silence of a Sunday morning I became conscious of others of a similar stamp moving towards a grass strip near the Serpentine, their jeans, duffle-coats, beards, hair and suitcase merged into one mass of sticky raffishness. The odd girl bursting out of her jeans walked along beside them trying to keep pace. Two players started running with a football and throwing it to each other.

'I haven't come to play that game,' I said. 'That's the only game they know how to play,' said a grave intellectual named Nicholas Tomalin, who was at that time a gossip-columnist on the *Daily Express*.

David appeared with Sandor in his car, staring out at our mob with mirth broadening over his face. 'We must be mad,' he said, coming over to me. 'Ah, our Honved friend has made it.' I said.

After some confusion, Karl, a wispy Burns figure, with a rich dissenting Scottish voice, and Tony, tall, enormously attractive and totally immersed in black leather, got their side, mostly players in jeans and jerseys, lined up, while David and I sorted our lot out.

By some strange twist of misunderstanding, we had thirteen a side, but that didn't seem to worry anybody. Our goalpost was a grandiose, awe-inspiring tree looking like John Charles, and during their first attack, Tony's team, running forward in one solid wave, carried ball and goalkeeper and almost the tree towards the direction of Marble Arch.

From the kick-off I flicked the ball to our Hungarian inside-left, and said: 'For God's sake do something.' He was still half-asleep muttering 'I want a woman' but the feeling of leather at his feet brought some sort of recollection to him of stadiums far away in Budapest, Puskas and Kocsis. He set off shaking off his randiness and after beating five prostrate men, cut towards the goal which was a pile of duffle-coats, beating another five men with one flick of his waist. I was running along beside him steaming, my lungs groaning and jerking after two minutes' running. There was the slapping of flesh as men who had rarely played the game before tried to tackle with their heads, backsides and necks. Sandor went past Jonathan Miller, who for some unknown reason was crouching, and still the Hungarian flew, majestically beating all and now coming up on the goalkeeper who was as big as a tank and a solid demon designer with the name Assheton Gorton; he swung his boot and crashed in a shot which was surely a goal, had I not been running vigorously towards Bayswater ahead of our champion. The shot hit me on the backside and bounced away and Sandor roared: 'You firker.'

We lost that game, although Sandor scored ten or eleven goals, but we would have surely won but for our defence.

At any rate these Sunday games were clarified as a craze and every Sunday from then on we used to meet by that John Charles tree and bash each other to pieces. As the word spread in the Chelsea pubs, more people came: con men in Bentleys and advertising men with brandy on their breath, and poets with woollen knickers as boot laces and intellectuals on motor scooters, and one day we played with a man with one leg who came crashing through our defence on his crutches.

A few weeks later we took a team up to Cambridge to play King's College, and this time we had an even better player than Sandor, another Hungarian who was living in a house that had partly been turned over for refugees by the owners. Sandor, somewhere, had found a woman and disappeared.

The night before the match the son of that household gave a party in the main sitting-room, and I was astonished to find in that jocular, boozy atmosphere, that we were surrounded by temporary beds in which a number of figures lay snoring contentedly.

The refugees had retired early, pulling off their trousers and yawning in their underpants and completely oblivious of the roar of Cambridge conversation.

The next day our Hungarian massacred the men of King's. His shooting was so strong that it drove their goalkeeper almost brutally into goal with the ball. He dribbled at will through their defence and we stood by and let him get on with it. It was a case of giving him the ball and letting him go away contentedly like a man on horseback in Rotten Row. Sweat poured off the men of King's who bravely acknowledged defeat by a master.

But our Hungarians faded from the scene and we never saw them again. It was a time for reorganization and planning with our limited resources. About this time, Brian Glanville, author and *Sunday Times* sports writer, was introduced to me by David Sylvester, art critic, over a dirty game of table soccer. I invited Brian along to Hyde Park for our Sunday games, and he accepted with alacrity, having like me had no opportunity to play since his schooldays at Charterhouse.

Presented with the chance of playing football as a rugged left-back, Brian's fanaticism for the game broadened, his hips grew larger, his voice boomed higher, he was convinced at last that he could kick a football in the right direction.

Both of us became involved with the intricacies of park football and whether or not a tree could be beaten by sheer skill alone. Our telephone conversations analysing the game often lasted a good hour.

The name of the club was eventually suggested by David Stone, and we became Chelsea Casuals during the autumn of 1957. But dissension was already creeping into the side. On wet, ghost-like evenings we would assemble like a group of *pieds noirs* in a Chelsea garage, where Tony White had a temporary job.

The question was who to leave out during the organized games which were creeping into the schedule. We had acquired a number of players, including a master-baker from Swiss Cottage, an Olympian goalkeeper, an escort of Princess Alexandra, a soap-sud salesman, a Chelsea butcher's boy, and a string of mysterious layabouts exuding beer and brandy breath.

These meetings became extremely tetchy with everyone disagreeing about who should play and who should be left out. An element of seriousness was creeping in and the pounding the Casuals got against the BBC at Motspur Park when Frank Bowling, the British Guianese painter, came on gleaming at half-time in perfect strip to hammer the ball into our own net, because he still had his eyes shut after an all-night session in a night-club, told us that something would have to be done quickly.

We were annihilated by the Old Etonians on their playing fields, the referee surprising our master-baker, who prided himself at having at least played reasonable football in the RAF, by controlling the game with a broken leg. 'You're like a pack of hounds,' said an O.E. contemptuously. But we managed to break one of their jaws.

About this time Brian and I, through a mysterious piece of luck, started training one night a week at the Queen's Park Rangers ground with yet another invention which had come into being: The Showbiz XI. There the glossy stars came and budding disc-jockeys – Ronnie Carroll and Glen Mason and Andrew Ray and Ziggy Jackson, whom we called 'bearded Ziggy'.

We used to do some lapping under the astute, patient care of the Queen's Park Rangers' trainer, Alex Farmer, play six-asides and then take a long bath. The organizer of the Showbiz team was the disc-jockey Jimmy Henney, who would sit like a contented sheepdog in Mr Farmer's treatment room being massaged on the calves. Everything then was 'fantastic'.

Those dark nights gave one the impression of a small, provincial railway station being invaded by a travelling circus full of lispy, showbiz chat. As towels were rubbed over ripe flesh, the latest jokes were recalled with howls of laughter and fat actors weighed themselves with much concern on the scales of the Third Division club.

The Showbiz team eventually were able to call on a number of former professionals and Wally Barnes, Billy Wright, and later Tommy Docherty have become almost fixtures in the set-up. But in 1958 they were still in their pioneer stage, so when we met in a game at Hendon that spring it was like two primitive waggon trains running into each other.

The mud came up to our waists and the Chelsea Casuals were again annihilated by 7–1. We were soon at a disadvantage, the crowd obviously fancying the Showbiz team in their gleaming black strip against our sombre, semi-laundered rags, our left-half was taken to hospital with a slipped cartilage and our inside-left was drunk, having consumed ten brandies on his way to the ground. After the game we discovered that the elaborate tea which had been laid on had been devoured by hangers-on.

From then on Chelsea Casuals gradually moved out of its cocoon in the park and became deeply committed to engagement on LCC pitches at Hackney Marshes, Wormwood Scrubs and Wandsworth Common, against sides with odd-sounding names – Shaftesbury Avenue Fire Station, Speedway Riders, Arsenal Supporters' Club, Western Union.

It was on these vast windy open spaces where goalposts were as numerous as gravestones in a city cemetery that we came under the harsh, hostile glare of teams who knew these pitches as well as their own palm sweats. We looked out of place in the little box huts without showers, where we were forced to change, mere shacks, in which twenty-two men and a referee were expected, for a small fee payable to the London County Council, to take their trousers down at the same time.

Brian had introduced Reg Drury to captain the side, a shrewd football writer bred on Hackney Marshes, a pencil-thin eagle-eyed East Londoner, who viewed our inept manoeuvres with undisguised horror through glinting steel-rimmed glasses. Reg, on one occasion at Hackney Marshes, as the other team arrived without proper strip to play us, complained: 'I wouldn't mind ordinarily, Brian, but I've got friends on the Marshes.'

Brian also introduced an Italian coach, a young blond Florentine called Piero, who tried to force us into some sort of coherent combination. Tears swelled into his huge eyes during the game as he bellowed at the fast disappearing centre-forward: 'John, don't run away.'

The selection committee, as it was, moved to my flat, but the atmosphere grew even worse. Tony White and Karl Miller had already formed a splinter group which moved to Battersea Park and became the club of that name. It was the quality of seriousness which was creeping into Chelsea Casuals which they objected to, so away they went over the river and into other mists.

In my flat we would sit huddled around my bed working out who was to play and why. Our left-half, a painter, who had introduced an element of Zen into his game, broke up one of these sessions when he made a long speech in my defence, saying that I was not sleeping at nights because there was an undercurrent of opinion in the team insinuating that I was a natural goalkeeper, and not a natural centre-forward. 'John needs time to think about this, to achieve a peace of mind which will tolerate such brutality. His sleeplessness is due to exterior disorders. He must be allowed to achieve a balanced mind. And I want to be captain.'

There was a loud barking sound from the rest of the team as the last of the Spanish *rosé* was drained, cantankerous sounds of disagreement.

Brian was right when he said these sessions were run on group therapeutic lines without the analyst. They had to stop.

So we advanced forward in disorder, although clad decently now in red strip, with the selection of the team nominally in the hands of Brian and myself, although usually before our team really caught on it took about fifty telephone calls to get a side at all.

The sickening Sunday dawns when the telephone would ring and a voice would wheeze down the other end of the line: 'I can't play today. I've got pneumonia.' 'Oh, for God's sake, why?' The groans of a wife beside one saying: 'Can't you tell your bloody muddy oafs to ring up at a reasonable hour?'

Dialling a number in Willesden for a London School of Economics student and the long wait down the other end as one hung on for a naked bleary-eyed form to pick up the receiver with a snort and apologize that he couldn't play because his corns were hurting. Tracking down a student of the Royal College of Art in Wandsworth and giving him elaborate instructions about getting to Wormwood Scrubs and that one would meet him at East Acton tube station at 10.15, and then the long wait and nobody coming, and the tubes rattling by in streaks of plunging red, and nobody coming, and Reg's long look in the dressing-room, lacing up his legs with a mile of bandage.

And the rainy mornings ringing the ground and the LCC park keeper saying: 'It's hoff,' and the delight in his voice as he rubbed it in. The dirty teams which we sometimes took on, such as one lot in the Fulham Sportsmen's League at Tooting Common, who threatened the referee with violence during the game if they lost and the referee meekly giving them a winning goal after the right-winger had crossed the ball a good yard over the line, so much so that he fell over in the long grass.

And the tactics of some of the dour Sunday players that one got to know, and learnt to give back; the centre-half who put his square skull in my mouth as I endeavoured to go past him and I bit hard on bone and bristle and took away a good lump as he came down on top of me and I said: 'Go easy.' And the nigglers, the weasel-faced inside-forwards from sweet factories and printing works who kept up an incessant: 'Ref, hey ref, ref, hey, keep your hands down, ref, penalty ref, hey ref, you bugger, ref, no goal, ref, off-side ref.'

And the players of a Sunday morning, the tall spade at Hackney Marshes, a temporary goalkeeper, with a blue corduroy cap, brilliant yellow jersey, pink shorts, white socks and new boots, smoking a fag in the goalmouth before the game, as nonchalant as a jazz pianist between solos. A full-back at Sandhurst saying: 'Permission to go up for a corner, Sir' to his captain, and being refused. The inside-forward we had transferred to us from the Royal College of Art, an ex-Rochdale professional, who never stopped giggling when he had the ball. David Miller, of the *Sunday Telegraph*, beating three men and running on to make a telephone call. Our 'Zen' left-half going through periods of meditation during the game by making quiet tackles on non-existent opponents. Our centre-half we picked off the park, after he had called us 'a bloody shower' and nicknamed 'Blondie'; a player of fickle disposition, whose sudden generosity would make us scream and Reg howl. Reg refusing to be congratulated after he had scored and muttering: 'All right, one's not enough,' Reg, who knows all the pros, pleasing a great hunk of a man called Strain in the dressing-room before a match: 'I know you son, Gravesend Reserves,' and a great chest swelling out in appreciation: 'That's right, that's right.'

But confusion grew less and less as Brian fanatically bore on from year to year with almost savage seasonal programmes with over thirty games on the schedule. The Italian coach had gone, Reg was still there as captain but the side had altered shape with an experienced Scottish element woven in incorporating a fastidious quality of professionalism, a hardness of play which swung the club's formations and turned them into a winning combination, with decisive victories against all the sides who had previously humiliated us. Brian still sits at the telephone with fantastic zeal for finding fixtures, so much so that I feel he could get a team out of the Zoo for the Casuals if necessary.

The other sides have grown into orderly groups too. It all goes with the emancipation of football, the smoothness of the new professional with his Op-Art kit rubbing off on the modest amateur. At any rate most of our rough edges have gone. The enterprising Tony White fixed up two tours of France for Battersea Park, one in Dieppe and one in Paris, which slightly flummoxed the French who perhaps expected firmer competition than they actually got, but the Battersea team, bleary-eyed, pursued a difficult task and were never disgraced although drugged by Pernod.

The teams increase, competition swells, there is a Queen's Elm league. Disorder, emotion and bloodshed can never be ruled out, we play what might be called LSD soccer, a pleasure only for the participants. The drug, at any rate, has taken a firm hold in ten years, as good a way as any of staying sane some say, although outsiders think we're barmy.

From *The Soccer Syndrome*, 1966

The Munich Disaster, 1958
GEOFFREY GREEN

[Green had been booked to cover the Cup tie between Manchester United and Red Star in Belgrade, but *The Times* ordered him to go instead to report a World Cup qualifying match at Cardiff between Wales and Israel: 'Life indeed is largely a matter of luck and timing and but for that strange throw of the dice I should now probably

86

be roaming the Elysian fields with the many friends I lost that day.']

Everyone will have their own memories of that dark February day twenty years ago when the world seemed suddenly to shift on its axis and disintegrate. For myself, having returned to London overnight from Cardiff, I went to a cinema that Thursday afternoon.

On emerging around teatime, the first thing I saw on the street was an evening paper billposter screaming out the dreadful news in the heaviest type. I ran home like a hare just in time to hear the telephone ringing. It was the office. For two hours they had been trying to make contact. Then the BBC rang. At that stage precise information on the casualties was scarce and confused. No one knew anything for certain apart from the stark fact that United's aeroplane had crashed on take-off at Munich Riem Airport.

Sometime after midnight I finally got home having written two pieces for the paper in the office and done four broadcasts at the BBC all virtually in the dark of uncertain knowledge. One of those broadcasts was in company with Walter Winterbottom, himself a former United player and at that time manager of the England side due to take part only four months later in the World Cup of 1958, in Sweden. Little was he to know at that moment that his team had lost three key figures, one in each department of its make-up: Roger Byrne at full back, Duncan Edwards at half back and Tommy Taylor at centre forward. For myself, on returning home, I went to bed and wept at the loss of so many friends.

When Jimmy Murphy[1] got back to Manchester and Old Trafford from Cardiff he had no inkling of what had happened. There were only three or four of the staff on duty, but a strained, unreal atmosphere seemed to hang in the air. Going into one of the offices he ran into a secretary who appeared white, dazed and scarcely able to speak. Then her tears began to fall; she stammered out the news and the enormity of the disaster struck him. Taking a bottle of whisky from a sideboard he quickly retired to his own office and wept.

By nightfall there were few people in Britain unmoved by the extent and nature of the tragedy. Manchester itself became a dead city as the blinds were drawn in every house as if somehow to keep out the truth and reality of it all.

1. United's assistant manager and manager of the Welsh national side.

87

H. E. Bates, the novelist, later epitomized the universal feeling in a tribute published in the *F.A. Year Book* of 1958–59:

At six o'clock, out of pure curiosity, I turned on my television set. As the news came on, the screen seemed to go black. The normally urbane voice of the announcer seemed to turn into a sledge hammer. My eyes went deathly cold and I sat listening with a frozen brain to that cruel and shocking list of casualties that was now to give the word Munich an even sadder meaning than it had acquired on a day before the war, after a British Prime Minister had come home to London waving a pitiful piece of paper and most of us knew that new calamities of war were inevitable.

In the end fate reaped a deadly harvest of eight United players (five of whom had played in the 3–3 draw the previous day), eight journalists, three Manchester club officials, two members of the aircrew (one the co-pilot) and two other passengers – a total of twenty-three from a full complement of forty-three who had set out on the flight.

The Departed

Players: Roger Byrne (left back), Geoff Bent (reserve left back), Eddie Colman (right half), Mark Jones (centre half), Duncan Edwards (left half), David Pegg (outside left), Tommy Taylor (centre forward), Liam ('Bill') Whelan (inside right).

Journalists: Alf Clarke (*Manchester Evening Chronicle*), Don Davies (*Manchester Guardian*), George Follows (*Daily Herald*), Tom Jackson (*Manchester Evening News*), Archie Ledbrooke (*Daily Mirror*), Henry Rose (*Daily Express*), Frank Swift (*News of the World*), Eric Thompson (*Daily Mail*).

Officials: Walter Crickmer (Man. United secretary), Tom Curry (Man. United trainer), Bert Whalley (Man. United team coach).

Crew: Captain K. G. Rayment (co-pilot), Mr W. T. Cable (steward).

Others: Mr B. P. Miklos (travel agent), Mr Willie Satinoff (Man. United supporter).

The Survivors:

Matt Busby (Man. United manager).

Players: John Berry (outside right), Jackie Blanchflower (centre half), Bobby Charlton (inside left), Billy Foulkes (right back), Harry Gregg (goalkeeper), Ken Morgans (outside right), Albert Scanlon (outside left), Dennis Viollet (inside left), Ray Wood (goalkeeper).

Press: E. Ellyard (*Daily Mail* photographer), Peter Howard (*Daily Mail* photographer), Frank Taylor (*News Chronicle* sports writer).

Others: Mrs Vera Lukić and baby, Mrs B. P. Miklos, Mr N. Tomasevic.

Without question that was the darkest day in British sport, more solemn and far reaching even than the Burnden Park crowd disaster when thirty-three people were crushed to death and suffocated during an F. A. Cup tie between Bolton Wanderers and Stoke City in 1946; more traumatic even than the Ibrox Park disaster later in Glasgow when over sixty people died in a pile-up on the exit steps of the stadium during the final minutes of a match between those traditional rivals Rangers and Celtic.

The significant difference lay in the fact that while those other tragedies, shocking though they were, seemed almost faceless and anonymous (except to the families involved), those young Manchester United players had appeared many times on the television screens of every front parlour the length and breadth of the country. To millions they had become identified in their many exploits almost as personal friends. Some years earlier, in 1949, a similar kind of accident had happened in Italy when the great Torino team – seven or eight of them then current members of the Italian national side – crashed into Superga Hill in their aeroplane on the way back to Turin from Spain. On that occasion, too, some half a dozen journalists travelling with the party had perished with most of the players. Like the plaque that has stood in the Old Trafford press box these past twenty years commemorating the deaths of those eight Munich air disaster pressmen, there stands in the Comunale Stadium in Turin a similar memorial to their Italian brothers. And over the portals of both grounds also are enshrined the names of the players who were taken before their time.

Yet the Superga disaster had by no means the same world-wide impact as Munich. This was brought home to me a summer or so later when on holiday in Spain. I was approached by a young Spanish boy. Anxious to earn a few pesetas, he offered to conduct me to the local bull-ring and a church or two. The afternoon sun was high and the heat simmered like an iron as he took on the role of experienced guide.

During our conversation he suddenly produced a grubby cigarette card from his trouser pocket. I could see it held the face of a footballer. Realizing I was from England, he asked if I knew of the player. I took the card into my hand. It was Tommy Taylor. I nodded my head, whereupon with dramatic use of his little hand he illustrated how the plane had crashed. Then, to my utter astonishment, he told how his village school had gone into mourning and had been closed for a week. I remember wondering at the time whether one of our own little schools back home would have reacted similarly had a Spanish football team perished likewise. I doubted it.

In June 1969 [eleven years after the event], the final findings of the Court of Inquiry into the Munich crash were published, after much controversy and backsliding by German officialdom.

The key witness in the inquiry which cleared Captain James Thain from blame for the disaster was a German pilot who was at Munich airport on the day of the crash. Herr Reinhard Meyer, a pilot since 1940 and an aircraft designer, was one of the first to reach the crashed aircraft. He told the British inquiry under Mr E. S. Fay that he 'was thinking about possible reasons for it and . . . was considering whether aircraft icing could have been the reason'. He said there was nothing like frost or frozen deposit on the wing of the BEA Elizabethan airliner as it lay at the end of the runway. There was melting snow only.'

The Fay Report comments: '. . . Herr Meyer was the only person to investigate the icing question within a short time of the accident. He looked with the eye of an experienced pilot and aircraft designer.' The inquiry finds that the cause of the crash was slush on the runway, and that it is 'possible but unlikely' that wing icing was a contributory cause.

Other findings of the inquiry, set up by the Prime Minister and the President of the Board of Trade in April last year, are that Captain Thain was not at fault with regard to runway slush, but that he was at fault with regard to wing icing. 'But,' the report adds, 'because wing icing is unlikely to have been a contributory cause of the accident, blame cannot be imputed to him.' The report also finds that Captain Thain, now aged forty-eight and a smallholder in Berkshire, was at fault in permitting his co-pilot – another captain – to occupy the left instead of the right-hand seat, 'but this played no part in causing the accident'. The report concludes: 'In accordance with our terms of reference, we therefore report that in our opinion blame for the accident is not to be imputed to Captain Thain.'

These findings are at variance with those of two inquiries conducted by the Germans, which declared that the decisive cause of the accident lay in wing icing and that runway slush was a further cause. The latest inquiry heard twenty-seven witnesses and the commission sat in London, Bremen and Frankfurt. The central witness was Captain Thain who, since the accident, has spent more than £1,000 trying to clear his name. He told the inquiry that before the unsuccessful take-off he and his co-pilot looked out of the windows and the wings looked clean. The Fay Commission examined a photograph produced by the German investigators. It was taken from the airport building just before the Elizabethan's departure. The photograph appeared to show no signs of snow on the wings. After examining an enlargement of the original negative, the Joint Air Reconnaissance Intelligence Centre decided that the whiteness on the wings may have been light reflected from the wet surface, and not ice as previously thought.

from *There's Only One United*, 1978

What I Owe to Football
ALBERT CAMUS

Yes, I played for several years at the University of Algiers. It seems to me like yesterday. But when, in 1940, I put on my boots again, I realized that it was not yesterday. Before the end of the first half, my tongue was hanging out like those *kabyles* dogs that one comes across at two o'clock in the afternoon, at Tizi-Ouzou. It was a long while ago, then, from 1928 onwards, I believe. I made my début with Montpensier sports club. God knows why, since I lived at Belcourt, and the Belcourt-Mustapha team is Gallia-Sports. But I had a friend, a shaggy fellow, who swam in the port with me and played water polo for Montpensier. That's how one's life is determined. Montpensier often played at the Manoeuvre Grounds, for no apparent reason. The ground was bumpier than the shin of a visiting centre-forward at the Alenda Stadium, Oran. I quickly learned that the ball never came to you where you expected it. This helped me in life, above all in the metropolis, where people are not always wholly straightforward. But after a year of bumps and Montpensier, they made me ashamed of myself at the lycée: a 'university man' ought to play for Algiers University, R.U.A. At this period, the shaggy fellow had gone out of my life. We hadn't quarrelled, it was merely that he now went swimming at Padovani, where the water was not pure. Nor, frankly, were his motives. Personally, I found his motive charming, but she danced badly, which seemed to me insupportable in a woman. It's the man, is it not, who should tread on the toes? The shaggy fellow and I had merely promised to see each other again. But years have gone by. Much later, I frequented the Padovani restaurant (for pure motives) but the shaggy fellow had married his paralytic, who must have forbidden him to bathe, as is the usual practice.

Where was I? Yes, R.U.A. I was very pleased, the important thing for me being to play. I fretted with impatience from Sunday to Thursday, for training day, and from Thursday to Sunday, match day. So I joined the university men. And there I was, goalkeeper of the junior team. Yes, it all seemed quite easy. But I didn't know that I had just established a bond which would endure for years, embracing every stadium in the Department, and which would never come to an end. I did not know then that twenty years after, in the streets of Paris or even Buenos Aires (yes, it happened to me) the words R.U.A. spoken by a friend I met would make my heart beat again as foolishly as could be. And since I am giving away secrets, I can admit that in Paris, for instance, I go to watch the matches of the Racing Club de Paris, whom I have made my favourites solely because they wear the same jerseys as R.U.A., blue and white hoops. I must say, too, that Racing has some of the same eccentricities as R.U.A. It plays 'scientifically', as we say, and scientifically loses matches it should win. It seems that this has changed (so they write to me from Algiers) so far at least as R.U.A. are concerned. It needed to change – but not too much. After all, that was why I loved my team so much, not only for the joy of victory, so wonderful when it is combined with the weariness that follows exertion, but also for the stupid desire to cry on evenings when we had lost.

At full-back I had The Big Fellow – I mean Raymond Couard. He had a tough time of it, if I remember correctly. We used to play hard. Students, their fathers' sons, don't spare themselves. Poor us, in every sense, a good half of us mown down like corn! We had to face up to it. And we had to play 'sportingly', because that was the golden rule of the R.U.A., and 'strongly', because, when all is said and done, a man is a man. Difficult compromise! This cannot have changed, I am sure. The hardest team was Olympic Hussein Dey. The stadium is beside the cemetery. They made us realize, without mercy, that there was direct access. As for me, poor goalkeeper, they went for my body. Without Roger, I would have suffered. There was Boufarik, too, that great big centre-forward (among ourselves we called him Watermelon) who always came down with all his weight, right on my kidneys, without counting the cost: shin-massage with football boots, shirt pulled back by the hand, knees in the distinguished parts, sandwiches against the post . . . in brief, a scourge. And every time, Watermelon apologized with a 'Sorry, son,' and a Franciscan smile.

I shall stop. I have already exceeded the limits set for me. And then, I am softening. There was good even in Watermelon. Besides, let us be frank, we paid him back. But without cheating, as this was the way we were taught. And at this point, I no longer want to go on jesting. For, after many years in which the world has afforded me many experiences, what I most surely know in the long run about morality and the obligations of men, I owe to sport, I learned it with R.U.A. That, in short, is why the R.U.A. cannot die. Let us preserve it. Let us preserve this great and good image of our youth. It will keep watch over yours, as well.

from *France Football*, 1957

Danny Blanchflower
BRIAN GLANVILLE

If one were to seek for the watershed between the old school of professional footballer and the new, one might do worse than look at Danny Blanchflower. Not that he was, in any strict sense, representative of either; merely that, as a great player of uncommon intelligence and versatility, he suffered under the regimen which ended with the

New Deal of 1961, while suggesting to those who came after it what they might become. By 1961, the erosion of social difference which followed our bloodless social revolution had already given pro footballers a much less working-class orientation than they'd had before the war. They no longer dressed in baggy suits, mufflers and cloth caps, no longer felt content with an Andy Capp life a few rungs higher than Andy Capp himself, their fan, might have. But Blanchflower, fluent to a fault, articulate to a paradox, fraternizing with literary editors and philosophers, writing for the intellectual weeklies and the posh Sundays, pointed the way to wider horizons still. Thus, though he played little or no active part in the crusade to abolish the iniquitous maximum wage, in 1960 and 1961, he had already given the pro footballer a new concept of himself; or what he might, in some remote future, become.

It is hard for me to write about Blanchflower, because I have known him for many years, and moderately closely. I say moderately closely, because Blanchflower is not an easy man to know well. The charm, the eloquence, mask rather than illuminate; there is a core of something secret, held back, concealed. Thus, one can say of him that he is intelligent, humorous, ambitious, competitive, even egocentric, but the inwardness of the man is elusive.

As a footballer, one could only admire him; it seems to me that he was indisputably a great player, with a vision of the game which was at once sophisticated yet simple; the qualities of the very best football. It was these characteristics which enabled him to be so fine a captain, at a time when football captaincy had grown to be little more than a question of tossing for ends before the kick-off. The freshness and originality of his approach to the game, combined with his remarkable poise, enabled him to give a team inspiration, confidence, and a sense of tactical purpose. He did it superbly with Tottenham Hotspur – and for a time, significantly, had the captaincy taken away from him. He did it just as well with a Northern Ireland team which, against all expectation, knocked Italy out of the eliminators for the 1958 World Cup, and reached the quarter-finals.

It has been said, possibly with truth, that the dominant force in his life has been his mother; once the pretty centre-forward of a women's football team, and Blanchflower's first coach. He was born and brought up in that hard, vigorous, bigoted city, Belfast, 'where they beat the big drum', as he once said; but there is nothing bigoted about him. He seems to have inherited the city's vigorous, robust humour, with none of its black undertones. He began there with Glentoran, joined Barnsley, in Yorkshire, as little more than a boy, from there went to Aston Villa and finally, in 1954, joined Spurs, thus coming to London, where he must always have felt he belonged, where there was an opportunity to grow, to prosper and to spread himself.

If one were to describe him, as a player, in one word, I suppose that word would be 'scientific'. Certainly he owed nothing to force. Wiry and fit, he carried little weight, and though he did not flinch from tackles, it was his positional play, his highly developed sense of anticipation, which made him remarkable. Nor was he ever very quick – except in thought. And if there were some who criticized his defensive qualities, it might be answered that he was a little unfortunate to come slightly before what would have been 'his' time; that of 4–2–4, and the specialized mid-field man. I remember, just after he had come back from the World Cup of 1958, his speaking enthusiastically to me in that great, grey clearing house of gossip and opinion, the Tottenham car park, of 4–2–4. What a good and simple idea it was, he said, simply to string a line of four defenders right across the pitch.

He was even, in season 1958–59, dropped from the Tottenham Hotspur team, and replaced by some young half-back whose name one can barely remember, on the grounds that he was not defensive enough. When, in March, 1959, he came back, it was to inspire the team to a marvellous six goal victory against Leicester City. You will deduce, from this, that he had to suffer a lot of pain for his uniqueness, his vigorous non-conformity. At Barnsley, at Aston Villa, then at Tottenham, he was never free from the reminder that he was, in the last analysis, a professional footballer, a paid servant.

It was at Barnsley, for example, that someone yelled at him for daring to be so unorthodox as to train with the ball. It would be many years before the Hungarians came to Wembley, thrashed England 6–3, and paved the way for a general acknowledgement that it really might be better to prepare for a ball game with a ball. Even as a youngster newly arrived in England, Blanchflower was shrewd enough to doubt the value of continued lapping, the mindless development of stamina. He has always believed – and it has come to be a heresy once more – that the great and dangerous forward may be dangerous precisely *because* he does so little: like a dormant volcano, always liable to erupt. This discussion, I recall, was provoked by a match against the Russian team, Tbilisi Dynamo. Their international outside-left, Meshki, had stood inactive on the wing for much of the time, but looked wonderfully effective when he did come to life. Today, when all is 'work rate', a player like Meshki – or Greaves – might be considered a luxury. Blanchflower, always superbly economic himself, knew better.

One may see him today, perhaps, as a bruised idealist; not cynical, but hurt. Professional football is, to some degree, a paradigm of the larger world. Young players enter it full of hope and enthusiasm, only to encounter the proud stupidity of directors, the ineptitude of managers, the violence of opponents, the shallow ephemerality of the Press. Thus Blanchflower, particularly aware and alert, was hurt more than most professionals.

There was, for example, the shock, as a very young international, of having the team's coach invaded by jolly, ultra-convivial men who turned out to be . . . officials. Where was the sense of high-minded purpose which he himself had brought to international football? And the awful anticlimax, the dazed disappointment, of the first inter-national match in which he played.

It was in October, 1949, against Scotland, in Belfast; and Ireland let in eight goals. Those were bad days indeed for Ulster football. The team, subject in any case to the whims of the Football League clubs, who need not release their players if they did not choose, met at the eleventh hour, and took the field with little hope, little in the way of history.

The Irish team stayed in Bangor, and Blanchflower spent a wretched night, trying unavailingly to sleep. 'The nervous anticipation of the big event had something to do with that,' he wrote. Then, in the small hours, when sleep seemed possible and imminent, a noisy band of Scottish fans arrived, and tore the peace of the night to tatters.

Blanchflower describes his recollections of that Saturday as 'mere shadows'. He was 'numb, dangling in a state of nervous suspension'. It is an interesting admission, given the absolute aplomb of his later career. Clearly he had none of the precocious *sang froid* of a Cliff Bastin or a Pelé who, as teenagers, could stroll untroubled through a Cup Final, or even a World Cup Final.

'The game that day,' wrote Blanchflower, in the *International Foot-ball Book*, 'swirled past me, over me, around me like a fog. I chased fleeting figures through it; but all in vain. I felt weak and exhausted as if I had no control over my movements; and everything I did seemed strangely irrelevant to the game.'

In parenthesis, the most intriguing thing about this passage is that it should be written by Blanchflower himself not, as in the case of almost every other footballer, by some assiduous 'ghost'. Blanchflower has a natural talent for writing as well as for football, but this is a subject to which I shall return later.

After the game, Blanchflower, 'slumped into the dressing-room, a pathetic figure sadly humiliated by bitter experience'. He was ashamed and disappointed at what he considered his total failure, and wondered if he would ever be chosen for his country again. Though there were excuses to lean on, he acknowledged that the main responsibility was his own. But he was well aware of the sad inertia which grips a losing team, of the whimsical methods of selection, of the lack of any leader to give the team direction and morale. At the same time, especially coming from the Second Division, he had been made to realize what a gap there was between club and international football, where there were so many good players about.

It was, by his own admission, Peter Doherty who recovered him for international football; Doherty who was one of the few figures in the game he has ever admired (another, I think, was Arthur Rowe, in his days as manager of Tottenham).

Doherty had shared Blanchflower's resentment of the slapdash, defeatist way in which Irish teams were put in the field. Like Blanchflower, he was an individualist, often a stormy one, and a wonderfully talented player. 'Always remembering Doherty,' he once said, 'I aim at precision soccer. Constructiveness, no matter what the circumstances, ball control, precise and accurate distribution, back in defence to blot out the inside-forward when necessary. I am described as an attacking wing-half, and I suppose that is correct. Sometimes I even score goals.'

Doherty's appointment as team manager gave Ireland, and Blanchflower, new life. 'Here was someone,' wrote Blanchflower, 'it seemed right should be in charge; a great player, an idol to some of us, a man we all respected. There was hope; something to believe in, something to fight for.' Doherty told them they had nothing to lose; 'the biggest step forward,' Blanchflower has said, 'was a psychological one.' This in turn led him to a developing interest in the psychological aspects of the game at large. Though the individual skills and abilities of the Irish team had improved, he was aware that what Doherty had done, above all, was to remove an enormous mental block. Once the Irish team had convinced itself that it was as good as anybody else, it proceeded to prove as much, on the field. The climax of Doherty's partnership with Blanchflower, if one may so describe what it virtually came to be, was reached in the 1958 World Cup.

Blanchflower, though his background was largely similar, had had a better formal education than Doherty. He was born in Bloomfield, a suburb of East Belfast, one street away from Billy Bingham, who would become his outside-right in that notable Irish team. Bingham and Danny's younger brother, Jackie, in fact, played together in the same boys' football team run by Mrs Blanchflower, after at first playing football in the street; a game in which Danny sometimes joined.

Blanchflower went to the local college of technology, to be trained as an electrician. In 1944, however, volunteering for the Royal Air Force, he was sent to St Andrew's University, for a short course in electrical engineering. It was a view into another, alien but beguiling world; the students, in their red gowns, represented a fortunate way of existence, a privilege of learning which had been denied to him. After this, he was subjected to another new experience, being sent to Canada for aircrew training. But the war was over, and he was still in Canada, before he could do any operational flying.

Returned to Belfast, Glentoran, with whom he had been an amateur, gave him £50 and £3 a match to sign professional, though until his demobilization, he played as a 'guest' for Swindon Town. In 1948, Barnsley signed him, and three years later, they transferred him to Aston Villa, a great club fallen on barren times.

Blanchflower has related, often enough, the traumatizing story of how he signed for Villa: travelling to Derby with Mr Joe Richards, the coal-owner who was chairman of Barnsley and later President of the Football League, in his chauffeur-driven car – then, when they reached Derby, being sent with the chauffeur to eat in the kitchen, while business was done in the hotel dining-room. What was he, after all, but a professional footballer; and, as such, one consigned to the kitchen and the tradesmen's entrance? This, though Villa paid £15,000 for him.

Further disillusion lay in wait for him at Villa Park. Villa may have been a very great team indeed up to the Great War, a goodish one in the early twenties, but ever since their relegation in the thirties, they had been a stagnant, disappointing club. Playing for them, Blanchflower matured both physically and technically, but there was none of the stimulus a player of his capacities required, no manager there to inspire and lead him as Doherty had done, little chance, season by season, of anything better than staying in the middle reaches of the First Division.

In 1954, he agitated long enough for a transfer to get it. He wanted London; and London wanted him. Both the great North London clubs, Spurs and Arsenal, were eager to sign him. Tom Whittaker, the manager of Arsenal, came up to Villa Park, met Blanchflower, and told him that of course he would be coming to Highbury, that Arsenal could match or top any offer that was made. But in the event, they couldn't. The bidding rose to £30,000, a larger sum than had ever before been paid for a half-back, and Arsenal's board of directors refused to allow Whittaker to go so high. The same kind of penny-pinching would lose Arsenal Denis Law, when he was a £55,000 rather than £100,000 player. Blanchflower never forgot it. He was convinced from that moment that there was something rotten in the state of Arsenal – like Villa, a great club fallen on mediocre times – and his scepticism would flair into a silly row, twelve years later. After a somewhat intemperate article in the *Sunday Express* criticizing Arsenal's treatment of an injured player, the club suspended him indefinitely from their Press Box.

Blanchflower has written amusingly of the cameo at Villa Park when he was due to be transferred; how the directors sat in the Board Room while he waited next door with a local journalist called Tommy Lyons, how it was Tommy Lyons, not Blanchflower, who was eventually and mistakenly called into the Board Room. Still, the transfer to Tottenham Hotspur went through, conducted by Arthur Rowe – who justified the price by saying, 'In nine matches out of ten, Blanchflower has the ball more than any other two players on the field – it's an expression of his tremendous ego, which is just what a great captain needs.'

From this you will divine not only that Rowe had a deep appreciation of Blanchflower's qualities, but that he was prepared to allow him to exercise them. In other words, he was a big enough man and manager himself to give Blanchflower free rein on the field; as a real captain. Yet Rowe, a sensitive, vigorous, idealistic, enormously stimulating man, had not much time to go at Tottenham. He had been bitterly wounded by the opposition and hostility of certain directors, manifested even during the most successful days of his push-and-run strategy.

The fact was, however, that Blanchflower was the last player to adapt himself to push and run. This game of wall passes, of immediate parting with the ball over short distances, was quite alien to his own, which was more deliberative. The beauty of push-and-run, in a way, was that it did not require any specific midfield general. Certainly Eddie Baily, the little English international inside-left, was a fine constructive player, but in fact, every player carried a field marshal's baton in his knapsack. Blanchflower liked to give the ball room and space; was always adept at chipping it, floating it, lobbing it. Endless, hurried movement was not for him; any more than it was for the brilliant little waif of an inside-forward, Tommy Harmer, a footballer's footballer who had been in and out of the Spurs first team for years, because he did not fit into the push-and-run formula.

Blanchflower and Harmer were to establish a marvellous, telepathic partnership. There could scarcely have been two more sharply contrasted figures. Though both had enormous technical talent, and what the Italians call 'a vision of the game', Harmer did it all by instinct while Blanchflower, besides the natural good instincts of a fine player, had his ratiocinating intelligence, as well. He was from Belfast, Harmer was a Cockney of the Cockneys, uneasy anywhere too far from Hackney. Yet they combined marvellously, each perfectly understanding the needs and intentions of the other, and they set up some famous victories; not least one which brought ten goals against Everton.

There were moments, not least when Spurs were awarded a free kick, when they appeared to be arguing. 'They really *were* arguing,' said a London journalist who, like Harmer, came from Hackney. 'Tommy's quite serious about it; he says, "Got to keep Danny down, you know!" '

Later, the partnership with Harmer would give way to one with the marvellously elusive John White, 'The Ghost', floating unobserved, by all but Blanchflower, into open spaces, unmarked positions, especially out on the left – where Blanchflower would reach him with impeccably accurate balls.

When Arthur Rowe, who had already been driven into one breakdown, had another and left the Spurs, he was succeeded by a very different manager: Jimmy Anderson. Anderson had, like Rowe – once a Tottenham captain – been with Spurs for many years, graduating from the position of third team trainer slowly and steadily up to manager. He was regarded essentially as an interim appointment: a figure without glamour or allure who, whatever hidden qualities he might have possessed, was unlikely to hit it off with a Blanchflower.

A crisis point was reached when Spurs lost to Manchester City, in the semi-final of the 1956 F.A. Cup, at Villa Park. Spurs, in the concluding stages, were behind, their attack making little impression on the City defence. In desperation, Blanchflower, in his capacity as captain, called the gigantic Maurice Norman, centre-half, up to inside-right. Norman was very tall, very heavy, rather clumsy, but undoubtedly a fearsome figure, particularly efficient in the air. The gamble might have worked, given a grain of luck; but it didn't. The other possibility, that of City exploiting a weakened defence, was the one which came about, and Tottenham lost, City went on to win the Cup.

Blanchflower was deprived of the captaincy, and for a long time steadfastly refused to resume it. He was not going to be captain, he said, in name alone: either he exercised the rights of a captain, or someone else could have the job; or the sinecure. At the end of that season, he was even, briefly, dropped. The announcement was that he was unfit. Blanchflower said this was nonsense, he was perfectly fit. 'I turned up at White Hart Lane all ready to go. I thought the lads were kidding when they told me.'

In due course the dim interregnum of Jimmy Anderson came to an end, but the manager who succeeded him was – if much more forceful – little nearer Blanchflower in temperament. Billy Nicholson had been a dour, conscientious right-half in the splendid push-and-run team, a Yorkshireman without frills or exaggerated ambitions, content to chase and tackle and cover till the cows came home. Some, cruelly, had said that he did Alf Ramsey's tackling for him. He was anything but a stupid man: his exceedingly shrewd tactical thinking had provided England with a plan to hold Brazil to a goalless draw in the Swedish World Cup of 1958; no other side had prevented Brazil scoring. But Nicholson, though subject to refreshing bursts of good humour, was in the main close, wary and cautious. Besides, a player of Blanchflower's stature and loquacity was not the easiest kind for a young manager to inherit. They had, inevitably, their ups and downs, but in the end they worked together in sufficient harmony for Spurs brilliantly to achieve the League and Cup double which had eluded every other club in this century.

I don't think I myself saw Blanchflower play at all till the middle fifties – I had been living in Italy – and was not, initially, too impressed. He was, at the time, being used at inside-right, a position which manifestly did not suit him. He hadn't the acceleration, nor the ability to turn quickly, while his many qualities of foresight and construction largely went begging. He regained his rightful position, of course, and Spurs, buying Dave Mackay from Hearts, transferred their ultra-attacking left-half, Jim Iley.

Blanchflower and Mackay were to form a magnificent partnership. By utter contrast with Blanchflower, Mackay was all muscle and flamboyance, capable of what might loosely be termed 'tackles' (he was to sober down in time) which made one's hair stand on end. He clapped his hands, he stuck out his barrel chest: he took, *ad infinitum*, what Peter Cook once called 'his long, boring throw-ins', he flung himself among flailing boots. He was essentially a hectic player, certainly not without skills, but with none of Blanchflower's cool, rational artistry. They complemented one another splendidly, though if I were asked which had the greater importance to the team I should reply, unhesitatingly, Blanchflower. This became very obvious when he retired, and Spurs all at once lost the direction and detachment which he had given them. Mackay, John White, Jimmy Greaves were all, in their way, remarkable footballers, but it was Blanchflower, finally, who gave the team its stamp and character.

I remember in particular a European Cupwinners' Cup game, at White Hart Lane, against Slovan, Bratislava. Spurs had lost the first leg, in Czechoslovakia, and they made a bad, nervous beginning. Maurice Norman, the centre-half, was clearly on edge, plunging and lunging at balls, committing himself and being drawn out of position. But there beside him was Blanchflower, like a groom calming a high-strung racehorse, slowing the game, covering mistakes, till at last Norman and the rest of the team settled down for an easy win.

Similarly, the triumphs of the 1957–58 Ireland side would have been unthinkable without Blanchflower; as they would have been equally impossible without Doherty. The team had in it a handful of very talented players, a few who were naturally gifted but unreflective, others who were frankly moderate. Among the most talented was Blanchflower's own brother, Jackie, at centre-half. A player of immense versatility, Jackie had begun with Manchester United as an inside-right, been turned into a right-half, and finally, with immense success, into a centre-half.

Danny admired him, as a footballer, a great deal, though they were temperamentally quite different: Jackie hadn't the same, consuming ambition as his older brother, and seemed prepared to make less stringent demands on life. In the 1957 Cup Final, when Manchester United's goalkeeper, Ray Wood, was injured, Jackie went in goal, and won Danny's admiration for the clever way he distributed the ball. Goalkeepers' distribution, indeed, has always been one of Danny's hobby-horses. Given this, and his love of paradox, perhaps it was explicable that one day, in the Burnley team coach, he should reach a point where he seemed to be advocating distribution as the chief quality any goalkeeper needed, where others might feel that the first duty was to keep the ball out of the net!

One of the chief reasons Danny enjoyed playing for Ireland with Jackie was that his younger brother's great all-round skill and confidence allowed him to be left chiefly to his own devices. Danny himself could go upfield and occupy himself with the build-up in midfield. But in February, 1958, Jackie was involved in the appalling disaster of Munich Airport, when the Elizabethan air-liner carrying Manchester United back from Belgrade crashed. Mercifully, Jackie himself escaped, but he was painfully injured, and never again graced a game for which he had been so well endowed.

This meant that Ireland had to find a new centre-half for the finals of the World Cup, in Sweden, and they manufactured one out of the tall, blond full-back, Willie Cunningham. Cunningham was a solid enough footballer, but he could aspire to none of Jackie Blanchflower's class, with the result that Danny had to play a much more cautious and defensive game. It is interesting – and rather sad – to speculate how much better Ireland might have done in Sweden, had Jackie Blanchflower played.

But the footballer who had the greatest affinity, both temperamentally and in his approach to the game, in that Irish team was Jimmy McIlroy. Dark-haired, pink-complexioned, modest and dry, McIlroy, at inside-forward, brought to football the same cool perfectionism, the emphasis on skill and science, as Blanchflower. They both thought about the game a great deal, they liked each other, perhaps a little warily – they were wonderfully humorous together – and they had the Irish team playing football their way; and Doherty's way. They delighted in working out new moves and strategies; such as the penalty-kick which involved both of them running into the area, the first pushing the ball forward for the other, following up, to shoot home. Blanchflower, as might be expected, was particularly good at taking penalties, success usually guaranteed by his cool composure.

On the right wing, the ebullient little Billy Bingham, later to become the Irish team manager, was a player of another mould, more of a force of nature. It was no use McIlroy and Blanchflower expecting Bingham to share their quizzical, rational approach to the game. If he had, no doubt they could have worked out some remarkable triangular schemes. But football is a house of many mansions, and there is always room, and need, for the gifted, instinctive player; as Garrincha, in that very World Cup, was to show with Brazil.

To qualify for Sweden, Ireland had to accomplish the 'impossible' feat of eliminating Italy, not to mention Portugal. The Portuguese had yet to reach their heights of the early sixties, when Benfica would produce a team to delight and dominate Europe, but they were no easy victims. As for the Italians, invertebrate though they may have shown themselves in away matches, they had the tradition of two World Cup victories behind them, and a crop of native talent laced and reinforced by *oriundi*, South American stars of Italian descent. In Rome, Ireland were obliged to put the tiny Billy Cush, a wing-half, at centre-half, but played so well and with such spirit that they lost only by a goal.

The following Autumn, they came to Wembley and, wonder of wonders, defeated England. Harry Gregg, the Manchester United goalkeeper by the time Munich came, and a great admirer of Blanchflower, worked wonders in goal. Clearly if the Irish were capable of that, they must have felt themselves capable of anything.

As they were. Early in the New Year, they were due to play Italy in mid-week in Belfast. M. Zsolt, the Hungarian referee, was held up in the fog and didn't get there, so that the teams had to play a futile friendly, instead. This didn't please an already violently partisan crowd, which became increasingly more violent as the referee lost control, and foul succeeded foul. The limit was reached when Beppe

Chiappella, the Italian right-half, jumped with both knees into the back of Billy McAdams, Ireland's centre-forward.

At the final whistle, with the score 2–2, the crowd brutally invaded the pitch and attacked the Italian players. Police and the Irish players helped them to escape; it was the kind of scene to which Blanchflower himself was totally alien.

For another of his qualities was his absolute sportsmanship on the field. No doubt he committed fouls now and again, but it is hard to remember any of them. Nor can one dismiss this by saying that the really gifted player has no need to indulge in roughness. A long, long line of Scottish international wing-halves bears depressing witness to the contrary. Violence was simply remote from Blanchflower's nature, and when it was visited on him, he became understandably bitter. One of the few occasions I can recall him being really angry was when, on a train journey, he was talking of a recent match at Everton, in which he had been brutally charged down from behind, the referee looking on with indulgence. Competitive almost to a fault, his career – at a time when so many vital matches turn into brawls – reassures one that competitiveness need not always turn into cynicism and viciousness.

A few weeks later, Ireland played Italy again and this time beat them, deservedly, 2–1. It was a triumph for Blanchflower and for McIlroy, who scored one of the goals. This time, both crowd and Italians alike seemed purged of anger, so that the Irish, by and large, were able to play the pure football of which they were capable. Their victory was an appalling blow for Italy, who thus failed for the first time to reach the finals, but it was an uplifting achievement for Doherty and little Ireland.

It is notable that Blanchflower, for his behaviour after the first, savage affair, was praised by Ottorino Barassi, the Italian Vice President of F.I.F.A. It was Blanchflower who had seen to it that each Italian player had an Irish escort from the pitch, moving Barassi to remark, 'Blanchflower is a man of many parts, and a gentleman.'

At the end of the season, he was deservedly voted Footballer of the Year, an honour which would be conferred on him a second time, when captaining Spurs to their successes.

There was another absentee from the Irish team which travelled to Sweden. Or rather, Billy Simpson, the big Rangers centre-forward, though he made the trip, was too badly injured to play. So Ireland had to manufacture, from their bare resources, another centre-forward as well as a new centre-half, and though they did amazingly well in the circumstances, they did not really manage it.

They stayed at a little seaside town called Tylosand, in a hotel above the beach, with a pitch situated picturesquely in a nearby wood, to play on. The atmosphere had none of the cold formality of the England party, where every man seemed to be looking over his shoulder. Doherty, though he never lost control of his team and its players, knew how to weld them into a cheerful family – and in Blanchflower and McIlroy he had mature lieutenants.

Their opposition was alarming: Argentina, re-entering the World Cup after long sulks and silence, Czechoslovakia – and the World Cup holders, West Germany. Clearly it would be a splendid achievement if they finished in the first two of their group, to qualify for the quarter-finals.

And they did. They beat the Czechs, they lost to the Argentinians, they drew with the West Germans, then, in a play-off, they beat the Czechs again. Finally, an exhausted and depleted team, they went down to the French, in the quarter-finals. Obliged, as we have seen, to mask his batteries, Blanchflower only came fully into his own, perhaps in the play-off against the Czechs, in Malmo. These, a few days earlier, had thrashed Argentina 6–1, and were locally the favourites against what was by now a scratch Irish side. But the wonderful morale of the Irish players carried them through. In extra time, with the score 1–1, Blanchflower floated one of his long, immaculate free kicks across the Czech goal, and McParland scored with a right-footed volley, to put the Irish, incredibly, into the final eight.

With seven injured players and the imbecility of a 210 mile coach ride to Norkopping, they had little real hope from the first. The French, thanks to the anomalies of the competition, had benefited from four days' rest, and it was clear that Ireland needed some kind of miracle. They did not get it, but if one of the ideas that Blanchflower, Bingham and McIlroy had devised had only been fully worked out, things might have been different.

For almost half the game, Jack was as good as, and better than, his master. Then the idea was put into practice, took the French by surprise – but it was not exploited. It involved a throw-in on the Irish right flank. The intention was for Blanchflower to throw the ball to

Bingham, Bingham, with his head, to flick it to McIlroy, and McIlroy to run through for a shot at goal.

It worked; up to a point. Blanchflower threw in, Bingham duly headed on, and McIlroy ran into the penalty area. But instead of shooting he squared the ball across the goal, and the chance was gone. France went on to score four times, and Ireland's brave attempt had ended in anti-climax. Still, it was a superb achievement to get to Sweden at all, and an even finer one to reach the quarter-finals against such strenuous opposition.

For the future, Blanchflower's greatest triumphs were reserved for club football with the Spurs. This, now, had a more fascinating aspect than it ever had in the past, for victory in the English Cup and League meant entry into European competition, the sort of thing which was meat and drink to Blanchflower, always looking for new challenges, new approaches, fresh aspects of the game.

He had settled in a pleasant house in a North London suburb with Betty, his second wife, and their three agreeable children. His first marriage, which came to an end while he lived in Birmingham, had been to an Ulster girl – and he was to marry a third time, to a South African. On arrival in London, he had begun an amusing column for the *Evening News* which, while it did not extend him, was often humorously inventive.

In season 1960–61, Spurs began the League season with a remarkable unbeaten run, and cantered on to win the Championship. They were essentially an attacking team, highly talented, if not a great club side in the manner of Real Madrid. Blanchflower, John White and Dave Mackay were perhaps their three outstanding players, but there were also the lean, professional Bill Brown, of Scotland, in goal, and the tremendously brave Cliff Jones, on the right or left wing. Blanchflower's clever crosses into the penalty area were as well tailored for his flying headers as Alf Ramsey's had been, a decade earlier, for the headers of Leslie Medley.

Looking back, Blanchflower has said that he enjoyed playing with them all; that there was no player whom he enjoyed playing with more than any other. There were times, he added, when Jimmy McIlroy would tell him he thought he played badly for Ireland, to which Blanchflower would reply, 'You don't play badly, you just play differently.'

The Ireland team had reached its apotheosis with the 1958 World

Cup. The following October, it lost at home, 5–2, to England. 'How England won 5–2 nobody knew,' Blanchflower said. 'We should have won 5–2. They were meant to have been playing 4–2–4; all they'd done was play two centre-halves to stop our two centre-forwards, and afterwards they went on like that for thirteen games.'

His account of the scene outside the England dressing-rooms, after the match, shows him at his best as a raconteur and a close observer. 'X of the *Daily* — is very excited, this is England's greatest victory for years, and he says to Walter Winterbottom, "Walter, would you say England was playing 4–2–4?" And Walter looks up, and he doesn't find the answer up there, and he looks down again, then he looks up, and he says . . . "Yes." And — says, "What I thought was so-and-so and so-and-so. And so-and-so and so-and-so and so-and-so and so-and-so." And then Bob Pennington of the *Daily Express* comes forward with a big smile, his rival, and he says, "Thank you very much, Walter. And now do you think we can have —'s views?" And all the little local journalists standing round, amazed at this quarrel between the big boys!'

Spurs won the 1960–61 Championship with a forward-line led by the powerful Bobby Smith, with Les Allen an excellent, incisive inside-left. The following December, however, they paid some £99,000 to buy Jimmy Greaves from Milan, so that Blanchflower was captaining a still more richly gifted side. At that time, he feels, Spurs and Benfica, the holders of the European Cup, were the two best club teams in Europe, Real Madrid having passed their zenith. The two clubs met in the quarter-finals, and Benfica got home by a goal. Blanchflower thinks that Spurs had two and possibly three good goals disallowed for offside, the first two in Lisbon – particularly one by Bobby Smith – the other by Jimmy Greaves, early in an exciting match at White Hart Lane. Spurs won it, hectically, by the odd goal, but it wasn't enough to keep them in.

Intriguingly, Blanchflower endorses the fast and physical nature of Tottenham's football in the second leg, although it was very much in the image of Mackay, rather than his own. Many of us criticized Tottenham for their methods; it is significant that Blanchflower, though they were so foreign to his own approach, should still feel they were right. 'It wasn't football,' he has said, 'but that was what was needed. If a team came out to play defensive football, the very thing it wanted was for the other side to play a rational, cool, elaborate game.' Others might think that pressure defeats itself, that the modern game has, for the last forty years, been built on the sudden breakaway, but Blanchflower's view is an interesting one.

He scored from a penalty-kick in that game: cool enough, as usual, to make a very good job of it, selling the excellent Costa Pereira, in goal, a dummy, then sliding the ball into the left-hand corner, after Pereira himself had moved left. Afterwards, Pereira told him that it was the first time anybody had sent him the wrong way. This penalty-kick had an interesting sequel, for a few months later, at Wembley, during the Cup Final, Blanchflower was called upon to take another one, against Burnley.

He was so convinced that Adam Blacklaw, Burnley's Scottish goal-keeper, would have seen his penalty against Benfica on television that he decided to try to send him the other way from Pereira. As he walked up to take the kick, Jimmy McIlroy, who 'used to take them for Ireland, and miss them, said to me, "You're going to miss it." I said, "I'm glad *you're* not taking it." ' And Blanchflower did not miss it. He duly sent Blacklaw to the left, and put the ball in, to the right.

The following season, he and Spurs had consolation, when they thrashed Atletico Madrid 5–1 in Rotterdam, to win the Final of the European Cupwinners' Cup. By this time, Blanchflower was 'assistant to the manager, whatever that meant', and on the morning of the game, Billy Nicholson decreed that there should be training. The team, already demoralized by its poor form over the past six weeks, resented this: all the talk was of bonuses, of who would and who would not be playing.

'I'd been playing terrible,' Blanchflower said, 'because uncon-sciously I was carrying my knee. I told them, "You're all afraid of this match. I deserve to play more than anybody and I don't know if I'm playing, and I'm not worrying. I'm going out to train. If you're not training, please yourselves; you can sit and play cards, if you like." ' The players trained – and they won.

From this, it can be deduced that Blanchflower might have become an exceptional manager; yet, while playing, he always denied any ambition to do so. He had, he said, been disappointed too often and one cannot imagine him suffering directors gladly. Even at Tottenham, where things had certainly improved since the fifties, 'I said that the team at Tottenham was bigger than the club, when I left. I felt that Tottenham never made the best of those years.' It may also be that

Blanchflower was too much the individualist, even the egoist, to have submitted to the grinding compromises of management. Shrewd about the psychology of footballers – I remember his once saying of a successful manager, 'X hasn't done anything. He's just sat there and sucked his pipe and given them confidence' – one nevertheless sees him as a lone wolf, impatient of stupidity.

He had by now become a 'fashionable' figure, taken up by such as Professor Ayer, the logical-positivist philosopher, author of *Language, Truth and Logic*, whom Blanchflower once reproached on a television programme for being superstitious, and Karl Miller, the young literary editor, then, of the *New Statesman*. Blanchflower wrote frequently for the *New Statesman*, sometimes very well, and later had a fruitful period on the *Observer*. One has always felt it a pity he left them to spread himself over the wider but less exacting spaces of the *Sunday Express*, for he seemed to have there the direction and discipline his writing demands. It is hard for a footballer who has, as Blanchflower admits, been 'adulated', and has reached such peaks, to buckle down to the needs of another *métier*; yet just as the tension between his own talent and the demands of organization probably brought the best out of him as a footballer, so a similar tension might bring the best out of him as a writer. A tendency to sentimentality, mild vendetta and a sacrifice of individuality to the fashions of American sports journalism might thus have been avoided.

Not surprisingly, perhaps, his admirations in literature have tended towards the romantic, in particular to Scott Fitzgerald, that doomed, gilded, perennial adolescent of the protracted nineteen-twenties. Though he writes, now, for the popular Press, his relations with it have long been uneasy; one remembers a ferocious *New Statesman* column, after the World Cup Finals of 1962, in Chile, which presumed that one writer must have come home to be sick into his well-advertised bowler hat. Misquotation, malice and the cynical kite-flying which he so often met during his playing career were not likely to be received by him with tolerance.

Despite the breadth of his interest, he testifies to the shock of leaving football; which he did, at last, in 1964. 'There's a strange awakening when you come out of the game, because we're all very spoiled in the game. You've had so much adulation. You've spent ten years having things done for you, Army style.'

Retiring, he embarked, with bright success, on television as well as journalism, and in 1967, became one of the commentators on the C.B.S. network of the first professional soccer league to be played in the United States. Beyond question one of the great footballers of his day, a great captain in an age when captaincy was moribund if not dead, his major contribution, perhaps, was to give the professional footballer a rational, articulate voice.

from John Arlott (ed.), *Soccer: The Great Ones*, 1968

The George Eastham Case
GEOFFREY NICHOLSON

George Eastham was born in Blackpool in 1936, the son of a professional footballer, and soon after leaving school at sixteen went to Northern Ireland to join the Ards club as an amateur. At nineteen he turned professional and agreed to transfer to Newcastle, who paid Ards £9,000 for him. He made a success there, in his first three seasons establishing himself as the tactician of the forward line; but a series of small personal differences with the club unsettled him, and towards the end of 1959 he made an oral request for a transfer, which he put into writing on December 11. His application wasn't formally acknowledged, but he had a conversation with Mr Hurford, the club chairman, who said he would help Eastham to find a job and would have certain work done on his house. Eastham's annual contract was due to run out on June 30, 1960; on April 29 the club told him that they intended to retain him for the 1960–61 season at his current wage; on May 3 the League was informed of this. By this time Eastham was even more determined to break with Newcastle. He wanted to come south, and for preference to Arsenal, who had shown some interest in buying him. He thought this would advance his football career, and also give him more scope to develop some sort of second-string job outside the game. Newcastle, who considered him indispensable to their attack, were just as anxious that he should stay with them. Exercising the only option left to him, Eastham refused to re-sign for the club; but on June 23 he was told he had been retained.

Two days later he again applied in writing for a transfer, but before the board met to discuss it, two events occurred which further aggravated the situation. Eastham had an interview with Charles Mitten, the team manager, who criticized him for his general conduct. And on June 27 the Newcastle *Evening Chronicle* quoted Mitten as saying: 'As far as I am concerned, Eastham won't be transferred. The board meet on Wednesday to discuss his application, but I have spoken to the chairman and he feels as I do. If he wants to play football, it will be at Newcastle.' As Mitten had allegedly predicted, the application was turned down. Eastham learnt this officially on June 30, the day his contract expired. He was no longer a paid or a playing member of the club; on the other hand, he was ineligible, under the terms of the League's retention laws, to play for anyone else. Four days later he left Newcastle to take up a job as a salesman with an old army friend of his father's, who had a firm in Surrey which manufactured cork and other insulating materials.

Eastham's next step was to apply to the Management Committee of the League under Rule Sixty-two (e) on the ground that he could not 'arrange his transfer with his club'. In stating their side of the case, Newcastle wrote to say that they had kept to the letter of the retain laws, and hoped that the Committee would 'uphold them in the stand they had felt bound to take'. On July 22 the Committee ruled that it was 'a matter entirely between the club and the player'.

Then Eastham tried another tack. He appealed under Rule Nineteen, which obliged the Committee to adjudicate on any dispute or difference between a club and a player. The League asked for more information, and meanwhile Eastham met Mitten informally. Mitten advised him to re-sign and to continue playing until Newcastle found a replacement for him; it would then be understood that Eastham would get his transfer by the end of the year. He still refused to re-sign, but in his letter to the League he made it clear that he was not crusading for a change in the rules; his only concern 'at that moment was to get a release from the club'.

On September 20 he met the Newcastle chairman – which, apart from the meeting with Mitten, was the only communication he had had with the club, oral or in writing, since the day he left – and this, too, apparently ended in stalemate. But perhaps it had its effect, for the next day Mitten was instructed by the club to try to arrange Eastham's transfer to Arsenal in exchange for cash and a substitute player. Eastham, himself, was not told about this, however, and on September 28 he asked the League once more to consider his case.

At this point it becomes a little difficult to read the club's collective mind. As late as September 23, Mitten was reported as saying to the *Newcastle Journal*: 'So Eastham will not sign . . . Eastham must realize that his decision makes it impossible for him to link up in any way with any other club, professional or amateur.' Since this report, and others of similar tone, were not immediately disowned, Eastham was entitled to feel puzzled by the reply he received from the League secretary. This said that as Newcastle had made it clear that they would discuss his transfer with any club, the dispute was presumably over. The secretary later admitted that he had been under a misapprehension when he wrote this letter; but on October 6 he suggested to Newcastle that they should circularize the clubs to say that they would consider offers for Eastham. He added that 'so long as that offer of retention is still alive and you are prepared to sign him, he cannot sign for anyone else either inside the League or outside.'

On October 6, too, Eastham's solicitors wrote to Newcastle to ask once more that Eastham should be put on the transfer list 'and at a fee which is not prohibitive'. They added: '. . . we must request a positive and satisfactory reply within seven days, failing which our client will be reluctantly compelled to take such steps as Counsel may advise to ensure the preservation of his livelihood and skill as a professional footballer.' The following week Newcastle redrafted and approved a circular letter to the clubs. But once more they maintained their silence towards Eastham. All he knew was that the playing season was entering its second month, and he was still apparently no nearer getting his release.

So, with the moral support of his boss and the backing of the PFA, he began legal proceedings on October 13. Against Newcastle United he claimed a declaration, and also damages and costs. Against the six directors and the manager of the club, individually, he claimed that their refusal to release him was illegal and *ultra vires* (i.e. exceeding their authority), and that, in effect, it amounted to a conspiracy to injure him. Against the Football League and the Football Association he claimed a declaration that their rules and regulations relating to the retention and transfer of players were not binding on him, and were in unreasonable restraint of trade, or illegal or *ultra vires*.

About five weeks later Eastham learnt, while he happened to be listening to his car radio, that Newcastle had agreed to transfer him to Arsenal for a fee of £47,000. However, although Eastham himself had now achieved exactly what he had been campaigning for, the whole affair had grown into a test case involving the basic rights of all professional footballers. Eastham therefore allowed it to be pressed to its conclusion, which was reached in the Chancery Division of the High Court in June, 1963.

After all the drama in the newspapers, it was a bit of an anticlimax, though not an unpleasant one, to meet Eastham himself early in October, 1960. A slight man, with fair, wavy hair, a pointed face which gave him a rather puckish appearance, and a soft, unassertive voice, he didn't strike you at all as one of nature's anarchists. But he was articulate and reasonable, and didn't doubt for one moment that he was in the right. There was no question of him going back to Newcastle after some of the things that had been said to his face there, and said about him to the Press. And with his natural stubbornness reinforced by the support of the people around him, he was prepared to hold his ground – even if it meant damaging his prospects in football beyond the point where they were worth repairing.

In a sense the worst part of the period of waiting was over. He had felt it acutely when he missed the opening matches of the season; but with every Saturday that passed, his anxiety to get back into the game had lessened. Or so he put it. But obviously this was, in part at least, a piece of rationalization. Even at that time he was planning his legal action against Newcastle; he was keeping in training; and he was very concerned that his rebellion should not give him the reputation of being a trouble-maker. When the deal with Arsenal went through, his delight and relief were obvious. And when the maximum wage was abolished, he was happy enough to give up his part-time salesman's job to concentrate on football. But if it had eventually proved that his only way back into soccer was via Newcastle, I don't believe he would have taken it. Ironically, within two years Eastham was at odds with his new club, Arsenal – and this time he got on the transfer list without having to ask twice. However, this second dispute arose out of methods of play not systems of employment. Eastham is a forward whose virtue lies in his positional sense and his ability to open up the defence by moving the ball, rather than blasting through aggressively with it; he sets up more scoring opportunities for others than for himself; in the jargon he is a ball player and a schemer not a runner or a striker. This suited Arsenal well enough during his first two seasons with them. But when Billy Wright joined the club as manager in 1962, he wanted to put more speed and physical strength into his forward line, and Eastham was dropped. Seeing no future for himself in this kind of set-up, Eastham asked to be released and was put on the transfer list in mid-September. Although the sale never went through – Arsenal found they needed Eastham, and he was only too happy to return to the side – the story illustrates how peculiarly vulnerable even a top player may be to changes of style and fashion in play. (There are fashions in cricket, too, especially among bowlers; but at least if a man is in form and has the figures to prove it, he can usually count on his place in the side.) It's little wonder, therefore, that having discovered their collective strength, the players should campaign so insistently for adequate safeguards.

After the law's customary delays, the Eastham case came before Mr Justice Wilberforce in the High Court on June 11, 1963, and lasted a week. It is worth some space as a type of action almost unknown to British sport, and as the classic exposition of the players' central grievances.

Mr Gerald Gardiner, QC, opening for the plaintiff, made it clear that this was a test action to determine the legality of the retain and transfer systems operated by the League and its member clubs, and of the general terms on which players were employed in England. He then described these terms as containing 'such restraints on the ability of professional footballers to earn their livelihood as – here I borrow a phrase of a Member of Parliament – would have been rejected with scorn by any intelligent apprentice in the Middle Ages'. And he outlined some of these restraints: the contract's emphasis on players obeying orders, living where they were told, etc.; the imposition of a maximum wage; and the restriction of the length of contracts to fifteen months. There would be no complaint, he said, if that were all. But there was also the registration system and the retain system by which a player had to stay with one club 'because the rings would put out of business any other employer who employed him'. By rings he referred to the FA, the League and, by extension, all the clubs in membership of the international body, FIFA.

Having described Eastham's career, the circumstances in which he had issued the writ, and the money that had been paid at the time of his eventual transfer to Arsenal, Mr Gardiner returned to his point about the injustice of the whole set-up: 'I regard this as a system from the Middle Ages. It is really treating men like cattle, and really the position is that they are paid slaves. The transfer fees paid are more than a player can earn during the whole of his playing life. It is rather like transferring shares in a company, or any other inanimate property.'

The following day he referred to the three changes in the system which had been introduced since the writ was issued. The first was that there was no longer a maximum wage. The second was that two-year contracts were now permitted, but he regarded these as inadequate: 'When a club wants to get a good team it can keep, and wants to employ players for five years, and the players want the security of a five years' contract, why they should not be allowed to do so, my friends will no doubt explain to your Lordship.'

The third change had been an increase in the amount of money payable to a player when he was transferred, but not at his own request. Previously he had been entitled to only £10; now if he was sold for £100,000, the employers got only £99,700, and the player £300 – 'which they say is very generous'.

Mr Gardiner then referred to the curious fact that purchased players did not appear on the club's balance sheet among the assets: 'If they bought an expensive herd of cattle, I apprehend that they would have to appear . . . I do not know whether it is from a sense of delicacy, or some process of law which I have not discovered, that the same does not apply to players.'

The judge commented dryly: 'Livestock at valuation – it would look a little insulting.'

'No more insulting to an individual than being bought and sold as cattle,' Mr Gardiner suggested.

Eastham then came to the witness box, and his quiet voice caused a little trouble at the start. 'You are in rather an outside-right position,' said the judge, entering into the spirit of the thing. 'Would you speak up so that people on the left wing can hear?'

A picture of the uneasy relationship between himself and the club emerged from Eastham's replies to the questions he was asked. There had been much trouble when he took his fiancée to a match at Blackpool in the teach coach, and another incident when, he said, he had been given the wrong information about a train time. So feelings had already become strained when, after he had made his written application for transfer, he had asked to see the team manager: 'Mr Mitten criticized me; he said I was big-headed; that my hands were too short and my pockets too long; and that I was unpopular with the players.' Eastham said he had replied that he hoped these criticisms weren't justified.

He agreed, on minor points at issue, that he had been told by Newcastle that he would get a transfer if he re-signed for the club, but said he hadn't believed it. And he denied that he had moved south to force Newcastle's hand; it had been simply to earn the money to keep his family.

The next witness was Cliff Lloyd, who expanded on the point made by Mr Gardiner that 'the rings' acted in concert to enforce the retain system. He explained that there was nowhere in the world except Australia – whose own Football Association had been suspended by FIFA for accepting otherwise registered players – where a man could find alternative employment if his club insisted on keeping him on the retain list.

The PFA would like to have players' contracts of up to ten years. It would give the clubs security, just as it would the players, and he didn't think it would be only the big clubs that would benefit. Under the present system, many third and fourth division clubs could not afford the fees that were being asked, and so non-League clubs were stepping in. He thought no more harm would come from the abolition of the retain and transfer system than had come from the abolition of the maximum wage: 'It has caused very little difficulty, and has done English football a power of good.'

Alan Hardaker, secretary of the Football League since 1957, produced the opposing arguments: 'If any of the restrictions of the retain and transfer system were removed, it would make it worse for the player, because both the club and player would have the same opportunity of deciding the length of the contract.' As an example of the indecision of players, he cited the case of a man who had asked for a transfer the very day after signing for Chelsea. He considered the length of contracts to be of minor importance; since clubs had been given the option of granting two-year contracts, very few of them had taken it up.

The importance of transfer fees could be judged by the transfer of Denis Law from Huddersfield to Manchester City for £55,000, a sum which had enabled Huddersfield to pay benefits to seven players and install floodlights at the ground. There could be no such fees unless the employers had a reasonable hold over the players, and without these fees 'a large number of clubs, including some in the first division, would go bankrupt'.

Mr Hardaker insisted again the next day that the loss of the retain and transfer system would mean complete anarchy: 'People in many parts of the country would very quickly find themselves without a football club.' And instead of being controlled 'by the governing bodies of football, players would be controlled by agents, as in the entertainment industry'.

Various Newcastle directors stressed that the offer to transfer Eastham if he re-signed had been made in good faith; Mr Wilf Taylor, a director of the club and a member of the League Management Committee, denied that there had been any intent to injure Eastham's career: 'He was a key man, the schemer, and we wanted to retain him'; and on July 4, after another fortnight had passed, Mr Justice Wilberforce delivered his judgement. He granted Eastham a declaration that 'the Rules of the Defendant Association and the Regulations of the Defendant League relating to retention and transfer of players of professional football, including the Plaintiff, constitute an unreasonable restraint of trade and are accordingly not binding upon the Plaintiff, and *ultra vires*.'

It was a long judgement ... and while Mr Justice Wilberforce described those 'Defendants and their Directors' who had appeared before him as 'reasonable men whose attitude to their players was as much paternal as proprietary', he rejected most of the arguments in defence of the system which they had put forward in court and during the years of controversy which preceded the case.

When Alderman McKeag, a director of the Newcastle club, learnt of the judgement he said: 'Eastham was only the puppet. If he hadn't done it, somebody else would have – the next week, the next year. The judgement throws a rock into the water, the ripples of which will extend to the farthest corners of the earth, wherever football is played.'

from *The Professionals*, 1964

Cock-a-Double-Do

A. J. AYER

It has been done at last. For the first time in this century a single team has won 'the double' – both the Football League championship and the FA Cup. Arsenal came near it in the thirties; Manchester United looked almost certain to achieve it four seasons ago; Wolverhampton Wanderers, who won the cup last year, were within a point of heading the League. Last Saturday Tottenham Hotspur brought it off. They had already won the League championship with a total of points which equalled the record set up by Arsenal thirty years ago; they had achieved the record number of wins in the League, including a record run of eleven matches at the opening of the season; their performance in away matches had given them yet another record. By defeating Burnley in the semi-final they had eliminated their most dangerous rivals for the cup. Leicester City whom they had to meet in the final were quite a formidable team. In League matches, though the Spurs had beaten them at Leicester, they had lost to them at home; in fact, Leicester were the first team to win at Tottenham this season. Nevertheless, the experts almost unanimously picked the Spurs to win.

The experts were right. The Spurs did win by two goals to nothing, but though a famous it was not a magnificent victory. On the day, as one of the Leicester players said a little sourly after the match, the Spurs were not 'super'. There have been many occasions this season when the Tottenham cock has had better reason to crow. They were not noticeably nervous, but they did seem rather jaded. The strain of living up to their reputation throughout the long League programme had taken its toll of them. Blanchflower, their right-half and captain, who more than anyone has been responsible for the team's success, looked a little tired; Mackay, the other wing-half, lacked something of his usual drive; the inside-forwards, White and Allen, were both a little out of touch. In fact, the Spurs owed their victory mainly to what some critics had thought to be their only possible weakness, their defence. In particular, their left-back, Henry, played a superb game. On this form, he deserves to play for England; it can only be the reluctance of the England selectors to disturb a winning team that keeps him out of the World Cup.

The Spurs lost the championship last season, when they seemed to have it won, because their mid-field play was let down by their finishing; they made the openings but failed to score the goals. This is an old fault of theirs, which even in this triumphant season has occasionally cost them matches that they could have won. For a long time on Saturday it looked as if this were again going to be their downfall. One wondered if a goal would ever come. White missed an easy chance in the opening minutes; just before half-time Jones had what seemed to be a good goal disallowed for off-side; Allen and Dyson missed open goals in the second half. It was not until the last quarter of the game that Smith, the centre-forward, beat a Leicester defender skilfully on the turn and scored with a shot which the goalkeeper had no chance to save. This goal was decisive. The Spurs belatedly took charge of the game, and it was no surprise when the left-winger, Dyson, headed a second goal to make their victory complete.

The greatest fear of the Spurs' supporters before the game had been that an injury at Wembley would rob their team of the double; as it did Manchester United four years ago. In the event, the game was marred by injury, but by an injury to one of the Leicester players. After less than twenty minutes, the Leicester right-back, Chalmers, hurt his leg in a tackle; he stayed bravely on the field, but was only a passenger at outside-left. For more than three-quarters of the game the Leicester side was practically reduced to ten men. Under this handicap, they played extremely well. Banks in goal, McLintock, the right-half who took Chalmers' place at back, and King, the centre-half, were outstanding; but the whole defence was resolute, and the forwards often threatened to break through, especially in the opening period of the second half. Leicester are not a conspicuously artistic side, but they are strong and fit and thrustful, in the tradition of Midland English football. If, as is probable, they deputize for the Spurs in the European Cupwinners' Cup next season, since the Spurs as League champions will be competing in the European Cup, and can hardly manage both, they should do very well.

It is idle to speculate what would have happened if Chalmers had not been injured. What can be said is that it is intolerable that the Cup Final should be vitiated year after year by injuries of this kind.

This is surely an occasion on which it should be allowable to introduce substitutes, as it already is in many international matches, at least up to half-time. There would have to be safeguards to prevent abuses, but they should not be very hard to devise.

How good is this Spurs side? Are they the team of the century, in merit as well as in achievement? By the very highest standards, they are not a team of stars. Blanchflower is a very great player, at his zenith the best wing-half that I have ever seen, but he is nearing the end of his career. Of the others only Jones, a wing-forward with the speed and swerve of a rugby three-quarter, could clearly command a place in a current world eleven. Of course they have good players besides these. Norman is a dominating centre-half. Mackay can play like a tornado. Though White is erratic, his intelligent play at inside-forward has won the team many of its matches; he has the positional sense of a great player. Smith, who is now the England centre-forward, has played better this year than he ever has before. He is a clumsy-looking footballer, and there are periods when nothing will go right for him, but he has more skill than one might think and he rises splendidly to an occasion. In the semi-final as well as in the final of the Cup, and in the critical League match with Sheffield Wednesday, which settled the championship for the Spurs, it was his well-taken goals that turned the scale.

Nevertheless, it is not so much to the individual merits of the players as to their team work that the Spurs owe their extraordinary success. They have kept very nearly the same side for two seasons, and they have in this season been very little disturbed by injuries. The result is that they have achieved a remarkable understanding. In their use of the open space, they resemble the famous Spurs team which won the League championship ten years ago. But whereas the 1950 eleven relied, under Arthur Rowe's management, exclusively on 'push and run', a style which is very beautiful to watch when it is successful but one which makes very heavy demands upon the players' energy, the present team has been able to blend this 'continental' style with the English long-passing method. One of their most considerable achievements has been their ability to pace a game, to conserve their energy between bouts of pressure: it has repeatedly brought them goals in quick succession. For this they owe much to their manager, Bill Nicholson, who was himself a member of the 1950 team, but still more, I think, to their captain, Danny Blanchflower, whose control of them on the field has always been intelligent and sure. At their best, I think they have been superior to any English team since the war, though the Manchester United side, which was broken by the Munich air crash, ran them very close. I am not sure that they are better than the great Arsenal side of the thirties, though it is perhaps in their favour that the game is probably played nowadays at a faster pace.

How will they fare next season in the European Cup? A fast, hard-tackling side like some of the West German teams might throw them out of their rhythm. Against a team of artists like Real Madrid, their own artistry should flourish. I cannot wager that they will beat Real Madrid; but if at any stage they are drawn against them, it should be a wonderful game to watch.

from New Statesman, 12 May 1961

Bobby Charlton
ARTHUR HOPCRAFT

Everyone who follows football has his favourite player; even the players do. The selection is bound to reflect something of the nature of the one who is doing the choosing. The favourite is not necessarily being named as the greatest player of all. We may admit, reluctantly, our favourite's weakness. What we are saying is that this particular player appeals to us more than any other. It has to do with his personality, his style of behaviour, perhaps importantly the way in which he compensates for his deficiencies. He is the player who may disappoint sometimes with a ragged, off-form performance, and yet over the years stays clear and bright in the memory. He is the player we bring to mind first when we ask ourselves what football looks like when we enjoy it most. The man I name for this role is Bobby Charlton.

The flowing line of Charlton's football has no disfiguring barbs in it, but there is a heavy and razor-sharp arrowhead at its end. It is the combination of the graceful and the dramatic which makes him so special. There are few players who affect a crowd's responses as much as he does. Something extraordinary is expected of him the moment he receives the ball. He can silence a crowd instantly, make it hold its breath in expectation. A shot from Charlton, especially if hit on the run from outside the penalty area, is one of the great events of the sport, not because it is rare, which it is not, but because the power of it is massive and it erupts out of elegance; he is never clumsy or desperate in movement; he can rise very close to the athletic ideal.

The persistent complaint I have heard made against Charlton, the one which keeps him out of the lists when some people name the handful of the world's greatest players, is that he avoids the fury of the game, that where the hacking and elbowing are fiercest Charlton is not to be found. But this is like dismissing Dickens from the world's great literature because he never went to gaol for throwing bricks at politicians; like denigrating Disraeli on the grounds that he was a third-rate novelist. Charlton's courage is geared to his special talents. I have certainly never seen him fling himself headlong across his own goalmouth to head the ball away from some opposing forward's foot. But I have seen him summon his speed and use his swerve to score goals when defences were swinging their boots at him with intent to hurt. Charlton has been felled so often in his career that he could not possibly have stayed so compellingly in the game for so long if he lacked nerve. I do not object at all that he has never been sent off the field for kneeing someone in the groin.

It is true, I think, to say that although he became an England international player when he was twenty it was in later years that he gathered full resolution for the game. He was never less than an excellent player, but he was past twenty-five before he became a great one. He flowered fully, and gloriously, for the World Cup in 1966, appropriately scoring England's first goal with a veering run from near the centre-circle and a characteristic shot taken in mid-stride. He scored another like it in the semi-final against Portugal. They are the kind of goals he will be remembered by. They are a great player's goals.

Yet Charlton is not just a scoring specialist. Being so fast and possessing the best body swerve of his generation, he made his name as a winger. In his early years as a professional his great merit was his ability to run past the defender from the left touchline and go diagonally on the back's inside to hit the ball at goal with either foot. This was the young Charlton, with most of his weight in his legs, whose speed and control of the ball were aimed almost exclusively at scoring goals. By his late twenties – he was twenty-eight in the 1966 World Cup – he had moved to a deep-lying centre-forward or inside-forward position, as the fulcrum of the attack. His accuracy with the ball at great distance was now used to shift, in one sudden pass, the point of action. These passes, especially if preceded by one of his sidesteps and a burst of acceleration, could turn the fortune of a game instantly. A moment's work of this calibre from him, perhaps at the edge of his own penalty area, could take his side out of an alarming defensive situation and have it menacing the other goal immediately. I saw him do this once against Liverpool and the moment stunned that ferocious crowd into silence.

Charlton makes his own rules for dealing with a football. He is a player to admire but not for younger ones to copy. When he strikes the ball he often has his head up high, instead of looking down over the ball as the coaches teach. He will flick at it with the outside of his left foot when leaning back looking at the sky. When players on his own side are unaccustomed to him they often find that the ball comes to them, having miraculously been 'bent' round some obstructing opponent, spinning violently and therefore difficult to control; only the best can take advantage of such passes, as Denis Law, Best and Jimmy Greaves (in the international side) all have. Charlton does not dribble with the ball in the sense that Best does, patting it between his feet, nor does he run with it as if it is tied by elastic to him, as in the case of Pelé, of Brazil, so that it bounces against his knees, thighs, stomach, ankles as he moves. Charlton kicks the ball close to the ground in front of him, often a long way in front, and runs like a sprinter behind it, almost as if there was no ball at all. No boy could possibly be taught such a method of playing football.

This run deceives defenders. They see the ball coming towards them, with Charlton well behind it, and they think they can reach it before him. Suddenly, just as they commit themselves, his right shoulder dips, his whole weight goes momentarily on his right foot, flat on the grass, and then he has sped past them the other way, kicking the ball in front of him as he goes. His own speed, coupled with the defender's impetus, often means that he is 10 yards clear before the defender has turned. To be beaten by Charlton's swerve is to be beaten for good. If the defender anticipates the swerve and turns in the right direction Charlton will clear the tackle expertly like a hurdler.

There is delicious exhilaration in watching movement like this. Crowds will him to repeat it, and if he gets the ball and pauses as if gathering himself for such a run the whole sound of the stadium changes from its baying or grumbling into an excited purr. If he decides the moment is not right, and releases the ball quickly with a merely sensible short pass, there is a deep groan of disappointment.

He has his bad matches, when his touch deserts him and the casual flicks and lobs skim away erratically, sometimes presenting the other team with the initiative they had lost. In games like these his shooting at goal can be laughably wild, and yet there is seldom laughter; the communal embarrassment is the same that settles around a wrong final note from the recital platform. Charlton hates these lapses. He reacts to them with something close to self-revulsion, like a man discovering a flea in his vest. He shakes his head wretchedly, apologizes to the company, and on his very worst days may keep clear of the ball for a while. More often he tries to compose himself, trapping the ball and striking it with an unusual, elaborate care. It is only now that he looks awkward. When Charlton is keeping his eye intently on the ball, as every good player is supposed to, then he is at his least effective. He is not a player's player, in the sense of being reliable, even though he is entirely professional in his attitude to the game; he is certainly a spectator's player, in the sense that he is a sight to watch.

His dejection in failure, even in the momentary kind, is more easily understood when Charlton has been met off the field. There is a natural diffidence in him, a sense of anxiety not to show himself up in public. His shyness was brought home to me first of all when he was twenty-one, unmarried and living in lodgings. I had some fairly harmless questions to ask him for the newspaper I was working for at the time, and the whole interview was conducted on the doorstep, with Charlton holding on to the doorknob, not being in the least obstructive but blushing and leaving words trailing indistinctly and ambiguously in the air. He said at the time that he had always found it hard to answer any questions about himself. Seven years later, when he was a much better player and going bald, he was still far from casual in conversation even in his own home, only showing a marked step forward in self-confidence when he was holding one of his children in his arms. He has done a good deal of talking to youth clubs and at sports clubs functions in recent years, yet there was a distinct nervincss in his voice when I heard him deliver a few impromptu sentences in a hospital's broadcast at half-time in one of Liverpool's midweek matches. He smokes more than would be expected of a man who is still one of the fastest movers in international football in spite of being thirty years old.

He gets the star footballer's profusion of flattery. His name is chanted to raise the spirits of ticket queues in the rain; vivid, coarse girls have to be held off by policemen when he gets in and out of the Manchester United coach; small boys write him letters of charming clumsiness and kick footballs with his autograph on them; he has been European Footballer of the Year, and a poll of referees has voted him Model Player. His wife is pretty, so are his two daughters, and he lives in a rich man's house in a rich man's neighbourhood. He is the classic working-class hero who has made it to glamour and Nob Hill.

Charlton's childhood was spent in Ashington, Northumberland, and he was a miner's son, living in one of those immensely long, pitshaft-straight rows of houses which characterize the area. Classically, for a workers' hero, he owes much to his mother.

Mrs Elizabeth Charlton is a grey-haired, handsome woman now. It is said in Ashington that when she was a girl she could dribble with a football as well as most of the boys. She was born into football and she knew the game and its ways as theatre mums know make-up and stage-doors. Her father was a goalkeeper, called 'Tanner' Milburn, and her four brothers were all fullbacks with League clubs, the Milburns, Jack, George, Jimmy and Stan. The greatest of all the Milburns, the centre-forward 'Wor Jackie', of Newcastle United and England, is her cousin. The story goes that when her eldest son (Jack Charlton, Leeds' and England's centre-half) first made her a grandmother she was asked by a friend in the street how the baby was, and she answered: 'Eee, the bairn's lovely. And his feet are fine, too.'

When Mrs Charlton talks about her sons her face takes on a brightness which strips the years away. One can see where Bobby got that exuberance of movement. She told me that when the two boys were babies – Jack is the older by eighteen months – she used to take them in one pram to Ashington's matches. She said: 'I used to leave them behind the dressing-rooms, and whenever the crowd roared they'd jump.'

Bobby went to a local primary school, which then as now was a hideous line of apexes in blood-red brick. There is a long, rectangular playground where the boys play football in engrossed tangles, their faces set fiercely against defeat. It was here that Bobby wore his first football strip, a set of maroon shirts with black shorts which were made out of wartime blackout curtaining by one of the women teachers. The school still has the set. Bobby was captain of the team which won the East Northumberland junior schools league championship wearing it. These matters are not taken lightly in Ashington.

The headmaster at the time was Mr James Hamilton, and I talked to him in his bed-sitter when he was nearing eighty and in retirement. He had a photograph on one wall of Bobby and some thirty other small boys with their arms folded across their chests. That was Bobby Charlton as school captain, he said. 'He didn't mention that in his book. He was too modest.' He produced another photograph of an unmistakable Charlton, at eleven years old, holding a trophy in the middle of his football team. Mr Hamilton is on one flank of the group and the sports master, Mr Norman McGuiness, on the other. Mr Hamilton said that when Bobby got through his scholarship examination for senior school he was directed to Morpeth Grammar School. He said: 'It's one of those snooty schools where they play rugby. We got him transferred to the grammar school at Bedlington.'

Both Charlton and his mother say that Mr McGuiness contributed more than anyone else to Bobby's development as a young footballer. I met him at the secondary school where he was now headmaster, a small, tightly made man of fifty-two with some alarming stories of contemporary adolescent indiscipline. He sounded glad to be able to talk about someone who had responded more readily to him; but he confessed he taught Charlton little, merely encouraged him. He said: 'There really wasn't much he could be coached in. My first memory of him is seeing this small, thin lad of nine playing football with the fourteen-year-olds and just waltzing through them. It didn't take a Solomon to see he had natural ability. Even at nine he had a body swerve and a natural check that would take the other man the wrong way.'

Mr McGuiness clearly had enjoyed running junior schoolboy football, its sudden revelations of talent delighting him, the general enthusiasm having its own charm and calling for special bending of the rules. He said that even then Charlton could hit the ball as strongly as the seniors, and his side used to win heavily. He said: 'But, you know, the thing was never to let the scores get too big. The unwritten law was that you didn't let anyone get into double figures.

After a certain stage of the game, if one side was winning easily, you just whistled everyone offside the moment they got into the penalty area.'

This was serious stuff, nevertheless. Mr McGuiness used to put his ten- and eleven-year-olds through six-a-side games in the playground after school three times a week. There was no resistance to the training. Then as now, as the current headmaster of Charlton's primary school said to me, Ashington boys were 'football daft'.

There was less devotion to football at Bedlington Grammar School, and the prompting hand which put Charlton in the game as a career still came from Ashington. The headmaster of the secondary school which Jack Charlton was attending was a remarkable man. Mr Stuart Hemingway came to approve of professional football, rejecting the prejudice he had held against it in his younger days, when he went to Ashington in the twenties. He had been a Foundation Scholar at Manchester Grammar School, he was steeped in church music, and he thought that education was the key to the emancipation of the unemployed working-classes. In Ashington they taught him that football was.

He too was in retirement when I met him, a thin, keen-faced man in his seventies, with sharp wit in spite of a wavering voice. He had been years ahead of his time as an educationist. He introduced foreign languages, and even school trips abroad, to a colliers' non-selective secondary school.

He remembered the sad deprivation of the Northumberland mining areas between the wars. He said: 'That was terrible poverty. In the summer the boys used to come to school in their bare feet to save their boots for winter – and for football. I was always against the professional game. I was against this chasing after schoolboys to turn them into footballers. Then I came to realize that this professional football was nothing bad at all. It was something good for them. It could be work. I think the footballer's wage then was about £4 a week.'

Once he had taken his boys out of the local schools league, to protect them from the tough competition which put the most talented ones into the public eye. Now he urged them into competitions so that they should not be overlooked.

He had played inside-right for Manchester University, and he retained his affection for the club he had watched in his boyhood,

Manchester United. By the time the Charlton brothers were in their teens he was well versed in the ways by which professional clubs pick up young players, and with Bobby he stole a march on the clubs' scouts. Soon after Bobby's fifteenth birthday he wrote to Busby at United. He had already advised Mr and Mrs Charlton that United was the best club for their younger son. Mr Hemingway, talking about Charlton as a boy player, used exactly the word that Mrs Charlton used when she remembered the excitement of watching him play. They both said: 'He used to *delight* people.'

Mrs Charlton, meanwhile, had been doing some coaching of her own. She and Mr McGuiness were determined that Bobby should get into the England schoolboys team. She said: 'The one thing we worried about was that he was slow off the mark.' She was handling the teapot, which is always handy for visitors to her house, and she jabbed it about the air to emphasize her point. 'I talked to Mr McGuiness about it and he said if we could quicken him up over 30 yards he'd be all right. Well, I asked ever so many men around here to take the job on, but they wouldn't. So I took him down to the park myself and got him doing sprints.'

It is an appealing picture: the fair boy and the brisk, pretty mother, she pacing out the distances and urging him shrilly on, a few bystanders nodding at each other and agreeing that 'Tanner' Milburn's lass would have her lad in the England team if anybody could. She said, smiling in hindsight at the humour in the situation: 'It was 20 yards, then back; 80 yards, back again.' Now she laughed outright. 'I don't know if it helped but Bobby got his cap,' she said.

Manchester United's chief scout, Joe Armstrong, a stocky, trundly old man now, with a round, lined face and wispy hair, watched Bobby Charlton play for East Northumberland schoolboys against Hebburn and Jarrow boys on February 9, 1953. He would remember the day until he died, he said. 'It was a thin morning, with frost on the ground, and we were peering through the mist. Ooh, I can see it all now.' He winced at the memory of the cold. 'Bobby didn't do so much that day, but it was enough for me.'

There was also a scout from the Sunderland club at the game. Mrs Charlton remembered that Bobby was disappointed because, after the match, this man went to speak to the goalkeeper on his side but not to him. She said: 'But then Joe came up, and he said, "I don't want to butter you up, Missis, but your boy will play for England before he's twenty-one." '

Mrs Charlton was informative about the way professional football clubs hunt for young players. She said that once it was known that Manchester United had made contact other clubs had representatives calling at the house almost daily. She said: 'They were offering us the world. One fellow offered £800. Another said he'd double whatever was the highest offer we'd had. He didn't even ask what it was. There was another fellow in the front room who said he'd got £550 in his brief-case, and we could have it there and then.'

All these inducements were illegal, but the practice was widespread. Ashington was not appalled by it all, but the Charltons were properly suspicious. Mrs Charlton said: 'Jackie Milburn told us not to be taken in by anyone. He said, "They'll all offer you the earth, but even if you say yes you might never get it." ' The scouts' persistence brought them to the house at all times of the day and night. Mrs Charlton said: 'I'd be cleaning the fireplace in the morning and I'd look round and there'd be another one standing behind me. There were times when we've had one in the front room and one in the kitchen.'

Eventually there were eighteen clubs asking for Bobby's signature. Joe Armstrong kept close to the family, and sometimes he had his wife with him. The education authorities were objecting to the retinue of scouts now following Bobby to every school match he played. Mrs Charlton said: 'Bobby had already decided it was going to be Manchester United. Joe had come first, you see. Joe used to say at the matches he was Bobby's uncle, and then he'd introduce his wife and say, "And this is his Auntie Sally." '

Busby saw Charlton play for the first time at a public trial for the England schoolboys' side at Manchester City's ground, and he decided he wanted him. Charlton left Ashington for Manchester in July 1953.

Nowadays a boy can join a professional club as an apprentice at fifteen, and if he does not match up to expectations he can revert to amateur status later on. But this was not the case in the fifties. As Charlton put it: 'You either went on the ground staff and spent your time cleaning toilets, or you went to work.' He took a job in an engineering works close to Old Trafford until he was seventeen, when he could sign as a professional. For a while he played in a youth side which used to win, against opponents trying to impress the United representatives on the touchline, by scores like 12–0 regularly. He said the experience taught him how to take rough treatment. His first League game came in the month of his nineteenth birthday, and he scored twice. As Joe Armstrong had forecast, he played for England before he was twenty-one.

Drama and gloss come to every star footballer, and Charlton has had more than most. He has travelled in a score of different countries, and he is accustomed to the pampering that surrounds valuable human cargoes in transit. Yet his wife says that every time he drives past a particular hotel in Sale, near Manchester, he points it out and tells her it was the first hotel he ever stayed in. He was fifteen at the time, and where Charlton came from boys might have seen the insides of off-licences but not of hotels, where people ate and slept. He said to me, his Geordie accent still clear: 'Well, at school that was the end. I mean, that was really something.' It was the first time, he said, he was conscious of being looked at.

Charlton was in the Munich air crash, and got out of it unhurt. He was playing for United soon afterwards. He has always said that it had no lasting effect on him, although it is difficult to believe that the shock did not linger. He played for England in the year of the disaster, and he has been in the national side ever since. For all that, it is true to say that it took him until his mid-twenties to find the authority of personality to complement and extend his abounding talents. Busby says that is because the great years of a player's career are those between the ages of twenty-six and thirty-two. No one can speak with more knowledge.

In the 1967–8 season I have seen less ease in Charlton's game than there was three seasons ago, but more wisdom and a new sense of responsibility. The sparse hair flops across the bald crown; the face is tauter than ever. No one can play eleven years of top quality football at his pace without showing the strain. But his speed still astonishes spectators and opponents. He can chase opposing, younger forwards from behind, make up a 10-yard gap and get in front of them to force them into parting with the ball. He is one of the very few players who can bring rheumy-eyed sportswriters to their feet in a press box. He has not been staled by knocks or mud or the dragging weight of repetition. He does not make a crowd think murder; what he gives them is delight.

from *The Football Man*, 1968

Denis Law
JOHN RAFFERTY

Denis Law, a slim, blond, whiffy-haired youth affecting a colourful modern style of dress, is, at eighteen years of age, the youngest player to be capped for Scotland since R. S. McColl sixty years ago. Such has been his success at Cardiff last month and at Hampden Park last week that on sheer football ability his selection for Scotland's team for years to come would seem to be more or less automatic.

Unfortunately, it is not just as simple as all that. There is a small question of field conduct occupying many of the minds that matter. This, to some, may seem strange, for it was those same minds which conceived the 'rummel 'em up' international tactics which disgraced Scotland just a few years ago. After the Hampden game on Wednesday Law was credited with having played to orders and worried and harried Danny Blanchflower off his game. This, of course, went a long way to disrupting the Irish attacking rhythm. Yet it was generally deplored later that young Law had been too rough about his task. It does seem all wrong that a youngster of no more than school age should be roughing a world celebrity and football master such as Blanchflower. Later an Irishman complained bitterly that he had never been kicked so much in a game but when asked about Law would only say: 'If that is him at eighteen I would not like to play against him when he is twenty-four.' But this is not the first occasion on which the young Huddersfield forward has drawn attention to himself. At Cardiff, in his first international, he had to be reprimanded by the referee for showing signs of retaliation when the game became hot – and him only eighteen too. Then it is a fact that every time the selectors watched him before he was chosen he was spoken to by the referee for serious breach of rules.

The selectors may have found an inside-forward but, at the same time, they have bought themselves a bit of trouble. It was inevitable this should happen, for Law has been described as resembling rock and roll singer Tommy Steele in appearance and former international Billy Steel in his play. It is just too much to resemble two such turbulent characters.

Law, at a very moderate eighteen years of age, is a long jump from the small, slim, fifteen-year-old boy sent from Aberdeen to Huddersfield to begin a football apprenticeship. He had been spotted by the brother of manager Andy Beattie playing for Powis School. When he arrived at Huddersfield station the waiting officials did not recognize him. No wonder. He looked so frail and slight and he wore thick glasses to correct a squint. This has gone and so have the spectacles. Now, after working on the ground staff and graduating through Huddersfield's five teams, he stands, a slim, wiry, confident athlete. He favours the clothes liked by those youths who bounce to the modern dance rhythms – the narrow trousers, the colourful socks, the elaborate footwear. He has all the brashness and love of a good time of that group.

Of his football ability there is no doubt. His fitness to be a profitable member of Scotland's team for the next ten years at least is equally clear. There is just this business of having him conform to the conventions. That is not so easy either. Try to change his style, try to tone him down too much, and as sure as a gun he will be ruined as a footballer. His cheek and lack of respect for the opposition go a long way to making him the player he is. Goodness knows we have had too many players showing too much respect for too long. We may say we do not like cheeky boys, but we must admit that when it comes to winning, a bit of cheek goes a long way and that goes for football, boxing, running or any other sport. Perhaps the modern, luxurious international atmosphere with the five-star elegance of Turnberry and the understanding of Matt Busby will take the rough edges off young Law. But for goodness' sake don't let us go too far and stifle him. Just ensuring that cheek does not become big-head would be enough.

from *The Observer*, 1958

Turf Moor, and Other Fields of Dreams
BLAKE MORRISON

> 5 kids still play at making blossoms fall
> and humming as they do 'Here Comes the Bride'.
> They never seem to tire of their ball
> though I hear a woman's voice call one inside.
>
> 2 larking boys play bawdy bride and groom.
> 3 boys in Leeds strip la-la Lohengrin
> I hear them as I go through growing gloom
> still years away from being skald or skin.
>
> The ground's carpeted with petals as I throw
> the aerosol, the HARP can, the cleared weeds
> on top of Dad's dead daffodils, then go,
> with not one glance behind away from Leeds.
>
> *V*, Tony Harrison

How they kept football from me for so long I don't know, but I was almost eleven before I discovered it – or should I say it discovered me. I remember the moment clearly. It was a Sunday morning in autumn and my father and I were sitting in adjoining armchairs in the dining room of our one-time rectory in Yorkshire, sunlight pouring in through the windows and over our shoulders. He had the *Sunday Times*, I the *Sunday Express*, and as I turned to the back page my eye fell on a photograph and match report. In an instant the wicked secret was out and I was doomed – another of the century's lost boys destined to squander the best years of his life failing to make the grade as a professional or simply supporting the wrong team.

Until that moment in the sunlight my only sporting interest had been motor racing: at Oulton Park and Aintree and Silverstone I'd seen Graham Hill and Jack Brabham, Roy Salvadori and Stirling Moss, Bruce McLaren and Innes Ireland battle it out in Formula One races; at home with Dinky toys, I'd recreate these races in the back yard or round the legs of my father's billiard table. It wasn't much of a participation sport for a boy, and it's hard to imagine a child of the 1980s or 1990s finding anything exciting about a noisy, polluting, past-you-in-a-flash car race. But these were the years when the British dominated the sport, drivers as well as manufacturers, and the 1959 championship – with Jack Brabham pushing his car over the line in the final race to wrest victory from Stirling Moss and Tony Brooks – had all the last-gasp enthralment of the 1988–9 soccer season.

There were other dramas, too – like the system we devised for smuggling two large families into the Oulton Park paddock on a single ticket (slip it out to the next person through the slats of a wooden fence), or the extraordinary practice (when the last race was over) of being allowed to drive round the circuit in your family saloon.

Then on that day in 1961 I picked up the family paper and, looking for motor-racing news, saw instead a muddy goalmouth, a bulging net, and what the poet Vernon Scannell once called 'the blurred anguish of goalkeepers'. I pored over the match reports and league tables like someone trying to get to grips with a foreign language. And straight away, the grip was on me. Only once since, after that European Cup Final in the Heysel Stadium, when I thought I could never bear to play or watch the game again, has it promised to set me free.

My son, a child of the 1980s, got the soccer virus at seven. Surely I must have known about football before I was eleven? But there were just eighteen children at our village primary school, and football was not played there at all, not even in the playground.

At home it was no better. My father had never played football, only rugby, and as the local GP in an under-resourced practice was confined to home, on call, most weekends; when he wasn't, it was Oulton Park we'd go to, not a football ground. My cousins from Manchester, the only children I saw outside school, were all mad about car racing, too. Isolated as I was, the rich kid in the rectory, it wasn't so surprising that football hadn't impinged on my world. Like sex later, it was something my parents probably preferred me not to know about.

Yet 18 miles away was the town of Burnley, not only my birthplace (in the district hospital) but home to one of the two great football teams of the day. By now, the point of my initiation, their greatest moment, when they won the 1959–60 championship, had already passed. But I was not to know that, and nor were any of the sports journalists who covered their games that autumn. Burnley were riding high, and even if they hadn't been it would never have occurred to me to support Leeds United, though the place we lived in was right on the Yorkshire–Lancashire border, almost as close to Elland Road as to Turf Moor. Who were Leeds United? Just some team languishing in a lower division. Whereas Burnley, as the autumn of 1961 gave way to the spring of 1962, looked on target for the double, and could boast a team of English, Irish and Scottish internationals: Blacklaw, Angus, Elder, Adamson, Cummings, Miller, Connelly, McIlroy, Pointer, Harris.

It was an exciting season but a sad one. The scrapbook I began, when I look at it more closely, reveals some odd gaps, and stops abruptly on 3 March, at which point Burnley were four points clear of Ipswich and five clear of Tottenham, with games in hand over both of them. (In the Second Division Liverpool made the pace ahead of Leyton Orient and Plymouth Argyle.) Thereafter Burnley's progress was too agonizing to record, and I have suppressed all memory of it apart from a rare win over lowly Blackpool: inexorably, Ipswich caught us and the games in hand were blown away.

But there was still the FA Cup, the very reason, some commentators said (as they always do), for the team's faltering in the League. Here my scrapbook details are much fuller: 6–1 over QPR; then Leyton Orient, 1–0 in a replay; Everton, 3–1; Sheffield United 1–0; and finally in the semi-finals a 2–1 win over Fulham, again after a replay. This left the final against Spurs, the Old Enemy, who came to Turf Moor for a league match just fourteen days before and drew 2–2. There were four goals again at Wembley, but this time it all turned to dust. Jimmy Greaves scored after three minutes; Burnley's equalizer early in the second half came from Robson, who somehow squeezed it in the narrow gap that Brown was guarding at one post – anything but a classic. This goal was cancelled out by the burly Smith just one minute later.

Then came a disputed penalty ten minutes from time: Blacklaw lost the ball to two challenging Spurs players (surely a foul), Cummings stepped in to breast away a shot by Merwin (never handball, ref) and the referee pointed to the spot. The decision was agony enough, but nothing compared to the slow-motion trauma of the penalty itself: tubby Adam Blacklaw dropping on one knee to his right as Danny Blanchflower stepped up and rolled the ball gently to his left. At the final whistle I did the only thing a boy could do in the circumstances: took my ball out on the front lawn and re-enacted the entire game, with certain crucial adjustments to the scoreline. This was the principle I'd learnt with my Dinky toys round the billiard table: a world of isolated make-believe, where the action replay, yet to be invented on television, ensured that your favourites could never lose. But to a growing boy there were shades of the prison house about these fantasy games: I wanted to play football myself, and that seemed to mean having somebody to play it with.

For the moment this possibility was remote. My younger sister soon tired of being put in goal and my long-suffering Aunt Sheila, who came to stay every school holiday and who one summer allowed me to amass a century against her on the back lawn, would not extend her tolerance of cricket to football. As for the three boys of my age at primary school – Simon, Stephen, and Jeffrey – they were so uninterested in football they used to satirize my obsession with it. In desperation I started going to a youth club in Kelbrook, 3 miles away, where there was five-a-side every Friday evening and where the intention was to form a fully fledged eleven-a-side village boys' team. My grave offence to tribal loyalties somehow got back to Simon, Stephen and Jeffrey, who took the piss relentlessly – 'Morrie, Morrie, football mad' – and eventually stopped talking to me altogether. Their persecution programme only strengthened my faith: I was now a martyr to football, a sufferer in the cause.

Forced to play alone, I began the process of transforming some rough and gale-swept ground in the paddock behind our house into a stadium of dreams. My father helped me clear the ground of stones, weeds, broken glass. We constructed goal posts from rusty old metal tubing and put some strawberry nets behind them. (To my dad's fury I left the nets there the whole winter until grass and weed began to grow through and they fell apart in our hands.) The touchlines were ribbon-scatters of sawdust, standard local league practice in those days. But one afternoon I discovered an old line-marker and some lime bags in an outhouse, from the days when the house had a tennis court. Clearing the cobwebs, I slowly grasped how the contraption worked: you poured lime into the heavy metal base, added water, stirred the sloppy mass with a stick until you had the right consistency, dropped the wheel into the metal slots that held it, and then went squeaking off down the side of the pitch.

In Kevin Costner's 1989 film *Field of Dreams*, an American on a farm hears the corn telling him to construct a baseball field at the back of his house. I had the same sense of mystery and religious calling myself, though for this Yorkshire field of dreams it was that line-marker which provided all the magic. The touchlines and penalty areas and centre circle would be a pale, indistinguishable yellow when I marked them out on the wet grass in the morning; by lunchtime, as the day dried out, they'd come up a brilliant white. I surveyed them from the main stand – a large earth mound running down one side of the field, separating it from our garden. It was a short pitch, 30 yards at most, and a bumpy one, narrower at one end than the other and with a ridge running across the edge of the penalty areas. But as far as I was concerned – Little Lord Fauntleroy on his earth mound, chairman, groundsman, manager, and twenty-two players rolled into one – these were the green expanses of Turf Moor or even Wembley.

I lacked only opponents, but these weren't hard to imagine, any more than it was hard to provide Ken Wolstenholme's commentary as I raced up and down. My favourite move was to pass back to myself in goal, then punt the ball high in the air and sprint up to the centre circle to head forward; a further rush, a volley on the edge of the area and with luck the ball might hit the roof of the net without bringing down the wonky crossbar as well. (Why was it always so much more exciting to hit the roof of the net, though all the manuals said that a low shot stood more chance of beating the keeper? Why is that sort of goal still so much more spectacular to see?) A line of elms and chestnuts ran down the side of the pitch opposite the grandstand, a kop that roared and swayed in the wind: if I timed it right there'd be a gust of wind at just the moment the strawberry net was bulging – the ecstatic crowd, or even Ken Wolstenholme moved to excitement by what had happened.

It was all very well but I'd have to put in some proper games of football – with real opponents – if I was ever going to be signed up by Burnley. Then one spring evening as I was dashing about the pitch and muttering Wolstenholmeisms to myself, Simon and Stephen were suddenly there at the field gate. I slunk over to them, shamefaced, caught in the act, only to find that they'd decided they liked football and, more to the point, had resolved to persecute Jeffrey instead. Things looked up after that, for me if not for Jeffrey; we started to play football at break and even managed to con the soppy new teacher at the primary school into letting us have a match during lesson time.

The Kelbrook team got off the ground, too, if only for two matches, one of which exposed me for the first time to violence (unthinkable in our school for a boy to be beaten up by another boy) and the other to the four-letter work 'f . . .': it was in the bath afterwards, I remember, that I half-innocently asked my mother what the word meant and knew from her fumbling evasiveness that it possessed a power I would want to test out again. Football and f . . . ing (whatever that was) were, I intuitively grasped, a long way from my mother's aspirations for me, which among other things included learning to play the piano. I dutifully went to piano lessons at the house of Mrs Brown, in Earby, until I arrived one Wednesday afternoon in the middle of live television coverage (rare in those days) of an England World Cup qualifying match. To have the football on television turned off and to be forced to practise the piano instead put paid to my faltering interest in that instrument. I have never been musical since.

Later, in September 1962, I moved on to a grammar school in Skipton and at last found boys even more manacled to football than myself. Undeterred that rugby, not soccer, was the official school sport, we would get to the playing fields early on games afternoons so we could use the oval ball as a round one (even heading it) before the games master arrived. And though soccer was in theory banned from the playground, the staff were happy to turn a blind eye to our break-time mauling outside the art room: there was a chalked goal on one wall, but to score at the other end you had to get the ball between the drainpipe and the ventilation-grate. Mostly we played with a tennis ball but if there wasn't one to be had we'd make do with a small stone instead. (Out walking at thirty-nine, I still find myself trying to steer small stones through gateposts or other imaginary goals.) For a time we even got away with using a Frido. It all ended the morning I sent a wayward shot towards a doorway at exactly the moment that Harry Evans, the notoriously fierce physics master, came whistling through it on his way to assembly. Like the Blanchflower penalty, I see it all now in horrible slow motion: his unexpected emergence; the Frido smacking him on his bald patch and leaving a neat imprint of mud dots across his forehead; his terrifyingly loud demand 'Who kicked that?'; me shuffling over in terror and contrition as he began to wipe the muddy print off with his handkerchief; an almost audible general sigh of relief that punishment went no further than confiscation of the ball and detention for all those of us who'd been playing. For half a term there was no playground football at all. Then the tennis-ball games resumed.

Playing regular rugby for the school would have made it difficult to pursue a soccer career, of course, but whether through design or lack of skill I rose no higher than captaincy of the third XV, where I played stand-off (lots of kicking, not much service to the three-quarters) and took all the penalties. This left nearly all my Saturdays free to go to Burnley and, later, to play for a team in Colne; only once was I caught out, when I had to bunk off from a third XV game in order to play in a crucial cup match at Lancaster, which we won 5–3 in a swirling wind that allowed me, for the only time in my career, to score direct from a corner.

Sundays were reserved for the phenomenally successful Barnold-swich Park Rovers Minor Side, which I joined at fifteen, just after the start of a season which ended with a long unbeaten run and the league title. I didn't think of myself as much of a player but both schoolyard practice and the solitary hours I spent at home modelling myself on Burnley midfield genius Gordon Harris did mean that I was highly trained and motivated. And there was one spectacular goal which helped me make my mark, at least as far as the local paper was concerned. ('Left winger Laurence Stocker raced away down the right wing before putting across a bullet-like centre. Blake Morrison, who had followed up field, came running in to head the ball into the corner of the net with the entire Hellifield defence left stranded': I still don't know if I meant it or just could not get out of the way.)

The team went on winning the following season, and soon there were rumours of scouts coming to Barlick in order to watch us: Liverpool, Leeds United, Burnley, Bury and Blackburn were all said to be 'taking an interest' and Preston manager Jimmy Milne himself turned up for one game. Finally an invitation came for six of us to go to Preston for trials. The local paper made much of the fact that I was among them, a grammar-school boy and doctor's son, but we all knew that it was the other grammar-school boy among the six, Seehan Grace, three years younger than most of us and a star sprinter, whom Preston must be after. Nonetheless, after two lots of trials, three of us were offered schoolboy forms.

It seems amazing now that we were so blasé as to refuse, but we were taking the advice of our mentors – Park Rovers stalwarts like Neville Thwaites and Teddy Bamber as well as Seehan Grace's dad, who ran the Barlick carpet shop and knew the score better than we did. Their view was that schoolboy forms wouldn't mean much – no more than a couple of games a season in the B-team. And though I was tempted to give it a go just to see what the level of competition was like, I didn't want to break ranks. Preston, in any case, were not Burnley. O-levels were looming, I'd begun to get interested in girls and poetry, and deep down I knew I'd neither the skill nor bottle to make a soccer career.

Still, I went on playing. Langroyd, the Colne adult side I played for on Saturdays, had a lousy sloping pitch and were no great shakes, but I was enough of a fantasist to persuade myself that the stocky young apprentice engineers and flabby, middle-aged mill workers who made up the rest of the team were in the same league as Gordon Harris and Ray Pointer.

We had a fantasist for a manager, too. Ernie, who had been a good player in his day and still sometimes turned out if we were one short, lived in a grim terrace in Earby with an outsize wife and mentally disabled teenage daughter. Football was his escape from the pressures at home, and he was even more obsessed with it than I was. Unfortunately, he was also a cheat, and had a habit of drafting in star players for one-off appearances in cup matches even if this meant forging their signing-on forms. He got away with it most of the time but there were two notable occasions when his cheating caught up with us. The first was a summer five-a-side tournament, when the Langroyd A-team were progressing steadily towards the final until, in the semi, 1–0 up with five minutes to go, one of our players went down injured. We didn't have a substitute and didn't reckon we needed one either but Ernie, taking no risks, illegally sent on someone from our B-team, an offence immediately spotted by a rival team manager, who reported it and had us disqualified.

Easier to forgive, in some ways, was Ernie's ploy when we found ourselves 1–0 down at half-time in a crucial quarter-final cup match in Skelmersdale: Langroyd had been beaten in the final the previous year, and we were determined to triumph this time. The game should never have started on the waterlogged pitch, and the rain continued to bucket down. Skelmersdale got a squelchy early goal and there was worse to come when our centre half was sent off after twenty minutes for taking a wild kick at a niggly opposition forward. In the dressing-room at the interval Ernie told us – and none of us disputed it – that since we'd hardly got out of our own penalty area there was no chance of our winning; the best thing would be for a succession of players to go down injured and be taken off, forcing the referee to recognize the error of his ways in not having called the game off. I couldn't bring myself to be one of the imposters, but there were a couple of players who made a brilliant job of shamming serious injury and when the second of these had been helped off, after seventy-two minutes, leaving us with eight men, the referee decided to abandon the match – the pitch, he said, with no exaggeration, was now unplayable. Judging by the whistling from the Skelmersdale stand, the crowd had clearly got Ernie's number: we were even booed as we left the ground for the team coach at the end. But Skelmersdale had the last laugh, invoking some arcane Lancashire League rule that if a game had been abandoned after seventy minutes the authorities had the right to allow the result to stand. Ernie was phoneless and it fell to me to ring the appeals committee to learn the result of their hearing, and to drive down to Ernie to break the bad news. I remember him, in his cramped front room full of ironing and football trophies, his nylon shirt covered in sweat, indignantly planning our next move. But there was none we could make: Langroyd were out of the cup, and my last season with them before I left for university was all but over.

My interest in Burnley was all but over, too. I had gone on watching them throughout the 1960s, but they were in steady decline and my memories of the period are random and fragmented. I saw newly promoted Liverpool come up to Turf Moor and win 3–0 with Ian St John thumping one goal straight up into the roof of the net from about 2 yards; I remember an Aston Villa defender squaring up to Willie Irvine (or was it another of Burnley's flash-in-the-pan forwards of that era?) then nutting him full in the face: we howled for his blood, a linesman had spotted it, and off he went. Clearest of all – I remember it as yesterday – there was the most spectacular own goal ever seen at Turf Moor, scored for Leeds United (just up from the Second Division) by Alex Elder, who won the ball near his own corner flag, brought it forward a yard or two then, without looking, lofted it back to Adam Blacklaw. But Blacklaw had advanced towards the edge of the penalty area, and would have had no chance anyway with Elder's overhit lob, which swung into the far top corner. The only goal in a 1–0 defeat by Leeds: things were never the same after that.

There were still the odd moments of glory, but not many. The last programme I have is against Arsenal – from 13 September 1969, two weeks before I left for university. Arsenal that day had Bob Wilson in goal, plus Frank McLintock, Bobby Gould and George Graham; the Burnley team was Peter Mellor, John Angus, Les Latcham, Brian O'Neil, Dave Merrington, Sammy Todd, Dave Thomas, Ralph Coates, Frank Casper, Martin Dobson and Steve Kindon. It was still a classy outfit – or should have been with Dobson, O'Neil and Coates there – but only Angus was left from the Cup Final side seven years earlier and the inexorable slide had begun. Two seasons later, in 1971, Burnley were relegated. They quickly climbed back up again, but only for two seasons, and then cascaded down until they reached the Fourth Division in 1985. In 1988 they escaped plummeting out of the Football League altogether by winning their last match: I heard it on the radio from a Suffolk garden, urging them on as if I were back on the terraces and this were a Cup Final, not a battle for survival.

Already by the end of the 1960s the crowds at Turf Moor had begun to peter out. In those days I went with Les, a manager at the Barlick Rolls Royce factory, and we'd park his warm, purring saloon a couple of streets away, before taking our place on the empty terraces or in the stand. But in the early 1960s I had travelled to matches with a carpenter named Geoff, in his battered old van, and we'd have to park miles away from the ground and walk; once inside, we'd stand behind the goal where the crowds were sometimes big enough for me to experience that feeling of being carried helplessly downwards, feet off the ground, after some particularly exciting goalmouth incident.

Intimidation, violence and vandalism we took for granted. Whenever I'm tempted to look back on that decade as some innocent age of pre-hooliganism, I remember my brush with a Stoke City fan when I was about thirteen. He was walking ahead of me as (in those unsegregated days) I looked for a place behind the goal. Catching sight of my claret and blue scarf, he abruptly stopped and wouldn't budge, so that when I gingerly tried to make my way past his looming bulk he could turn and snarl: 'Who the f . . . do you think you're pushing?' He grabbed hold of me, dangled me in the air in front of him, drew his fist back and was about to belt me when a mate of his called him off: 'Leave 'im Mick, it's not worth it, he's nobbut a little 'un.' He put me down: 'Just f . . . ing watch it next time.'

Violence had its own momentum and needed no excuses. I remember the story of a friend beaten up in Skipton bus station. 'Hey, you're t'c . . . what's been cleverin' roun' town all evenin'.'

'Nay, ah've been in Keighley – ah've just got off t'bus.'

'That's nowt to wi' it.' Thump.

At the Heysel Stadium, and again after Hillsborough last year, I wondered whether the violence and tragedy that attend football might not kill off the pleasure I've always taken in it. But there's no sign of that. On the contrary, with my young son's fantasies to look after as well as my own, I've renewed my interest. That interest began as a kind of vicarious dream, and it still operates on that level. Listening to Burnley's great escape act the other season, I wasn't thinking how fortunate I was not to be there, squalidly ending my playing days at the bottom of the Fourth Division. I was wondering why the call from the Burnley manager hadn't come yet, and staying fairly close to the phone in case it did.

from Harry Lansdown and Alex Spillius (eds.),

Saturday's Boys, 1990

Away
HAROLD PINTER

GUS: What town are we in? I've forgotten.

BEN: I've told you. Birmingham.

GUS: Go on! (*He looks with interest about the room.*) That's in the Midlands. The second biggest city in Great Britain. I'd never have guessed. (*He snaps his fingers.*) Eh, it's Friday today, isn't it? It'll be Saturday tomorrow.

BEN: What about it?

GUS: (*Excited*) We could go and watch the Villa.

BEN: They're playing away.

GUS: No, are they? Caarr! What a pity.

BEN: Anyway, there's no time. We've got to get straight back.

GUS: Well, we have done in the past, haven't we? Stayed over and watched a game, haven't we? For a bit of relaxation.

BEN: Things have tightened up, mate. They've tightened up.

(GUS *chuckles to himself.*)

GUS: I saw the Villa get beat in a cup tie once. Who was it against now? White shirts. It was one-all at half-time. I'll never forget it. Their opponents won by a penalty. Talk about drama. Yes, it was a disputed penalty. Disputed. They got beat 2–1, anyway, because of it. You were there yourself.

BEN: Not me.

GUS: Yes, you were there. Don't you remember that disputed penalty?

BEN: No.

GUS: He went down just inside the area. Then they said he was just acting. I didn't think the other bloke touched him myself. But the referee had the ball on the spot.

BEN: Didn't touch him! What are you talking about? He laid him out flat!

GUS: Not the Villa. The Villa don't play that sort of game.

BEN: Get out of it.

(*Pause.*)

GUS: Eh, that must have been here, in Birmingham.

BEN: What must?

GUS: The Villa. That must have been here.

BEN: They were playing away.

GUS: Because you know who the other team was? It was the Spurs. It was Tottenham Hotspur.

BEN: Well, what about it?

GUS: We've never done a job in Tottenham.

BEN: How do you know?

GUS: I'd remember Tottenham.

(BEN *turns on his bed to look at him.*)

BEN: Don't make me laugh, will you?

(BEN *turns back and reads.* GUS *yawns and speaks through his yawn.*)

GUS: When's he going to get in touch? (*Pause.*) Yes, I'd like to see another football match. I've always been an ardent football fan. Here, what about coming to see the Spurs tomorrow?

BEN: (*Tonelessly*) They're playing away.

GUS: Who are?

BEN: The Spurs.

GUS: Then they might be playing here.

BEN: Don't be silly.

GUS: If they're playing away they might be playing here. They might be playing the Villa.

BEN: (*Tonelessly*) But the Villa are playing away.

145

(Pause. An envelope slides under the door, right. GUS *sees it. He stands, looking at it.)*

GUS: Ben.

BEN: Away. They're all playing away.

from The Dumb Waiter, 1960

The Soccer Conspiracy Case
ARTHUR HOPCRAFT

In January 1965 three of England's best-known footballers were sent to prison for four months after their conviction in what was called The Soccer Conspiracy Case. They were Peter Swan, the Sheffield Wednesday centre-half who had played nineteen times for his country, David Layne, the Sheffield Wednesday centre-forward, and Tony Kay, a wing-half, formerly of Sheffield Wednesday but at the time of the disclosure playing for Everton. The gist of the case was that all three, while playing for Wednesday, had conspired to prevent their own team from winning a match to facilitate a betting coup. A few months after the case the three players were suspended from football for life by the Football Association, which meant that any form of officially recognized football anywhere was barred to them. Kay and Swan had pleaded not guilty in court.

The case made a wretched winter for British football. Seven less well-known players and former players were sentenced at the same time on similar charges to terms of imprisonment ranging from four years to six months. The exposure was the work of the *People*, the Sunday newspaper, whose reporters did their job resourcefully and ruthlessly, and the dirty shrapnel of the explosion nicked and wounded people all round the game. Such a revelation was bound to make the public ask each other, blackly, how much 'fixing' of matches was going on which was never discovered. This fear struck at the very roots and heart of football. The footballers, once found guilty, were bound to suffer the complete punishment.

While the tale was being told little sympathy was invited for the men concerned, although Mr Justice Lawton, passing sentence, said he accepted that the Sheffield Wednesday players were involved 'really by chance' and on one isolated occasion; they presented him, he said, 'with the most unpleasant part of my duty'. Excuse may never be possible, but at least the personal tragedy of the event should be acknowledged. The fallen, ruined hero is no figure for callous scorn. Some respected men in the game have given their names to appeals for the players' reinstatement. There is kindness here but also, I think, a failure on their part to recognize the significance of the case. Perhaps it is a matter of being too close to the game to see the extent of the damage. A court conviction on a charge of 'fixing' football is not just a nasty blotch on the wall, but a jagged hole in the fabric. Two or three more like that and the whole structure falls in rubble.

Of the three men I have named, Kay was the most colourful player, and he was notably articulate. He was twenty-seven at the time of the case, and he had played once for England, against Switzerland. He was an extremely tough, quick, enterprising halfback, of the combative, all-action kind: very much the type of player whom Sir Alf Ramsey developed in Nobby Stiles for England's World Cup victory. Stiles played magnificently for England. It is fair to ask whether he would have been given the chance if Kay had been available. That thought was very sharply in my mind when I went to see Kay in Liverpool in 1967.

He looked haggard, although not in the debilitated sense of a man gone to seed. He looked what he was still: a hard-driven athlete, the flesh tight on the bones. He had red, scrubbing-brush hair, and he wore thick-rimmed glasses. He exuded an exaggerated ruefulness, a bitter and aggressive self-mockery. There was a distinct television-age, showbiz edge to the back-street wit. 'The cops have it in for me; must have,' he said. 'Have you ever heard of anyone being booked for parking by a copper on a horse? That's Anthony's luck.'

Kay was brought up in Sheffield, [where] he learned about life and football, which amounted practically to the same thing for him . . . He knew working-class austerity as people know sweat, through the pores, not book-learnt or observed in passing. Money was important because there was not much of it about. Everton bought him from Sheffield Wednesday for more than £55,000.

The face has a flare of insolence, and now that he had much to regret he played up this component in his personality, telling stories of the persecution and recurrent disaster in his life with a chirpy, gritty comicality. 'Wasn't I always in trouble?' he said. 'Well, I nearly got killed more than once, didn't I? Look how the crowds used to get at me.'

He launched into a story about a match in London, which ended with a mob of the home crowd's fans yelling for his blood round the exit. He walked out disguised in the home team manager's long overcoat and trilby. He said: 'When I got in the coach I took 'em off and tapped the window at the crowd. You should have seen 'em,' and he bared his teeth wide and crooked his fingers on either side of his face, like talons.

Then he said: 'There was that time in Italy when the crowd was at me. "Kay, Bastardo, Bastardo." They were behind this wire grille (bared teeth and crooked fingers again). I banged the ball at their faces. So what happens when we come off at the end? I'm there, with our team in the dressing-room, and I'm standing at the tunnel thanking everyone, and I go up to this Italian trainer, who's only about 7 feet tall. I hold my hand out, and what does he do? He's only got both me arms pinned behind me back. And all the Italian team's giving me one as they go off the field.'

The resentment poured out of him, as he built up a picture of a victimized upbringing. The voice teetered up into a thin malevolence, the voice of childhood's tormentors: 'Right, you've been very, very naughty, and now we're going to rattle your little arse. Whack. Sort that out.'

Kay, the bolshie; Kay, the whipping-boy; Kay, the misunderstood; Kay, the unlucky: he overstated his battering from life, and his fumbling resistance, with the skill of a natural comedian who is beginning to believe the letter as well as the spirit of his material.

'I've always hated referees,' he said. 'To me they're all no-marks. Otherwise, they wouldn't be there. Who are they? All the week they're sitting there in offices, scribbling away, scribble, scribble, and on Saturday afternoons they're on the field with all the big men, and they're saying, "Right, now you do what I tell you or you're going in my little book." ' He did a wickedly observed impersonation of a hunchbacked, myopic referee writing in a notebook, his hands up by his nose. He said: 'I've seen blokes kicking lumps out of each other, and what's the referee doing? He's wagging his finger and making a great production out of moving the ball 3 foot back for a free kick.'

Kay's sadly funny performance was the more disturbing because in his comment on authority, and its view of him, there was a strong thread of truth. As a player he was undoubtedly one of those eruptive influences which infuriate referees. He was known for his bitter tackling and only tough men were prepared to take the consequences. Kay insisted to me that he was a marked man not only in the opposition's dressing-room but in the referee's as well, and he added that he did not mind telling referees so. One of his troubles was that he was never discreet in what he said or what he did. He said to me: 'I was naïve.' He was right. He knew most of the tricks of the trade, but not the most important trick of all, which is to appear not to.

The more Kay talks the stronger is the conviction borne in on the listener that his misfortunes were impelled from inside him. Like everyone else the influences he assimilated from his environment were an imperfect blend; but is it the mixture or the chemistry which makes a man? Kay was embattled against the world, pretty well all of it, so that ultimately he was working against himself. Even in trivial, everyday matters, such as his relationship with road traffic, his progress was interrupted by violent incidents of bizarre complexity, in which his saving grace was to be found in his comic, fatalistic hindsight. One accident, as he described it, involved the inexorable will of some dauntless old lady, launched come what might for the distant haven of the opposite pavement. There was also snow and a steep hill. Then: 'So all of a sudden I'm waking up in me mini, upside down, and this geezer's shouting all sorts at me out of his bedroom winder.' On another occasion the slapstick disaster ends: 'So here I am, can't move a limb, being wheeled about the station by a porter on a trolley.'

Kay managed to squeeze a few wicked, retaliatory jokes out of his prison sentence. He said that the prison governor was 'a wild football fan, and he couldn't get enough of the game'. Kay said that he and his friends were given full rein to train the prison football team, and that the governor refereed most of the matches himself. 'We only lost one game out of fourteen,' Kay said, adding with a look of feigned distaste, 'and that was because the other lot brought their own referee; the game was *bent*.' He laughed. He said that the first warder he met in gaol was a little man – most villains in Kay's life are little men – who greeted him with: 'Yes, it's through people like you I never win the pools.' Kay said: 'I thought to myself, "Hullo, Anthony, you've found yourself one here. It's your luck again."' He encountered the warder later when the man was a linesman at one of the matches. The story is a symmetry of irony:

'The governor was sold on us. I gave 'em all hell, you know. He used to say, "Well done, young Kay." Well, this little warder – the bad one – he kept sticking his flag up and shouting at me every time I touched anybody. After a bit I said to him, "Why don't you piss off?" He was furious. He said, "I'll have you yet." So I ran across to the governor – he was refereeing again – and I said, "Excuse me, Sir, can't you do something about this linesman? He keeps on at me. I can't concentrate." So the governor went across to this warder, and he said, "Not so much noise, please, Mr So-and-so." ' Kay's eyes glinted at the memory.

To judge from Kay's conversation, his attitude to authority always had that cynicism. He reminds one of the bad lad at the back of the class, or the hard case in the barrack-room, who recognizes the sneaking respect, and often fear, that the man in charge has for the ones who won't conform. Such men seldom appeal for help, and when they do it is to exploit the boss's sense of importance. Kay told me this story about a match against Fulham:

'I was up against Jimmy Hill, and he was up there towering above me. Every time I went up for the ball there he was, just leaning over the top of me. I thought, "Right, I'm not having this all the game. Next time we go up I'll have his shorts off him." Well, up we went, and I shoved me hand out and I missed 'em. Instead I caught him right between the legs. He screamed the place down. But he kept with me afterwards, all over the field. I went to the ref. I said, "Hey, ref, look at this maniac with the beard. Look at the way he's after me." It worked.' Kay's relished little triumphs can only be properly understood by someone brought up where people never play cards for matchsticks.

I was warned before I went to see him that Kay might be sad; that if the gloom was on him he might even weep. He anticipated my wariness. He had stopped crying, he said, although when he was first told that he could never play football competitively again, he confessed: 'I never cried so much in all me life.' He said it looking straight at me, using the words like a showbiz catchphrase, but not smiling. He knew he had been overdoing the clowning. 'It just hides the tears,' he said. 'You can't cry all the time. You get a reputation for it. No one wants to know after a bit. They say, "Oh Christ, I've got to put up with this crying gett again." You can't just give up, can you?'

It was plain that he had been deeply hurt by what had happened to him; he was convinced it had been imposed and not brought upon himself by himself. Every six months, he said, he wrote to the FA, asking if they would reconsider his registration. He did not really think they ever would. People in Liverpool, he said, were friendly and sympathetic towards him. That salty city would never snub a man like Kay. He was as much one of Liverpool's own, pugnacious and at least pretending cunning, as if he had been born there.

But his life was not pleasing him, to say the least of it. At the time I was talking to him he was a family man living away from his wife, and a bookmaker not sure that there would be another year's wages out of his betting shop. What had he been doing since prison? 'Just going round in circles,' he said. 'Getting nowhere.'

He had been playing football, surreptitiously, in scratch matches, giving another name when he was asked, keeping an eye open for men hanging about with cameras. He was training twice a week, and I could believe it when he said: 'I really push myself.' He did much of his training at a school gymnasium, often giving practical instruction to the boys. He said, the edge going out of the voice for the first time: 'They all want to take me on, you know. They think, "Oh, this old Tony Kay, he's finished." I like to get 'em trying to get past me on the outside, and I'm leaving 'em behind, and I'm shouting, "Come on, what are you waiting for, you lads?" '

There was a lot of heart in Kay as a player. Professional sport made him, tested him and broke him. He is one of football's tragic casualties because he was so strongly equipped in nearly all his aspects. His counsel said in court, after his conviction: 'He has given up for £100 what has in fact been one of the greatest careers of any footballer. He was tempted once, and fell.'

from *The Football Man*, 1968

The World Cup Final, 1966
HUGH MCILVANNEY

The greatest moment in the history of English football came at 5.15 this afternoon when Geoff Hurst shot the magnificent goal that made certain of the World Cup. It was Hurst's third goal, England's fourth, and, coming as it did in the final seconds of extra time, it shattered the last remnants of German resistance.

Germany had equalized with almost the last kick in the regular ninety minutes, and they had just gone within inches of repeating the blow in extra time when Seeler lunged in on a headed pass by Held. But Moore took the ball coolly out of defence and lifted it upfield to Hurst 10 yards inside the German half. The referee was already looking at his watch and three England supporters had prematurely invaded the pitch as Hurst collected the ball on his chest.

At first he seemed inclined to dawdle-out time. Then abruptly he sprinted through in the inside-left position with a German defender pressing him. As Tilkowski prepared to move out, Hurst swung his left foot and drove the ball breathtakingly into the top of the net.

The scene that followed was unforgettable. Stiles and Cohen collapsed in a tearful embrace on the ground, young Ball turned wild cartwheels, and Bobby Charlton dropped to his knees, felled by emotion.

Almost immediately it was over, and the honour that had escaped England for so long had been won. Soon the players, who had forgotten the crippling weariness of a few minutes before, were hugging and laughing, and crying with manager Alf Ramsey and the reserves, who must go through the rest of their lives with bitter-sweet memories of how it looked from the touch-line.

'Ramsey, Ramsey,' the crowd roared, and in his moment of vindication it was a tribute that no one could grudge him. Eventually, Moore led his men up to the Royal Box to receive the gold Jules Rimet trophy from the Queen, and the slow, ecstatic lap of honour began. 'Ee-aye-addio, we've won the Cup,' sang the crowd, as Moore threw it in a golden arc above his head and caught it again.

England had, indeed, won the Cup, producing more determined aggression and flair than they had shown at any earlier stage of the competition. In such a triumph there could be no failures, but if one had to name outstanding heroes they were Hurst, Ball, Moore and the brothers Charlton.

Hurst, who just a month ago appeared to have only the remotest chance of figuring in the World Cup, had emerged as the destructive star of a feverishly exciting game, becoming the first man to score a hat-trick in the final. Ball, who looked like a boy, had done the work of two men. Moore, showing again that he is stimulated by the demands of the great occasion, played with an imaginative self-confidence that made it unnecessary for anyone to ask who was the England captain.

Beside him, Jack Charlton was a giant of a player. And through the whole performance there ran the inspiration of Bobby Charlton. In the first half, when the foundations of England's victory were being laid, it was his relentless but unhurried foraging, his ability to impose his experience and his class on the team's play, that counted most.

Every one of the others responded superbly and if some were sometimes short of inspiration, none ever lacked courage, or total commitment.

Of course, the Germans were on the field, too, and they let England know about it, often enough. They may regret now that they set Beckenbauer to mark Charlton, for the young half-back had little opportunity to exploit his attacking genius until it was too late. Held and Haller, with tremendous early assistance from Seeler, did plenty of damage, but ultimately it was Tilkowski and his defenders who were left to try to save Germany.

They tried mightily but in the end England's spirit broke them. Germany had already won the World Cup, England had not, so they had a right to accept defeat with pride. They did, and the crowd cheered almost as much for their lap of honour as for England's.

Wembley was charged with an atmosphere it had never known before. Long before the teams appeared the great crowd was chanting and singing. It might have been Anfield (England did wear red) and there can be no greater tribute.

When the band of the Royal Marines, who had played a tune for each of the sixteen competing nations, came to play the National

Anthem it was sung as it may never be sung again. *Deutschland über Alles* boomed out in its wake and the battle was on.

The Germans began rather nervously, standing off from the tackle and letting the England forwards move smoothly up to the edge of the penalty area. Charlton and Peters were able to work the ball along the left at their leisure and there was anxiety in the German defence before the cross was cleared.

Charlton wandered purposefully all over the field, bringing composure and smoothness wherever he went, again making comparisons with di Stefano seem relevant.

One of Hunt's few imaginative passes set Stiles clear on the right and his high cross beat Tilkowski before Höttes headed it away. The ball was returned smartly by Bobby Charlton and Tilkowski had so much difficulty punching it away from Hurst that he knocked himself out.

The goalkeeper was prostrate, the whistle had gone and the German defenders had stopped challenging by the time Moore put the ball in the net. The crowd cheered in the hope that next time it would be the real thing.

Jack Charlton, carrying the ball forward on his forehead with a skill that would have done credit to his brother, moved swiftly out of defence and his finely judged diagonal pass let Peters in for a quick powerful shot from the edge of the penalty area. Tilkowski, diving desperately to his left, punched the ball round the post. Hurst met Ball's corner on the volley but sent it much too high.

At that point Weber chose to give one of the agonized performances that have been one of the German hallmarks in the competition, but Mr Dienst quickly let him know that he was fooling nobody.

Peters emphasized the eagerness of the England attack by surging in from the right to shoot the ball only 2 ft wide from 25 yards.

Then, stunningly, in the tenth minute England found themselves a goal behind. And it was a goal that anyone who had watched their magnificent defensive play earlier in the tournament could scarcely believe. Held glided a high cross from the left wing and Wilson jumping for the ball in comfortable isolation incredibly headed it precisely down to the feet of Haller, standing a dozen yards out and directly in front of Banks. Haller had time to steady and pivot to turn his right-foot shot on the ground past Banks' right side.

It took England only six minutes to reassure the crowd. Overath had been warned for a severe foul on Ball and now he committed another one on Moore, tripping the England captain as he turned away with the ball. Moore himself took the free kick and from 40 yards out near the left touch-line he flighted the ball beautifully towards the far post. Hurst, timing his run superbly to slip through the defence much as he had done against the Argentine, struck a perfect header low inside Tilkowski's right-hand post.

Moore held one arm aloft in the familiar gladiator salute while Hurst was smothered with congratulations. It was another reminder of the huge contribution West Ham have made to England's success in this World Cup.

Bobby Charlton reasserted himself with a sharp run across the face of the goal from the right and a left-foot shot. It troubled Tilkowski but he gathered it at his second attempt. The Germans retaliated through Haller, who was just beaten by Banks in a race for a through pass but the most sustained aggression was still coming from England. Moore, playing with wonderful control and assurance, was driving up among the forwards, joining intelligently in the moves initiated by Bobby Charlton.

Unfortunately, however, Charlton could not be in two places at once. Time and again the attacks he conceived from deep positions cried out to be climaxed with his killing power.

After Ball had been rebuked for showing dissent he took part in one of England's more effective attacks. Cohen crossed the ball long from the right and Hurst rose magnificently to deflect in another header which Tilkowski could only scramble away from his right-hand post. Ball turned the ball back into the goal mouth and the Germans' desperation was unmistakable as Overath came hurtling in to scythe the ball away for a corner.

Not all the uneasy moments were around Tilkowski, however. First Ball and then Cohen toyed riskily with Held near the byline. Jack Charlton, maintaining the remarkable standard of his World Cup performances, had to intervene with a prodigious sweeping tackle on the ground to get them out of trouble. It cost him a corner and the corner almost cost England a goal. The ball went to Overath and from 20 yards he drove it in fiercely at chest height. Banks beat it out and when Emmerich hammered it back from an acute angle the goalkeeper caught it surely.

When a Wilson header into goal was headed down by Hurst, Hunt appeared certain to score. But when the Liverpool man forced in his left-foot volley Tilkowski was in the way. Soon afterwards a subtle pass from Charlton bewildered the German defence but Peters could not quite reach the ball for the shot.

The hectic fluctuating pattern of the first half was stressed again before the interval when Overath hit a bludgeoning shot from 20 yards and Banks turned the ball brilliantly over his crossbar.

Bobby Charlton, moving through on Moore's pass early in the second half, fell after being tackled by Schulz but the claims for a penalty were understandably half-hearted. Cohen was making regular runs on the right wing but his centres were easily cut out.

Mr Dienst was at his most officious but he was entitled to reprimand Stiles after the wing-half had bounced the ball in disgust at a harsh decision. Hunt was crowded out in the last stride as he met a cross from the left, but after five minutes he had a hand in England's second goal.

He pushed a pass to Ball and when the winger shot Tilkowski pushed the ball on to the outside of his net. Following the corner Hurst's shot from the left was deflected across goal by Schulz, and Peters, strangely neglected by the German defenders, came in swiftly to take the ball on the half volley and drive it into the net from 4 or 5 yards.

A free kick given against Stiles was guided accurately above the English defenders by Emmerich, and Weber should have done more than head weakly past. In the last seconds of the ninety minutes the English supporters were silenced by an equalizing goal.

Charlton was doubtfully penalized after jumping to a header and from the free-kick Emmerich drove the ball through the English wall. As it cannoned across the face of the goal it appeared to hit Schnellinger on the arm but the referee saw nothing illegal and Weber at the far post was able to score powerfully.

From the kick-off in extra time England swept the Germans back into their penalty area. Ball had a wonderful shot from 20 yards edged over the crossbar by Tilkowski. Then Charlton hit a low drive that Tilkowski pushed against his left-hand upright.

The Germans looked weary but their swift breaks out of defence were still dangerous. Emmerich moved in on Banks but when he passed Held was slow to control the ball and Stiles cleared. Then Held compensated for this by dribbling clear of the entire English defence and turning the ball back invitingly across goal. But there was nobody following up.

When England took the lead again in the tenth minute of extra time they did it controversially. Ball made an opening for himself on the right and when the ball went in to Hurst the inside-forward resolutely worked for a clear view of the goal. His rising right-foot shot on the turn from 10 yards was pushed against the underside of the crossbar by Tilkowski and when it bounced the England players appealed as one man for a goal. The referee spoke to the Russian linesman on the side away from the main stand and turned to award a goal. The delayed-action cheers shook the stadium.

Then we were up yelling and stamping, and slapping one another as Hurst shot the last staggering goal. The sky had been overcast all afternoon, but now the clouds split and the sun glared down on the stadium. Maybe those fellows were right when they said God was an Englishman.

England – Banks: Cohen, J. Charlton, Moore, Wilson: Stiles, R. Charlton, Ball: Hurst, Hunt, Peters.
Germany – Tilkowski: Höttes, Schulz, Weber, Schnellinger: Haller, Beckenbauer: Seeler, Held, Overath, Emmerich.

Referee – D. Dienst (Switzerland)

from The Observer, 31 July 1966

Mr Sugden
BARRY HINES

He walked into the changing room as clean and shining as a boy down for breakfast on his seaside holidays. The other boys were packed into the aisles between the rows of pegs, their hanging clothes partitioning the room into corridors. Mr Sugden was passing slowly across one end of the room, looking down the corridors and counting the boys as they changed. He was wearing a violet tracksuit. The top was embellished with cloth badges depicting numerous crests and qualifications, and on the breast a white athlete carried the Olympic torch. The legs were tucked into new white football socks, neatly folded at his ankles, and his football boots were polished as black and shiny as the bombs used by assassins in comic strips. The laces binding them had been scrubbed white, and both boots had been fastened identically: two loops of the foot and one of the ankle, and tied in a neat bow under the tab at the back.

He finished counting and rolled a football off the window sill into his hand. The leather was rich with dubbin, and the new orange lace nipped the slit as firmly as a row of surgical stitches. He tossed it up and caught it on the ends of his fingers, then turned round to Billy.

'Skyving again, Casper?'

'No, Sir, Mr Farthing wanted me; he's been talking to me.'

'I bet that was stimulating for him, wasn't it?'

'What does that mean, Sir?'

'The conversation, lad, what do you think it means?'

'No, Sir, that word, stimult . . . stimult-ting.'

'Stimulating, you fool, S-T-I-M-U-L-A-T-I-N-G, stimulating!'

'Yes, Sir.'

'Well get changed, lad, you're two weeks late already!'

He lifted the elastic webbing of one cuff and rotated his fist to look at his watch on the underside of his wrist.

'Some of us want a game even if you don't.'

'I've no kit, Sir.'

Mr Sugden stepped back and slowly looked Billy up and down, his top lip curling.

'Casper, you make me S I C K.'

'S I C K' penetrated the hubbub, which immediately decreased as the boys stopped their own conversations and turned their attention to Mr Sugden and Billy.

'Every lesson it's the same old story, "Please, Sir, I've no kit." '

The boys tittered at his whipped-dog whining impersonation.

'Every lesson for four years! And in all that time you've made no attempt whatsoever to get any kit, you've skyved and scrounged and borrowed and . . .'

He tried this lot on one breath, and his ruddy complexion heightened and glowed like a red balloon as he held his breath and fought for another verb.

'. . . and . . . B E G . . .' The balloon burst and the pronunciation of the verb disintegrated.

'Why is that everyone else can get some but you can't?'

'I don't know, Sir. My mother won't buy me any. She says it's a waste of money, especially now that I'm leaving.'

'You haven't been leaving for four years, have you?'

'No, Sir.'

'You could have bought some out of your spending money, couldn't you?'

'I don't like football, Sir.'

'What's that got to do with it?'

'I don't know, Sir. Anyway I don't get enough.'

'Get a job then. I don't . . .'

'I've got one, Sir.'

'When then! You get paid, don't you?'

'Yes, Sir. But I have to gi' it to my mam. I'm still payin' her for my fines, like instalments every week.'

Mr Sugden bounced the ball on Billy's head, compressing his neck into his shoulders.

'Well you should keep out of trouble then, lad, and then . . .'

'I haven't been in trouble, Sir, not . . .'

'Shut up, lad! Shut up, before you drive me crackers!'

He hit Billy twice with the ball, holding it between both hands as though he was murdering him with a boulder. The rest of the class grinned behind each other's backs, or placed their fingers over their mouths to suppress the laughter gathering there. They watched Mr Sugden rush into his changing room, and began to giggle, stopping immediately he reappeared waving a pair of giant blue drawers.

'Here Casper, get them on!'

He wanged them across the room, and Billy caught them flying over his head, then held them up for inspection as though he was contemplating buying. The class roared. They would have made Billy two suits and an overcoat.

'They'll not fit me, Sir.'

The class roared again and even Billy had to smile. There was only Mr Sugden not amused.

'What are you talking about, lad? You can get them on, can't you?'

'Yes, Sir.'

'Well they fit you then! Now get changed, QUICK.'

Billy found an empty peg and hung his jacket on it. He was immediately enclosed in a tight square as two lines of boys formed up, one on each side of him between the parallel curtains of clothing. He sat down on the long bench covering the shoe racks, and worked his jeans over his pumps. Mr Sugden broke one side of the square and stood over him.

'And you want your underpants and vest off.'

'I don't wear 'em, Sir.'

As he reached up to hang his trousers on the peg, his shirt lap lifted, revealing his bare cheeks, which looked as smooth and bony as two white billiard balls. He stepped into the shorts and pulled them up to his waist. The legs reached halfway down his shins. He pulled the waist up to his neck and his knees just slid into view. Boys pointed at them, shouting and laughing into each other's faces, and other boys who were still changing rushed to the scene, jumping up on the benches or parting the curtains to see through. And at the centre of it all, Billy, like a brave little clown, was busy trying to make them fit, and Sugden was looking at him as though it was his fault for being too small for them.

'Roll them down and don't be so foolish. You're too daft to laugh at, Casper.'

No one else thought so. Billy started to roll them down from his chest, each tuck shortening the legs and gathering the material round his waist in a floppy blue tyre.

'That'll do. Let's have you all out now.'

He opened the door and led them down the corridor and out into the yard. Some boys waited until he had gone, then they took a run and had a good slide up to the door, rotating slowly as they slid, and finishing up facing the way they had come. Those with rubber studs left long black streaks on the tiles. The plastic and nailed leather studs cut through the veneer and scored deep scratches in the vinyl. When they reached the yard, the pad of the rubber studs on the concrete hardly differed from that in the changing room or the corridor, but the clatter produced by the nailed and plastic studs had a hollow, more metallic ring.

The cold caught Billy's breath as he stepped outside. He stopped dead, glanced round as though looking to escape, then set off full belt, shouting, across the concrete on to the field. Mr Sugden set off after him.

'Casper! Shut up, lad! What are you trying to do, disrupt the whole school?'

He gained on Billy, and as he drew near swiped at him with his flat hand. Billy, watching the blows, zig-zagged out of reach, just ahead of them.

'I'm frozen, Sir! I'm shoutin' to keep warm!'

'Well don't shout at me then! I'm not a mile away!'

They were shouting at each other as though they were aboard ship in a gale. Mr Sugden tried to swat him again. Billy sidestepped, and threw him off balance. So he slowed to a walk and turned round, blowing his whistle and beckoning the others to hurry up.

'Come on, you lot! Hurry up!'

They started to run at speeds ranging from jogging to sprinting, and arrived within a few seconds of each other on the senior football pitch.

'Line up on the halfway line and let's get two sides picked!'

They lined up, jumping and running on the spot, those with long sleeves clutching the cuffs in their hands, those without massaging their goosey arms.

'Tibbut, come out here and be the other captain.'

Tibbut walked out and stood facing the line, away from Mr Sugden.

'I'll have first pick, Tibbut.'

'That's not right, Sir.'

'Why isn't it?'

''Cos you'll get all the best players.'

'Rubbish, lad.'

'Course you will, Sir. It's not fair.'

'Tibbut. Do you want to play football? Or do you want to get dressed and go and do some maths?'

'Play football, Sir.'

'Right then, stop moaning and start picking. I'll have Anderson.'

He turned away from Tibbut and pointed to a boy who was standing on one of the intersections of the centre circle and the halfway line. Anderson walked off this cross and stood behind him. Tibbut scanned the line, considering his choice.

'I'll have Purdey.'

'Come on then, Ellis.'

Each selection altered the structure of the line. When Tibbut had been removed from the centre, all the boys sidestepped to fill the gap. The same happened when Anderson went from near one end. But when Purdey and Ellis, who had been standing side by side, were removed, the boys at their shoulders stood still, therefore dividing the original line into two. These new lines were swiftly segmented as more boys were chosen, leaving no trace of the first major division, just half a dozen boys looking across spaces at each other; reading from left to right: a fat boy; an arm's length away, two friends, one tall with glasses, the other short with a hare-lip; then a space of two yards and Billy; a boy space away from him, a thin boy with a crew-cut and a spotty face; and right away from these, at the far end of the line, another fat boy. Spotty Crew-Cut was halfway between the two fat boys, therefore half of the length of the line was occupied by five of the boys. The far fat boy was the next to go, which halved the length of the line and left Spotty Crew-Cut as one of the end markers.

Tibbut then selected the tall friend with glasses. Mr Sugden immediately selected his partner. They separated gradually as they walked away from the line, parting finally to enter their respective teams. And then there were three: Fatty, Billy, and Spotty Crew-Cut, blushing across at each other while the captains considered. Tibbut picked Crew-Cut. He dashed forward into the anonymity of his team. Fatty stood grinning. Billy stared down at the earth. After long deliberation Mr Sugden chose Billy, leaving Tibbut with Hobson's choice; but before either Billy or Fatty could move towards their teams, Mr Sugden was already turning away and shouting instructions.

'Right! We'll play down hill!'

The team broke for their appropriate halves, and while they were arguing their claims for positions, Mr Sugden jogged to the sideline, dropped the ball, and took off his tracksuit. Underneath he was wearing a crisp red football shirt with white cuffs and a white band round the neck. A big white 9 filled most of the back, whiter than his white nylon shorts, which showed a slight fleshy tint through the material. He pulled his socks up, straightened the ribs, then took a fresh roll of half inch bandage from his tracksuit and ripped off two lengths. The torn bandage packet, the cup of its structure still intact, blew away over the turf like the damaged shell of a dark blue egg. Mr Sugden used the length of bandage to secure his stockings just below the knees, then he folded his tracksuit neatly on the ground, looked down at himself, and walked on to the pitch carrying the ball like a plum pudding on the tray of his hand. Tibbut, standing on the centre circle, with his hands down his shorts, winked at his Left Winger and waited for Mr Sugden to approach.

'Who are you today, Sir, Liverpool?'

'Rubbish, lad! Don't you know your club colours yet?'

'Liverpool are red, aren't they, Sir?'

'Yes, but they're all red, shirts, shorts and stockings. These are Manchester United's colours.'

'Course they are, Sir, I forgot. What position are you playing?'

Mr Sugden turned his back on him to show him the number 9.

'Bobby Charlton. I thought you were usually Denis Law when you were Manchester United.'

'It's too cold to play as a striker today. I'm scheming this morning, all over the field like Charlton.'

'Law plays all over, Sir. He's not only a striker.'

'He doesn't link like Charlton.'

'Better player though, Sir.'

Sugden shook his head. 'No, he's been badly off form recently.'

'Makes no odds, he's still a better player. He can settle a game in two minutes.'

'Are you trying to tell *me* about football, Tibbut?'

'No, Sir.'

'Well shut up then. Anyway Law's in the wash this week.'

He placed the ball on the centre spot and looked round at his team. There was only Billy out of position. He was standing between the full backs, the three of them forming a domino : : : pattern with the half backs. The goal was empty. Mr Sugden pointed at it.

'There's no one in goal!'

His team looked round to confirm this observation, but Tibbut's team had beaten them to it by just looking straight ahead.

'Casper! What position are you supposed to be playing?'

Billy looked to the Right Back, the Left Back, the Right Back again. Neither of them supplied the answer, so he answered the question himself.

'I don't know, Sir. Inside Right?'

This answer made 1: Mr Sugden angry. 2: the boys laugh.

'Don't talk ridiculous, lad! How can you be playing Inside Right back there?'

He looked up at the sky.

'God help us; fifteen years old and still doesn't know the positions of a football team!'

He levelled one arm at Billy.

'Get in goal lad!'

'O, Sir! I can't goal. I'm no good.'

'Now's your chance to learn then, isn't it?'

'I'm fed up o' goin' in goal. I go in every week.'

Billy turned round and looked at the goal as though it was the portal leading into the gladiatorial arena.

'Don't stand looking, lad. Get in there!'

'Well don't blame me then, when I let 'em all through.'

'Of course I'll blame you, lad! Who do you expect me to blame?'

Billy cursed him quietly all the way back to the nets.

Sugden (commentator): 'And both teams are lined up for the kick off in this vital fifth-round cup-tie, Manchester United versus . . . ?'

Sugden (teacher): 'Who are we playing, Tibbut?'

'Er . . . we'll be Liverpool, Sir.'

'You can't be Liverpool.'

'Why not, Sir?'

'I've told you once, they're too close to Manchester United's colours, aren't they?'

Tibbut massaged his brow with his fingertips, and under this guise of thinking, glanced round at his team: Goalkeeper, green polo. Right Back, blue and white stripes. Left Back, green and white quarters. Right Half, white cricket. Centre Half, all blue. Left Half, all yellow. Right Wing, orange and green rugby. Inside Right, black T. Centre Forward, blue denim tab collar. Tibbut, red body white sleeves. Left Wing, all blue.

'We'll be Spurs then, Sir. They'll be no clash of colours then.'

'. . . And it's Manchester United v. Spurs in this vital fifth-round cup-tie.'

Mr Sugden (referee) sucked his whistle and stared at his watch, waiting for the second finger to twitch back up to twelve. 5 4 3 2. He dropped his wrist and blew. Anderson received the ball from him, sidestepped a tackle from Tibbut then cut it diagonally between two opponents into a space to his left. Sugden (player) running into this space, raised his left foot to trap it, but the ball rolled under his studs. He veered left, caught it, and started to cudgel it upfield in a travesty of a dribble, sending it too far ahead each time he touched it, so that by the time he had progressed 20 yards, he had crash-tackled it back from three Spurs defenders. His left winger, unmarked and lonely out on the touchline, called for the ball, Sugden heard him, looked at him, then kicked the ball hard along the ground towards him. But even though the wingman started to sprint as soon as he read its line, it still shot out of play a good 10 yards in front of him. He slithered to a stop and whipped round.

'Hey up, Sir! What do you think I am?'

'You should have been moving, lad. You'd have caught it then.'

'What do you think I wa' doin', standing still?'

'It was a perfectly good ball!'

'Ar, for a whippet perhaps!'

'Don't argue with me, lad! And get that ball fetched!'

The ball had rolled and stopped on the roped-off cricket square. The left winger left the pitch and walked towards it. He scissor-jumped the rope, picked the ball up off the lush lawn, then volleyed it straight back on to the pitch without bouncing it once on the intervening stretch of field.

Back in the goal, Billy was giant-striding along the goal line, counting the number of strides from post to post: five and a bit. He turned, propelled himself off the post and jump-strode across to the other side: five. After three more attempts he reduced this record to four and a half, then he returned along the line, heel-toe, heel-toeing it: thirty pump lengths.

After fourteen minutes' play he touched the ball for the first time. Tibbut, dribbling in fast, pushed the ball between Mr Sugden's legs, ran round him and delivered the ball out to his right winger, who took it in his stride, beat his Full Back and centred for Tibbut, who had continued his run, to outjump Mr Sugden and head the ball firmly into the top right-hand corner of the goal. Billy watched it fly in, way up on his left, then he turned round and picked it up from under the netting.

'Come on Casper! Make an effort, lad!'

'I couldn't save that, Sir.'

'You could have tried.'

'What for, Sir, when I knew I couldn't save it?'

'We're playing this game to win you know, lad.'

'I know, Sir.'

'Well, try then!'

He held his hands out to receive the ball. Billy obliged, but as it left his hand the wet leather skidded off his skin and it dropped short in the mud, between them. He ran out to retrieve it, but Sugden had already started towards it, and when Billy saw the stare of his eyes and the set of his jaw as he ran at the ball, he stopped and dropped down, and the ball missed him and went over him, back into the net. He knelt up, his left arm, left side and left leg striped with mud.

'What wa' that for, Sir?'

'Slack work, lad. Slack work.'

He retrieved the ball himself, and carried it quickly back to the centre for the restart. Billy stood up, a mud pack stuck to each knee. He pulled his shirt sleeve round and started to furrow the mud with his finger nails.

'Look at this lot. I've to keep this shirt on an' all after.'

The Right Back was drawn by this lament, but was immediately distracted by a chorus of warning shouts, and when he turned round he saw the ball running loose in his direction. He ran at it head down, and toed it far up field, showing no interest in its flight or destination, but turning to commiserate with Billy almost as soon as it had left his boot. It soared over the halfway line, and Sugden started to chase. It bounced, once, twice, then rolled out towards the touchline. He must catch it, and the rest of his forward line moved up in anticipation of the centre. But the ball, decelerating rapidly as though it wanted to be caught, still crossed the line before he could reach it. His disappointed Forwards muttered amongst themselves as they trooped back out of the penalty area.

'He should have caught that, easy.'

'He's like a chuffing carthorse.'

'Look at him, he's knackered.'

'Hopeless tha means.'

Tibbut picked the ball up for the throw in.

'Hard luck, Sir.'

Sugden, hands on hips, chest heaving, had his Right Back in focus a good thirty seconds before he had sufficient control over his respiration to remonstrate with him.

'Come on, lad! Find a man with this ball! Don't just kick it anywhere!'

The Right Back, his back turned, continued his conversation with Billy.

'S P A R R O W!'

'What, Sir?'

'I'm talking to you, lad!'

166

'Yes, Sir.'

'Well pay attention then and get a grip of your game. We're losing, lad.'

'Yes, Sir.'

Manchester United equalized soon after when the referee awarded them a penalty. Sugden scored.

At the other end of the pitch, Billy was busy with the netting. He was standing with his back to the play, clawing the fibres and growling like a little lion. He stuck a paw through a square and pawed at a visitor, withdrew it and stalked across his cage. The only other exhibit was the herd of multi-coloured cross-breeds gambolling around the ball behind him. The rest of the grounds were deserted. The main body of the collection was housed in the building across the fields, and all round the fields a high wire fence had been constructed. Round the top of the fence strands of barbed wire were affixed to inward-leaning angle-irons. Round the bottom, a ridge of shaggy grass grew where the mower had missed, and underneath the wire the grass had been cut in a severe fringe by the concrete flags of the pavement. The road curved round the field in a crescent, and across the road the row of council houses mirrored this exact curve. Field Crescent.

Billy gripped a post between both hands, inserted one raised foot into a square in the side netting, then, using this as a stirrup, heaved himself up and grabbed hold of the cross-bar. He hand-over-handed it to the middle and rested, swinging loosely backwards and forwards with his legs together. Then he let go with one hand and started to scratch his arm pits, kicking his legs and imitating chimp sounds. The bar shook, and the rattling of the bolts turned several heads, and soon all the boys were watching him, the game forgotten.

'Casper! Casper, get down lad! What do you think you are, an ape?'

'No, Sir, I'm just keeping warm.'

'Well get down then, before I come and make you red hot!'

Billy grasped the bar again with both hands, adjusted his grip, and began to swing: forward and back, forward and back, increasing momentum with thrusts of his legs. Forward and back, upwards and back, legs horizontal as he swung upwards and back. Horizontal and back, horizontal both ways, hands leaving bar at the top of each swing. Forward and back, just one more time; then a rainbow flight down, and a landing knees bent.

He needed no steps or staggering to correct his balance, but stood up straight, smiling; the cross-bar still quivering.

Applause broke out. Sugden silenced it.

'Right, come on then, let's get on with this G A M E.'

The score: still 1–1.

1–2. When Billy, shielding his face, deflected a stinger up on to the cross-bar, and it bounced down behind him and over the line.

2–2. When the referee, despite protests, allowed a goal by Anderson to count, even though he appeared to score it from an offside position.

A dog appeared at the edge of the field, a lean black mongrel, as big as an Alsatian, sniffing around the bottom of the fence on the pavement side. A second later it was inside, bounding across the field to join the game. It skidded round the ball, barking. The boy on the ball got off it, quick. The dog lay on its front legs, back curved, tail up continuing the line of its body. The boys ganged up at a distance, 'yarring' and threatening, but every time one of them moved towards it, the dog ran at him, jumping and barking, scattering the lot of them before turning and running back to the ball.

The boys were as excited as children playing 'Mr Wolf'. Carefully they closed in, then, when one of them made his effort to retrieve the ball, and the dog retaliated, they all scattered, screaming, to form up again 20 yards away and begin a new advance. If Mr Sugden had had a gun, Mr Wolf would have been dead in no time.

'Whose is it? Who does it belong to?' (From the back of the mob as it advanced, leading it when they retreated.) 'Somebody go and fetch some cricket bats from the storeroom, they'll shift it.'

In the excitement nobody took any notice of him, so he looked round and saw Billy, who was stamping patterns in the goalmouth mud.

'Casper!'

'What, Sir?'

'Come here!'

'What, Sir?'

'Go and fetch half a dozen cricket bats from the games store.'

'Cricket bats, Sir! What, in this weather?'

'No you fool! To shift that dog – it's ruining the game.'

'You don't need cricket bats to do that, Sir.'

'What do you need then, dynamite?'

'It'll not hurt you.'

'I'm not giving it a chance. I'd sooner take meat away from a starving lion than take the ball away from that thing.'

The dog was playing with the ball, holding it between its front paws, and with its head on one side, trying to bite it. However its jaws were too narrow, and each time it closed them its teeth pushed the ball forward out of reach. Then it shuffled after it, growling and rumbling in its throat. Billy walked forward, patting one thigh and clicking his tongue on the roof of his mouth. The other boys got down to their marks.

'Come on then, lad. Come on.'

It came. Bouncing up to his chest and down and round him. He reached out and scuffed its head each time it bounced up to his hand.

'What's up wi'thi? What's up then, you big daft sod?'

It rested its front paws on his chest and barked bright-eyed into his face, its tongue turning up at the edges and slithering in and out as it breathed. Billy fondled his ears, then walked away from it, making it drop down on all fours.

'Come on then, lad. Come on. Where do you want me to take him, Sir?'

'Anywhere, lad. Anywhere as long as you get it off this field.'

'Do you want me to find out where it lives, Sir, and take it home? I can be dressed in two ticks.'

'No. No, just get it off the field and get back in your goal.'

Billy hooked his finger under the dog's collar and led it firmly towards the school, talking quietly to it all the time.

When he returned they were leading 3–2.

A few minutes later they were level 3–3.

'What's the matter, Casper, are you scared of the ball?'

Mr Sugden studied his watch, as the ball was returned to him at the centre spot.

'Right then, the next goal's the winner?'

One to make and the match to win.

End to end play. Excitement. Thrills. OOOO! Arr! Goal! No! It was over the line, Sir! Play on!

Billy snatched the ball up, ran forward, and volleyed it up the field. He turned round and hopped back, pulling a sucked lemon face.

'Bloody hell, it's like lead, that ball. It's just like gettin' t'stick across your feet.'

He stood stork fashion and manipulated his foot. Every time he turned his toes up water squeezed into the folds of the instep of his pump.

'Bugger me. I'm not kicking that again.'

He placed the foot lightly to the ground and tested his weight on it.

'I feel champion, bones broke in one foot, frostbite in t'other.'

He unrolled his shorts up to his neck and pushed his arms down inside them.

'Come on, Sugden, blow that bloody whistle, I'm frozen.'

The game continued. Sugden shot over the bar. Seconds later he prevented Tibbut from shooting by tugging his shirt. Penalty! Play on.

Billy sighted the school behind one outstretched thumb and obliterated it by drawing the thumb slowly to his eye. A young midget walked from behind the nail. Billy opened his other eye and dropped his hand. More midgets were leaving the midget building, walking down the midget drive to the midget gates. Billy ran out to the edge of the penalty area, his arms back at attention down his shorts.

'Bell's gone, Sir! They're comin' out!'

'Never mind the bell, get back in your goal!'

'I'm on first sitting, Sir. I'll miss my dinner.'

'I thought I told you to swap sittings when you had games.'

'I forgot, Sir.'

'Well you'd better forget about your dinner then.'

He turned back to the game, then did a double take.

'And get your arms out of your shorts, lad! You look as if you've had Thalidomide!'

Play developed at the other end. Billy stayed on the edge of the penalty area, forming a trio with his Full Backs.

'How can I stop to second dinners when I've to go home an' feed my hawk?'

All the toys had disappeared from the playground, some of them growing into boys as they walked up Field Crescent and passed level with the pitch. They shouted encouragement through the wire, then shrank and disappeared round the curve.

They were replaced by a man and a woman approaching in the same direction, on opposite pavements. The man was wearing a grey suit, the woman a green coat, and as they drew level with the field they merged on to the same plane, and were suddenly pursued by a red car. Three blocks of colour, red, grey and green, travelling on the same plane, in the same direction, and at different speeds. Stop. Red, grey and green. Above the green of the field, against the red of the houses, and below the grey of the sky. Start. The car wove between the two pedestrians, drawing its noise between them like a steel hawser. A few seconds later the man passed the woman, grey-green merging momentarily, and seconds later the woman opened a garden gate and disappeared from the scene, leaving the man isolated on the Crescent. Silence. Then the burst of a motor bike, Rrm! Rrm! revving behind the houses, fading, to allow a thunk of the ball. A call, an echo, an empty yard. A sheet of paper captured against the wire by the wind.

12.15 p.m. The winning goal suddenly became important, no more laughter, no more joking, everybody working. For most of the game most of the boys had been as fixed as buttons on a pinball machine, sparking into life only when the nucleus of footballers among them had occasionally shuttled the ball into their defined areas: mere props to the play. Now they were all playing. Both teams playing as units, and positions were taken seriously. In possession they moved and called for the ball from spaces. Out of possession they marked and tackled hard to win it back. A move provoked a counter move, which in turn determined moves made by players in other segments of the pitch. The ball was a magnet, exerting the strongest pull on the players nearest to it, and still strong enough to activate the players farthest away.

12.20 p.m. Billy jump, jump, jumped on the line. 'Score, for Christ's sake somebody score.' Tick tick tick tick. Sugden missed again. He's blind, he's bleedin' blind. Sugden was crimson and sweating like a drayhorse, and boys began to accelerate smoothly past him, well wide of him, well clear of his scything legs and shirt-grabbing fists.

Manchester United came under serious pressure. Sugden retreated to his own penalty area, tackling and clearing and hoping for a break-away. But back it came, back they came, all Tibbut's team except the goalkeeper advancing into Sugden's half, making the pitch look as unbalanced as the 6.1 domino.

But still Sugden held them, held them by threatening his own players into desperate heroics. But it had to come. It must.

12.25 p.m. 26. 27. Every time Billy saved a shot he looked heartbroken. Every time he cleared the ball, he cleared it blind, giving the other side a fifty-fifty chance of possession, and every time they gained possession, Sugden threatened him with violence, while at the same time keeping his eyes on the ball and moving out to check the next advance. So that a sudden spectator would have been surprised to see Sugden rushing forward and apparently intimidating the boy on the ball.

For one shot, coming straight to him, Billy dived, but the ball hit his legs and ricocheted round the post. Corner! Well saved, Casper. No joke. No laughter.

It was a good corner, the ball dropping close to the penalty spot. A shot – blocked, a tackle, a scramble, falling, fouling, W H O O S H, Sugden shifted it out. 'O U T. Get out! Get up that field!'

Billy scraped a lump of mud up and unconsciously began to mould it in his fist, elongating it to a sausage, then rolling it to a dumpling, picking pellets from it and flicking them with his thumb, until nothing remained but a few drying flakes on his crusty palm. He scraped another lump up and began again; rolling, moulding, flicking, then he pivoted and wanged it across the goal at the posts. F L O P. It stuck, and when the next shot came towards him he dived flamboyantly and made an elaborate pretence to save it, but the ball bounced over his arms and rolled slowly into the net.

G O A L!

Tibbut's team immediately abandoned the pitch and raced across the field, arms flying, cheering. Billy raced after them without even bothering to pick the ball out of the net, or look at his own team, or at Mr Sugden.

from *A Kestrel for a Knave*, 1968

George Best
GEOFFREY GREEN

At one stage in the late 1960s there were four Bests who were appearing currently on the stage of the Football League – an Irishman, an Englishman, a Scot and a Bermudan. One was a goalkeeper and three were forwards. But only one of them was THE Best. Born in

Belfast in 1946, a child of Gemini, he was christened George; he stood 5ft 8½ins in height; was frail-looking at some 10½ stone and was always the one to catch the headlines.

Thumb through the glossy magazines or the humblest football rag, the odds were he would be staring out of a page, fixing attention with luminous eyes, a lush Beatle hair-style and a quizzical expression which suggested that while he alone may know the hundredth name of Buddha, it was all a bit of a joke anyway. Words, words, words: analysed, x-rayed and photographed, it has all been told before about this phenomenon of a football scene. In a few years he became a cult of youth, a new folk hero, a living James Dean who was a rebel with a cause. The cause was clearly defined – the welfare of his club and country and to prove himself the greatest player in all history.

The rebel in him was two-fold and contrary – the creator of a new image for football – yet one who turned back the clock in a search for individual freedom in an age of conformity and method within the game. He was a son of instinct rather than logic. He was touched, mauled and buffeted by the crowd off-stage and on the field. Yet he did not suffer an inflated ego nor a wounded sense of revenge. Like breathing in and breathing out, it was all merely part of the business of life.

Certainly there were flaws in his complex psyche. There could come the sudden upsurge of angry retaliation to something brutal; sometimes a childish taunting provocation, the figurative thumbing of the nose at some frustrated opponent; a mischievous irreverence; he was difficult to pin down in personal affairs. A pied piper in one sense, he was an elusive pimpernel in another. He was a Leonardo da Vinci who wantonly threw away his paint brushes and his genius. Yet he was generous, a lost child who loved to do tricks. One of these was to drop a penny piece on the toe of his shoe, then flick it up into his top breast pocket. He never failed.

People persistently inquire his place in the hierarchy of the game. Where does he stand in relationship to Stanley Matthews, Tom Finney and the rest of the cavalcade of the past? Everything is relative from age to age. The genius of one would be the genius of another. Once Reuben Bennett, the coach of Liverpool, a Scotsman, remarked to me: 'Wee Patsy Gallacher, of Celtic, was as good as Pelé and Eusebio rolled into one.' 'And,' laughed the Liverpool players around us, 'to think that he weighed no more than eight stone when wet!' They had heard this claim a hundred times.

Once I put the question to Arthur Rowe, the architect of Tottenham's fine 'push and run' days in the early 1950s, and to Blanchflower, later his captain who carried forward the White Hart Lane spark into the 1960s: 'Place in order of preference Matthews, Finney and Best.' Rowe at first hedged: 'Diamonds are diamonds, rubies are rubies and pearls are pearls,' he replied evasively. But when Blanchflower voted for Best, Rowe was inclined to agree.

Blanchflower's reasoning ran: 'Stanley was a supreme dribbler who would tax even the most ruthless, sophisticated defences of today; but he was primarily a provider. Finney was perhaps a better all-rounder than Matthews. He could play anywhere in a forward line and besides that was a free goalscorer. But George Best gets my vote. A master of control and manipulation, he was also a superb combination of creator and finisher; he, too, could play anywhere along the line. But more than the others he seemed to have a wider, more appreciative eye for any situation. He seldom passed to a colleague in a poor position. He was prepared to carry the responsibility himself.

'But basically, Best made a greater appeal to the senses than the other two. His movements were quicker, lighter, more balletic. He offered the greater surprise to the mind and eye. Though you could do nothing about it, you usually knew how Matthews would beat you. In those terms, he was more predictable to the audience. Best, I feel, had the more refined, unexpected range. And with it all there was his utter disregard of physical danger. Think of his ability to beat giants like Ron Yeats, well over 6 foot, in the air. He had ice in his veins, warmth in his heart, and timing and balance in his feet.' I would second Blanchflower's opinion.

Genius is a much overworked word. Yet when Best, after a stuttering homesick start, first settled down at Old Trafford as a skinny schoolboy of fifteen, Manchester United felt that they were in the presence of an evolving genius with an individual expression. From the first, the word went out from Sir Matt Busby: 'Don't try to change this boy's style. Let him develop naturally. The rest will come in time.' Now Busby draws on his pipe and says: 'George Best was possibly the greatest player on the ball I have ever seen. You can remember Matthews, Finney, Mannion and all the great players of that era, but I cannot think of one who took the ball so close to an opponent to beat him with it as Best did.'

As for Best, his own hero remains di Stefano, of Real Madrid. Voted Footballer of the Year both at home and in Europe concurrently in 1968, Best was the sharp point of the attack in the centre; the figure 11 on his shirt meant nothing. A marked character, the hatchet-man tracked his every stride, and if anything is certain it is that he will not play to his fifties like Matthews or Billy Meredith.

Yet his dedication was complete in his earlier days, his nerves non-existent. Once, before a big European Cup tie, he was calmly drinking Bovril with me at a crowded bar under the Old Trafford stands while other players, already changed, were anxiously living out the last tense moments before the kick-off in the dressing room. With only twenty minutes to the whistle, he had to be reminded that he was playing and still unchanged. Whereupon he departed, to perform in a kind of radiance, destroying the opposition as he has done so often. Benfica, among others, will always have cause to remember him.

Best himself was a gipsy at heart. His mother was more than partial to drink. I do not think that George ever took drugs, although he became virtually an alcoholic. Yet he was a dear person and we always remained friends. He gave a house-warming party in the Wirral one fabulous Saturday night. There were so many policemen round the house it was like trying to get into the Kremlin. I had a camera with me and took some pictures – which nearly caused a scene. Best had an exclusive contract with the Express Newspaper Group and one of their photographers saw me with my camera. He went up to Best and said: 'Who's that guy taking photographs?'

'Oh, don't worry about him,' Best replied. 'He's an artist, he's just doing it for fun.' And that was the end of it.

When he was playing for Fulham in the 1970s he took me out to lunch one day at some Italian dive in the King's Road and we sat there until 5 p.m. while people paid homage to him. He told me that he was still up to his old tricks – womanizing, drinking and so forth. He had just been to America where he had a house near the beach. But he said that he rarely reached the beach because, to get there, he had to go through a bar – and that was that as far as the beach was concerned. He always stopped at the bar – 'on the edge of the penalty area' so to speak.

from *Pardon Me For Living*, 1985

Even the Scots Had Tears in Their Eyes: The World Cup, 1970

HUGH MCILVANNEY

If anything could restore spirits bruised by the sad and undeserved expulsion of England from the World Cup it was the sight of Brazil surging, like a man o' war with nuclear armament, into the final of the competition for the fourth time.

Whatever happens in the Aztec Stadium here tomorrow, and clearly the most likely occurrence is a Brazilian victory, Pelé and Tostao, Gerson and Rivelino, Jairzinho and the rest have demonstrated that the richest flowering of football is still to be found in the southern latitudes.

That statement is no slight on the deposed champions, who will accept it as sufficient tribute that the most exciting and dangerous team in the world regard them as equals, to be respected to the point of apprehension.

Judged by all objective criteria, England should be in tomorrow's final with Brazil, meeting fire with ice in a classic collision of the European and South American philosophies of the game. Italy are there, and no one should carp about their presence. But the contrasting memories of how they struggled from beginning to exhausted end against West Germany and the ease with which England dominated the Germans, until the wide crack in Bonetti's nerve let them through, make it impossible to believe that Italy would have beaten England.

Sir Alf Ramsey's team are out because the best goalkeeper most people have ever seen turned sick, and one who is only slightly less gifted was overwhelmed by the suddenness of his promotion. In sport disaster often feeds upon itself but this was a sickeningly gluttonous example.

Those who ranted smugly in distant television studios about the tactical blunders of Ramsey were toying with the edges of the issue. Errors there were, and Ramsey in private has acknowledged one or two, but the England manager is entitled to his claim that his side were felled by something close to an act of God.

There are people who would offer prizes to anyone who could

quote an occasion when I have been sentimentally pro-English, but I was one of many outsiders who were moved by the champions' harsh experience in Leon and by the way they took it. 'I had a lump in my throat. I had to get out of the stadium before anybody noticed tears in my eyes,' said one Scottish international player. 'You just had to be affected when you saw a team with all those qualities – fellows like Mooro and Ballie and big Geoff and Mullers – getting the message like that. I'm telling you this competition lost something special when it lost them. Anybody who calls it nobility isn't far wrong.' Those who wince at that as soggy chauvinism should have heard it delivered in a West of Scotland accent.

That Scot, and quite a few Englishmen, had the good fortune to be moved in a more uplifting way three days later when Brazil, whose fuse had gathered sparkling momentum with each succeeding match in the tournament, exploded thrillingly to fragment Uruguay's stubborn defence.

The 3–1 victory was much more than a reiteration of all the virtues Europeans identify with Brazilian football: it was marvellously persuasive evidence that this side, like the best of their predecessors, reinforce genius with good sense, grace with athletic strength and art with tactical calculation.

Much of this was represented in their response to the goal they lost to Uruguay after eighteen minutes. A carelessly misdirected pass by Brito was punished by the inspired cunning of a centre from Morales, but Cubilla, in controlling the ball, was forced to an inhibiting angle, and his shot was hit slackly. When Felix, an emotional choice on whom Mario Zagalo has expended an excess of loyalty, reacted by dancing along his line like a novice ice-skater and allowing the ball to bounce languidly into his net, despair might have been general.

Gerson did clutch his head as if he had heard a terrible noise, and even the powerful captain, Carlos Alberto, looked broken for a moment. But Pelé ran through the demoralized lines to retrieve the ball and bring it back for the kick-off. In this, an unforgettably brilliant World Cup for him, he has shown an uncanny awareness of what is relevant (the crowd's cheers are no more than a bonus far out on the borders of his mind), and in that instant he knew the most meaningful thing was to play ball-boy.

'My first concern here, in Mexico,' he said afterwards, 'was to play a full World Cup. I have never been fit to complete all of Brazil's matches before. But now we have got this far I am determined to win. I am told I seem to be some kind of father figure now. If that is true it is only because I have the greatest experience of the World Cup. But, of course, I do have a special place in Brazilian football. I can talk to the other players. I can get them to do things that perhaps no one else could. This is something that has come naturally, not something I have worked to create. But I am happy to make use of it.'

In his efforts to calm and steady the team, Pelé has the required quorum of rationalizing influences. Three is an acceptable number and in 1958 Brazil had Didi, Zito and Nilton Santos. Now Tostao, who has all the cool, imperturbable shrewdness expected of men from Minas Gerais, a state that produces politicians as freely as others produce coffee, is an obvious lieutenant. And Gerson, though his volatile nature is inclined to dramatize disappointment, is too intelligently attuned to the realities of the game to be misled for long.

It was Gerson who first exposed the crippling flaw in the man-for-man marking of the Uruguayans. From the start he had been subjected to the ruthless proximity of Cortes, who stayed close enough to use the same shaving mirror. With Pelé similarly crowded by Montero Castillo, the effects could have been serious. But Gerson has the uncommon advantage of thinking as fluently as he talks.

'First I went to the left, then I went to the right. Then I moved up to the edge of their penalty area and still he stayed with me. So I decided there was one place to take him. They were interested only in defending, so I took him back to our penalty area. That meant one body out of the way of our attackers. I told Clodoaldo to go forward and do my job, that I would stay behind with the number 20. Clodoaldo scored our equalizer from my position. Then the whole game was changed and we could not lose.

'At half time I asked Zagalo if he approved of what I had done. He had no complaints. The only other change he wanted was that Rivelino should move a little to his right in midfield to give Pelé and Tostao room to make their moves on the left. They made good use of the room.'

Tostao in fact has spent the last year learning to employ his humbling talents without the luxury of space. Since his prodigious beginnings in the game he had functioned much as Pelé does, seeking the ball in the middle of the field and moving forward to beat tackles, creating trouble from deep positions.

'But when I came to play regularly with Pelé in the national team I realized I would have to change my style completely. There was too much risk of duplication. I saw that I would be far more effective if I operated as a pivot for the attack, staying forward as much as possible and giving first-time passes to the others as they came through.

'I developed the knack of playing with my back to the goal. My main function is to offer the maximum number of options to the other attackers, to draw defenders out of position and exploit the gaps with those one-touch plays.'

That he is now arguably the most consummately skilled exponent of this technique is no surprise to those who have followed his career. He is, in equipment and attitude, an astonishing amalgam of the finest in the European and South American approaches to football: the best of both worlds, an artist who turns economist if the going gets hard.

The will needed to transform his style in one year was no greater than that which enabled him to overcome the injury inflicted on his left eye by blows from a knee and a football. Detachment of the retina was minimal but it necessitated an operation in Houston, Texas, and the loss of vital months of action on the run-in to the World Cup.

As recently as the week before the tournament started, Tostao, disturbed by painless but unsightly haemorrhaging in the eye, had a psychological crisis and was ready to return to Brazil. A telephone call to Doctor Abdala Moura, the Brazilian ophthalmic surgeon who operated on him in Houston, brought reassurance.

The doctor, a football addict and supporter of Tostao's club, Cruzciro, flew to Mexico to watch the young forward play against a Leon side and told him that even if he had more bleeding in the eye he could turn out in a match the same day. Tostao's confidence was renewed and Brazil felt they were on their way to winning the World Cup.

Whether they do or not, Tostao will return to Houston to have the cause of the haemorrhaging removed. It is deduced to be the result of an allergy to the catgut sewn in during the operation.

The prospect of more surgery was only a fringe shadow on the bright optimism of the Brazilian camp after the defeat of Uruguay. They appreciated that Italy are formidably calculating, but are content to suspect that they will be faced by the man-to-man covering favoured by Uruguay rather than the more subtle zonal marking of the English defence Zagalo has defined as the best he ever saw. Any advantage the Italians gained by playing all their earlier matches at substantially higher altitudes has, they are sure, been balanced by the draining effects of those murderous two hours against Germany. Whoever wins tomorrow will claim permanent ownership of the Jules Rimet trophy, for both have two successive victories to their credit, but Brazil's dominance is a postwar phenomenon and they have the right to consider themselves favourites.

Pelé is now hard pressed to restrain their exuberance. As he stood in the sunshine by their model swimming-pool in Guadalajara before they left for Mexico City one had time to notice a great deal more than the remarkably low instep and the wide spread of toes that give him unlikely feet for the world's outstanding footballer. He took trouble to emphasize that Italy, with their frustrating competence at the back and Riva at the front, have still to be beaten. But he found it difficult to forget how great Brazil are.

Watching the Brazilians reach tentatively for a dream made us remember the scene in Leon on Sunday night when the England players had reconstructed a nightmare. As in all nightmares the central figures and events were at once familiar and unfamiliar. Bonetti was somehow not Bonetti.

'The cat didn't look like the cat out there,' somebody said. 'That first goal were a Weetabix goal,' one of the players added. 'And the second wasn't all that much. But you've got to feel sorry for Peter. Banksie seemed to have got over Montezuma's on the Saturday night and he was playing about with the ball on Sunday morning. He was in the side and then keeled over at the team meeting and Peter was told he was in about half an hour before we left for the ground. No wonder he was a bunch of nerves. If he'd had a lot of the ball early on he might have sorted it out, but there was hardly anything to do before Beckenbauer stuck that one in. In that sort of situation goal-keepers have no chance to find their feet.'

Sunday afternoon did nothing to improve Banks's condition. He was watching the quarter-final on a delayed television transmission. And England were a goal ahead when his room-mate, Alex Stepney, came in with the shattering news. The team doctor, Neil Phillips, who had seen his obsessive conscientiousness come to nothing, had the additional pain of telling Banks that Stepney's report was all too accurate.

Outside at the swimming-pool the players tried to make themselves believe they were out. Naturally, they wondered about the timing and the nature of Ramsey's substitutions. Several could be persuaded to agree that Bobby Charlton should not have been called off, that Lee should.

Perhaps neither Lee nor Peters should have been fielded in the first place, but for me the only specific criticism to be made of the England manager is that, once he had Bell warming up on the touch-line, the player should have been pushed on without delay instead of being withheld until Germany had scored and the change assumed the appearance of a panic measure.

Sadly, all that is now a footnote to this World Cup. Tomorrow belongs to Brazil and Italy, and principally I believe, to Brazil.

from *The Observer*, 21 June 1970

The Brazilians, 1970
HANS KELLER

I.

Footballers are not generally given to weeping at tense moments – more to praying and blessing themselves (in Roman Catholic areas) or to ritualistic removals of dentures (Nobby Stiles), to emerging last, or penultimately, from the tunnel, touching the ball one last time before shaking the referee's hand (Dave Mackay), and the like. What seems to be needed is a strictly statistical survey of which specific superstitions are the most effective: this, after all, is science, and we want to treat the game ever more scientifically – or you do, anyway, if you are a loyal supporter of the perennial search for substitutes for skill and invention, and therefore want England to win the World Cup.

Amongst the weepers one remembers were Eusebio (when Portugal were knocked out of the 1966 competition) and Bobby Charlton (when England won it and when Manchester United won the European

Cup): it appears that, invariably, the weepers are players who love the game at the bottom of the money. But until Brazil's win over Czechoslovakia – up front and in midfield the greatest football I have ever experienced in my life, overpowering without a display of power – I had never yet seen a player break into tears right in the middle of a match, and not at a competition's most critical stage either. Pelé had received that sovereign 50–yard pass from Gerson (forty cigarettes a day, which means that he smokes while training), had uniquely trapped it in the air with his chest and, challenged, had scored with calculated timing and exactitude. It was, of course, a very great goal, but the young Brazilian player who was overcome by tears must have seen them before, at yet more critical junctures. There was something more than the goal behind those tears, and I think we can feel what. This young star cannot have been much more than ten when Pelé was twenty – already at the height of his refined powers, with one of his four World Cups behind him. The child must have been amongst the master's most perceptive worshippers – and, years later, must have become gravely worried when Pelé, like all football virtuosos approaching thirty was duly said to be 'overrated', 'nothing like what he used to be', 'finished', droppable: an ineluctable part, this, of thinly rationalized football mythology, with its hostility against those who are felt to have presumed above their station, and with whom fate, time, can be relied upon to catch up. As the young Brazilian buried his face in his hands, he felt the hostile myth had been exploded, as indeed it had. Yet for me, the moment of epitomized truth came with Pelé's chip from behind the middle-line (which, at sea-level where he is used to playing, might well have gone in; it was only a yard or two out). Here was everything: daring skill, electric intelligence, and that greatest of human capacities – for new ideas flowing from one's discovery of changed circumstances (the keeper had left the goal-line), ideas which compel you to depart, meaningfully and drastically, from accepted conventions, tactics, intended moves . . . The crowd's applause itself was significant: it wasn't fanatical, nor an expression of that explosive gratification a goal produces. What one heard was the more dignified sound of admiration.

The newspapers had predicted Czech and English victories over Brazil. It was the same old myth, applied collectively: Brazil were overrated, not what they used to be, their football philosophy was getting old. And then Brazil beat both of them, with five goals of the highest calibre, and without an element of chance in their making. England, in pathetic contrast, have so far produced a single goal, against Romania, a cross aimed nowhere in particular being followed by a header aimed nowhere in particular: it landed at Geoff Hurst's feet, and he turned and left-footed well, but if anybody is going to win the World Cup that way, there must be something wrong with the World Cup.

2.

On 29 May, two days before the World Cup, Radio 4's *PM* show invited me to look into the future. This is what I said:

Anyone who tells you he knows who's going to win the World Cup is a charlatan, because nobody, least of all sports writers, has seen enough of all the strong sides involved to be able to form a realistic opinion. But I can tell you who won't win it, and who ought to win it.

Second answer first: who ought to? That's easy, so long as you believe in quality, which you probably don't – because you, whoever you are, are likely to be nationally prejudiced. But if quality – skill, imagination, invention – if quality counts, there is only one possible winner, and that's Brazil. The Brazilian footballer is in a class of his own, and compared to his performance, ours looks Second Division stuff. But then, many a Second Division side has knocked many a First Division side out of the FA Cup, so it could happen again, on the World Cup level. But should it? Shouldn't one's loyalty to quality be absolute? It is certainly touching to find that the majority of Mexican football supporters seem to be supporting, not Mexico, but Brazil. They have a point.

Have we got one? I doubt it. As I said, I can tell you who won't win, and that's England. Sir Alf Ramsey's is a Second Division mind; he has this enormous ability to make second-rate footballers play beyond their capacity. But he makes jolly sure that he's selecting second-raters in the first place. From the moment he dropped Jimmy Greaves from his last World Cup team – one of the few Brazilian players, as it were, in this country – he lost the loyalty of such world-class onlookers as Danny Blanchflower and George Best. He's done it again now: he's dropped Peter Thompson. And if he can help it, he won't play Peter Osgood. In defence he's strong. But this World Cup, as opposed to the last, won't be won by defenders. The climatic conditions may well be such that Dave Mackay's old motto – 'There's no substitute for skill' – will come unreservedly true.

Well, then, if you want to support a substitute for skill, that's entirely up to you, and jolly bad luck to you.

It made quaint listening, I daresay, but perhaps it doesn't make stale reading now – whereas when you read what our brainwashed sports writers wrote three weeks ago, you can hardly believe those senses of yours that went on reading: you, too, had been brainwashed. The issue is serious: why did people who spend their lives in football show no foresight? I don't know more about the game than they, but I do refuse to be brainwashed by fashions, however official, however seemingly successful.

While reality has won in reality, it has not yet won in people's heads. True, they are gradually coming round, but with two steps forward they take one back and three sideways. We now hear that the Brazilians – who, unlike the Italians, had won every single game up to the final, and then won 4–1 against the world's ablest defence – were 'the most entertaining side'. They are indeed; they are also the best. We went out 'difficult to beat', as Ramsey put it. Anybody playing two forwards is difficult to beat. But even nine people bunched together in the box can't be sure that the others won't score – and then where are you, if your most effective strikers are amongst your defenders? The Brazilians don't worry about not letting anything in. They allow for individual errors, which are inevitable anyway. If you are defence-minded, you work on the illusory assumption that individual errors can be avoided. Errors in attack don't matter, unless you do nothing but err, as England did. The Brazilians just make sure that they play enough talent to score more than they give away (19–7!). Of course, for a good attack you need more talent than for a good defence.

And individual talent at that. All our puritan rubbish about sacrificing individuality to team-work and work-rate has been exploded hell-deep. Alone amongst all, the Brazilians constructed and created every one of their nineteen goals in six matches, most of them in intricate moves. Pelé, striker and midfield man rolled into one, now creates as many goals as he scores. And the Brazilians' creations are as individual as their solo feats: they play to each other's individualism, expecting each other to expect their unexpected ideas, born of situations which, properly analysed, show these inventions to be discoveries – ideal solutions. It follows that, theoretically, an opposition with equally sudden, realistic counter-ideas could outwit Brazil – if it had the wits, and the constructive thoughts in its turn.

Instead, the toughest, the fittest, the hardest-working, the best acclimatized, the most methodical, the most systematic were all beaten in sovereign style. Where the going was tough, there invariably came, after prolonged testing, the moment of positive, flash-like outwitting: it was all over. The fittest surrendered to Tostao, whose recently detached retina seems to have prevented him from heading a single ball in the entire tournament, and to Gerson, whose forty cigarettes a day seem to prevent him from running. (If I remember aright, he ran only once, or tried to: when he was overjoyed after his goal in the final.) What we hear is that irrational talent and skill, irresponsible feeling, animal grace, have won the day over method and strategy. But have Pavlov dogs reason and method? Is not the supreme achievement that combination of instinct and reason which is imagination, and which makes reason itself seem instinctive? Behind one of those Pelé passes which produced goals unforeseen by the most methodical defence lay more thought than you found in any ninety minutes of England's play.

Was our World Cup victory, then, itself an illusion? Yes. At home, we played in the easiest group, drew with Uruguay, beat the Argentinians 1–0, had one good game against Portugal, and needed – for the first time in history – extra-time to beat West Germany. Surprise. The world's admiration was not forthcoming. Brazil, away, played in the toughest group, and beat everybody with goals which – hitherto, I have always resisted this comparison – approached works of art. They didn't take their chances: they made them, complexly, out of what seemed nothing to methodical mindlessness. The world's admiration is forthcoming.

from *The Listener*, June 1970

Goalies
FRANK KEATING

Frank Swift was the first goalkeeper to dominate the 6-yard box of my consciousness. He had hands as big as Joe Baksi and, on tiptoe, the peak of his cap could touch the crossbar. Raymond Glendenning would always describe him on the wireless as 'the big fellow'. Then came the first colour photographs, and a shot of Bert Williams turning one round for a corner, wings outstretched in flight like a tacking

Spitfire, inspired me to ask my mother to knit me a similar polo-neck jumper of canary yellow.

Swift became a journalist and, representing the *News of the World*, died in the Munich air crash in 1958. The last I heard of Williams he was headmaster of a School for Goalkeepers in the Black Country. In the earlyish 1950s Bert vied for the yellow badge of courage with another Midlander, Gil Merrick, who in the space of three hours on either side of Christmas 1952, let in thirteen goals against Hungary. Thereafter, with his sad toothbrush moustache and spaniel eyes, he always looked like the boxer, Jack Gardner, when Bruce Woodcock was hitting him.

Back in the mists they were called 'net-minders'. In an essay on his craft in 1900, the Southampton polo-neck, Jack Robinson, began: 'We do not grow on trees. Many imagine us custodians of the sticks are as plentiful as berries in autumn. I concede there are thousands who consider themselves keepers of the goal, but you must remember there are thousands upon thousands of men who consider themselves poets. And just as there are poets and poets so there are goalkeepers and goalkeepers.' Quite.

Far earlier than that, in *Football at Westminster School*, H. G. Benham had defined the very beginnings for every mittened Horatius. 'A goalkeeper is a duffer or funk-stick. If any player who was playing out showed any sign of funk or failed to play up, he was packed off into goal at once, not only for the day, but as a lasting degradation. On the other hand, if any keeper made a good save of a goal, he was called for immediately to play out, and thenceforth he played out always.'

Since when, of course, the Netminders' Union has become a pretty closed shop. It is not in the least bit chauvinist to say the British have been remarkably well blessed. Offhand, since Glendenning's 'big fellow', I can rattle off a litany of last-liners – Hopkinson and Hodgkinson, Swindin and Bartram, Springett and Ditchburn, Kelsey and Sprake, Uprichard and Gregg, Lawrence and Stepney and Brown. Not forgetting Bonetti 'The Cat' . . . nor Montgomery of the Sunderland save . . .

Oddly, Scotland have seldom fielded reliable 100-per-centers. Their glorious talents are reserved for those playing 'out'. I suppose the most celebrated tartan goalie remains John Thomson, who was capped at twenty-two in 1930 but a year later died after diving at the feet of a Ranger. At his memorial service, the theme of the requiem was, 'Greater love hath no man that that he lay down his life for his friends.' His ghost is said still to haunt the 6-yard box at Celtic. On braw and wintry full-moon nights at Celtic Park you can still, apparently, hear the eerie, desperate, high-pitched shriek of 'Mine!'

My own particular favourite was the Fulham gloveman a quarter of a century past. When Tony Macedo was good he was very, very good – but when . . . But we loved him. He once lost us a semi-final of the Cup. But we knew he'd got us there in the first place. He was a magnficent madcap. The old *Manchester Guardian* football correspondent, H. D. Davies, may well have seen Macedo the week before he wrote that it was 'axiomatic that goalkeepers, like wicketkeepers, were "a slate loose" '.

Then Gordon Banks rewrote the rules, re-drew the geometry, upped even the courage. I was in Mexico for the 1970 World Cup, but was covering another match and never saw for real Banks' save against Pelé, of Brazil and the Universe. On television it is all over and done with in a blur. But the journalist, John Moynihan, was actually behind Banks' net as:

Pelé hurtled in, leaping over Mullery, and all for one were shouting 'Goal!' and rising to acclaim the 'King'. Then an outrageous flash of movement, a combination of sprawling arms and legs. Banks was suddenly over to the right of goal laying sideways with his left leg thrust out straight, his other bent at right angles and his groping right hand scooping the ball up and over the crossbar. Banks, in this attitude of a praying mantis after spinning to a new twig, had played the ball up and away with an extended palm into oblivion. It tumbled over the bar and rolled slowly on to the other side of the net with the sudden abatement of an ocean wave after breaking on a rock. And one wondered, amid all the shouting and screaming and commotion, whether England's goalkeeper had broken his arm and suffered grievous damage; he lay on his back with his shoulders on the grass, his colleagues standing around too nonplussed to yell their praise. Already the moment had become a legend, a piece of unique folklore, a gymnastic impossibility. 'Did you see that!' roared Harry, turning round to me. His nicotined fingers were trembling with tension. 'Christ! Did you see that!'

Clemence and Corrigan were taking turns in Banks' jumper by the time the hero lost an eye in a motor accident. Now England's Peter Shilton, geometry and agility allied to a rousing, bullying, muscular presence, is considered one of the best in the world and a formidable successor to Banks.

And yet, there remains a goalkeeper who plays, week in, week out, in the English Football League, who might, when grandchildren come to write history books, figure with far more twirly gold-leaf script. Up among the jerseyed gods will be Pat Jennings, once of Watford and Tottenham Hotspur, now of Arsenal. He recently played his hundredth game in goal for Northern Ireland.

Jennings, still the same soft and gentle fellow who came over from Newry twenty years ago, is thirty-eight now. He cannot have long times left between the sticks. If fathers care about such things they should summon their sons to go to see Jennings keep goal before he picks up the gloves from the back of his net for the last time, shakes hands with his opposite number in the wintry sunset, and clatters down the tunnel forever.

Like Swift and Williams of my boyhood, Jennings keeps guard of his cluttered stage of bodies and boots and braying, brawling, breathlessness, with athleticism, bravery, grace and chivalry. The olde tyme hero. And I always fancy he, too, plays even that teeny bit better in his yellow jersey.

from Long Days, Late Nights, 1984

How We Taught the Turks the Meaning of Worship:
Leeds in Turkey
COLIN WELLAND

If Soccer is the new religion I've just met the twelve Apostles. There they sat in Ankara Stadium, Turkish pastries wrapped around their faces, hurling healthy abuse at an inept Romanian referee, chatting 'intimately' from stand to pitch with Don, and Billy and Norman and swinging with reckless defiance on bank after bank of bloodthirsty Turks. 'Super Leeds,' they cried. 'Super Leeds' – their arms thrown wide in salute – and, passionately, they believed every word.

'Super Leeds' were performing a quiet, ultra-professional suffocating job on a local side all torrid and volatile, full of bounce but with no real football brains. As a policy it was predictable, and to be honest, it was boring. It was also completely inconsequential to the roaring enjoyment of an expeditionary force of twelve Leeds fanatics bent on football and a bloody good time.

Two thousand miles they'd come. Moving with the speed of light infantry – and under the cover of a blue-black sky – they hit the unsuspecting Turkish capital before last Tuesday's dawn . . . and soon even this city, well used to the petulance of old Mother Earth, was shuddering to its very foundations.

Mind you, who'd have guessed? We must have looked quite a respectable lot boarding the plane at Heathrow. A couple of local businessmen and wives, a Yorkshire League ref and son, who won the trip in a newspaper competition (people actually fill them in), a muck-and-brass-type company director travelling alone – and (here's the crunch) four Bradford publicans who, with a master window-cleaner called Big H, provided the party's real firepower. These last five were ready for anything. Inevitably anything wasn't available – but they sure made the most of what was.

On second thoughts perhaps Turkish Airlines should have realized when during the solemn search for arms Gilbert (who looked like Charlie Williams and had a voice to match) earnestly requested that the Arab passenger in long flowing robes be given another good do – as he looked like their kid – and he wouldn't trust *him* as far as he could throw him. Surely their suspicions should have been roused when, once airborne, Big H stood proudly and introduced himself to the crowded, sweaty cabin as H. Bower window-cleaner, no job too large or small – as the rest laced the Turkish coffees with duty-free Scotch explaining that that's how its done 'in the Gaelic'.

A wiser, more worldly crew would have radioed ahead crying 'Siege.' But then, despite their reputation, they're a kind-hearted lot, the Turks, and fate is often cruel to the kind.

Ankara, although the capital, is by our standards quite an unsophisticated place. Football there is still a game, not a creed. The men are gentle and cling to one another's arms. The women, though no longer veiled, are essentially demure.

Still, we were there to enjoy ourselves, and we set about doing just that. A guide was summoned to show us the sights. An earnest strip of a lad he was, a student, briefed in local ethnological history, eager to trace for us in detail the development of Turkish ceramic art. Give us our due, we gave him a hearing – enjoyed it – but it took a fleeting glimpse of a shapely ballerina flitting across the open doors of the

State ballet rehearsal rooms to really fire our dormant imaginations. In a flash we were in with the chat. 'Dame Margot Fonteyn! Yes! Lovely!' The girls were kind and tolerant and we swept out triumphant to the sun and the mountain air and the spread of our chests.

Ankara was fast becoming our oyster when Leeds flew in and somebody mentioned football and the match. The match! What a fantastic experience that was – not the game, the event. The city, naïvely new to European football, was engagingly enthusiastic. Curious knots of locals clustered about us smiling, clutching our hands. We were proud to be Leedsites, here, miles from anywhere. We patted heads like newly descended gods as exotic sounds and smells crowded our senses.

Suddenly across the compound staggered an unearthly figure. It was hairy, wild-eyed and uttering weird cries, strangely familiar. 'A ticket lads – a ticket?' wailed the creature, his face festooned with mosquito bites. Eight days on the road he'd hitched from Leeds. We pressed him to our bosoms, tended his wounds and gave him a ticket. As he sobbed out his thanks we rebuked him and reminded him that in spite of all he was still British.

And so were we, like it or not. Once inside, Her Majesty's Consul opened his paternal arms and sat us firmly in his private enclosure surrounded by armed troops thoughtfully and insistently provided by the largest standing army in Europe. From what, we asked, were they protecting us? Kindness?

Leeds came, and saw and contained – like benign Victorian grandfathers . . . but this was football à l'Orient, immune from 'civilizing' influences. It was a game in which goalkeeper and penalty-taker embrace before the shot, linesmen throw bouquets of flowers to the crowd and bonfires and rockets celebrate a goal.

Afterwards we sat like kings surrounded by adoring Turks who whistled Leeds admiringly through their teeth. Superior beings will scoff at those who travel 2,000 miles to see a game of football. But our lives were enriched by this particular journey.

By necessity I had to leave the following day with half the week still to go. I flew home with the team and their speedily sobering chat of Leicester on Saturday and the points. I left behind the new Gilbert, and Big H and the rest lunching at the Embassy . . . But later that evening, secure in the belief that language barriers just don't exist they'd be swopping yarns over black, sweet Turkish coffee with our new-found Ankaran friends.

I cannot help feeling that this beautiful city will look back with affection not only on the visit of Leeds United but of their twelve supporters.

from *The Observer*, 17 September 1972

Three Managers
BARRY NORMAN

1. BERTIE MEE

Bertie Mee was rather disappointed when his own football career came to a premature end. Not that it had been much of a career, really. He was an outside-left with Derby County before the war, in the days when teams marched boldly forward in the famous 2–3–5 formation and outside-lefts were nippy little blokes like Bertie Mee.

He'd had his dreams of glory, naturally, but these were all frustrated soon after the war when injury put him out of the game. 'It was a great disappointment, certainly,' he says now. 'But I hope I'm a realist as well as an optimist. The fact is, I was no good – not good enough anyway. I would have played League football at a low level but I'd never have made a First Division player and I like to be first in whatever I do.'

This, actually, is quite an assertive statement, coming from Bertie Mee. As a rule he delivers his remarks in a precise, formal manner as if handing down the tablets or, more likely, as if everything he says is likely to be taken down and used at some later date to embarrass him. Not a suspicious man perhaps, but certainly a cautious one.

Still, it could be that, as manager of Arsenal, he feels he *is* number one or, as he would put it, first and, if so, it's a tenable theory.

Since he became manager in 1966, somewhat to his own surprise (he had, after all, joined the club only in 1960 as a physiotherapist), Arsenal have won the Fairs Cup and done the double and been runners-up in both the League and FA Cups. Other managers may claim comparable records, but Mr Mee is possibly alone in feeling confident enough to proffer advice to Brian Clough.

'Every club suffers a let-down after winning the League,' he said. 'I faced this the season after we'd done the double. I bought Alan Ball at Christmas, but it was too late. The problems, really, were in the first three months.

'The thing is: when you're young and you've done it all, what do you do for an encore? If you're Jack Nicklaus or Lee Trevino you go on and do it again. It's easy enough, perhaps, for one man to capture that sort of drive, but how do you instil it into eleven men?'

It's on this subject that he had been advising Mr Clough. His own solution, he said, had been to drop people ruthlessly from his team and make them fight for their places. He has also bought new players, for example, the £200,000 Jeff Blockley.

Tentatively, I put forward the theory that it was only fairy gold anyway – that the same £250,000 or so went wearily from one club to another in exchange for one player or another; a great fat wad of greasy notes.

Mr Mee agreed that, broadly speaking, this was so, but nevertheless prices were absurd. He himself, of course, was not responsible for that situation, but . . . 'I can't afford to stand aside and watch. I have a wife and children to support.

'The game has reached a stage where success or failure is measured by the result of each match. If you lose it's a real crisis for three or four days, or until your next win. There's no comfort in failure at all. You have to win and keep on winning – the spectators demand it.'

The double team of 1970–71, of course, did exactly that, but it was still criticized for being dour, hard and unattractive. Did such criticism hurt? Mr Mee said it didn't and, clearly, neither wild horses nor even wild Charlie Georges would force him to say otherwise.

'These days,' he said, 'a manager has a number of priorities – 1, you don't lose; 2, you start to win; 3, you don't lose away. Now, fifteen years ago, that was enough to win the League championship. Today it's not. Today you have to win everything at home and two out of three away.'

I said that, with this kind of pressure, it was a wonder that he still enjoyed his football, and he said that, on the whole, he didn't. 'I enjoy it when we're not playing or when there's ten minutes to go and we're leading 5–0. Otherwise I don't enjoy it at all. The pressures are tremendous and they're reflected in the high cost of players. It's a panic measure by some clubs to pay over the odds in an attempt to achieve success – like Malcolm Allison buying Rodney Marsh last season and Brian Clough paying a high price for David Nish.

'I suppose I could be accused of the same thing by buying Ball and now Blockley. But I bought Blockley as cover for Frank McLintock, who is thirty-two, and because I don't want a situation such as Leeds have where they're desperately trying to find a centre-half because Jackie Charlton is waning.'

This pressure, though – was it greater at Arsenal than at any other club? On account of the traditions? Yes, he thought possibly it was. Arsenal, after all, was the number one club; always had been.

'I can't imagine any more attractive job in football than the one I have here,' he said. Even so, surely it was inhibiting to have that bust of Arsenal's first great manager, Herbert Chapman, glowering at him every time he walked into the stadium.

Mr Mee, caught off guard perhaps, permitted his eyebrows to rise fractionally in surprise. 'Herbert who?' he said. 'Bust? What bust? Where is it? I've never seen it.' For a moment I was fool enough to believe him but, of course, he was really making a joke. Mr Mee doesn't make many jokes and when he lets one slip he doesn't tele-graph its coming.

'Naturally,' he said, 'I can't concern myself with what Herbert Chapman did. The past is dead; it's only tomorrow that counts, although I think I can say with due modesty that, bearing in mind what had happened over the previous twelve years or so, the success ratio since I took over has been quite high.'

Indeed it has, so was there anything left for him to achieve? 'Yes,' he said. 'I should like to win the European Cup, something that no other manager has done.'

Well, hang on, I said. I mean, Matt Busby and Jock Stein . . . Mr Mee regarded me across his desk with mild contempt. 'I meant, of course, something that no other *Arsenal* manager has done,' he said.

2. MALCOLM ALLISON

In the long run, said Malcolm Allison, the answer might well lie in psycho-analysis. He waited, with a defensive grin, for the laugh.

Psycho-analysis, I said, not laughing (and indeed it would take a bigger and braver man than I to laugh at Malcolm Allison), for his footballers? Exactly, he said. Brazil had psychiatrists attached to their football squad so why not Manchester City?

After all, there he was with potentially the finest bunch of players in the land, trained to a hair, almost indecently fit, erupting with skill and yet they were pretty damn nearly bottom of the League.

'It's not ability they've lost,' he said. 'It's confidence and what do you do about that? Ask advice? No. You get plenty of advice offered but you don't go seeking it. If any manager knew the answer he'd win everything every year.

'There's nothing physically wrong, you see. Players these days are stronger, run faster and jump higher than ever before. But we're not nearly so professional at sorting out the mental side of the game. We don't use psychiatrists. We should, though, and eventually we will. It'll come, I'm sure of that. As a matter of fact I've been thinking about it seriously for a couple of years.'

We eyed each other solemnly across his office. 'Yeah,' he said. 'You can imagine the gags, can't you? "Here, look what old Mal's got there – right bunch of nut cases."

'It's a matter of convincing the players that a psychiatrist could find out why they're playing badly, why they're not happy in their work. And they aren't happy at the moment: they're bloody miserable. They don't like losing any more than I do.'

Meanwhile, and until the climate is right for the club psychiatrist to be appointed, failure brings other problems in its wake. New rumours spring up every day – Lee's going, Doyle's going. The football gossip columns hint at a berserk and panic-stricken Allison booting his entire squad out of Maine Road. Untrue, he said, all of it.

'I'm a person who makes quick decisions and one of those decisions was that I wouldn't sell any player until I could replace him with a better one and where do I find better players than the mob I've got? God, it's an unbelievable game, football.

'I can tell the exact minute when they're going to start playing badly. They play the first half, they're putting it together, playing great – and then the whistle goes and in the dressing-room everything's gone. It all falls apart – and there's not a thing you can do about it.

'I can talk to them, sure. I do. I talk to them individually, I talk to them in groups. I tell 'em I believe in them – but until they start believing in themselves again they're not going to get the results.'

Wasn't it possible, though, to trace failure back to its source; to pinpoint the moment when things started going wrong? He looked at me with justifiable scorn. Blimey, hadn't he tried that?

Well, then, how about Rodney Marsh? City were top of the League when he joined them; two weeks ago they were practically bottom. Was he perhaps the wrong kind of player for this team?

'No,' said Allison, 'that's nonsense. You can't blame anything on Rodney Marsh. It may be that because he came here with a reputation as an artist, a brilliant ball player, the others felt they ought to show the crowds that they can play a bit, too. That might have upset the rhythm a little but it's hardly Marsh's fault, is it?

'I bought him because he's got more skill than anybody else in English football, he can score goals and he's just got that thing. He affects people – like Bestie, Cassius Clay or Tom Jones. I don't know what it is but he's got it. Besides, I like his originality. He's got the sort of footballing brain that can spot the other team's pattern of play and know just where and how to break it up.'

He prowled about the office in his track suit, a naturally worried but still philosophical man. The situation was serious but not desperate, or desperate but not serious depending on the level of his optimism.

He said: 'Just before the season started I went and looked at the stadium. It was great. The pitch looked great, the stands looked great. The players were confident, the spirit was good. I thought, "Christ, what a season we're going to have."

'I was proud. I looked at all these things and I thought, "It's there. It's all there." ' A long, rueful pause, 'And it *is* all there.

'Losing a few games doesn't change anything really. It just puts you in your place, makes you realize you're not infallible. You see, my players were over-confident. That's what started the whole thing.

'Even when they were getting beat, they were still over-confident, up to a certain time. I remember Arsenal had the same trouble the year after they'd done the double. We went down to Highbury and won and Bertie Mee said to me, "What do I do, Mal?" and I said, "I don't know, Bertie. You just work." That's all we can do here – just work. I always reckon I'm luckier when I work harder.

'But we've had bad patches before – just after we got promoted, then when I got suspended and the team didn't win in twelve matches and again after we won the championship. Anyway, this season's only a quarter of the way through.

'Not that anybody likes the present situation. The players say they can't go into a pub, can't talk to the next-door neighbour. They're ashamed to go into town and it's no consolation that Manchester United are doing just as badly.

'There's no comfort in that. I mean, I can't go and swop worries with Frank O'Farrell. I can't talk to any managers. All they could advise me on is tactical things and I'm not bothered about them. It's the players' state of mind that causes all the trouble and maybe I haven't worked hard enough on that.

'And yet, in a way, I quite like this situation. I get a certain pleasure out of being down and knowing that I've got to get this right and that right.

'That's what I'm here for. It's what my job's all about.' A helluva job, I said. 'Yeah,' he said. 'Sometimes you think, "I don't need all these pressures; I'd like it a bit easier," and then you think you'd like to go and work at a smaller club, maybe abroad, and have a quieter life.'

He stared wistfully out at the car park and then he said: 'Ah, but what the hell! If you've made a bit of a name for yourself they'd expect things of you wherever you went. There'd still be pressure. So, finally, I reckon I'm better off where I am.'

3. BERT HEAD

If Bert Head were playing Monopoly, someone remarked with more wit than charity, he'd buy the Old Kent Road instead of Mayfair. Not true at all. He started the week by trying to buy Mayfair (assuming Ted MacDougall at £220,000 can be so described), but Frank O'Farrell landed there first.

Mr Head may have finished up with a package deal of three lesser properties at £280,000 the lot, but it would still be unkind to liken them to the Old Kent Road, begging Millwall's pardon, of course.

As it happened, only one of the new Palace acquisitions, Iain Phillip (£110,000 from Dundee) was on display, since Paddy Mulligan (£75,000 from Chelsea) was poorly with a sore throat and Charlie Cooke (£85,000 from Chelsea) was ineligible. Thus Mr Head was in the frustrating position of a gambler limited to putting only a third of his stake on the table. 'Don't equate today's result with the £280,000,' he said afterwards. 'It's not fair.'

Palace had been played on to the pitch with much canned music –

though not, oddly enough, 'Hey, Big Spender' – and the record of having failed to score in their last six matches.

This distinguished run they stretched to seven without any trouble at all. A flick over the bar early on by Craven, an optimistic thump by Hughes, an even more optimistic scissors kick by Craven again and two or three uninhibited long-range drives by Hinshelwood were about the best they could muster.

Yes, said Mr Head later, you could say Palace were still in the market for another player. A striker? 'Call him what you like,' said Mr Head. 'Some bugger who puts the goals in, anyway.'

Norwich, actually, were quite well equipped with buggers like that. Bone scored the first after twelve minutes, a corner and a scene of total chaos in the Palace penalty area. Fifteen minutes later Paddon got the second, amid similar panic, with a header.

Meanwhile, Phillip – neat but not gaudy – was dividing his attentions between Bone and Cross and doing quite well. His colleagues treated him with polite reserve, as though they hadn't been formally introduced yet, and rarely gave him the ball. He shouldn't feel too slighted by that, however, since they rarely gave it to one another either. 'Phillip?' said Mr Head. 'He'll be all right once he's settled down and sharpened up. The lads were a bit disjointed today. They'd lost confidence, don't believe in themselves any more.'

On the whole, though, he was encouraged by the thought of the players he'd signed. 'Not a bad week's work,' he said. 'Of course, I'm still a bit sore about MacDougall, but he's gone so there's no point in talking about him, is there?'

True. But it was a lot of money he'd spent nevertheless. Didn't it worry him, gambling all that on three players? 'It's the way prices go, isn't it?' he said. 'Of course they're ridiculous – a £100,000 transfer is nothing these days. It's like bananas – they used to be two-a-penny, but they're not any more. No, I'm not worried, though. You back your fancy, that's all. It's the occupational hazard of being a manager. The day I lose any sleep through worry is the day I pack it in.'

On the field Norwich had skated the first half and eased up a little in the second when, to do them credit, Palace did look somewhat more businesslike. Even so, just before the end the slow handclapping started, somebody waved a banner saying 'Head Must Go' and Bone came off, being, in the elegant phrase of his manager, 'knackered'.

So once again Palace are in their familiar position near the bottom of the League. 'Well,' said Mr Head, 'we're in the process of building traditions here. I didn't buy these players on a short-term basis, just to get us out of trouble. If you're spending that much money you have to think long-term. You have to think of getting into Europe, otherwise it takes years to get the money back.'

In any case, he said, though he's invested £750,000 in players in the last four years he has got most of it back by selling others. 'Anyway, look at it this way: if I spend half a million pounds this season which I might, it'll seem an awful lot. But I may not spend any more for another five years. You have to judge it, not week by week, but over a length of time.'

He was not, then, feeling in any way desperate? 'We're never desperate here, mate,' he said. 'We're never desperate here.'

from *The Observer*, 1, 29 and 15 October 1972

Stuck in
GORDON WILLIAMS

He had always had nerves before a game, worse if there were people watching. Glenryan was a village halfway between Kilcaddie and the smaller town of Bridge of Kilmorchan – the Brig. Twenty or so men and boys were on the touchline of Glenryan's cinder and grass pitch. They'd been known to attack visiting teams.

Baldy Campbell made him even more nervous. The great fat man in the belted gabardine raincoat and flat checked cap was watching the second eleven for only one reason – to see if any of them were fit to move up into the big team. One silly mistake could ruin his chance. He put the rest of the chewing-gum packet in his jacket pocket. The new chiclet slipped about between his teeth and tongue until he'd bitten through to the gum. He always felt the same way before a game, nervous, half-thinking he wasn't good enough for the team, wondering if he'd play a stinker. He'd been playing almost every Saturday, morning and afternoon, since he was about twelve or thirteen and he was still nervous. Nobody else knew just how seriously you took it, how much you hoped that one day you'd play a blinder and a strange man would come up to you after the game and write your name down in a wee book and ask you if you wanted a trial with Rangers or Aston Villa or Leicester City. Or even Ayr United – he wasn't fussy. Nobody else knew that you thought of each game as a tightrope along which you walked hoping you wouldn't fall off. You had a feeling that the rest of the guys in the team didn't think you were good enough to be playing, so you couldn't really think of them as pals.

You ran out on to the pitch wondering whether your studs were hammered in properly, would a nail come up through your sole, were your laces tied tight enough. Your thighs seemed darker and hairier than usual against white shorts. During the kickabout you didn't exert yourself, you took the odd shot at goal, you jumped up and down feet together, you rubbed your hands against the cold, you sneaked a look at the other team – who always seemed bigger and stronger and more sure of themselves. You wondered which one you were marking, was he a hard case or a fantastic sprinter or a tremendous dribbler? Did you really need to go to the lavvy again, or was it just nerves?

The first ball you got was the vital one, if you bungled it you'd probably have a stinker. You saw the houses and the trees and the people but you didn't think about them. After ten minutes you'd know what kind of a game it was, hard and fast, a kicking match, a walkover, a hopeless defeat? Once you knew that you could fit yourself into it, play as well as possible. But the beginning was the worst, waiting for your first ball.

As they lined up for the kick-off he saw Baldy talking to his crony, Joe Overend. Were they talking about him? All Joe had said was that Baldy would be coming to their game, he never told you who Baldy was supposed to be interested in.

His first kick came after a few minutes running up and down behind the forwards. He saw it hit somebody's shin and run loose. He was able to trap it and look up before Glenryan blokes came at him. At this stage in the game, everybody was full of wind, there was no time to hang about.

He hit it up the left-wing, wishing there had been time to make sure it went to one of their forwards. It landed near enough to Sammy Muir to make it look intentional, so maybe he was going to have a good game. As he ran about there seemed to be two parts of his brain. One followed the ball, deciding when to tackle and when to fall back. The other seemed to talk back to him, as though he was really two people, one making a speech to the other.

Go in hard. No time for fancy-work in juvenile football. Go in hard and don't waste time. One day play like Bobby Evans. Not really fond of playing wing-half. Centre-forward best position. Be Billy Houliston. Rummle 'em up.

One thing you've got – iron determination. Hard as nails. Don't care about being hurt. Only get hurt if you go in half-hearted. Do or die.

After half an hour the pattern was there. Glenryan's inside-right, the man he was marking, did most of the dribbling in their team. He was a nifty dribbler, fancy with it, too. Hands splayed out at his sides, palms towards the ground, copying Willie Woodburn of the Rangers, the spread-out hands.

Just before half-time Glenryan got the first goal. A long ball came up from their defence and by the time Dunky saw that he was nearest to it he was caught in two minds whether to go for it in the air or wait to collect it after the first bounce. On the greasy, melting surface, his feet slipped as he first went forward and then decided to run back. The ball bounced over his head. Big Colin Thompson, their right-back, tried a sliding tackle on the fancy inside-right, but he flicked the ball forward and did a neat little hurdling jump over Colin's scything legs. Swaying his head from side to side to confuse the goalkeeper he ran forward into the penalty area and shot it into the net just as Bobby Black, Cartneuk's centre-half, crashed him to the ground.

Cartneuk's goalie, Billy Forsyth, sat on one leg, the other stuck out in the mud, looking accusingly at his defenders.

Dunky spat. It was his fault. He made a tight mouth and shook his head.

'What was the fuck'n matter wi' you?' demanded Bobby Black, glowering at Dunky.

'Piss off.'

Bobby Black was fond of shouting the odds about other players' mistakes. Dunky thought Bobby didn't like him because he was the only one in the team who'd gone to the Academy, which a lot of the guys called a toffs' school.

The whistle went and they walked over to the dressing-room hut, where Baldy Campbell stood with Overend. Dunky went inside for a new bit of gum. The sun was shining, although it was cold. Overend had oranges for those who felt thirsty. Dunky didn't bother. What did Baldy have to say? Men who ran football teams were funny buggers. They never saw the game the same way as you did. Some of the guys always made a point of buttering up Baldy, getting in their versions of what'd gone wrong, trying to put the blame on somebody else. He didn't. He was lucky to be in the team at all, he supposed, yet he wasn't going to smarm up to anybody. If Baldy didn't like the way he played too bloody bad.

'You're not covering each other enough,' was Baldy's pronouncement. He spoke quietly, not annoyed that they'd lost the first goal. Although he was big he had very small eyes. Funny eyes. Different from the rest of him. His mouth said one thing, but his eyes seemed to be watching you listening to him, as though his eyes were separate from the rest of him. Dunky blew his nose, thumb against one nostril, snort, head bent forward so that it would miss his legs, middle finger against the other nostril, snort. Spit. It could be a bad sign, Baldy not being annoyed. Hundreds of guys wanted to play for Cartneuk. He didn't have to persevere with players. If he didn't think you were any good he just let you go. You had to fight to get a game, let alone become a regular.

'That inside-right's the danger man,' said Joe Overend. Normally he was in charge of the second team, a scruffy wee man who was very friendly towards everyone – and who told tales to Baldy all the time. You had to be careful what you said to Overend.

'I want the full-backs to play closer together,' Baldy said. 'Concentrate on the middle, their wingers is nothing hot.'

Dunky bent down and touched the dried blood on his knee, thinking that it would nip later on when he had to scrub the embedded cinders out of the skin.

'And Logan,' went on Baldy, 'don't be scared to take your man, if he thinks you're scared of him he'll do what he wants.'

Dunky nodded. Who the hell was *scared*?

A slight stiffness after the half-time rest. Get stuck in, that's what Baldy wanted. All right, I'll show you who can get stuck in.

At school it was all sportsmanship. You didn't play to win, oh no, you were told off for fouling. The referees were all schoolteachers, you couldn't play it hard or they'd give you a dressing-down, as though you'd been caught wanking in class. But once you were out in real football it was different. The ref could only give fouls against you, not treat you like a wee boy. And

Baldy was only interested in playing to win. As long as you didn't give away penalties or get sent off Baldy didn't care what you did. He didn't care what the other team said, either. He said there was only one way to play the game. Hard – to win. He believed in real football, not a lot of namby-pamby schools stuff. If you got in trouble he was on your side. As long as you were one of his players he would stick up for you.

The hand-waver trapped the ball near the touchline. Go in – hard as nails. Dunky leaned back as his left leg swept round from behind, knocking the inside-right to the ground, forcing the ball over the line. He shot up his hands and shouted 'Our ball' but the referee gave the throw-in to Glenryan. It was a short one to the outside-right. Dunky took a kick at it through the outside-right's legs.

'Hey watch it,' shouted a man on the touchline. The outside-right looked over his shoulder at Dunky. The ref gave another throw-in to Glenryan. This time it went into the middle. Dunky moved forward, taking up position to cover any breakaway attacks, aligning himself with Bobby Black and the full-backs. Another ball to the inside-right, who'd taken up position at the touchline, near halfway, giving him room to trap and move forward. Run out to block him. Body jack-knifed, eyes on the ball, never take your eyes off the ball. Go in – hard as nails. The inside-right put his foot on the ball and dragged it back out of range of Dunky's jabbing boot. Then he pushed it forward, past Dunky.

Up and after him. The wing-half must never stop running. Keep harassing him, don't give him a moment to get control. Thought so, like all fancy guys he wanted to hold on to the ball, work it a bit, show off. Dunky came up, cold air rasping on his throat. As the inside-right swung back his right leg to cross he went in, left foot first, knees together, throwing himself at the ball, seeing only the ball.

The swinging boot caught him on the knee. The ball skidded a yard. Bobby Black cleared it. Dunky drew in a gasping breath and bit his lower lip. His knee was in agony. Teeth clenched, he went on swearing until the pain faded. Limp a couple of steps, nothing wrong with it, bite your lip, all right. That was deliberate, pretending he couldn't stop his kick. Well, he'd asked for it now, the dirty rat.

The next time the inside-right came running up with the ball Dunky went in from the side, right hip thumping into the guy's side. At that speed he had no chance. Up you go, fancy pants.

'You dirty bastard!' roared a man on the touchline, his face red with anger, shaking his right fist. Dunky ignored him. Spectators meant nothing. Fancy pants made a great show of standing up in pain, rubbing his back, stretching, agony on his face.

They fell back for the free-kick. The ball was scrambled away. Overend was shouting them on. Glenryan didn't look so hot now. Like all village teams they were stronger than they were skilful. You had to have years of playing in the streets, a tennis ball on cobbles with twenty a side, sometimes under the streetlights, a tin can if there wasn't a ball – that's what you needed. Village boys were never nippy enough.

Go in hard. Their outside-right with the ball, dribbling up the wing. Glenryan's supporters stepping back to give him room. Sammy Muir was out there with him, but Sammy wasn't so hot at tackling. Go out to the wing, cover Sammy. The outside-right coming past Sammy on the outside, pushing the ball forward with the outside of his right foot. Choose your moment, then go in hard. Get the ball or man, both if possible, either will do, a free-kick out here won't do any damage.

He took the outside-right and the ball and himself over the line, crashing through the spectators, putting up his hands to protect his face, falling. Men shouting at him, a face looking down, an angry face.

As he got up a bare-headed man kicked his leg.

'Take that ye wee pig!'

Dunky spat at the man's feet and trotted, not too quickly, back on to the pitch. The outside-right knelt to replace his shin-pad. No foul! The ref must be blind. Still, you took what you could get. From the throw-in he muscled in on their right-half and came away with the ball. You had to try and *feel* them coming at you from behind, keep running forward, make ground. About now.

He jumped as he ran and the boot that came from behind only scraped his ankles, not enough force to trip him. Pretending to make for the wing he pushed it inside to Sammy Muir, stroking it with the inside of his right foot.

Sammy to Joe McNenemy. Joe going across the field, small and left-footed, he'll have to turn back again to cross it, his right foot's only for standing on. Move up for the cross. Light not so good, difficult to see the ball against the mud and cinders. Watch Joe's body, that'll tell when it's coming. Joe's cross. Coming from the right, kicked with the left foot, ball curling in towards the goal. Don't chase in after it, enough forwards in there already. Hover on the edge of the box, move this way and that following the scramble. Here it comes, high ball. One of their guys going to jump. Go up with him, push yourself up, elbow out in his chest, go in hard. Full strength header, back into the goalmouth.

Glenryan's centre-half took a mighty swing at the dropping ball, trying to volley it a mile. He misconnected. The ball hit the outside of his ankle. Before their goalkeeper could move across to cover the deflection the ball had spun, quite gently, in a series of bounces, into their net, a full-back entangling himself in the rigging as he tried to rush back and hook it clear.

After that they seemed to play for only a few more minutes and then the whistle went. Ah well, a draw wasn't bad, Glenryan were a strong bunch on their own ground.

As they ran towards the dressing-hut the Glenryan supporters were waiting for them, in a small bunch, directly between him and the door of the hut. He kept up with the rest. They ran through the men, ignoring their shouts.

There was a bucket of cold water in the dressing-room. He wiped the worst of the mud off his torn knee, dipping one of his socks in the bucket. Baldy didn't say much till they were dressed and out of the hut again, having shaken hands with the Glenryan team, fouls seemingly forgotten.

Carrying his boots and socks, dirty strip and pants, shinguards and spare laces in his small brown case, Dunky walked with the team to the bus stop, listening to what Baldy was saying. Funny how much some guys talked about a game once it was over.

'You'll get your postcards about next Saturday during the week,' Baldy said as some of them left to get the bus to the Brig. It was almost dark now. Upstairs on the bus, Sammy Muir dragging on a fag like a grown man, Baldy sat next to Overend, the guys in the seat in front twisting round to speak to him, the same guys who always smarmed up to the big man. Dunky sat with wee Joe McNenemy. His knee was getting stiff. He'd have to scrub it with hot water and iodine or it might go septic. At Kilcaddie Cross Baldy at last spoke to him, just before he left to catch the scheme bus.

'No' a bad second half, Logan,' he said. 'We'll mibbe see about trying you out in the first team.'

'Oh great.'

Baldy looked at him, big face under the flat cap.

'Aye, just a bit more weight and you'd do fine.'

On the way down in the scheme bus he thought of all the balls he'd had during the match and how he could have done better. Christ, wouldn't it be great if Elsa Noble could come and see him playing for Cartneuk first eleven! That would impress her, dead right it would. Or maybe Baldy would mention him in the report he put into the paper. His father would have to read that. Then he might admit that he *could* play football . . .

'Get tore into these Victoria people,' said Baldy. He patted each player on the shoulder as they passed him and clattered down the tunnel. 'Don't let us down,' he shouted after them.

Bigtime! Running out of a proper dressing-room and down a wee tunnel and out into the sunshine. A real football stadium – only a junior ground, of course, but it looked bigtime, with the wee wall round the pitch and the folk standing on the little terracing. The first-team strip was the same as Hearts, maroon shirts with white collars and white pants, black stockings with white bands. All sorts of people were watching, Baldy had said. Scouts from big clubs. He'd told them how he'd been given this strip by Hearts when they took one of last year's first team on to the groundstaff. That was to make them feel bigtime. Baldy knew what he was doing, all right. It was guff but you wanted to believe it.

He and Sammy Muir were the only two from the second team. Sammy was a wee terror, smoked like a demon and yet could run like wildfire. He hardly knew the rest of the first team. Bigtime guys. He didn't run about too much in the kickabout, it was a hot day and they'd need all their wind for later on. This was his big chance. Keep the heid, that's what Joe Overend had said. Keep the heid. There was nobody in the crowd he knew. He trapped the ball and set it up for a cross. Have to impress them, show I'm good enough. Right foot. Not bad. Norrie Picken, their goalie, caught it and rolled it out to the forwards. He ran round to the corner of the penalty box, chewing hard, sleeves still rolled down to his wrists. Nice white cuffs. Made you feel neat and sharp. Like Willie Bauld, neat and deadly.

They lost the toss and changed ends, running through the oncoming Victoria team. The goalies shook hands, nobody else did. They looked a hard lot, sort of scruffy, too, they had Airdrie strips, white with the big red V down their chests. This way they'd face into the sun. In the second half it would be lower, better angle for dazzling them.

The ref looked round the two teams. People shouted. He watched the centre-forward's feet. The ref raised his whistle. Wait for it – the centre-forward had jumped the gun. The new ball, round and *lovely*, as bright as a Belisha beacon, was replaced on the spot. Then the whistle. God make me play a good game.

No wonder the first team hadn't lost since Christmas. They were fantastic. He hardly had any work to do. Victoria didn't have a hope. He took the ball off one of them easily, tackling the way you were taught, boot jammed in hard, knee over your boot, body over your knee, hit ball and man hard, bring it away, don't hold it too long, look for a man. Going up the left side of the field he saw Sammy and another of their forwards, but they were marked. A man came to tackle him. He cut in, switching to his right foot. Then he crossed it to the right wing. Had the scouts seen that? It went to their outside-right, McLatchie, all smooth and elusive. Nothing came of the cross. He fell back. Victoria must be *some* good or they wouldn't have reached the final. Most of the players had new laces on their boots, white on dark leather, the whole *thing* was neat and bright.

Victoria had a good inside-left, a very solid guy who could dribble like mad. Strong, too. After they'd seen two or three of his runs they began to tackle him in pairs, trying to crowd him off the ball.

In from the side, hook the ball away with the right foot. Missed! Going down on his left knee he curled his right leg round the guy's shins and hooked the feet from him. The ref shook his head when the Victoria guy raised his arms for a foul. Somebody else got the ball down field. The Victoria guy rubbed his knees.

'You try that again an' I'll kick yur face in,' he said.

'You and what army?'

'Jist watch it.'

Some guys thought they were very bigtime. Big mouths was more like it.

They scored the first from a corner, a header, easy as winky. While they all ran to clap their centre-forward on the back the Victoria defenders argued among themselves. Their goalie should have got it.

That made you feel great. You were going to murder them. He could hardly believe it when the next came, a couple of minutes later. It was the first real thing Sammy Muir had done, flicking the ball over the right-back's head, running round him, belting it from just inside the penalty box. When you saw it hitting the net you felt like screaming, as though a bright light had flashed in your head. They mobbed Sammy, hugging and kissing him. He wasn't nervous at all now. Then it was three, McLatchie dribbling right to the line and then cutting it back for Archie Kennedy to bang it in. Three up at half-time! Look at us, people! They ran into the wee tunnel, their studs clattering on concrete.

'No' bad, lads, you're doin' okay,' said Baldy.

He sat on the bench that ran round the room, his head resting on somebody's jacket, panting slightly.

'Score another three and show these people,' said Joe. 'They're a load of rubbish.'

Some guys shouted the odds and some combed their hair and some scratched their balls with both hands and some horsed about and some sat still and looked on. Baldy moved about, chatting quietly, a huge man in a pair of trousers that would've fitted an elephant. He made you feel you were somebody. You wanted him to speak to you, to give some sign he thought you were playing well. The lads said that if Cartneuk won the Scottish Cup Baldy would say 'No' bad, lads' and then tell you off for not scoring another ten goals. McLatchie had once scored four goals for the first team and all Baldy had said was, 'Pass it about more, lad, you're gettin' a bit selfish.' It made you want to laugh. Or to do the impossible and see what Baldy said then.

'Don't get carried away,' he said as they stood up to go out again. 'Ye havenae won till the final whistle, remember that.'

'What does he want, jam on it?' said somebody. They got a fair roar as they went out again.

This is what it would be like playing for Rangers, knowing you were in a *real* team, too good for anybody else, bigtime. He watched the inside-left. He thought he was a real hard man. Cheek of the rat, threatening *him*!

Up they came, Victoria must have had a real telling-off in their dressing-room. They looked angry. How about that then, he thought, as Jimmy Clark, their centre-half, shouldered the inside-left to the ground and cleared half the length of the pitch. He was near enough to hear the Victoria inside-left have a go at Jimmy.

'I'll do you,' he was saying.

Jimmy spat and sniffed.

So that's what he was, a rough guy? Right then, let's get tore into them.

He went for the inside-left's ankles the next time he was near him, tapping the right heel so that his toe went on the wrong side of his left foot, sending him flying face first.

The ref gave a foul for that, although he put on an innocent face and held up his hands as though he couldn't believe it. The other Victoria forwards seemed like weak nonentities, not worth bothering about. Jimmy Clark had the same idea as he had. They both got near the inside-left and when the foul was taken they rammed him in the back as the ball came down.

The ref didn't give a foul. He was weak!

Victoria were getting bad-tempered. Their backs began to take fly-kicks at people. Faces were pushed together and fists clenched. Great fun. Beat them hollow then finish them off.

One of them got Sammy Muir in a two-footed tackle. Sammy went down so heavily they thought he was really injured. Joe Overend came running on to the field with his dripping sponge, his jacket flying at his side.

'Fuck me,' said Sammy, lying on the grass, the rest of them looking down at him. 'Is ma ankle broke?'

'They're asking for what they get,' said Jimmy Clark. Joe gave Sammy a last rub and then walked back to the wee stand.

So they wanted a kicking match? Right. Let's get tore in properly. Next time he'd tramp on the bastard's hands. All the people who watched him thought he was a coward. They all remembered him being frightened of the horses, of Blackie McCann, of guys at the dancing, of Telfer. There was only one way to show them.

It was the only way to play. To hate the other team. To want to destroy them. Jimmy Clark tripped a guy when the ball was at the other end of the park. Two of their forwards charged the Victoria goalie so hard he was actually crying. Two Victoria guys sandwiched McLatchie, almost breaking his ribs. The ref was hopeless, he ponced about and hardly saw anything. The crowd was going mad, especially the Victoria supporters. They were well beaten so they had to shout about something.

He hated the bloody lot of them.

The inside-left started another of his runs, this time moving out into the shadow of the stand, a thick-necked guy he was, very sure of himself, a hard man, thought he was Torry Gillick or somebody.

He beat one man, then hit the ball down the wing and started after it, quite fast. There wasn't much point in tackling him, the idea was to fall back and let him come to you, but what the hell, they were three up, he could take a chance.

He started out for the ball, body leaning forward, sprinting as hard as he knew how. The inside-left had his speed up now, going to make a dash down the wing.

Hit him, go on, hit the bastard.

There was a blinding sickness in his face and head. Everything went black. His stomach tried to heave up. The pain in his face made him want to vomit. He saw things but didn't understand what they were. People had a hold of his arms. He tried to say something, but they were miles away. He heaved up again. Shocks of agony went through his head. He couldn't hear what the voices were shouting. It was a dream. A dream . . .

He woke up in a bed and thought for a moment it was still Saturday morning. A white bed, white blankets? Not at home. A big window. Where was he?

Then Joe Overend and his mother were coming towards him. They were looking at his face. He put up his hands. There was a bandage over half of his face. The game!

'How're ye feelin', Dunky?' Joe asked.

His mother looked as though she'd been crying.

'What happened?'

As he spoke he felt his mouth funny. His tongue was thick and sore. He ran it tenderly along his teeth. At the front he could only feel soft stuff. His mother leaned over him. Looking away from her he saw other men in white beds.

'Your nose is broken and you've lost two front teeth, oh Dunky, thank God you're all right.'

'What happened?'

Joe patted his mother's back.

'You'll be all right, son,' he said. 'You should see the other guy. Huh, he'll no' be out of plaster for months.'

He couldn't believe it at first. He didn't remember a thing about it. Joe said he'd charged the inside-left like a tank and sent him flying on to the wee wall, breaking his arm and two fingers. He must have broken his nose when he hit the guy, Joe said. Before anybody could get near enough one of the other Victoria guys had run up and booted him in the face, knocking out his front teeth. They'd run him to the Ayr hospital in Joe's van and then fetched his mother.

'The ref says he was sendin' you off anyway,' said Joe. 'You and the geezer that kickt you. Och, don't bother your head aboot it. Dunky, we'll claim proveycation, he was threatenin' quite a few o' the lads.'

'Did we win?'

'Of course we did. We are the people, eh?'

They X-rayed him and found nothing worse and his mother came to collect him later that night. They got a bus from Ayr to Kilcaddie, folk looking at his bandaged face, his mother acting as if he'd broken his skull.

'I'm all right,' he kept telling her.

When they got home he was still feeling chirpy, but suddenly he had another attack of vomiting and she put him to bed.

'I'll be all right, I'll be at my work on Monday no bother,' he said.

At least it had saved him from having to decide what to do with himself. A great way to spend a Saturday night.

But it was his own fault, he knew that. He'd behaved like an animal and he'd got what he deserved. The big day all ruined, just because of sheer animalistic hate. He'd wear false teeth for the rest of his life, serve him right. And what about the other guy? Maybe his arm wouldn't set properly, or his fingers. What kind of job did he have? Christ, he'd behaved no better than a criminal. His father had always been right, he *was* unnatural.

No, that was soft, to think like that. The other guy had asked for all he got. Bad luck, that's all it was. Or bad timing. He should've been more clever. If you were going to put the mockers on another player you had to do it the canny way. Learn to get away with murder, that was the motto. He'd been carried away. It was a lesson learned. Know better the next time.

Thinking about the next time made his stomach rise. The same sickening shock echoed through his brain, the breath-catching, heart-constricting shock you always got from a bang on the nose. He lay completely still, hands holding the blanket, eyes closed, trying to hold it down.

from *From Scenes Like These*, 1968

Pretty Bubbles
SEBASTIAN FAULKS

The team bus was winding through the plantations of Sri Lanka in 1981. We were on a cricket tour and one of the party was David Lacey, the *Guardian*'s football correspondent. Lacey is one of those people who lack the capacity to forget. His knowledge of films was more encyclopaedic than that of either of the two professional film buffs on the trip, and when it came to football we used to cluster round him at the end of the coach to listen, like boys at a fruit machine.

'Okay, David,' I said. 'Name all eleven players in the West Ham team that won the FA Cup in 1964.'

'You'll have to give me a minute,' said Lacey, and closed his eyes in the tight concentration that preceded these spectacular feats. We watched the beautiful hills slide away beneath us and felt the coach swerve to avoid another bullock cart.

'Right,' said Lacey, and opened his eyes. 'Standen, Bovingdon, Birkett, Moore, Bond, Boyce, Peters, Brabrook, Byrne, Hurst, Sissons.'

Blimey. Even I sometimes had trouble remembering Bovingdon, and West Ham were my team. They had become so in that year, 1964, when I was eleven. Before that I had vaguely supported Spurs, because they were good, but not with the passion of ownership. So in the quarter-finals of the Cup I had decided that I was going to pick a team. West Ham seemed the right choice. No one else at school supported them; they were in the First Division, but near the bottom and thus in need of my support; and they were in the running for the Cup. I didn't know where West Ham was (Reading was our closest league team) and I had no idea that they had a reputation for classy, attacking football. I was lucky in my choice. One of my equally ignorant contemporaries picked Arsenal.

Three great years: the FA Cup in 1964; the Cup Winners' Cup in 1965; and in 1966 England won the World Cup, with, as everyone knows, Moore, Hurst and Peters. I felt I couldn't have picked a better team, even though we never did much in the league. When we played well, no one could touch us.

I didn't see West Ham in the flesh until 1967 when I went with a schoolfriend who was a Chelsea supporter. I stood next to a man with a cap who kept on shouting 'Come on, you Irons.' I didn't know what he was talking about, and it has always struck me as odd that an East End team should have a nickname which in cockney rhyming slang (iron hoof/poof) should lay them open to mockery, especially with such a shaky defence. There were plenty of exciting players on display that day. Hurst, Sissons and Peters for West Ham; Charlie Cooke, Tambling and Osgood for Chelsea. Yet it was to none of these that the eye was drawn, but to a defender: Bobby Moore. Much has been written about his style, but it was truly extraordinary. His anticipation was such that he seemed to be in a position to intercept a pass before the player on the other side had even decided to unload. He always gathered the ball moving forwards, so that at least three opposing players were wrong-footed and immediately had to go into reverse. Sometimes Moore would then step over the ball and turn the first challenger before releasing a 30–yard pass into the path of the winger; sometimes he would hit the ball flat and hard up to Ron Boyce ('Ticker' to the faithful) who would busy around the centre circle with it for a while before moving it on to Hurst or Peters.

Waves of applause rolled down towards Moore from the loving West Ham fans; every move he made was stamped with authority, every gesture made you certain he was the world's master of defence. Sometimes he could be almost too domineering; midfield players would lay the ball back to him when they might have taken it on. When he made the fatal mistake against Poland in the qualifying match for the 1974 World Cup, it was unbearable. The casual way he dragged the ball back inside to turn the tackler was a copy of the movement he had been successfully completing every Saturday for fifteen years. It was as if Denis Compton had been out at a crucial moment in a Test match to the sweep he had himself perfected. In my view that one error did nothing to tarnish Moore's career. On the contrary, by showing that he was human, like any other player, it made the riveting and masterful performances of his pomp seem all the more remarkable.

Even the Arsenal crowd was charmed. My first trip to Highbury came the following year. The ground made Upton Park look a bit down-market, to be honest. Arsenal had this greenhouse affair by the tunnel, the stadium was huge and, to a bright-eyed schoolboy, the red of their new shirts was dazzling. The Hammers looked all right, though. They played the better football, but their forwards kept getting chopped down by Simpson and Storey in the Arsenal defence. Even my Arsenal friend grimaced in embarrassment when Simpson was cautioned for another knee-high swing at West Ham's number 9.

This was a slow, gangling centre forward of about nineteen who had been brought in to replace Johnny Byrne. His name was Trevor Brooking and he had been in and out of the team for a couple of seasons. My reaction was 'Forget it.' Byrne was a real old centre forward with greased-back hair; he didn't play with a fag in the corner of his mouth, but it seemed implied. This youth Brooking was one-paced, kept falling over and didn't use his height in the air. 'Lovely build, that Brooking,' said the man next to me. 'That's about all,' I piped back bravely.

Time, Ron Greenwood and a hidden talent proved me wrong. Brooking became, with Keegan and Shilton, the light of his generation. Between the end of the Charlton era and the start of the Robson–Lineker age, these three were the only thing that made England worth watching. Yet Ron Greenwood's first move on being appointed England manager was to drop his old protégé. He brought in Ray Kennedy, a converted striker whose idea of creative midfield play was to gather the ball, then very slowly pass it to the opposition. Throughout his England career Brooking was accorded his place only grudgingly. If the manager could find a plodder – a Trevor Cherry, a Ray Kennedy, someone who was supposed to have a higher work rate – then Brooking would be dumped. Kennedy finally declared in a huff that he had not been picked often enough by England and didn't wish to be considered again. That he should have been capped at all is one of the more remarkable aspects of English football history.

Brooking and Keegan grew old, but they did not lose their edge. I remember watching them against Italy at Wembley in 1977. Brooking chipped the laziest of near-post goals, so top-spun, so languid, it barely had the strength to make it. But up rose Keegan, a foot above his taller markers, and headed through the only 6 inches of air space not covered by Zoff into the top right-hand corner of the net. In the second half the roles were reversed. Keegan slipped his marker with a scurrying, muscular turn; Brooking, as usual, conjured space, and slid the ball home, lazily, falling backwards. I remember his FA Cup-winning goal – a rare header from a mis-hit Stuart Pearson shot – and most clearly of all the goal he himself rates as his best. It was in the Nep Stadium against Hungary: he cut in (if that's not too active a word for Brooking) from the right wing, looked up and uncurled a 35-yard swinging left-footer that lodged with a crunching finality between the far upright and the stanchion. We were impressed, particularly those of us who find it difficult to get the ball airborne at all with the wrong foot. Brooking remarked in his autobiography that he assumed when young that a professional must be equally good with both feet, so he just practised until he was.

In the 1982 World Cup Finals both Keegan and Brooking had been injured, but were fit enough to be considered for the crucial game against Spain, which England needed to win by two clear goals. Neither was selected. Greenwood preferred Tony Woodcock to Keegan and Graham Rix (Rix!) to Brooking. For seventy minutes England panted and sweated, but no one looked likely to score a goal. With twenty minutes to go, Greenwood brought on Keegan and Brooking. Keegan missed a chance he would have taken if he had been warmed up. My recollection is that Brooking was in possession about eight times. He lost the ball twice in the tackle. Twice he passed it square or just disposed of it. Twice he opened the defence to create respectively England's best and second-best scoring chances of the match. And once he went clean through to see his shot ricochet off the goalkeeper's outstretched body. It was the team's closest effort. If he could do that in twenty minutes, you wondered what he might have done in the course of the match. What successive managers could never swallow was the first statistic – twice losing the ball in the tackle – which, to be fair, was not untypical. Always keeping possession in the tackle is pointless if you cannot then do something with the ball – a fact no England manager, not even Greenwood, has ever really accepted.

Brooking was the most beguiling and most skilful player West Ham have produced in my time. His famous dummy, his ability to lose a man by shrugging his shoulders and shifting his weight, were made more remarkable by the fact that – lovely build apart – there was something essentially quite ungainly about him. But what made his game so ravishing to watch was his ability to make other players look ordinary, or even stupid. This he did with his passing. It might be with one of his characteristic near-post balls, when the big guns were gathered at the other side, but most exquisitely it was with the pass placed casually into no-man's-land. Crowd and defenders would look on for a moment in disbelief. Then suddenly it would dawn. The ball was not rolling into no-man's-land at all, but on to the one diagonal that would take the accelerating striker clean through the previously unbreachable defence.

The West Ham crowd was spoiled by this kind of thing for years. They loved him for it and they applauded every time, but they took it as their due. Such talents, however, as the present West Ham team sadly demonstrates, come only once in a lifetime. I went to Upton Park for Trevor Brooking's final game. It was against Everton whose then newish goalkeeper, Neville Southall, allowed them an improbable 1–0 victory. It didn't spoil the occasion, however. Brooking was called back for a lap of honour after the game, and the crowd gave him as fine a tribute as any man could ask for. In that ten or fifteen minutes of cheering and applause I think they registered their gratitude for the joy he'd brought them over so many winter Saturdays. I have not had the heart to go back to Upton Park since.

from Harry Lansdown and Alex Spillius (eds.),
Saturday's Boys, 1990

A Present for the Wife: Tottenham in France
HUNTER DAVIES

We had to be at London Airport at two o'clock on the Tuesday to board a BEA charter plane for Nantes in France. As we were checking in, a TV crew were standing waiting, their lights at the ready. 'Must be waiting for Martin,' said someone and the others agreed. But when Martin appeared, the one and only Martin of the moment, the cameramen weren't at all interested.

The Spurs party consisted of thirty-five people. There were sixteen players, eight directors and officials, ten journalists and Mr Broderick of Cook's who'd arranged the trip.

It was a normal-sized party for a British football team going into Europe. The cost of the plane was about £1,500. Spurs usually hire their own plane when they play abroad as it's more convenient, letting the Press for once join the inner sanctum. But no fans are allowed on the team plane.

Mr Broderick spends his whole life organizing football trips, for clubs like Spurs, Chelsea and others, plus the England team. He'd recently taken the England party to Switzerland. He prefers going with the England team, though not for snob reasons. 'With the England team, there's a nice atmosphere because it's mainly old friends meeting each other again. With a club, they see each other every day of the week.'

At Nantes airport, there were photographers and a TV crew waiting to meet the Spurs team as they climbed out of the plane. Greetings were exchanged with the Nantes officials who said there would be a reception next day, Wednesday, for the Spurs directors and the Press. Bill Nicholson thanked them but said he was more interested in visiting the stadium. It was agreed he could see it at eleven the next day.

The local Press went straight for Chivers, running after him and shouting Mee-ster Chee-vers. They got him to pose with a toy pistol, pretending to shoot. His legend had preceded him, even to Nantes, wherever Nantes was. None of the players had the slightest idea, or were even interested.

We went by coach to the Central Hotel in Nantes, a modest, medium-sized hotel, nothing like as posh as most of the English hotels Spurs use. Bill Nicholson had chosen it personally, vetting the rooms and meals. He'd come over on a quick trip the week before, mainly to scout on the Nantes team. As usual, he'd left nothing to chance, but he'd been even more meticulous this time, as it was Europe.

Playing in Europe is both an end and a beginning for the top British clubs. It's in their minds all season, knowing that if they finish high enough in the English League, they will end up qualifying for one of the three European competitions the following season.

Spurs were now in the second round of what's called the UEFA Cup – the Union of European Football Associations Cup. Each round is played on a home and away basis, with the winner on aggregate of the two matches going into the next round.

Sixty-four teams had started off from every footballing country in Europe back in September and several famous ones had already been knocked out, such as Leeds United and Atletico Madrid, though traditionally the first round is looked upon as a walk-over for the big clubs. It had been for Spurs, playing the Icelandic amateurs. But now it was serious. Having a good run in Europe can keep a club going for nine months, a whole season in fact. It keeps the players on their toes, the fans happy and brings in money to the club.

They knew they would have a hard struggle with Nantes. They had twice won the French League in recent years so they'd had good experience of European football (Celtic had knocked them out of the European Cup in 1966). Although French football journalism is of a high, nay, intense level, French football is not as well supported as English. Nantes' average gate is considered very good for France, 18,000, only half that of Spurs.

The Spurs directors were making no bones about what a pleasure it was to be in Europe again, but many of the players were coming on strong about it being a drag. The ones who'd played in France before were telling the others there was no chance of any talent after the match. The French didn't like the English. Their girls wouldn't even dance with you, unless you paid them a fortune. Now Germany, you always had a good time in Germany.

We checked in quickly at the hotel and the players went into their own dining-room for a light tea while the Press and directors went into the main dining-room.

As they waited for their meal, the players were all comparing their rooms. 'How's your TV? Only one of mine's got colour. Got a bar? We've got a bar. Cyril's got a swimming-pool in his room.' They were complaining, in their usual inverted fashion, about the hotel. They all thought it was pretty crummy with no facilities. It wasn't luxury by any means, but very French with a kind staff and a friendly atmosphere. The players ordered toast and tea and had hysterics when the toast arrived wrapped in plastic, like babies' rusks. They tried to butter it and immediately it disintegrated into crumbs. But there was strawberry jam which they loved.

After tea most players put their heads out of the front door. It was raining and dark. Several had wanted a walk but when they saw the rain, they went back to the foyer, sat chatting or played cards. The regular card players, Joe, Gilly, Mike and Cyril, had got down to it the minute tea was over without looking at the weather.

Phil, Roger, Jimmy Neighbour and myself decided to chance it and we made a dash between showers. We got 50 yards from the hotel and took shelter in a souvenir shop. Phil picked up a pair of moccasins and indicated that he wanted a larger size. The assistant nodded and went to get bigger ones. Phil spread his arms about 2 feet wide and she nodded, though beginning to think she'd got the order wrong, or was serving a madman. Phil put one finger up and said One, he only wanted one, then left the shop.

Roger picked up a paper knife and was pretending he was going to throw it at the wall. The lady took it from him and held it in front of her chest, defending herself, convinced they were madmen, trying to push Roger out of the shop.

Roger came out at last, laughing. 'She said Sootie, Sootie. What does that mean?'

Dinner for the players was at seven thirty, served in the same dining-room. Bill spent at least an hour going through the menu, standing in the middle of the room and reading it out, getting them to choose by a show of hands what they wanted. Not just for the meal they were about to have, but for the next day's meals as well. It was a job Johnny Wallis could have done, or Mullery, or the head waiter, or anyone.

The choice of main course was veal or steak. At the table I was at, Phil and Roger and Jimmy had steak but left almost all of it. It arrived with a little daub of garlic butter on the top and they tore at it furiously, swearing, and wiped all marks of it from their steak. They all said they hated garlic. Phil even washed his hands on his napkin, pouring water on them from a jug, in case he'd been contaminated. I ordered beer but the players couldn't. The hotel staff had been given instructions that no player could have beer or alcohol of any kind, at the table or in his room, not till the match was over.

Bill, his orders finally completed, went to eat with the directors in the main dining-room. When he'd gone, the bread pellets started flying and then the grapes, but nothing out of hand and no clothes or tables were ruined. The waiters were amused, when they weren't pointing out to each other which one was Cheevers.

Throughout the entire meal, all four courses of it, the card school played cards non-stop, dealing on the table over the vegetable soup, trout meunière, the steak and the fruit salad, all of which was delicious, much better than any English hotel food, that's if you don't mind garlic.

As we left the dining-room, Roger saw a notice above the door which said 'Sortie' and asked what it meant. I said exit. 'That's it. Sootie. That's what she said.'

After dinner, they all sat around in the hall, the card players still hard at it. The Press decided they'd go out and see the town, plus me, and Mr Broderick, the Cook's man. We all discussed our plans loudly, about the night-clubs we were going to, knowing the players were confined to barracks.

As we went out the front door, Eddie Baily and Johnny Wallis were standing there, four square and resolute. They were on guard to make sure that no players sneaked out with us.

Next day the morning paper, *Nantes Océan* had a picture of me on their front page, coming down the ladder from the plane. Beside me were David Miller from the *Telegraph*, Colin Malam of the *Sun*, Steve Curry of the *Express* and Nigel Clarke of the *Mirror*. The caption underneath said 'The stars of the celebrated Tottenham team arriving at Nantes airport yesterday.' That kept the team in jokes all day.

At eleven o'clock, I went with the players for a brief visit to the stadium, then they went back to the hotel to put in the time till lunch, going through their usual monastic rituals, no fun and no alcohol, simply playing cards or taking an occasional walk round the block, hour after boring hour.

Meanwhile, I went with the Press and the Spurs directors to a slap-up reception at a hotel 10 kilometres out of Nantes, given by the Nantes Football Club. We had lots of wine, a three-hour lunch and several speeches. The big lads from the Paris Press had now arrived, wheeled out for the match, to show the local lads how to write correct captions. They knew the names of every Spurs player. All of them seemed to be from *L'Equipe*.

Back in Nantes, I went shopping in the afternoon with a couple of directors. We went to a superb cheese shop, taken by a Nantes director. Mr Groves, the bachelor, bought six. Then he bought six bottles of Muscatel. Back at the hotel, you could tell the players from the directors. One lot had bought souvenir dolls and the other carried wine bottles and smelled very strongly of cheese.

While the Press and the directors had been enjoying themselves hugely all day, lapping up the entertainment which the players' success had brought them, the players themselves had still been hanging about the hotel. They were obviously feeling the strain of waiting. They'd just finished a one and a half hour team talk from Bill. He'd gone through every Nantes player in detail. They couldn't wait for the match. They were all fed-up and bored rigid with waiting.

We left the hotel by coach at seven fifteen. By now the hotel was full of Spurs supporters – seventy of whom had just arrived. Suddenly the foyer had become crowded with middle-aged Englishmen in their best Sunday suits and supporters' club ties, wandering round wearing blue and white rosettes and ogling the players.

The streets to the stadium were crowded but the bus got through fairly easily. Along the final stretch were rows and rows of stalls selling nougat, hot dogs, sweets and drinks, ham rolls and other delicacies. Unlike a British ground before a match, nobody seemed to be selling rosettes, scarves, badges or other football souvenirs. Food and drink seemed to be the only line for all the street traders. The crowds too appeared different, older and better behaved, a lot of them wearing tartan berries. There were no gangs of young hooligans trying to assert themselves or looking for fights. But inside the stadium, they made just as much noise if not more than a British crowd. When the songs started, the whole crowd joined in. At Tottenham, it's just the Park Lane end who sing the songs. The French crowd communally sing, the way they do at Welsh Rugby Union matches.

The dressing-room, like the stadium, was spartan and seemed to be made entirely of concrete. On the benches round the dressing-room was a new bar of soap and a new blue towel for each player to use, still in their wrapping papers. Most of the players pocketed the soap in its wrapper. 'Another free present for the wife.'

Peter Collins, who was suffering from diarrhoea, was given some pills by the Spurs doctor and told not to eat anything for twenty-four hours. Then, along with the directors, the doctor discreetly withdrew, leaving the manager and the players to get on with their rituals.

A French official opened the dressing-room door and looked in and Philip Beal shouted at him. Philip beckoned with his hand, wiping his bottom and saying in English that there was no lavatory paper. Everyone laughed, thinking it was another Philip Beal joke. A few minutes later the official reappeared with a packet of paper and everyone cheered as he threw it across the room to Philip.

'Well played,' said Roger Morgan. That was his catch phrase of the moment. He'd said it to every waiter in the hotel since we'd arrived in Nantes.

'It's good to have one joker in the team,' said Eddie Baily heavily and sarcastically. 'A joker always helps.' He was busily massaging Steve Perryman's thighs with warm oil.

'Is that why you bought Roger,' someone shouted. Everyone was looking at Roger, to see how he reacted. They were no doubt thinking of an article in the previous week's *People* in which Roger Morgan had been described as one of Bill Nicholson's expensive mistakes. Roger must have been very hurt. It hadn't been his fault that he'd been injured and not played in the first team for a year.

Roger made a face, his head bowed, pretending to be hurt and embarrassed, but laughing, putting it on, not at all worried by the joke at his expense. Roger is one player who'd be very difficult to humiliate by sarcasm. Not because he's thick-skinned, or even conceited, but because he takes it all as a joke anyway. He'll try hard, but not playing for the first team is not the end of the world to Roger.

Underneath the table was a brown cardboard box. Bill Nicholson picked it up, put it on the table and opened it, saying there was a present inside for everyone.

'They asked me for a list of things you'd like, but I don't know which one they chose,' explained Bill. 'If it had been me, I'd have given you a comb and a pair of scissors each.'

The players ignored the joke, having heard it a hundred times before, and rushed forward to get their presents. They'd been individually wrapped in green paper and tied with a bow, just like a Christmas present. Roger was first to tear his open so they all watched, deciding to keep theirs nicely wrapped up. Another free present for the wife. Inside was a black present box containing a Waterman's propelling pencil. 'Great,' said Roger. 'The box on its own will do as a present.'

'Made in Hong Kong, mine says,' said someone, pretending to read the label.

'Nantes,' said Mullery.

'Nantes-sense,' said Chivers, walking across the room to the shower, repeating his joke on the way, but still nobody got it.

An official appeared and told Bill that the teams were to come out five minutes before the kick-off. The match was to begin at eight thirty. It was now ten past eight. The room was getting quieter. The time for jokes was over, if you could call them jokes. It had been self-conscious noise and chatter, an outlet for their nerves.

Joe Kinnear was doing exercises on his own in a corner. Outside, inspecting the pitch, he'd been shivering. An evening chill had descended, but he was obviously nervous.

Martin Peters asked Bill if he knew the referee. Bill said he was an East German but he'd forgotten the name, which was unlike Bill Nicholson. Martin thought he might be the same East German ref they'd had in the World Cup. Bill said he didn't think so.

None of the players had programmes. In an English dressing-room, the players are always amply supplied with free programmes. I had got one at the hotel from a French journalist. It was a simple four-page, folded-over programme, full of adverts. Leslie Yates, a freelance journalist who writes the Spurs programmes, had come specially to Nantes so that his sixteen-page Spurs programme would be full of information about the Nantes players and club. I handed the Nantes programme to Bill. No, it wasn't a ref he knew.

Martin Peters went into the shower room with a ball and started banging it back and forward against the walls. Eddie Baily moved on from Perryman's thighs to rubbing Gilzean's chest. Johnny Wallis was strapping up ankles. Mike England was putting a new strip of elasto-plast on a cut on his forehead. Phil Beal and Mullery were rubbing vaseline on their faces – to stop the sweat going into their eyes during the match. Bill Nicholson went out of the room again. He told Eddie to lock it and let no one in. He'd knock three times to get back. The room was hot and fetid with embrocation. It was more of a crowded concrete cavern than a dressing-room, with no direct light and no ventilation, just a couple of small holes in one corner of the ceiling.

Bill came back, almost bursting the door down in his rage, swearing and cursing. 'They've changed their bloody strip. They told me last week they'd play in yellow. They always play in yellow. That's why they're called the bloody canaries.'

The players tried to look equally concerned and serious. A few joined in the curses, pleased to have something to vent their anger on, an outside body they could all have a go at. Mullery asked why they'd changed their minds.

'For the bloody French TV,' said Nicholson. 'The TV want them to play in green.'

Everyone groaned even louder this time, all cursing TV, saying you should never do anything for those TV cunts. I couldn't see what all the fuss was about. As Spurs were going to play in white, their normal colour, it could make no difference if Nantes played in green as opposed to their normal yellow.

'Have you brought any others,' said Nicholson to Johnny Wallis. 'Pat will have to get changed.'

Pat was out at the lavatory. I'd forgotten he always plays in a green jumper. Someone shouted down the corridor for him. When he came back, he was already wearing green. He looked annoyed, when he heard what had happened. Roger handed him a red shirt, to try it on, but Pat said it was OK. He went to his corner and searched around till he found a yellow shirt. He said that would do. Bill went to wash his hands.

Everyone calmed down again, the curses dying out as the talking stopped once again and only the stamping of boots could be heard and the stretching of arms and legs in last-minute exercises. Eddie Baily called out the time – fifteen minutes to go. There was a knock at the door and the referee came in, very quickly, catching everyone by surprise. He tapped Pat on the shoulder and pointed to his boots. Pat turned them over to be inspected. He moved on as Pat was holding up his boots, going round the room so quickly that he hardly seemed to look at more than one pair of boots. Bill tried to grab him as he came round the room and was going out of the door.

'They've changed their shirts,' began Bill. 'It means our goalie is now in yellow, will that be . . .'

But the ref had gone, pushing straight past Nicholson, ignoring him. Bill made a face when he'd gone. The players whistled. 'Not much of an inspection that,' said someone.

'East German, eh? said Eddie. 'I wonder if he was a POW in the . . .' But he tailed off in mid-sentence, unable to think of a suitable insult.

Bill went to the middle of the room and began addressing his players. They sat silently, each of them taut and gleaming, ready for action. Bill had his head bowed and was moving his hands and arms nervously, walking back and forwards, talking loudly and urgently. There was a feeling of embarrassment, as if the players felt worried on his behalf. They were already completely keyed up. Their minds were on the match. There was only three minutes to go. Nothing he could say now could make much difference, not at this late stage.

'The last time we played in France,' began Bill, 'I know you all remember it. You know what happened. I don't have to go over it. We thought we'd have it easy. But we didn't, did we? I don't want a repeat of that. I want you to go hard, but keep your feet down. Even one foot off the ground and you'll be for it. Don't give that referee any excuses.'

The last time in France had been four years ago at Lyons. Olympique Lyonnais had beaten Spurs 1–0 and went on to knock them out of Europe. That was the night that Mullery was sent off, a night not to remember.

Bill went over a few more points, then finished suddenly. It was as if all he'd been doing was nervously clearing his throat, thinking aloud. His mind was seething with details but he knew that it was too late. He stood in silence, the players watching.

'Now no arguing with the ref either,' said Mullery, taking over the silence, becoming keen and captain-like, clapping his hands, moving forward so everyone could see him. 'We've got to go very hard for the first ten minutes. Don't let them get settled. *Hard* all the time. OK lads.'

They were sitting with their heads bowed. A couple of the reserves exchanged looks as Mullery spoke, quickly, and then looked away. All five reserves were in bulky blue canvas track suits – Roger Morgan, Collins, Daines, Ray Evans and John Pratt. They looked like convicts in a work party.

'One minute to go,' said Eddie Baily. Nobody spoke. It was now like a death cell. As if they were all going out to an execution.

'If you beat this lot,' said Eddie, 'you'll be in the last sixteen. Then after that you'll be in the last sixty-four.'

He was trying to reduce the tension, but as always they were ignoring Eddie's jokes.

'Right, bayonets on,' shouted Eddie as a whistle went in the corridor. 'Over the top. Let's have you!'

They all stood up, stamping their feet. Bill had been busily tidying up the already tidy room as Eddie had been joking. He suddenly beamed and looked expansive and benevolent. As usual, he patted them on the back and wished each one by name the best of luck.

Then he went to the shower room where he washed his hands yet again and put on his jacket. He helped Eddie to lock the dressing-room door and then followed the players into the tunnel where they were waiting, lined up, just below the entrance. There was a roar as both teams went out together and a blaze of fireworks lit up the night sky.

The trainers' bench reserved for the Spurs team was just to the left of the centre stand, three wooden forms which we all crowded on to. Just a couple of yards behind us, well within spitting distance, was the crowd, separated by a 6-foot-high wire fence. The crowd were in good temper and gave Bill, Eddie and the Spurs substitutes a cheer as they sat down.

'Get out there,' said Bill, turning to his reserves. 'Get the feel of the turf.' They were a bit embarrassed, not wanting to draw attention to themselves in their baggy blue track suits, only being reserves, but they went out reluctantly to join the first team in white for the pre-match kick around, then they returned hurriedly and sat down. The crowd gave them a derisive cheer. They were screaming in our ears, trying to get us to turn round, shoving beer and bread through the wires, but nobody did. 'Bloody frogs,' said Eddie Baily.

The ball was wet and greasy and from the beginning the Spurs forwards seemed unable to control it. When they tried to collect the ball it bounced off their legs to a Nantes player. When they did get a passing move going, it ended with someone hitting it too far in front. Chivers at last collected a ball well but was robbed before he was ready and gave up without chasing the man who'd robbed him. Eddie screamed abuse. Bill hung his head.

The Nantes team came tearing through the middle right from the beginning, very confident on the ball and in their running. They were doing immaculate wall passes, scattering the Spurs midfield before them, and the crowd was roaring and cheering. For the first half hour, they had it almost all their own way, apart from a couple of isolated raids by Spurs. Even high balls up the middle to the tall Spurs strikers were getting nowhere. Chivers and Gilzean were having no luck. Only Jimmy Neighbour looked dangerous, beating their full back easily and tearing up the wing, but his centres were not finding their men and he was soon starting to take on one man too many and losing the ball. But he alone looked sharp and on form.

My ears were numb well before half-time. Eddie kept up a continuous stream of abuse, cursing every Spurs mistake when they lost the ball and then screaming orders when the Nantes forwards started thundering towards the Spurs penalty area.

He screamed at Steve to mark number 8, or Gilly to come back, or Jimmy to run wide. He was working himself into a frenzy, yet none of them could hear him. Only when a Spurs player was running down our side of the pitch, right beside us, could his voice he heard. He yelled at Phil Beal, but Phil deliberately ignored him. He yelled at Mullery to urge the team on. Mullery shouted back that he was fucking doing it.

Bill was shouting as well, yelling at Chivers to get moving, but mostly his shouts were sudden blurted-out oaths of panic and fury, burying his face in his hands as once more the Spurs forwards failed to get anywhere. Eddie literally never stopped. His instructions were really a running commentary, shouting out what people should be doing even when he knew they were miles away, hoping by osmosis he might get through to them. Sometimes he just shouted out names, over and over again, screaming at the top of his voice. Sometimes it was sheer gibberish. He jumped on the bench once, putting his knees up in the air, his signal for Chivers to get running, hoping he might be seen by Chivers if not heard. The crowd behind furiously booed and jeered, thinking he wanted Chivers to get the boot in. This wasn't true. Not once did either of them exhort any player to rough stuff. They were concerned with their players getting rid of the ball quickly and intelligently, avoiding bodily contact if anything. When a foul was given against Spurs they were furious with their own players for having got into such a position, though it didn't stop them from cursing the ref whenever he seemed to be favouring the opposition.

When it was one of Spurs' three big stars at fault, Eddie was all the more abusive. 'Bloody internationals,' Eddie was screaming. 'Look at them. Play for England but they won't play for us. GET MOVING! DON'T BLOODY STAND THERE! Useless. Too much publicity. It's gone to his head. He won't try any more.'

Half-time came suddenly, in the middle of a stream of Eddie's curses. We followed the players slowly to the dressing-room, letting them get settled. They sat quietly, not looking at each other. Johnny Wallis got some bottles out of a crate which had been left for the Spurs players. It was all Vichy water. There was no tea, which was what the players wanted. They were too limp to be furious. They stared into space, avoiding each other's eyes, hanging their heads, exhausted on their benches.

Bill stood silently for a bit, his face red and contorted, controlling himself as much as possible.

'You're not getting in. You've got to get in first. You're just letting them do those wall passes.'

He went round the defenders individually. He told Mike England and Phil Beal to keep up their covering and to watch numbers 7 and 10 breaking through from behind. He said nothing to the forwards. He was furious with them and they knew it. They were furious with themselves, dejected and utterly miserable. Slowly they all started to stand up, looking round, bemused, asking for a drink, looking for some stimulus, some diversion, anything to avoid Bill.

'It's just Fishy water,' said Eddie. 'And there's no bloody glasses either.' I went down the corridor and got some glass coffee cups which was all I could find.

'We don't want any mistakes at the back,' Bill was saying when I returned. 'No silly goals.'

The second half was much the same. Nantes had most of the ball and were still as quick and inventive as ever, especially in midfield. Spurs were sluggish and had no inspiration up front, but the defence was still managing each time to break down the Nantes attack on the edge of the penalty area.

Everyone on the Spurs bench knew that the Spurs forwards were playing badly. It was one of those away games where they seem to hide, to go numb, to stop thinking at the vital moments. Jimmy Neighbour was still trying hard, but Chivers was showing little of his skills. Admittedly he was getting few good balls from his harassed midfield men and not once did the ball bounce his way, but all the same, he made not one chance for himself. You could sense the team praying for him to turn a half chance into a goal by sheer brilliance and bring himself and the whole team to life.

Gilly was showing a lot of heart, but was getting nowhere. Fifteen minutes before the end, he was brought off and Roger Morgan was sent on, his first appearance in the first team since he'd been injured exactly a year ago. It seemed a rather desperate measure considering he was a long way from being back to first-team form, but Bill was obviously hoping for some miracle.

'Do it for us, Roger,' exhorted Eddie, pushing him on.

The reserves stood up to make room for Gilly on the bench. Someone gave him Roger's track suit and helped him to put it on. He sat at the end of the bench, his face shattered with effort, sweat streaming from every pore. Around his head was a halo of steam. He was like a defeated racehorse, frothing and steaming from being pushed almost beyond endurance.

Roger had no chance to show what he could do, though he made one good cross, which was what Bill had told him to do.

Eddie kept up his screams. The crowd behind were now getting angry with him. They'd started by laughing, then had taunted him and now they were furious. They were convinced that he was egging his players on to foul. When Chivers got his name taken, just before the end, Eddie had tomatoes thrown at him from behind.

It was a goal-less draw. Spurs could have scored, when Jimmy had a chance towards the end, but it would have been unfair if Nantes had been beaten. They had played well and had the majority of the play. They'd been well drilled, had run well and intelligently, and their defence had successfully blotted Chivers out of the game. They'd shown none of the inferiority complex about Chivers the local Press had led us to believe.

In the dressing-room the players were a mixture of anger, sadness and disappointment. On the way into the tunnel, as we followed the team, a couple of reserves whispered that now we'd see something. Bill would have to say something. No, he wouldn't go for Martin, said one of them. The Big Fellow's now too famous for anyone to criticize him, even on a bad game.

The players collapsed exhausted. Bill stood in the middle, his head bowed, saying nothing.

Martin Chivers was the last to sit down. As he did so he muttered loudly, 'Poor team, poor team.' It was a sort of reflex remark, getting in first, as if he expected to be assaulted.

'I never said they were a poor team,' said Bill sharply, looking at Chivers, suddenly angry. 'Never at any time did I tell you they were a poor team.'

Chivers hadn't meant it like that. By criticizing them he was really blaming Spurs for not doing better, and himself. He hadn't meant to accuse Bill of misleading them. Bill couldn't have warned them more about Nantes, piling on the details of the strength of their team. In turning on Chivers' remark, Bill was really attacking Chivers, as they both knew.

'They were a poor team,' repeated Chivers sullenly, knowing that Bill had said the opposite. Perhaps he meant that Spurs might have beaten them if they'd been told beforehand they were a poor team. If so, it was a silly line of attack. On the night Spurs had been the poorer team.

Chivers was looking for something to say, a way of getting words out, any words, to convey an emotion, a feeling of depression. 'A poor team,' he said again, shaking his head. The lack of logic was a red rag to Bill but he was struggling to control himself.

'You mean *we* had some poor players,' said Bill. He was standing feet apart, shaking slightly, his head up, looking straight at Chivers. He hadn't named any names, but there was no doubt which poor player he was referring to.

'What do you mean?' said Chivers, becoming suddenly violent and animated. Up to now he'd been deliberately sullen, waiting for the real attack to come so that he could plead self-defence.

'What do you know about it? You never praise us when we do well. Never. You never do. What do you know about it? You weren't out there. You didn't have to do it. It's easy to say we didn't do well, bloody easy . . .'

'I've bloody well been out there,' said Bill, determined to finish the argument. 'I know what it's like. I've been through it. What are you talking about? We had some poor players tonight. That's what I'm saying. Some of our players weren't trying. That's what I'm saying.'

'You weren't out there,' continued Chivers, repeating himself once again, but beginning to weaken. It was too early to admit any failings. In his mood of tension, fraught and straight from the field, he was still caught up in his confused mood of bitterness.

Bill waited for him to continue, more than willing to see the argument through, to say to his face what he really wanted to say, but there was a sudden commotion behind him on the table. The anger and the heat and the half-finished fury suddenly began to disintegrate.

Someone had asked for a towel. In throwing a clean one across the table, Eddie Baily accidently knocked one of the glass cups on to the floor where it shattered, spreading broken glass under the players' bare feet.

Bill left Chivers and got down on the floor and used some soiled tie-ups to sweep the glass under the table out of the way. The players all started talking loudly, jeering at Eddie for his mistake, trooping into the showers to get washed. Soon there were the normal post-match noises and discussions, players showing injuries to Johnny and asking for bandages, going over mistakes made, chances lost.

Chivers didn't move. Everyone else was soon back from the showers and busy putting on their clean clothes, but Chivers sat in his filthy, sweat-sodden, matted strip, just as he'd come from the field. He had one leg across the other, leaning on one elbow, staring straight ahead, menacing, and threatening, yet beaten and fed-up. What's the point. What do I get out of it. Why do I bother. I tried my hardest out there. I wanted to win. I didn't go out there not to try. But that's all I get.

Mullery started singing 'Oh what a beautiful morning' very loudly and badly, knowing he was singing it badly, going right through with all the words, carrying on when people groaned and told him to shut up. After all, it had been a goal-less draw, a good away result. There was the home match still to come.

Someone shouted to Eddie to open the door. They couldn't breathe. The place was like an oven. Eddie unlocked it and opened both doors, swinging them back and forward to make a breeze.

'Close the bloody door,' said Mike England, who was getting dressed just beside the doors. French officials were hanging around outside, trying to stare in. 'They're like monkeys out there.'

'One says open it, one says close,' said Eddie. 'Bloody hell.' He closed both doors and locked them, banging them hard. There was a knock, then another knock, then another. He opened them furiously, ready to give a mouthful to some monkey. Mr Wale, the chairman, came in followed by the directors. They crept in rather than walked in, nodding to Bill, not saying anything, sensing the atmosphere, standing demurely against the wall, looking round, talking quietly to each other.

There was another knock and in came Mr Broderick, the Cook's organizer. He went to help Johnny pick up all the dirty clothes and pack the bags – they'd brought a huge canvas holdall this time, not their normal basketwork skips. Bill helped as well, passing over filthy boots and dirty socks. When Bill finished, Mr Wale went into a corner with him where they talked very solemnly.

'The chairman wants you all to go to this reception,' announced Bill apologetically when the directors had trooped out again. 'Don't worry. We'll only stay fifteen minutes. There'll be a buffet there but don't forget there's a meal back at the hotel, if you want it.'

Chivers had started to move at last. He was now in the shower, having peeled off his dirty clothes in a pile at his bench. He'd brightened up a bit, now he'd pushed himself back to life. Bill, Johnny and Broderick were packing away Chivers' dirty strip with the rest of the gear.

Chivers came back to his seat and stood drying himself beside Mike England. 'Did you hear that supporter,' said Chivers. 'Shouting at me I should have scored six.'

'They know nothing,' said Mike, quickly, eagerly. 'They know bloody nothing. I heard one as well. They know nothing.'

'You're right. Nothing at all.'

Mike started gently whistling, quietly and in tune, not a pop song but a piece of Tchaikowsky, from the Nutcracker Suite. He was in his smart three-piece suit. He'd washed the vaseline out of his hair and the battle out of his body and looked like a young managing director about to summon his board of directors.

Some British reporters arrived when the players were ready and were allowed in. They went to Chivers and to Mullery, taking it in turns to talk confidentially in their ears. One had heard the rest of the evening's football results and everyone stopped talking to listen to his news.

On the coach Bill Stevens, Spurs' assistant secretary, was given the job of chucking off the French kids. While it had been waiting, quite a few had crept on and were hiding behind the seats. Chivers was their main target. He signed autographs good-humouredly. The bus was surrounded by French fans, waving and smiling. If the crowd felt they'd been robbed by the draw, which is what an English crowd would have thought after a similar performance, they weren't showing it. They were still as fascinated and as pleased to see the Tottenham team, especially Chivers, as they'd been before the match.

The reception was being given by the Mayor of Nantes at the Château des Ducs, a towering castle in the middle of the city, with a drawbridge and a wide moat.

It was all lit up when we got there with powdered flunkeys everywhere and a magnificent buffet laid out. The reception was in two large rooms, with a closed-circuit TV in the smaller room, so that the guests there wouldn't miss the speeches being made in the other. The

Press were also invited, French and British, plus both teams and officials and assorted local dignitaries. Mr Wale and Mr Cox replied in English on behalf of Spurs, thanking the Mayor and people of Nantes for their excellent hospitality, the best they'd experienced in many years of going abroad.

The players stayed about half an hour in all, then Bill said they could go back to their hotel.

Most of them drank lagers in the hotel bar till about one or two o'clock and then went to bed, glad it was all over.

On the plane next morning, only Gilzean was moaning, at least moaning on about France, saying it was his third French trip and he still didn't like it. He preferred any country except France. But the rest were all very cheerful, greatly relieved to be going home, carrying dolls, bottles, souvenirs and other presents.

Champagne was served on the plane, though it was only eleven o'clock in the morning, but I didn't see any of the players drinking it. The directors and the Press managed to have their share.

Chivers was now agreeing he'd had a bad game. He admitted it. He said nothing had gone right for him. He'd been heavily marked and had lashed out in the end out of anger, which had been silly.

Bill Nicholson chatted to a few of the reporters, saying who had had a good game, such as Phil Beal. Jimmy Neighbour had tried hard, he said, though he might have got the ball over more often. He had no praise for Chivers, Peters or Mullery. He nodded towards them as he spoke, not wanting them or the other players to hear.

Later, he told me that he was worried that Chivers was becoming a player who could only play brilliantly at home.

'All they have to do is play it simple. That's the answer, but they won't do it. When you get into difficulties, when the opposing team are doing well and not letting you do anything, all you do is play it very simple till things go your way.'

He opened a newspaper and divided the page in three with his fingers, describing how play could be kept safely in the middle third if things were going badly, even if it meant changing from one flank to another without beating anyone or going forward. He went over passes which had been thrown away. He analysed one move where Peters had tried to pass between two Nantes players and failed when he should have made two simple angle passes.

'I don't know what comes over them. Mackay and Blanchflower, they could get a grip when things were going badly, but this team doesn't seem to be able to do it. They've been told often enough what to do. And they *can* do it. I know they can. I don't know why they don't. It sickens me.'

In the cool clear light of a new day, did he agree with some of Eddie's screams in the heat of the match that some of the players suffered from too much publicity? Surely that couldn't have any effect on their play?

'Players can easily become too confident and arrogant. I don't mind confidence, but it leads to lack of self-criticism. That was what was wrong with some of them last night. They weren't self-critical. Good players like that shouldn't make mistakes, ever. That should be the aim. but if they do make one mistake, that should be it. They should be so furious with themselves that they vow never to do it again. But they won't admit mistakes, so they don't try harder and do better. *Everyone* can do better.'

It was a perfect flight, completely different from the dark and rain and turbulence which we'd had when flying out to the unknown. There was sunshine all the way home and we had a perfect landing at London Airport.

So what can be done, if his players won't do things simply and they won't be self-critical?

'Work at it,' said Bill grimly. 'Work at it. That's all we can do.'

from *The Glory Game*, 1972

A Player's Diary
EAMON DUNPHY

28 SEPTEMBER

We have Carlisle at the Den tomorrow. Another home win, and we will be really up there in the top five. And the best part of the season for us is yet to come. But there is a bad atmosphere, a lazy atmosphere, a kind of brooding greyness hanging over the place.

What we are doing is going to Crystal Palace on Mondays. We get changed, and finally start around 10.45. We have ten minutes running around doing exercises. Then we have twelve-a-side because the apprentices are there too. Two-touch football on a very narrow pitch. So everyone kicks the ball into each other's balls, and it is over the roof and all over the shop. I'm in goal one end, Gordon Bolland is in goal the other. So one whole morning – nothing. On Tuesday we go out and run our cobs off for half an hour, then we get the ball and play five-a-side. So again, nothing. Wednesday we have off. So there seems to be nobody really interested in correcting our basic faults, in working at the game.

The balance of the side is not right yet either. We have got a kid playing outside left who is not ready yet. Dennis is sitting on the bench tomorrow, which is ridiculous. He is one of our more positive players. It is obvious that without him we are not such a good side as we are with him. It is only a matter of time, until we lose a game, and then Benny will put him in. Then Benny will say, 'Now we are back to our best. This is us.'

But I cannot understand why he does not do it now. Why do we have to lose before we pull ourselves together? Why not work and organize ourselves now?

29 SEPTEMBER

Millwall 1 Carlisle United 2 'No way can we lose this game. Carlisle never beat us at home. Not many sides do, but certainly not the Carlisles of this world.' That was what we went out thinking. It was just a matter of waiting for the goal to come. We will get the first goal, and then start playing a bit, and the other one or two will come. We've done it 100 times, we've done it 200 times. Same old thing; dead easy.

They were desperate. They had lost at home, they had lost everywhere. They lost one game 6–0. So we started off. The pitch was bumpy, and it was very windy. In the first quarter of an hour we had one, maybe two, chances. Just little flurries, but nothing occurred. We were all kind of suspended in mid-air. No one was doing anything. But we were not worried. 'We will get a chance, and it will be in the back of the net.'

We did not respect them. A lot of them were just waiting for us to score. But there was one little guy in midfield who was working his heart out. Positive, making runs, tackling, jumping, getting involved. He seemed to be one of the few players on their side who wanted to play. I just looked at him and thought 'Ten out of ten for effort, but you are wasting your time.'

So half-time came and it was o–o. We were kicking into our favourite end in the second half. We had got the wind as well. Everything was right. A couple more near misses. Alfie missed an absolute sitter. That should have been the first goal.

Sides do not lose at the Den; they commit suicide. They wait for you to score. They offer you the game on a plate. Carlisle had offered us the game on a plate, but we had not taken it.

Now there was uneasiness, the first hint of doubt; a bit of desperation crept in. Alfie's miss was crucial. You think, 'That's ominous. We won't get an easier chance than that. This is not going to be the day.'

They began to see that there was nothing to be afraid of. They were beginning to play a little bit more. They were beginning to think they could win. And we were beginning to realize we could fail to win. And then we thought, 'We will switch it on.' But we could not. It just got worse and worse. In the middle of the second half it just got unbelievable. Nobody could pass the ball, nobody could find it, nobody wanted the ball, nobody wanted to do anything at all positive. People were putting their heads on their chest, and looking around, blaming other people. And everybody was getting edgy.

Then, ten minutes from the end, Brownie – he is overweight and having a nightmare – *blasts* a ball back to Kingy. Kingy had no chance. It flew past him, hit the post, and came back into his arms. He turned round and lashed it upfield. One of their defenders headed it out, Gordon hit it first time, and it was in the back of the net.

I could not even raise my arms. I was embarrassed. We did not deserve it. I did not do a war dance. I just stood there and said, 'Well, thank Christ for that! We have got away with it again.' Everyone was pleased now, it was a matter of holding out for eight or nine minutes. Well, we did not even think in terms of holding out. We thought, 'That's it, it is over.' We knocked it about for five minutes. They had jacked it in, except for that last desperate spurt every away team makes.

Some guy hit an aimless ball into the box. Kitch – there was not an opponent near him – headed it back to Kingy. But Kingy had come out instead of staying on his line, hadn't given Kitch a call, and it was in the back of the net. It bounced twice, and we thought Kingy had it. Always gets those balls, he is good at it. But not this time. It was Kingy's fault basically. Because he did not shout. Again it is all part of this thing he has been going through. It's predictable. You knew it had to happen some time. But you never thought ... And now it is 1–1. Christ! I held my head in my hands and thought, 'This is unbelievable!'

And this paralysing feeling came over me. There was no answer to it. So anyway, we had dropped a point. We got a little desperate, but I knew we would not get it now. There was no real desire to win.

Now they were steaming, Carlisle. They could not believe it. Energy! Positive runs! They were calling for the ball; they were knocking it around; they were 10 feet tall. Transformation. To come to Millwall and get a point!

So they boot a ball upfield, a fellow gets it, Kingy comes tearing out of his box, scythes the winger down. For no apparent reason. Free kick. Fellow takes it. The centre half has come up, heads it, it hits Kitch and then the back of the net. In the net!

I looked around again. I could not believe it. It really was like a bad dream. It is impossible to lose at home to Carlisle any time, but having been 1–0 up with ten minutes to go, it was unbelievable.

We went off and got in the bath. We had been diabolical. We had produced the kind of football that our training had threatened all season. Inept, grey, sterile, nothing football. No energy, nothing.

Nobody said anything. We just sat there, disbelief on everybody's face. Muttering about Kingy, muttering about this, muttering about that. And I was angry. I had not played well. I was annoyed at that. But I was not so much annoyed because we had not played well, but because the signs had been there for a good two weeks.

I don't like getting drunk, but tonight I feel, 'I'm going to get drunk.' There is nothing else for it.

I have never felt ashamed about Millwall until today. I have felt proud about them always. The character, the skill, the results we have got away from home ... you are proud to play for Millwall. You think, 'What a good set of lads. What a good club to play for.' But this ... it was such a waste. To get beaten like that!

30 SEPTEMBER

So I came home last night and had a few drinks. But it doesn't help. When you wake up in the morning, you think, 'It didn't happen' or you try to block it out. But it happened. And when you read the Sunday papers you soon learn that it did.

Sunday is very much a down day anyway. You build up all week emotionally and physically to Saturday. You get really wound up, then bang! Saturday afternoon it all comes out. Even the games that look diabolical to people watching, games where nothing has been achieved, nothing creative anyway, you come off the park thinking, 'Gotta get in that bath. Jesus!' You have put everything into it physically and emotionally, oblivious of the fact that it is drivel. And by Sunday you are no good for anything.

When you've won, it isn't so bad. Alan and I both have this routine of getting the Sunday papers, looking at the League table, working out who is playing who next week, where it will leave us – 'five points behind, but if they lose it'll only be three', all that sort of thing. But when you've lost like we did yesterday, when even you are conscious you've been in a load of rubbish, the Sunday papers you do not need.

1 OCTOBER

This morning everyone seemed to have forgotten last Saturday. We are at Sheffield on Wednesday, Forest on Saturday, and the feeling is, 'Well, we'll try and nick something there.'

The lads are sick, I suppose, in their own way. But footballers are resilient. They bounce back quickly as a group. Jokes, birds, you talk about anything. Even football. Some of the lads do anyway. When you get older you start talking about the game a bit, seeing things you never saw before, feeling responsible for things you never felt responsible for before. It becomes more difficult to shrug things off.

So we started training. A bit of running to get warmed up, then we were going to have this practice match. Lawrie was handing the bibs out. And he walked past me. 'That is very odd of him.' I thought nothing of it; just a little bit perturbed. I looked after him, and he was giving out first-team shirts. And he was giving one to Robin Wainwright . . . and he gave one to Dennis . . . and I looked around . . . 'I'm dropped! No! But I am!'

I could not believe it. I could not think for a minute. And Benny was standing there as if nothing had happened. No one said anything to me.

He had given me a reserve shirt. 'Play in midfield,' he said. How do you react? It was like somebody had plunged a dagger in my back.

237

I was so hurt. Not so much because I was dropped, but because they had done it like that.

And they could not do it to me! I was choked. I had been playing reasonably well; certainly better than a lot of other people. And I cared! I was part of it. This was me, this was the lads. And then BANG! I'm out of it.

So he said, 'Let's have the first-team lads over here. You lot go and have a kick about at the far end.' So they had all gone away, the lads, for a team talk. And I went up the other end with the youngsters. I could not believe it.

I could feel tears welling up in my eyes, but I thought, 'Nah, that's no good.' So I just stood there for about five or ten minutes. I don't know how long it was. I can't remember how long the talk went on. The young lads were knocking it about, and I looked round, and there was this little group, and Benny was talking to them. And you feel so left out.

And there's the hurt. It just happens. A snap of the fingers, and you are gone. Out. All the commitment, all the emotion, all the hard work, all the belief. Everything gone. Because some idiot fooled around at the back in the last eight minutes on Saturday.

And my first reaction then was to walk out. There and then. But I thought, 'No, anybody can be dropped. Now you have got to show you are a man. Now you have got to show you are big.'

So I made a few jokes with the young lads, picked my chin up, and started playing this practice game. I did my best, I worked hard, and funnily enough I started playing really well. Because again there was this strange feeling of relief. 'Sod it. I'm out of it.' So I just enjoyed myself for half an hour. And all the time, at the back of my mind, I was wondering, 'What am I going to do? How am I going to react? What do I do now?'

Seven games of the season had gone. And after all the struggle, all the worry, all the dreams, you are on the scrapheap. That is what the reserves is, when you are twenty-eight. No one had said a word to me. It was the same as if I had never given a damn. They had treated me as if I had never tried.

And I *had* tried. In the games where Dennis had been out, and there was no one there to take responsibility, I had taken it. I had covered for people, I had worked, I had shouted, I had bawled, I had grafted, I had tackled – which I cannot do very well – I had done all of that. And I was missing Dennis being alongside me doing things, because he takes a lot of that responsibility. I took all that on my own shoulders, tried to do the right thing, tried to do more than my whack, to make up for the fact that he was not there. All the time waiting for him to get back into the side so we could get it organized again. Like we had done in the latter part of last season. It never entered my mind that I might be dropped.

It had, funnily enough, when Franky had been playing so well. I thought, 'Well, Dennis is going to come back in, and he just might drop me.' But then I had played well in a couple of games, I had made the goal against Wednesday, and I had played well in the first half at Swindon when things were rocky. I had pulled the side together, and I thought I had done very well. So I said to myself, 'Now it's OK. You won't be dropped.' I thought he would drop Gordon Hill. I wanted Dennis back in the side.

But he had dropped Gordon Hill and me. And he brought this lad Robin Wainwright in. He has done well in the reserves, and should be given a chance. But he is not a midfield player, he is a winger or a striker.

So I reacted by playing as best I could for the reserves in that practice match. Trying to be manly, trying not to be small-minded. And when we finished I went to see Benny. When I walked through the door he said, 'What do you want?'

'You know what I want,' I said. 'I want to leave this place. I want to leave within a week. I'm finished here.'

'Out of the question,' he said. 'You're too good a player.'

So I said, 'I don't care why you have dropped me, I don't want to discuss it. Team selection is your business. But I'm finished with it. I have put too much work in, too much commitment, too much caring to be messed around like that. You did not even tell me before that I was dropped. I find out when a guy walks past me with a shirt. That's you, that is this club. No more for me. I'm finished. I want to leave. And if you do not let me leave, I'll leave anyway.'

'Out of the question. Calm yourself down.'

I did not talk about why he had dropped me. I do not believe in discussing team selection with managers. They have got a reason, and whatever the reason is, it is good enough. It is their job. You don't have to take it, if you don't believe it is right.

I was in a terrible temper. My hand was shaking, I could not talk properly. I was hurt more than angry.

So I said, 'I'll wait ten days. And if you don't let me go, I'll go anyway. Don't put me on the sheet, don't take me with you.'

'What about the money?'

'You can stuff the money,' I said. 'I don't care about that.'

So I went home. I phoned Sandra first, and told her what had happened. I walked in and just burst out crying. I sat here for quarter of an hour, and I just cried.

I had never cried before about football. Never ever. But this time I did. I don't know why. Maybe it was the hurt, the injustice of it. But that has happened before. Every year, the first sign of the team having problems and it is me he drops. He tells me that he thinks the world of me as a person, but when we lose games the first person he sorts out is me. I do think he likes me. I think the reason he does drop me every time is because of a weakness in him. He is the kind of person who would sooner hurt his friends than his enemies. But I did not think it would happen to me again.

The other lads were surprised. Alan said, 'It's scandalous.'

I had not looked for sympathy. When you get dropped, players come up to you and say 'Diabolical.' They always say it whether they mean it or not. But when it happens to me, I try and avoid them. I don't want them to say it, because it does not mean anything. It is not real. What is real is what goes on the teamsheet. The rest is rubbish.

2 OCTOBER

Being dropped is something everyone in the game has to face. Manchester United dropped Bobby Charlton once. How do you face it? Yesterday I came home and I just cried! We went into Bromley in the afternoon shopping. But it's eating into you the whole time. You can't think about anything else for one minute. You go home and you are restless, edgy. The whole time you are thinking, 'What am I going to do?' I was in great doubt whether I should go to the ground today, or stay away. I didn't know what to do. Whether to jack it all in again, or go. Maybe go in for the money, sit on the bench as twelfth man, which means a lot extra on your wages. Or say 'Stuff the money' and keep out of it altogether.

But I went in this morning, and had a long chat with Benny. He called me into his office. He was hovering around me all morning, which is what he does when he knows you have got the needle with him. He called me into his room and said, 'Have you changed your mind about going on the teamsheet? Do you still not want to be in it?'

So I said, 'Leave me out. See how you do.' I said I wanted no part of it. I'm not going to sit on the bench or in the stand, tearing my guts out every week, wanting them to win in one sense, but basically wanting them to lose, because I cannot get back into the side until they lose. But he said, 'Come as thirteenth man; and get your money. Don't be a fool to yourself.' So in the end I agreed.

4 OCTOBER
Sheffield Wednesday 3 Millwall 2   So we went up to Sheffield. I wasn't on the bench, I went as thirteenth man. You go into the dressing-room before the game, and you smile and say, 'All the best, lads.' What does that mean? If they do well you stay out. And when they get beaten, as we did last night, what do you do? You act. Because you can't come in with a big smile all over your face saying, 'Great. Now you've been beaten I can get back in.' Everybody else is sick. But you aren't. You are pleased. So you come in and make faces; pretend that you are sick like the rest of them. But everyone knows that you are acting.

I sat in the stand with John Sissons, who is injured. I was sitting among some Millwall supporters too. They were all saying, 'Cor, you not in, Eamon? What a liberty! He should have dropped someone else.' You can't say anything. And they say the same to everyone when they are dropped. Some of them mean it, some don't.

The game was a shambles. Terrible. First half was diabolical. Kingy kept like a clown, gave away two goals. And he was being watched by Manchester City. Their scout left before the end. But while they are out there what am I doing? I'm sitting in the stand, wanting them to lose, but unable to show it. Because there are people around, I've got to pretend to want them to win. I can't jump up in the air when Sheffield score. Which I want to do. And when Millwall score I'm sick, but I have to jump up in the air. And there is this terrible conflict the whole time. And it is the same for everybody who is dropped.

You are always pleased when they have been beaten, because it means you are a candidate again. You are sick for the lads, of course, but your predominant emotion is delight.

I went into the dressing-room afterwards. People were throwing their boots off disconsolately, swearing a lot. I looked at Dennis. He shrugged his shoulders. He wasn't surprised. He looked as if he was past caring. Another confirmation for him of what he thinks about Millwall. I couldn't look at Alan. He is my closest friend, but I couldn't go to him. Because I was still isolated. I had not been part of the defeat. You aren't just isolated from the good things when you're out of the side, but from the bad things too. The lads who played and Benny are sharing the gloom, just as it would be their joy to share if they had done well. So I kept quiet. I sat down and read the programme for the fiftieth time, and tried to grab half a cup of tea. There was me, Benny and Jack while the lads were having their baths. Benny was walking around shaking his head. There was nothing he wanted to say to me; and nothing I wanted to say to him. He went to the mirror to comb his hair, as he always does before having to go and face the directors' room.

Now that's another tough situation. It's always tough for a manager to face that when his team has lost. It is not so much facing your own directors. That comes later. It is the guests and the opposition directors and other managers saying 'Unlucky' and not meaning it.

For the reserve, after about half an hour, when you've helped Jack Blackman get all the gear together, it isn't so bad. By then the lads have forgotten the game and you are all one again. Particularly for an away game like Sheffield, where you are staying overnight. You go off and have a few beers together. And you can feel part of it.

But Benny put a curfew on. So we didn't go out, just had a drink in the hotel lounge. There was a pretty bad atmosphere really.

What does a manager do? Benny could say, 'Go on, have a few beers and please yourself.' But it is difficult.

If I was a manager, I would tend to think there was no use in punishing people if they have done their best. And at Millwall they invariably have done their best. Let them go out and have a few beers, win or lose. But it is early season. We have a game on Saturday, so we have got to keep ourselves reasonably fit. The danger is that the lads could go out and drink a lot, pull a few birds and it ends as a four-in-the-morning job. And then you travel back the next day, so there is only Friday to recover.

But I think that players feel much more responsible nowadays than they did. There are far fewer cheats around. Certainly not at Millwall, which is one of the greatest things about the place. Over the years I've played there, one of the greatest joys has been that they have had no bad people. The one or two that came Benny got out quickly. We've always had good lads.

I've seen a few bad ones elsewhere. Going away with the Irish team there have been lads over the years who don't care whether they win or lose. They are looking for something else out of it: the 'big time'.

There is an element of that left in the game, but it is going very quickly. One thing I've always hated is the image of the hard-drinking, hard-living professional sportsman who goes out and stomps all over the world. That was part of the game when I first came into it in Manchester. I remember going out with a couple of the other players one Friday night to the dogs, then on to a nightclub. We were playing the next day, and I was really worried, guilty. And they said, 'Nothing to worry about. This is what it is all about.' And to a large extent at that time it was. Particularly in Manchester, there were a lot of playboys around and a lot of placcs to go. But there is not a lot of that left in football now.

And that has been one of the joys at Millwall. Players are honest. And Benny is normally good. He lets the players go out more often than not. And I think that is right. If a player goes out on a Wednesday night and even if he gets drunk out of his mind, if he is a good pro he will know what he has done. He will make up for it on the Saturday. He will give you that much more because he had that liccncc on Wednesday.

Last season we played Everton in the Cup. We went to Torquay for four days beforehand. It is a fantastic place down there for the nightlife. It was in January. London was terrible. But down there it was really nice. A warm atmosphere and a carefree air about the place. It was quiet, because it was out of season, but there was still a fairly hectic social life. The first couple of days we were down there we went out. Benny was really good and took the leash off. We found a club and had a few drinks. We did not really look after ourselves for those four days. We took liberties. On the Thursday we went back to London to go up to Everton.

I think Benny knew we had stayed up late and drunk more than we should have done. And I think he had done it to relax us. We went out and played like fury. We fought and we battled. It was a hell of a game, and we got a hell of a result.

So we asked if we could go to Torquay before the next round. Benny said yes, so before we played Wolves we went down there again and had a ball. We played really well again at Wolves, even though we lost.

These were isolated instances of us taking liberties. You could not do it every week and get away with it. But if you have got good lads it proves you can let them off the leash, and they will still produce the goods. Especially if you pick the right time.

5 OCTOBER

Lawrie did it again with his damn bibs this morning. We were having a five-a-side. On Friday mornings the first team normally play the reserves in little five-a-sides. And Lawrie gave me a first-team jersey, and gave Robin Wainwright a reserve-team jersey. Of course I thought I was back in the side and Robin thought he was dropped. So Robin naturally was really angry, and he couldn't get it together, and it destroyed him. I was angry too, because I did not want to come back like that. I knew it wasn't fair that he should be dropped after one game in which he had not done badly. And I knew that the lads would not think it fair either. It was really eating me. I played for half an hour, stumbling all over the place, confused, wondering what was going on. And Robin is confused too. I can see his face and the lad is choked. He has had one game after being at the club for ten months. And then they drop him like this.

I looked at him at the end of practice as if to say, 'Sorry, son, I think it is a liberty, but what can you do?'

So we went back to the ground, and Benny put up the teamsheet. And I wasn't playing. Robin was still in. So I made a beeline for Lawrie and said, 'What the hell were you playing at with those bibs? You give me a first-team jersey, and Robin a reserve one?'

'Oh,' said Lawrie, 'that was just coincidence. I gave the vest to you because you were standing nearest to me.'

Just a simple little thing, but that really hurt. It shows how you can be treated in this game. In the course of a morning you are in and out of the side with a snap of the fingers. Because you are told nothing, you have to watch for signs all the time. And then someone's incredible unthinking action destroys a morning for you.

Nottingham Forest 3 Millwall 0 Now we are in the depths. Today
Franky Saul got sent off. Stupidity. He deserved to be sent off. They
are a pretty moderate side, who we play again on Wednesday in the
League Cup. And we will beat them. We have got the needle with
them, because they were 1–0 up when Franky was sent off and not
playing well. But when they got us down to ten men in the second
half, they started taking the mickey, and buzzing around, and doing
all sorts of things. Dennis said to one of them on the way off, 'You
had better save some of that energy for Wednesday night.' Because
they are going to need it. That is the incentive we need to knock
them out of the League Cup. We will be steaming from the start.

Franky felt diabolical afterwards. From the stand I thought it was
quite right that he was sent off. He had had a go, stuck the nut on a
fellow, for which he was booked. Then he went in very late a few
minutes afterwards. There was nothing else the referee could have
done. But he was raging.

You have to sympathize, because the implications of being sent off
are so bad. You lose a lot of money, missing three games, and you
could lose your place in the side as a result. I think Franky thought
that if he was going to be sent off anyway, he wished he had done
the fellow properly. There's nothing worse than being sent off when
you haven't really done any damage. You feel you might as well have
done some.

The lads felt we had done all right until Franky was sent off. That
was the turning point. So everyone was fairly angry. I've never seen
a case where players say it was right someone was sent off. It's very
hard to see your own fellows in a bad light. Unless someone has
thrown a killer punch and caught the other guy on the point of the
chin, you never feel it is right.

It is a horrible thing, the long walk. You go in alone, and the old
boy (every club has this old boy) comes in and unlocks the dressing-
room door for you, and sympathizes. Franky came and sat on the
bench afterwards. He was fuming all the game.

Alfie and Dennis in particular were furious. It was another confirmation for them of the troubles we have been having with referees.
The lads felt he shouldn't have been sent off. I thought he should.
But I was sitting in the stand. A non-combatant, a rational critic. That
is the thing about being thirteenth man. You are watching the game

through reasonable eyes. And that has got nothing to do with football or any other sport.

So the lads have the needle with Forest. The general feeling was disgust at them. Because until we went one down, they had not looked anything. They had looked a load of bottlers really. Dennis was very angry. He said, 'We'll stuff them on Wednesday night.'

But then, where do we go from here? By beating them we will be reacting to something that happened today. It won't be something we have created ourselves.

Before the season started I said this was going to be a cataclysmic year for Millwall. Either way. And it is, I think, beginning to happen now. We have got guys in the side overweight. You have got the keeper who is in a terrible situation because of his contract. And it looks to me as if he has blown his chance now. Manchester City have watched him twice – today and last Wednesday – and both times they have walked out before the end. A £100,000 buy, and he is making mistakes. Elementary mistakes. It is not the lad's fault. He is in a diabolical situation. He is trapped. People react stupidly, they make mistakes, they get desperate. I have tried to tell him . . . but he can't help it. He talks to journalists, he makes these ridiculous statements to the papers.

You could say he is childish, but he is desperate. He feels his whole life's ambition – to play in the First Division – within his grasp. And there is nothing he can do to realize it. He has worked hard for it for four years. Brave, skilful, competent at his job, great at his job, and it has not happened. He must look at our side, and see this shambles we have been for the last month – the last three games anyway; it seems like a month – and despair. It has only been a week. We had won our previous three games; it seems like a month since then.

Alf walked in after the match today, and said, 'I wish I would break my leg!' He is sick, sick about the club, sick about the way he sees it run. Because he thinks about it a little bit. So am I sick.

That is what hurts more than anything. A good club, a good side, we should walk away with this League. With Dougy in the side . . . a great little player, Dougy, always done well for us, always does a good job. And he dropped him. Bang! Out! Now Dougy has broken his ribs in the reserves. He dropped Dougy and played this kid. Then Dennis got injured, and he left him out for three weeks.

He has destroyed it; destroyed the delicate balance. We went through nine months of last season as one of the most successful sides in the Division; seven or eight months, anyway, from October onwards. And he has taken all that for granted and destroyed that delicate thing. He thinks that you can muck around with the mechanism of a team, and still come up with the same answers. And you cannot. It is delicate. Take one or two players out of a side, move one or two players around, and you have ruined the whole thing.

Everybody was moody on the coach coming home tonight. The directors were moody, Benny was moody. There were bad vibes all round.

Basically you are all in it for the glory. And glory is not something you share. It is your glory. You only achieve it together. But you don't share it. Everyone sets out to achieve it, and the team is your means to that end. The togetherness is your means to achieve it, but once you achieve it, it's yours. Relationships in a football team are tenuous. They are not true friendships – very rarely, anyway. It's more a shared experience, on a not very deep basis. Of course most friendships are based on common ground, shared experiences. But in football these days, shared experience means shared money.

When the bad times come, it is every man for himself. Unless there is very good leadership. If not the relationships begin to crack up. Because sport is basically a lonely thing for every individual in it, even in team sports. Teams are basically individuals. A group of individuals.

You talk about team spirit and being together. But you always find in practice, when the bad times come, the cracks come, it's every man for himself. Because there is glory and money and your career at stake. And that entails backbiting, snidiness, scapegoating and a whole host of other things.

7 OCTOBER

Watching two games from the stand has been really instructive. Seeing the Second Division as it really is. It is a much less complex thing than one thinks when one is playing. You go out to play Forest, who really are terrible. But before you go out, and when you are out there, you're thinking in terms of this tremendous task. 'Christ, we've got to beat these.'

Sitting in the stand, out of it all, cool and objective, you see the game in a different light. You realize just how many balls go astray. You see so many players trying to do really difficult things. The full back will have the ball. He's got a simple ball on, and a very difficult ball on. Now here is a player in the Second Division. A good player with a fair amount of ability, but no genius. Winfield of Forest, for example. A good player, but not a great player. He can strike the ball well. If he has got someone 30 yards away who is free, he will hit him nine times out of ten. Most professionals can. But put him in a situation where there is a little bit of pressure, and he is not content with that.

There were twenty-two players out there on Wednesday. Four or five were doing the simple things. The rest of them – the ball was flying all over the place. You would get a lad in space. He would get the ball played to his feet forwards. And he would try to turn unbelievably quickly and knock a ball under pressure. Pressure that he only imagined. There was no one near him. He was so used to thinking like that, instead of controlling it, looking up and playing a simple ball. He was doing things in his head at 90 miles an hour. The worst thing that has happened to my game in the last two years is that I've lost my composure. What I was good at was putting my foot on the ball, and knocking it around. Doing the simple things well, and slowing it down.

Part of the problem is getting older. You get to know the game better, and you get to feel more responsible for things. You start to feel you can influence things. That's great. But it is also dangerous. You start trying to do things that are not within your scope. And you start feeling responsible for things that aren't your responsibility.

This happens partly because lads know, especially in the lower divisions, that the one thing that keeps them in the game is their application. Their dedication. The intensity with which they approach the game. Which leads them to this feeling that they have got to go out and punish themselves for ninety minutes. This is crucial to players, particularly in the lower divisions. It is one of the most important things in the game at the moment – the idea that you somehow have to suffer.

That is what really distinguishes English football – the amount of people willing to do that. And that is what also destroys English football. On the Continent, or in the First Division, you get fellows who feel they don't have to do that in the same way. They will do it on the ball. They will take responsibility and play. It takes as much courage to play, to get on the ball and be composed.

All of those lads out there yesterday were honest. That was the one distinguishing feature. Of twenty-two on the field, sixteen or eighteen, the great majority, were totally honest. Within a certain definition of honesty, which is: 'Run your cobs off, whack everything you see, and then chase it.'

Carlisle in many ways are the best side I've seen. In many respects they were crap. But they had two things going for them: simplicity and honesty. They were never going to give in.

They weren't technically a good side. They had a few players who could play. But there must be sixteen or eighteen sides in the Second Division with more. Balderstone is a tremendous, gifted player, and they played off him. They are one of the better footballing sides in the simple things. They did try to play.

And Les O'Neill is unbelievable. He is useless if you use any of the textbook criteria. All he has got is a heart as big as the Den. A real human dynamo, as they say in Fleet Street. He kept them going. They were dead and he would not stop. He was kicking and fighting and chasing.

Well, he can play a little bit. But it's his tremendous character that distinguishes him. Living proof of the triumph of the spirit. There are definitely fifty better midfield players in the Second Division. But I will bet none of them have a good game against him. Because he sickens you. At the end of the game you feel, 'Well, thank God he is off my back at last!' You were sick of him. He never left you alone.

He never gave it away when he had it. And he never left you alone when you got it. He was up your backside the whole time. Not dirty, but biting, fighting, niggling, chasing. If he couldn't get up and head it, he would get up and put off the fellow who was going to head it. And as soon as he got it he gave it to the nearest man. Simple. He never gave it back to you. He was like Nobby Stiles when he was playing well. A pain in the ass. And that is the greatest thing in the lower divisions.

Or in any division. Leeds, for example. What a terrible team to play against. A pain. You try and take a throw-in. They have got everybody picked up, a man in front of the winger, and a man on you. You can't even take a throw-in. It demoralizes you. After half an hour you think, 'Oh hell, we can't even take a throw-in and get the ball.' It is terrible, especially for skilful midfield players. There you are, a skilful player, and you can't get the ball. So you start trying that bit more desperately. Then you get this throw-in. And you still have no chance. There used to be no question. It was at your feet and away you went. Not now. Not against good sides. They have got everyone picked up. Everyone. That is what the coaches are telling everyone to do.

Now that is very unimportant in one sense. But in another sense it is crucial. Because you are taking your throw-in. A throw-in you have 'won'. According to the books you 'win' a throw-in. And you look to throw it one way. No good. You go for another option. There aren't any. And the crowd is yelling, 'Get on with it, book him, ref . . .' and the referee is whistling, so you throw a fifty-fifty ball. And you lose it. That is the first time. Second time you get exactly the same thing. And then it gets to you. You think, 'Oh, for pity's sake . . .' And that is the way games are won and lost. That is the way it is. Multiply that by fifty and that is what Leeds have done.

Again, Jackie Charlton goes up and stands in front of the goal-keeper for corners. Now you need your goalkeeper – he is crucial at corners. But he can't see the ball. Jack Charlton is standing in front of him. So straight away you are handicapped. Then he starts jumping up and down on the line. Pushes the full back. Pushes the centre half.

The first time you may get it away. The goalie somehow will get a desperate fist to it. But after about six corners, the keeper is thinking, 'This fellow is driving me mad.' And he will stop. He won't go for the next ball. And Allan Clarke comes up and puts it in the net. So Leeds are 1–0 up. And why? Because Jackie Charlton has been driving people mad on the goal-line. That is football the way those people want to play it. You cannot beat them. You have to join them.

Les O'Neill is like that. After half an hour you are saying, 'Oh no, not him again.' He is a pest. You get the ball and his leg sneaks through and knocks it away. That's all right the first time. But after about twenty minutes you cannot get on the ball. Every time you do, there is this pest pestering you. Driving you mad. And if you have got eleven fellows doing that to the other team you can stop them doing anything in the end. Because what happens then is that when you have the ball, the other guy thinks, 'Here is my chance to get away from this pest', and he goes off and leaves you. You are a midfield player and you are marking a skilful player in the opposition. Right up his backside all the time. He can't find any space and he is sick of you. So your team gets the ball. And you run and take up a position. So he thinks, 'I'm not going after him. If it breaks down and I go out here I might get the ball in space for once.' But what happens is that you now have space and so you can go on.

That is how games are won and lost in English football. More so at the lower level. But Leeds have developed that into an art. Nobody outside the game knows what it is like. It is like some fellow running up to your desk or work bench all day and sticking a pin in you then running away. The cumulative effect is drastic. By the second half you have had it with Jackie Charlton. You don't want to see him ever again. Norman Hunter is down the other end. Every time you get the ball – bang. He comes crashing in. That is the way they do it. Leeds, when they have got the ball, can play. Brilliantly. But they felt that was how they destroyed teams. Not by football. But by that. They played football once they had destroyed them.

Given how close English football is – how little difference there is between most sides – doing all these little things tips the balance in your favour. You drive them mad.

And that is what Carlisle have. I can see them driving people mad. Sheffield Wednesday, for example. A much better side on paper. But you would only have to do that to Craig for ten minutes.

But that is also the trouble with English football. Everyone is doing it. I've been doing it, and I'm meant to be a little ball-player. And that shouldn't be necessary. You have to have an element of it. But to be a good side you have also got to be able to play. It isn't necessary for everyone to be doing that. And the real problem, from what I have seen in the last couple of games, is the way it affects the good players.

They start trying to be even more intricate than they were before. If you have the ball and you want to lay off a simple ball, whatever the other bloke is trying to do shouldn't bother you. It bothers you when you are trying to do a little bit on the ball. Something a bit creative.

But what I've seen suggests that simplicity and creativity are often much nearer to being the same thing than we think. Simplicity is creativity a lot of the time. When you are being driven mad by someone you tend to start trying to squeeze things through gaps that don't exist; trying to produce the killer punch once and for all. He drives you crazy, and in the end the whole thing becomes crazy. Whereas if you are calm and try and play simple football, you still can.

Not every side does it for one thing. In the two games I've watched, Wednesday and Forest haven't done it to any great extent. But everyone is conditioned to it. So that even though it wasn't happening, people were expecting it and reacting as if it was. As soon as you put your toe on the ball you are expecting someone right up your ass. Because a lot of the Second Division is like that. You don't have time. So in the end you become a side who doesn't have time, because you won't give yourselves time. It is all part of the Second Division syndrome.

In the Second Division you do have less time than in the First. In the Third you have even less. What that means is that when you've got the ball some fool will come charging at you to put you under pressure. In the First they know they can't charge at Bobby Charlton, Johnny Giles or Billy Bremner. They will do you, bcause they are very very good. But in the Second Joe Bloggs gets it. And they think, 'Well, if we go at him and dive in, he'll give us the ball a lot of the time.' And that is why they do it. But if Joe Bloggs begins to learn that the guy diving can be beaten. . .

But that is the thing about the Second Division. Nobody ever seems to learn. Everyone accepts the game in the diver-in's context. That is what has happened to the game at the moment, and that is why it is so poor. People have settled for this lower level where kick and rush and bite and fight are the order of the day. No one has been brave enough to say, 'No. We are not getting involved in that.'

from *Only a Game? The Diary of a Professional Footballer*, 1976

Jock Stein: A Hero Worshipped by His People
HUGH MCILVANNEY

The larcenous nature of death, its habit of breaking in on us when we are least prepared and stealing the irreplaceable, has seldom been more sickeningly experienced than at Ninian Park in Cardiff on Tuesday night.

Those of us who crowded sweatily into the small entrance hall of the main stand to wait for word of Jock Stein's condition will always remember the long half hour in which the understandable vagueness of reports filtering from the dressing-area lulled us into believing that Jock was going to make it through yet another crisis. The raw dread that had been spread among us by his collapse on the touchline at the end of the Wales–Scotland World Cup match gave way to the more bearable gloom of acknowledging that the career of one of the greatest managers football has known would have to be ended by immediate retirement.

Then – off in a corner of that confused room – Mike England, the manager of Wales and a deeply concerned first-hand witness of what had been happening to Stein, was heard to say that he was still 'very, very poorly'. There was no mistaking the true meaning of those words and suddenly the sense of relief that had been infiltrating our anxieties was exposed as baseless. We felt almost guilty about having allowed ourselves to be comforted by rumours. Then, abruptly, we knew for sure that the Big Man was dead and for some of us it was indeed as if our spirits, our very lives, had been burglarized.

Of all the reactions to Stein's death, none meant more than that of the thousands of Scotland's travelling supporters who learned of it haphazardly but with eerie swiftness as they got ready to celebrate a ragged draw against Wales that should guarantee their team a passage to the World Cup Finals in Mexico next summer. They are, given half an excuse, the most raucously exuberant fans in the game but as midnight neared in Cardiff on Tuesday they wandered through the streets in subdued clusters, sustaining the unforced atmosphere of mourning that pervaded the hundreds who waited silently in the darkness outside Ninian Park after the last hope of reviving the stricken man inside had been abandoned.

There is no doubt that the Scots have a highly developed capacity for the elegiac mood, especially when there is a bottle about, but what was to be encountered in South Wales last week was no cheap example of the genre. When travel-soiled units of the tartan expeditionary force interrupted their morose drinking to propose toasts to the lost leader, anybody cynical enough to see such behaviour as just another maudlin ritual doesn't know much about the way the power of Jock Stein's nature communicated itself to millions of ordinary people.

His achievements in football were monumental but they can only partially explain his impact upon and relevance to so many lives. Perhaps he was profoundly cherished simply because he was a true working-class hero – and that is a species which is disappearing almost as fast in industrial Scotland as elsewhere, if only because the values that governed its creation are being relentlessly eroded day by day. Even the common misery of unemployment has not halted the fragmentation of a sense of community that once seemed indestructible.

In an age when, if I may quote a line from my brother William's latest novel, it is as if 'every man and his family were a private company', Stein was the unpretentious embodiment of that older, better code that was until not so long ago the compensatory inheritance of all who were born of the labouring poor. No one was ever likely to mistake him for a saint, or even for a repository of bland altruism. He could look after himself and his own in the market place or anywhere else, but there was never the remotest danger that he would be contaminated by the materialism that engulfs so many of those who find prosperity through sport or other forms of entertainment.

These days it is hard to avoid having the eardrums battered by some unlikely pillar of the New Right who – having persuaded himself that a largely fortuitous ability to kick a football or volley a tennis ball or belt out a pop song or tell a few jokes more acceptably than the next man is actually evidence of his own splendid mastery of his fate – insists that the dole queues would fade away overnight if people got off their arses, got on their bikes and showed the enterprise that has carried him to what he imagines is glory. Stein's whole life was a repudiation of such garbage.

He was utterly Scottish, utterly Lanarkshire in fact, but his was the kind of loyalty to his roots that made his principles universal.

His father was a miner who was a miner's son and Stein himself worked underground until turning belatedly to full-time professional football at the age of twenty-seven. During a long, incalculably rewarding friendship with him, I heard him say many memorable things and some of the most vivid were inevitably about the game he loved and the great practitioners of it, but he was most moved and most moving when he talked of that earlier phase of his working experience.

There was a dynamic, combative quality to most of his conversation (mischievous wind-up was a favourite mode and, though he did not drink alcohol, he occasionally dipped his barbs in curare) but when the subject was mining and miners a tone of wistful reverie invaded his voice.

'I went down the pit when I was sixteen (at first I was working with ponies – it was still that era) and when I left eleven years later I knew that wherever I went, whatever work I did, I'd never be alongside better men. They didn't just get their own work done and go away. They all stayed around until every man had finished what he had to do and everything was cleared up. Of course, in the bad or dangerous times that was even more true. It was a place where phoneys and cheats couldn't survive for long.

'Down there for eight hours you're away from God's fresh air and sunshine and there's nothing that can compensate for that. There's nothing as dark as the darkness down a pit, the blackness that closes in on you if your lamp goes out. You'd think you would see some kind of shapes but you can see nothing, nothing but the inside of your head. I think everybody should go down the pit at least once to learn what darkness is.'

Phoneys and cheats did not flourish in his company during four decades of involvement with senior football. As a player he was shrewd, well organized and strong rather than outstandingly gifted, though he made a fundamental contribution to the rich streak of prize-winning enjoyed by the Celtic team he joined unexpectedly for a fee of £1,200 after modest seasons with Albion Rovers and a motley troupe of non-League men at Llanelli in South Wales. He became an influential captain of Celtic and when his playing career was ended by an injury to his right ankle that left him with a noticeable limp for the rest of his days, it was clear that he would make a manager.

His old employers were certain to be impressed by his successful introduction to the trade in charge of Dunfermline, for he gave that humble club the Scottish Cup by beating Celtic in the final tie, and after a further rehearsal period with Hibernian he went back to Parkhead as manager in 1964. It was a genuinely historic return, perhaps the most significant single happening in the entire story of Scottish football.

All of Stein's family associations, centred on the Lanarkshire villages of Blantyre and Burnbank, were vehemently Protestant but he had never hesitated for a second over first identifying himself with a club traditionally seen as carrying the banner for the Catholic minority in Glasgow (and throughout Scotland) and when he emerged as Celtic's first non-Catholic manager he became a living, eloquent rebuke of the generations of bigotry surrounding the Rangers–Celtic rivalry.

Under him, Celtic dominated the whole range of Scottish domestic competitions to a degree that stamped him, in his context, as the supreme achiever among the world's football managers. Nine League championships in a row is in itself a record no one can ever hope to equal but it was the triumphant lifting of the European Cup in Lisbon in 1967, a feat that had previously proved beyond the most powerful British clubs, that set him totally apart in the annals of the sport. That other legendary Scot Bill Shankly got it just about right when he held out a fellow miner's hand to Stein after the brilliant defeat of Inter-Milan and said in his coal-cutter voice: 'John – you're immortal.'

Celtic in Lisbon performed with irresistible verve, representing perfectly Stein's ideal of blending athletic speed and competitiveness with imagination, delicacy of touch at close quarters and exhilarating surges of virtuosity. Of course, when all Stein's technical assets had been assessed – the vast tactical awareness that owed nothing to coaching courses, the precise judgement of his own and opposing players, the encyclopaedic retention of detail, the emphasis on the positive while eradicating the foolhardy – the essence of his gifts as a manager was seen to reside in something more basic and more subtle: in his capacity to make men do for him more than they would have been able to do for themselves.

Stein's allegiance to Celtic withstood more than one attempt to coax him to switch dramatically to the manager's chair at Rangers and it was sad that when his connection with Parkhead was eventually severed in 1978 he should leave with a justified feeling of grievance about how he had ultimately been treated. By that time he had survived a warning of skirmish with heart trouble and a car crash that almost killed him in the summer of 1975. Many men would have throttled down there and then but he had been a compulsive worker around football most of his life and when the manager's job at Leeds United was offered he decided, at the age of fifty-five, to move south.

However, two months later he received the call millions of admirers believed he should have had years before and was given control of the Scotland team. He took them to the World Cup Finals in Spain in 1982 (the Soviet Union kept them out of the last twelve on goal difference) and after a match last Tuesday notable for its tensions and controversies, never for its quality, he had the result required to open a way to the Finals of 1986. But suddenly the strains that have been mounting mercilessly over the years, strains whose ravages the obsessive in him insisted on belittling, proved too much for a system weakened by that earlier illness and, most crucially, by the desperate car crash of ten years ago.

The pain of his death from a heart attack dug deepest into his wife Jean and into Rae and George, the attractive, stong-minded daughter and son of whom he was so proud. But there were many others in many places who felt last week that they did not have to go down a pit to know what real darkness was.

from The Observer, 15 September 1985

A Particularly Violent Day
JAY ALLAN

Eight a.m. at the Schooner Bar, Aberdeen. A young lad, Ray, joins three others who are waiting for the bar to open: Jim, Mole and Strath. He is told, as all the others will be, that twenty-five have already left Aberdeen on the 7 a.m. train – some to check out the shops in Glasgow for a new jumper or jacket, and some who simply couldn't sleep for sheer excitement and anticipation of the day ahead. You leave on the first train and come home on the last, if you've got the bottle.

A heavy key turns in the door and the four walk in, shampooed, shaved, with gold chains on their necks and about £180 worth of clothes on each. Jim is first at the bar: 'What yous for then, boys? Me and Strath's startin' with orange. So's Mole. Ray?'

'Ah, make it a pint of lager and lime, seein' as it's Celtic.'

They all laugh. On days like this it's always tough, especially after the match, and that's they way they like it. Jim has a bottle of Pils for good measure.

With vintage UB40 playing, the boys grab a table slowly, in ones and twos. More trendies enter the bar. Many have had very little sleep, but they don't care. It's Celtic today and they've been speaking about it for weeks.

By 8.25 a.m. there are around thirty-five in the bar, mostly discussing rubble in the town last night or what they're wearing, or the possibilities of rubble at Scottish and English games. Usually some

Aberdeen boys travel to England but not on the big ones – and Celtic certainly is a big one. A couple of lads from Torry are meeting two lads from Leeds, and there's always a few Scallies from Liverpool, but never more than ten. They can come with Aberdeen as long as there's not too many of them – because it's Aberdeen's mob, not Aberdeen plus somebody.

8.35 a.m. Now there's about sixty in the bar. One large group round a small table is the nucleus of the mob, an unwritten but accepted fact. There are about twenty-five of the elite, and even within that there is a scale of rank, though not many discuss it. Major decisions like train times, time to leave bars for the match or for rubble, and routes to avoid police, are decided amongst these top boys, and of these lads there are normally no more than two major decision-makers, or as some would say, leaders. For two years I was one of the leaders, and to the majority of young Casuals I was the number one, although Ray was always there, too.

'Got any hash?' Jim shouts over to Glennie, who's just walked in. 'Lovely little half-quarter of black here, my sons. Don't worry, we'll get wasted on the train.'

One of the under-fives is handing out new north-east firm stickers. There's around fifty under-fives and more big lads are jumping off buses and taxis, panicking that they won't have time to get their tickets. For different reasons – wages lost at cards or simply because they're out of a job – there are normally one or two, sometimes three, 'tappers', who get 50p or £1 from as many people as they can to pay for the train, food and a couple of pints. I have seen a young tapper clear a card school of £50 from 50ps given to him by those in the school.

As we walk to the platform the usual railway coppers are there, looking for drink. The same half-dozen cops – as long as you keep the joints under the table and don't get caught jumping the train, they're alright, not like the real filth in the town. 'Well Mr Allan,' said one PC, 'I see there's a good team of you going today.'

'Aye, there'll be a sound when this lot hits Glasgow, I'm nae jokin!'

As the train pulls away at 9.06 a.m. there are just over 200 Casuals and around twenty-five scarfers (or Christmas Trees, as we call them) on board. They are not our enemies – far from it, we've saved their skins a few times. The Casuals and scarfers, however, never go together in the town of an away game. It's not that all scarfers hate

258

fighting, but Christmas Trees usually fight when they lose a game. For us fighting is the game. You get boring games like St Mirren and good games like Celtic. Almost all Celtic and Rangers' fans want to play. They may throw stones and run from us, but they all enjoy the game.

The lads are now settled in. There are fifteen card schools and seven or eight groups of hash-smokers. A couple of lads manage to get their half-bottles of vodka and orange on, hidden down their balls. Most like to keep control of their senses. Some like to drink what they can to dull the sight of the hundreds behind the handful they might be running into.

I play on the big boys' table while the going is good. The same old faces are there: Watty, Turdie, Gregg, Big D and two more who wait for dropouts. There's always an audience of ten or a dozen, and plenty look-outs to shout when the guard comes on so that one or two jumpers can hide in between the seats. An old favourite of the jumpers is to sit on the bog with your jeans and pants to the floor and leave the door saying 'Vacant', so that any punter will just get embarrassed and go elsewhere, and the guard won't check a vacant bog.

In the school, pots of £30 and £40 are not rare for three-card brag. The most I won was on a train to Hibs – £74. When we got to our usual bar in Edinburgh my round was eighteen pints of lager, two tops and three lime, sixty fags and four pies. That was a score gone for a start, but it's the accepted thing to do, to stand your hand when you're in the winnings. And quite right, too.

Another ten Casuals come on at Stonehaven, and a handful at Montrose, but from then on you're no longer in your manor. Now you're entering jute territory. Many good rucks have been had in Dundee, but it's harder now because, as in Aberdeen, the police are very well organized, and there are so many when you play Dundee, or Dundee United, there's always the same faces. It's not so much one football team against another (although at games of high importance it can make confrontations even more violent), it's more one city against another.

The next stop is Perth, home of St Johnstone. Although they have a small, violent mob, they're a bit primitive – still skinheads – and there aren't that many of them.

Stirling is half an hour from Glasgow and sometimes some of the younger lads (the under-fives) get off here. That's because if it's an early train then all the big boys go for beers and the under-fives are left alone on the streets of Glasgow. If there are too few on an early train then they'll just get off and wait for the next train, and more under-fives for back-up.

Once past Stirling, the adrenalin really starts to flow. The lads get restless and the card schools stop. Tension is high not through fear (at least not generally) but through overwhelming excitement and anticipation. For sure there will be the usual police presence, sneering down their noses at us. 'Scum,' they'll say, and we'll look at them just long enough not to get pulled up. Even some of the coppers are recognizable from previous games. How feverishly hated they are – hated more than the lads we've travelled to fight.

There will also be representatives of other mobs there to suss out how many are coming off this train. Maybe Rangers or Motherwell will be there, waiting for a train to Edinburgh, or a couple of West Ham ICF or Scouse Scallies just up for the day to see what this Aberdeen mob is like. They'll have read about the mob in *The Face* or *The Maker*, or seen it in a real paper like *The Observer*. However, I think even football thugs, while realizing that all the fashion and violence is real, know that stories about us in gutter press newspapers are glorified beyond all recognition.

The corridors of the train are full now, and the doorways are solid. The time is 12.30 p.m. and everyone wants to be on the platform first. Your boat at the front of the mob, that's the business.

As the train slows down to stop, casuals are filing out of the train, bursting with excitement. We're in Glasgow once again – magic! We wonder what's going to happen this time, and hope it's as mental as Rangers was earlier this season.

The scene is pretty much standard. There's about twenty uniformed cops in the building, and quite a few vans just outside. (It's a funny thing that coppers are supposed to be such heroes for stopping violence, when sometimes I think they love it more than we do. Nothing pleases them more than dragging a young thug by the hair into their van, knees in his ribs and kicking him in the legs or back. They always make sure they don't hit your face and let you sue them. I have witnessed a cop with a Hearts scarf outside Tynecastle shouting: 'Come on then, you Casual bastards,' and when the Casual he was challenging booted him in the legs, he whisked him off into a nearby car and charged him with police assault. There's got to be something wrong there, surely.)

As usual, Paul and a couple of mates (Aberdeen Casuals from Glasgow) are amongst the welcoming party which includes two lads from Edinburgh, seven from Fife, the twenty-five that travelled on the 7 a.m. train, sixteen boozy Hazelhead Casuals from a minibus and three cars-full whose drivers just had to show the lads their new motors.

All in all, there's just short of 300 of the best boys. There will be a couple of hundred more on the specials, mainly younger boys, but this is our service crew. We are told immediately that three under-fives got done by Motherwell (the Saturday Service) on their way to play Hibs in Edinburgh. It's quite common for small groups to get rucked when they're looking around the shops.

Three Scousers, Liverpool Scallies, are the only English spies today. We don't mind them looking on 'cause they'll tell their lads back home how Aberdeen's got a good big firm and they're all mental.

The police start walking towards us and the lads don't even bother with all the bullshit. 'If you want to see the game move along now!' It's time to head into town anyway.

Whenever your mob gets off a train, out of a bar or out of the ground it always looks so much bigger. I don't know exactly why it is, but walking in a mob of 200 or more is a fantastic feeling – it's probably the security and the feeling of power. It's also magic watching all the amazement on the public's face, the pointing fingers. I think most of them realize it's not them we want to harm. The punter out walking and shopping is no target, the days of running down streets with shaved heads, braces and DMs, smashing house windows, are past. I wonder what they got out of that.

No. What the modern thug wants is to fight his opposite number in different areas and cities from his own. They want to fight us. We want to fight them. I've even seen thugs from Aberdeen witness for an opposition Casual in Edinburgh and vice versa. I think they just know that when it's down to courts it's them against us, no matter which city you're from.

Everyone heads for one of three or so bars that are big enough to hold the bulk of the lads. Today it's beside Central Station. It's well situated, has plenty of room and a good juke box. When we get about 25 yards from the bar some of the boys start running, making sure they get their whistle wet before the rest of the lads. Bottled Becks is the order of the day – tastes great and doesn't bloat you up like pints of lager or beer. Also, they're easy to carry through mobs of youths queuing to get served, or easily popped into your jacket to be drunk in the street or even thrown at opposition Casuals that you can't catch. We seldom throw things. Hand-to-hand combat is much more fun than throwing bottles and stones at each other. Glasgow has been famous for years for its running stone fights, and heavy bottles of Irn Bru are a definite favourite with the locals.

It's 12.45 p.m. now and most are on their third bottle. There are about 180 in the Central Bar and around forty in Tropics round the corner. There's more chances of a go when there's fewer of you.

Just before 1 p.m., Finlay comes up to our table and reports that two of our under-fives just got wasted outside Austin Reed's and one of them is away to hospital. Some of the lads have already gone looking for the bastards. Suddenly someone runs in and shouts: 'Celtic's outside, c'mon.' There's a huge rush to the door, the bar staff watch in amazement as the lads bottleneck, swaying and pushing, dying to get out and into them. It's a bit of a disappointment when we get into the street to find there's only about forty Celtic, and as soon as our under-fives know the lads are behind them they steam into Celtic. They don't stand long. As we make our way back inside a white cop van pulls up. Shit! That's all we need. Now they know where we are for sure and they'll keep tabs on us till we're off their patch. That's the best thing about Glasgow – you can be walking in an escort and suddenly you're on your own again. They don't give a shit if there's trouble, just as long as it's not on their manor.

1.15 p.m. now, and the suggestions start over when we should leave for the match. The eager lads say 1.30 p.m.; the boozers say 2.30 p.m. 2.15 p.m. is decided by me, Ray and Big D.

By 1.30 p.m. some of the lads are feeling the drink, and confidence is high. One of the top lads, Flakes, says with a laugh: 'Look around boys! What a fuckin' mob we've got, we're gonna waste Celtic, we're gonna fuckin' kill them!'

'C'mon then boys, it's a quarter past, let's go, let's go do it,' Ray says. I look at my watch – 2.15 p.m. I take a last long swig of my Becks and the whole bar starts swilling large gulps down their throats. A couple of boys look really pissed off – they've just paid for pints. But when the top lads go, everyone goes.

Passers-by stop and stare as more and more and more youths file out of the bar like a Paul Daniels hanky trick. I always think: 'Jesus, no way were we all in one pub.' We're joined by nearly 100 under-fives, the lads from Tropics and quite a few latecomers off the football special train. All in all there are around 350–400 of us. The sun is shining and all the lads are smiling. This is what we live for; this is what life is all about. I wish this walk to Parkhead would last forever, though I hope we won't just be walking all the way.

We like fighting other teams' Casuals best – that's who we really want. But, especially with the Old Firm, there's thousands who want to fight just like us, but are scarfers and hate even the Casuals of their own team. Aberdeen Casuals must be the most hated group of people in Scotland. We like it that way, it means that more people are willing to have a go.

It always starts the same. Going to Parkhead, some lads start punching the odd face and then the first time there's a decent mob of Celtic together everyone just goes for it non-stop until we get to the ground, and hopefully get a few hooks inside too. (This day turned out to be an exceptionally good one to remember.)

'Fuckin' magic, the cops are off.'

'Brilliant. OK boys, let's do it.'

'Come on, let's get nearer the front.'

Everyone is talking now, everyone knows it's time. There's plenty of Celtic scarfers on their way to the ground.

A corporation bus passes jammed with Celtic (Tims) and on the top deck they're all banging on their windows and shouting, 'You're fuckin' dead you Casual bastards.'

Just in front of us the bus stopped and to my amazement the shouters got off. Me and Big D were nearest so we didn't hang around, I butted the nearest one to me and Big D hooked another. It was as though a starting gun had been fired. The fifteen or so are joined by twenty more Celtic from a bar and fighting is breaking out everywhere at the front. Every corporation bus that passes is solid with Tims, and the under-fives are doing in their windows. Lots of Celtic get off further up and join the barncy.

2.30 p.m., London Road is a riot. There's a mob behind us getting bigger all the time, and there's a huge mob in front of us. Meanwhile me and twenty others are chasing thirty mods and skinheads up some side road – might as well waste them too. The bastards are too fast, though, and we just manage a punch off one face and a boot in the hip. Two lads kicked some scooters over.

Back in the main street there are unbelievable scenes, typical for Glasgow. It's now a stone and bottle affair – they won't stand and fight. They run up really close, throw their stones and bottles, then run like hell for more arms. At least six or seven shop-keepers run out to put their tin shutters down.

In the buses now Celtic are kicking out their own windows, and throwing anything they can get their hands on, from coins to their Irn Bru bottles. The chaos lasts a good five minutes before the first police van arrives, but the next six vans are very close behind.

At the bottom of the mob, the police grab any they can see still fighting. From experience, most of the lads know to stop when the bill steam in. It's just not worth getting lifted. Having said that there are a few charged at every game. Some don't see the bill in time, some are too involved in the ruck, and some are too pissed to give a damn.

Russell from Hazelhead, one of the boozers from the minibus, is thrown in the van along with two Celtic scarfers. As vans scream up through the street to the top fight, bodies scatter everywhere and most Aberdeen head along one side road. Two Aberdeen Casuals are lifted, and about five more drunken Celtic fans.

By now just about everyone is together again, and we're in an escort. Quite a few of the boys are sporting cuts and scuff marks, but everyone is smiling. Jesus! we just ran Celtic from both sides and by the end we were well outnumbered. Everyone talks at once, discussing their part of the action. No doubt, some exaggerate, some lie. But one thing is for sure – Aberdeen Casuals did very well. We showed the bastards, we showed them alright.

Now most of the boys have had a taste, there's nothing will stop them. Everyone is totally psyched up now, ready for anything. 'That's us 'till after the game now, boys,' says Ray, and we know he's right. There are now seven police on horseback, four vans, and about forty-four foot cops. One way or another, our mob is now about 300 strong – God knows where the rest went. Only around five were lifted. I suppose there were a few who couldn't handle the pressure on London Road and did a shoot. Some may have chased Glasgow boys too far and got lost or wasted. Still, at least three-quarters of the boys are still left, and they will run from no one now.

By 2.45 p.m. we are being escorted through the car park at Parkhead. Some Celtic bears are shouting abuse at the other side of the horses, things like: 'Come to the Barras and we'll fucking kill you, by the way,' and 'Ma wife an' her mates could do yous, ya bastards.' All of course said with the usual growl of the Glasgow accent. They speak like dogs bark.

Most of the English are terrified by the Glasgow accent, but although there are a lot of hard areas and hard men in Glasgow, the same could be said of every big city in Britain. Their reputation is definitely exaggerated.

When we get through the turnstiles, we make our way up to the terrace. The Rangers end is segregated; we have half and Celtic the other. There's a large gap in the terrace between sets of fans, heavy barriers and about 100 police trying to keep it that way.

There are already about 200 Casuals at the top of the Aberdeen support. Stories filter through that five of the boys originally with us in London Road split from the mob and got jumped. Rob's hand is cut pretty bad, Bones has got a nasty cut on his cheek, and poor Gab is away to get a glass cut on his hand stitched. When I see Rob's hand I say: 'What the hell happened to you then, eh?'

'Oh we got jumped. I'm nae jokin', there was about twenty of them. We stood, though, but they had bottles or glasses clean out of a bar.'

2.56 p.m. The players come out to massive roars, and both supports burst into song. The crowd is 43,000; Aberdeen have around 9,000 of them. After kick-off, Aberdeen force a corner straight away. The fans reply with one arm in the air, swaying 'Come on ye Reds!' All the Casual mob start singing 'Ran away, ran away, ran away . . .' to the Celtic on the other side of the segregation. And for the first time we get a glimpse of the Celtic trendies – a pathetic-looking lot. There are only 150–200 of them, and it looks like none of them are even eighteen. 'What a shit mob.'

The game is going very well. Midway through the first half, the Dons have the edge in a very tight match. Roy Aitken and Willie Miller are bouncing opposition players all over the park. There's the usual thundrous roar from the jungle every time a decision goes against Celtic. Of course, a lot of the lads are more interested in a slagging match than a football match. Whenever Celtic come out with one of their beloved religious (or anti-religious) songs like *Roamin' in the Gloamin'* or *Soldiers are We*, all the lads wave their hands in the air and conduct the massive orchestra of Glasgwegians with rum on their breath and vodka-injected oranges in their pockets. I don't pretend to understand the Catholic/Protestant hatred, or how they slander the Queen and the Pope respectively. As far as I'm concerned both are good, gentle and peace-loving people. Surely neither could properly be described as a bastard?

Most of the Casuals do watch Aberdeen when they play, and do genuinely love the club and players, but for some the only good thing about winning is that you get a good bounce at the goals. Also, it makes the away fans mad, and therefore more willing to come ahead after the game.

The half-time whistle goes, me and a few lads go out of the terrace into the back to see if there's any chance of a go. 'Who's that skinhead down there, eh?' Terry points down to a bonehead beside one of the entrances. 'Come on,' he says, 'let's find out.'

Terry: 'Hey skinhead, who are you?'

Skinhead: 'Ah'm no Celtic, I fuckin' hate Celtic.'

Tel: 'Well you're no Aberdeen with a skinhead, are you?'

Bonehead: 'Ah'm wantin' to fight wi youz against they Tim bastards.'

The skinhead pulls up his jumper to reveal a Union Jack t-shirt, proving at least that he certainly isn't Celtic.

Terry, pissed off with talking, punches him in the mouth and says: 'Fuck off, no skins in our mob. We fuckin' hate Rangers anyway.' The skinhead doesn't seem too impressed, so Terry runs in again, punches him and boots him until it sinks into the boy that we weren't wanting him to stick around and go for a few beers with us after the game.

Some of the lads managed to get some rubble in the bogs, but apart from that, it was a quiet half-time, and now, at 3.56 p.m., everyone is back on the terrace to watch Celtic kick-off.

Proving how big the influence of the fighting is, I can't remember exactly the score of the match but I know that we won and when our first goal of the match went in it was the usual scene. All the players celebrate, Fergie and Garner jump on to the track, hands in the air. And all the Casuals and scarfers bounce and shout hysterically. The whole Aberdeen sings a deafening 'We're gonna win the league,' followed by all the Casuals with appropriate hand signals singing 'one nil, one nil . . .' to the tune of *Amazing Grace*.

Aberdeen scored the winner and the Reds are still bouncing on the terrace when a familiar song with a real volume and feeling goes up from the Celtic support: 'You're gonna get your fuckin' heads kicked in.' To this they receive the usual reply of everyone waving their hands in the air to a high-pitched *woo woo*'s or maybe just a round of applause for coming out with such an original song. One thing is for sure, though, there's going to be rubble after this game. There's going to be thousands of mad Celtic, a few hundred who're pissed off at the doing they got on London Road, and about 150 Celtic Casuals. At full time the adrenalin is high. No doubt some are a bit wary and some are a bit scared but for the bulk it's smiles all round – time to steam in again.

Before the game, because people take different forms of transport, drink in different bars or go shopping instead, the mob is never all there. But straight after the game you can see properly how many boys you've got. Today we're pretty impressive. Looking back at all the heads I reckon there must be around 500; certainly no less than 450.

Everyone sticks together now. You're OK with a mob, but leave it and you're in trouble. Heading towards the first street of Celtic supporters, some of the lads are weaving their way to the front with anticipation. Suddenly a stone comes flying towards us, quickly followed by another, and then a half-bottle (empty of course). The effect of this is like the starting gun at the London Marathon; the Casuals wade in in droves. Celtic stand their ground. A really violent flare-up has started, and Celtic are running from everywhere to join the fun.

By the time the police wade in, minutes of mental battles had taken place, and for some time it's a relief – they are totally knackered. Nobody has really won this battle. A few of us got hit; a few of them got hit, the best thing is that there's been a good battle and, when outnumbered, the lads stood no problem. Two more of the boozy Hazelhead lot got lifted and a couple of Tims were thrown in the van as well.

That's the good thing about Celtic and Rangers – when they lose the match they do go mental. And because there are so many of them, you're battling all the way to the station.

Unfortunately, we've picked up a large police escort again, and four or five vans stretch the length of the mob (about 100 yards). There are five or six horses, too. The police have crushed everyone on to the grass verge and pavement at the side of the road, and we take the long way to Queen Street.

Some boys right at the front are striding out as fast as they can go without running, trying to get a fight without being seen by the coppers. There's a mob of about forty Celtic just in front of them across the road and the usual constant stream of Celtic fans heading for the city centre. Something has to happen soon.

It does. To the great joy of the lads, there's about 100 Celtic Casuals, and we get our chance. Aberdeen stream across the road and there is total panic. Horses are turned where Aberdeen are fighting, and at least two folk are knocked to the ground by them. Another few are arrested. When the police eventually pull Celtic back up the road and settle the Aberdeen lot back to walking, it's clear that there's little chance of more rubble as the police are greatly reinforced. Nearly 100 police in all are escorting Aberdeen. It's usually possible for small groups to break away from the escort, but the bulk will be escorted all the way to the station now. A few times the mob runs to try to shake the law, but with their radios and vans they make those attempts useless.

Thinking the day is over, quite a lot – over 100 – start to jog to Queen Street station trying to catch the 5.25 p.m. special back to Aberdeen. Mostly they're the under-fives or the lads with nagging birds. The bulk will take the 6 p.m. service train; a hardcore will wait for the 7.25 p.m., which unfortunately is the last train to leave Glasgow for Aberdeen.

When we get to Queen Street it's pretty obvious that there'll be no more violence, at least until the police escort is thinned down. About twenty-five of us go into Samuel Dow's bar, just next to the station. Pints are bought and we all sit down to talk about the day's events. It's been a good day for the Aberdeen Casuals. Came to Glasgow, ran amok, won the match, and still have a chance of some more. With most of the lads packed safely on their way home, Celtic Casuals will get braver and start milling around the station. Also, Rangers have to come back from Paisley, and Motherwell's Casuals will probably go home from Edinburgh via Glasgow.

During the discussion we find out that Watty, Brooner and Arsenal Steve are lifted, along with a dozen lesser-known Casuals. The Scousers we met off the train are now in Dow's with us, and they start

268

educating some of the lads on how to screw bandits – quite easy with a bit of plastic strimmer wire on metal slots or 10ps wrapped in silver paper and put into 50p plastic slots. One of the Scouse Scallies takes Telboy and Glennie to the next-door bar to show them how it's done. With so much unemployment in Liverpool, Scousers are the Kings of fraud. They can fix your electricity meter with a wire or rub off a signature on credit cards with brake fluid and sign their own names. They know the lot, and I suppose with no job and no prospects it's not really surprising.

Twenty minutes later the bandit frauders are back, pockets bulging with 10p pieces. They got £16 in total, and that emptied the machine.

'Anyone knockin' around outside, Tel?'

'Naw, naebody, and there's still heaps of coppers – watching this bar, too. There's no danger of another go now, no chance!'

As we leave Sammy Dow's at 7.15 p.m. it's soon apparent that Terry was right. The bill have sharpened themselves up a bit now, though it's got to be said that they didn't do well today. Quick pop into Casey Jones for a quarter-pounder, and then we get straight on to the train.

It's always annoying that you can't take drink on the train for the way home. Trying to keep you sober on the way down so that you don't fight at the match is fair enough, but when you've been in the bar for a few beers with your mates and you're not going to get home until 10.30 p.m., it's a bummer not being able to take a couple of cans to ease the boredom of the return journey. This journey is as boring as usual, and some of the lads go to sleep. We're all relieved when it pulls into Aberdeen station. It's 10.35 p.m. Magic! – there's time to nip up to Tammels to see the second half on the box.

When we get to Tammels, the upstairs lounge is mobbed with Casuals all watching the match, and we manage to see the winning goal and a couple of sways and bounces from our mob in the terrace behind the goal. Most of the lads will stay in the top bar until 1 a.m. but those with suitable clothing to get into discos will do so.

Me, Ged, Clouse, Gregg and a couple of others go to Gabriel's night-club, where there's an excellent sound system, chilled bottled beers, and plenty talent. By the end of the night (2.30 a.m.) all of us are well boozy. Ged and Gregg come with me to my flat while Clouse and the other lads make their way to the taxi rank. There are always about forty or fifty folk hanging around the stance until at least 3 a.m.

and sometimes 4 a.m. There are always a few girls hanging around, and hundreds of late-night revellers join the queue to get their taxis home. It's a real social centre at weekends. You might well get yourself invited to a party and get laid. Or you can get into a barney with some bikers or drunken mannies who start on you. Worst of all, you can get lifted. The police are never very far away – they only get out of sight long enough for a fight to start and then swoop in, hoping for arrests. On a Saturday night pounds are spent on chipping the white paint off their cars, and blue paint off their vans. Not just by Casuals either.

It's 3 a.m. when we get home, and it's time for bed but what a good time we've had. We look forward to Dundee Utd at home next week, but we'll rememeber today for a long time as a particualrly violent day.

from *Bloody Casuals: Diary of a Football Hooligan*, 1989

'The White Nigger'
DAVE HILL

'I used to call Howard "my white nigger". Now that is a compliment. It was the only way I could find to describe that I thought he was OK.'

TOMMY SMITH

The football culture of Merseyside has, for twenty-five years, represented one of the most passionate distillations of Liverpool's collective grass-roots identity. To support Liverpool or Everton is not simply to consume an afternoon's sporting entertainment, or even to follow the fortunes of a team. It is to participate in a ritual celebration of all the working-class characteristics that Liverpudlians of red and blue alike recognize as marks of distinction. The things that have become clichés, the wit, the knowingness a streetwise cut above the average – these account for part of it. Everton in the sixties was known as soccer's School of Science. Liverpool's players were canny and cultivated. But there were other qualities which the Merseysiders prided themselves on too, Liverpool in particular: dogged, resilient, nothing airy-fairy, and, if required, ready to mix it with anyone.

At Liverpool that reputation was formed under Bill Shankly. 'If you're going to fight for something, fight till you drop. That was Shanks's way of playing the game,' says Tommy Smith. In European competition, the qualities of true-grit solidarity-under-fire came to be contrasted with the perceived cynicism and sneakiness of the club's great European rivals, especially those from Italy. The Heysel confrontation has a historical explanation. A notorious previous European Cup encounter between Liverpool and an Italian side had taken place in 1965, the Red's first foray into European competition. The opposition was Inter Milan and the two teams met at the semi-final stage. Travelling to defend a 3–1 lead from the Anfield leg, Liverpool's players were subjected to an all-night barrage of motor horns and church bells on the eve of the game. Some dubious refereeing helped Inter to a 3–nil win and led to persistent rumours that the official had been bribed. The incident has entered the folk memory of the Liverpool FC fraternity, preserved with a prejudice echoing the English football establishment's habitual characterization of Mediterranean teams – excitable; untrustworthy; fatally flawed by the so-called 'Latin temperament'.

Liverpool supporters and Liverpool teams would never countenance such defects in their own ranks. Even at the height of their fame great individuals like Roger Hunt, Kevin Keegan and Kenny Dalglish never put vainglorious whims before the good of the team. Craft was encouraged, great skill highly prized, but unbridled ostentation – now, that could be a mixed blessing. The florid, intuitive player of extravagant gifts but dubious consistency was unlikely to be tolerated under the Anfield regime. After all, he might give the ball away. There had been eloquent flair players, running wingers like Peter Thompson and Steve Heighway whose job it was to go past opponents if they could, and the crowds had warmed to them. But these were also team men and temperamentally seen to be sound. Nothing suspect about them.

The Liverpool teams of Shankly, Bob Paisley and his short-lived successor Joe Fagan were united by this philosophy. If the club's Orange foundations had never been flaunted or actively promoted, on the field of play the Protestant work ethic was alive and well: blood, sweat and discipline a plenty, with no unnecessary ritual – and, of course, home with the silverware year after year. Given the unyielding stereotype to which they were routinely compared, black players were assumed to be about as suitable at Anfield as a ham sandwich in a synagogue. They, like all those swarthy Continentals, were generally regarded in English football as flashy, superficial and untrustworthy.

One football journalist recalls discussing the matter with Bob Paisley: 'If you ever talked to Bob Paisley and you asked him about various coloured footballers in private conversation, he'd say, "The trouble is, these sort of people, they don't tend to get stuck in, and they tend to get discouraged very easily." I don't think he was the least bit racialist . . . he just thought that in his experience, coloured footballers tended to get upset when things started going wrong, and drop out of the game. So he tended to be looking at them rather more critically than he'd look at other people.' Paisley is not recalled as expressing these views with malice. Simply, he was adhering to the prevailing wisdom of the football world at the time. At Everton, the same attitudes prevailed. Brian Labone was Everton's centre-half and captain throughout most of the sixties and early seventies, when Harry Catterick, an old-school disciplinarian, was manager of the team. He confirms that all the usual assumptions, about bottle, about reliability, about how 'they' won't go out when it rains, were commonly held in the Everton dressing-room. Gordon Lee, the Goodison manager from 1977 to 1981, was well known for his dislike of foreign players and black players, and in the opinion of former Everton stars, would never have signed one. It was hardly a break with tradition. Trebilcock, the Cup Final hero, had gone almost as soon as he arrived. Cliff Marshall, the local black winger, had failed to make a major impact. Some say that Marshall had all the skill but lacked competitive will. Others say that his spirit was so sapped by intimidation from crowds and opposing players he was emptied of the desire to play.

Liverpool, meanwhile, were the last club likely to take what they would have perceived as a risk. Their rituals were established, their preparations routinized to the point of fetishism. 'I'd . . . suggest that something as simple as superstition could be at the heart of the matter,' wrote former club captain Phil Neal. 'I reckon some of the coaches fear that a change in the training pattern could burst the Anfield bubble. It's a very old-fashioned club in many respects.' The system was the thing and the players Liverpool liked were the sort who would conform to it. And, of course, you couldn't rely on these 'coloured lads', could you? Everyone knew that.

It was into this environment that Howard Gayle took his Liverpool 8 sensibility, a native scouser and yet an outsider in a revered institution of his own home town. Gayle was a winger, a ball-player, a guy who could beat one man, beat two men, beat three men. He had a lot of ability. But, not, apparently, enough for some. 'It's quite ironic that we've not had a lot of coloured players,' Mr Robinson reflected, lightly, 'but the local community hasn't really thrown an outstanding one up. It's rather strange that it's happened in other areas. We had Howard Gayle who was locally-born. He had a good spell here but he really wasn't up to the standard that we required.'

It is not a point of view that everybody shares. 'At the age of sixteen or seventeen he was a very good player. He had the toughness and everything. I know for a fact that at Liverpool they were very disappointed that he didn't come through.' This is Tommy Smith's assessment of Howard Gayle's talent. Lawrence Iro, who knows both Gayle and John Barnes, offers a comparison of the two. 'OK, John Barnes is a great player, and he's got that little bit of craft. But Howie was fast ... faster than John Barnes will ever be.' Another of Gayle's team-mates, goalkeeper Bruce Grobbelaar, expressed a high opinion in his 1986 autobiography. But in the end his explanation for Gayle's failure to flourish is much the same as Smith's. Grobbelaar is the latest South African-born player to appear in a Liverpool shirt. Having moved to Rhodesia as a child, he had been drafted into the army there, and fought against the black guerrillas – 'terrorists', as Grobbelaar calls them – fighting to bring down Ian Smith's white supremacist regime. After a spell of goalkeeping in North America, Grobbelaar became a celebrity the hard way at Anfield. His early performances were littered with mistakes in vital games and he earned the nickname 'The Clown.' Subsequently proving his prowess as a marvellously gifted 'keeper, his attention-seeking activities on the field of play have made him a favourite with the Anfield faithful and have seen him hailed by the football media as the kind of individual who, to them, is meat and drink – a 'personality'.

But despite his early brushes with the derision of Liverpool partisans, Grobbelaar seems to have remained blissfully oblivious to the sensitivities of those around him. The passage in his ghosted book devoted to his relationship with Gayle speaks volumes for an inability to understand that there are some things some people should never be expected to laugh about, especially coming from a white South African: 'I do know that ... Howard Gayle was none too keen on me. There is always a lot of chat and winding up in the Liverpool dressing-room, and the first team players, quick to pick up on my "Jungle Man" nickname and my military service background, warned the coloured Howard Gayle that I would be after him.'

Grobbelaar goes on to describe an incident involving himself, Gayle and Olympic decathlon champion Daley Thompson who visited the team in training one day. The episode revolves around a racial 'joke' Grobbelaar made to the two of them, an astonishingly crude personal remark. 'Daley promptly fell into fits of laughter,' Grobbelaar reports, 'but Howard was not at all amused and found nothing to smile about.'

Thompson is a man whose consciousness with regard to his own colour is, by his own account, entirely different from that of Gayle. In fact it is not a characteristic by which he choses to define himself at all. But, then, it is not colour itself that has required race to become an issue among black people, but the attitude of whites to the characteristics they believe go with it. The peculiarities of Thompson's upbringing appear to have shielded him from the worst of the institutionalized diminution of black people's lives that is routine in Liverpool 8. Of racially-mixed parentage and educated in an otherwise all-white private school in Sussex, he has been spared the worst that British racism can offer. Submerging himself in sport, his strange, solitary lifestyle increased his isolation from the rest of the world. He rationalized 'race' to himself as a non-issue and took a dim view of other black athletes who did not. A revered figure in his chosen career, Thompson had spent his whole life refusing to acknowledge that racism, or anything else, could stop him from getting to the top. What else was he going to do but laugh?

But for Howard Gayle, racist 'humour', from Grobbelaar or anyone else, was not something his own heart would allow him to tolerate. He talked back. He fought back. He knew how to turn a cutting phrase himself and did not leave the talent untapped. But Gayle's resistance was not acceptable to some of those around him and there is no doubt that he paid for it. 'The funny thing is that I rather liked Howard Gayle,' wrote Grobbelaar, 'and if he hadn't carried around a great big chip on his shoulder he could have become an English international . . . If he were to allow [his] ability to take over and express himself in football terms he could still be a truly outstanding player.'

'Get rid of that chip, and you'll go far,' is how one club insider recalls Gayle being addressed by an illustrious Liverpool player. And how he was put to the test. One year at the players' Christmas party a comedian was hired to entertain. As part of his act the comic walked up to where Gayle was sitting and emptied a bowl of flour over his head: 'Now try walking into fucking Toxteth,' announced the funny man, or words to that effect. Gayle kept his cool. But the effort required to keep smiling in the face of such attentions would try the patience of a saint.

There are many who claim that Gayle was no angel. Under Shankly and Paisley, Liverpool players who got their names in the papers following this indiscretion or that seemed inexorably to find their way first on to the subs' bench, then into the Reserves and on to the transfer list soon after. People's memories of Gayle are fogged with speculations about one dubious propensity or another – speculations, though, are all they are. The club, meanwhile, put pressure on him to move out of Liverpool 8 and break contact with the area altogether. But though Gayle agreed to live somewhere else, he was not willing to desert his friends, whatever reputation the club attached to them. He was not willing to abandon his roots to keep Liverpool happy, not physically, not emotionally, not politically. The club could not begin to understand why.

So was it lack of ability that counted against Gayle or was it a question of 'character'? What word in English football parlance is more pregnant with value judgements? Consider the different things 'character' would have meant to Howard Gayle from Liverpool 8 compared with every other person in his vicinity at Liverpool Football Club. For them, 'character' meant submitting to the culture of the club. For Gayle, it meant the opposite. It could only count against him.

Howard Gayle played just five times for the Liverpool first team. The first, in October 1980, was a run-out as substitute away to Manchester City. The second could not have been more different. Liverpool were embroiled in a contentious European Cup semi-final with the formidable West German champions, Bayern Munich. The first leg at Anfield had seen the home team held to a goalless draw. Afterwards, the Bayern captain Paul Breitner had been reported as describing Liverpool's tactics as 'unintelligent'. Liverpool prepared for the second leg determined to make Breitner eat his words, but they had problems. Injuries had forced them to draft in a couple of reserve defenders. Howard Gayle made it on to the substitutes' bench.

In a furiously combative atmosphere Kenny Dalglish, the ace in Liverpool's pack, limped off the pitch within a few minutes of the start. Manager Bob Paisley, in what has been described by the then team captain Graeme Souness as 'an inspired use of the tactical substitution', sent Gayle on with instructions to take on the German defence.

Bayern, it seems, had no prior knowledge of this young fringe player, dribbling with the ball at high speed in a manner that was utterly untypical of the usual Liverpool style. 'Howie ran them ragged,' wrote Souness. And for an hour that is precisely what he did. The Germans resorted to kicking him. '[Liverpool] might have had a penalty just before the half hour,' wrote the *Guardian*'s David Lacey, 'after Gayle went sprawling after being tackled from behind . . . Gayle's strength and speed were of sufficient concern to Bayern for them to foul him regularly.' Jeff Powell, writing in the *Daily Mail*, enthused: 'Liverpool . . . found in Howard Gayle a substitute of such remarkable confidence . . . while he was unsettling Bayern with his black muscularity and aggression, the survivors were piecing together a performance of immense concentration, enduring discipline and inspiring morale.' Note the seemingly automatic association of 'aggression' and 'muscularity' with the racial category 'black'. But even so, a consensus around Gayle's performance emerged, from press and players alike. 'Howard's performance was outstanding,' says David Johnson, who played alongside Gayle that day. 'It was gritty, it was hard and it was courageous.'

Ten minutes from the end, Johnson, struggling with a torn muscle, lobbed the ball hopefully infield towards the Bayern goal. Ray Kennedy came through from midfield to score a priceless away goal. In the dying seconds, Karl-Heinz Rummenige equalized, but the away goal counted double and Liverpool were through to the Final against Real Madrid. Bayern had never been beaten at home in Europe and they had very nearly won at Anfield. It was an extraordinary performance, a Liverpool true-grit classic.

But for Howard Gayle the night ended in bitter disappointment. After being booked for retaliation – and Gayle insists the referee was conned – he was removed from the fray twenty minutes from the end and replaced by Jimmy Case. 'I was told,' says Gayle, 'it was to prevent me from being sent off.' Paisley's logic was that he could not risk

276

being reduced to ten men with extra time on the cards. It might have been an arguable case, but it was hardly a vote of confidence.

Others, though, hailed Gayle as a rising star. The following Saturday he played a full first-team game away to Tottenham. With Johnson and Dalglish both walking wounded, he linked up with the nineteen-year-old Ian Rush in a new-look attack. The match ended in a 1-all draw, Gayle scoring for the visitors. His last two first-team games were both at Anfield, where he enjoyed 'a good reception'. In the first, against Sunderland, he was substituted in a lack-lustre 1–nil defeat. In the second, against Manchester City again, Liverpool won by the same score and Gayle hit the post with a powerful header. Robert Armstrong in the *Guardian* filed the following report on the Tottenham match: 'A few more goals of quality by Gayle, who swept Lee's pass into the net after twenty-five minutes, and Johnson may have more than injury to overcome to regain his place. The impressive pace and timing of Gayle's runs, which bemused Bayern Munich, could well restore a dimension and width to Liverpool's attack missing since the dropping of Heighway. Significantly, both Gayle and . . . Rush have . . . shown they possess the nerve and flair required for the major occasion.'

It was not an assessment with which the club concurred. At the end of the season they offered Gayle a contract with just a cost-of-living wage rise – hardly a hint that he featured in their future plans. Wounded, Gayle reconsidered his position and asked the club to circulate his name. He went to Fulham on loan and had spells at Newcastle, at Sunderland, where he fell out with Lawrie McMenemy, and at Birmingham City, where he fell out with old-guard autocrat Ron Saunders. He ended up at Stoke City, a shadow of his former self. It was not until Don Mackay took him to Blackburn on a free transfer that his career picked up again and his gifts of pace, strength and timing began exerting themselves once more.

To many at Liverpool, Gayle's subsequent career simply proves that the club was right to let him go. To others, that heroic night in Munich will stand for ever as a clue to what might have been, with confidence, with encouragement, with a little bit of faith. Gayle's performance has made its mark in two different histories of Liverpool Football Club. One is within the club establishment of staff and supporters as the night the local black kid turned a vital game – a footnote in the record books; funny he didn't last. The other belongs in the folk memory of black Liverpool's disenfranchised football lovers. It is the story of the night that Liverpool Football Club decided that a black boy from Liverpool 8 could not be relied on to do his home town proud.

from Out of His Skin, 1989

The Long March from Vicarage Road: Watford in China
MARTIN AMIS

Fearing the worst – and hoping for the best possible copy – I expected Watford to play the China card. That is to say, I expected half the squad to play pontoon and drink beer in their hotel rooms, while the other half would play pontoon and drink beer out by the pool. I expected the team's only cultural concession to their historic tour would be the odd racist taunt, the occasional self-destructive experiment with rice wine and one or two requests for a Chinese takeaway. How would these stormy individualists fare, how would they cope, in the unsmiling termitary of Red China?

Wearing a Billy Bunter suit, a banded boater, purple sunglasses and a diamond earring, Chairman John gazed down fondly at his protégés. Kippered and sallowed by the twenty-four-hour flight, in regulation blazers, flannels and club ties, the players impassively awaited their baggage in the chaotic kiln of Peking airport. For a moment they looked far more inscrutable and regimented than the quacking Chinese who bustled about them . . . I knew at that moment that all my expectations were misplaced. And so it proved.

The Press has often been blamed for the poor image of footballers and football in general. There *is* a tacit conspiracy in Fleet Street, but it is a conspiracy of silence. Off the field, and especially away from home, footballers behave so outrageously that it's a full-time job looking the other way.

And yet, one by one, the Watford squad approached the Hall of Preserving Harmony, peered into the Pavilion of Universal Tranquillity and passed through the Gate of Benevolence and Longevity.

Somewhat reluctant, homesick and disorientated, they broached the Forbidden City, and emerged as very creditable ambassadors.

The man responsible for this as for so much else at Watford, is the manager Graham Taylor. Seven years ago Watford were a nothing club in the dregs of the Football League. Elton John, a fan since his schooldays in Pinner, took over the chairmanship, injected a good deal of money (the usual estimate is £1,600,000) and hired Taylor from Lincoln City. Last season Watford finished runners-up to Liverpool in the first division. But Taylor wants more than success from his players: he wants to form them as individuals. It is a little-known fact, for instance, that the Watford team are contractually obliged to do seven hours of community work each week. Footballers are often no more than chattels to their clubs; and when the game is finished with them, they blunder out into the world like stranded adolescents.

The day after our arrival Watford turned out for a joint training session at the Workers' Stadium, the 80,000–seater where they would play China the following night, the first of two meetings with the national side. Taylor was wearing full strip and throwing off as much sweat as anyone in the ninety-degree heat. 'Work! One touch and go! *Give* it. *Go*. *Give* it. *Go*.' Stocky, grinning, intense, Taylor puts his men through their hoops with a spurring candour, a flattering brutality. There is intimacy in his bellowed orders: he is the canny schoolmaster who knows all your soft-spots, who forces you beyond your limits and then sues for peace with a slap on the back.

Elton John (also present, in Humpty Dumpty outfit, baseball cap and purple shades) would later admit that it was Taylor who had saved him from the traditional immolation of the rock-star life. Elton had showed up to a Watford match, looking more like Big Ears than usual and bearing all the signs of bodily abuse. Taylor summoned him to his house that night and offered him a pint glass brimmed with brandy. 'Here. Are you going to drink that? What the fuck's the *matter* with you?' I can well imagine that sharp, pinning stare. Elton mended his ways, and not before time. All superstars, it seems, must get off the fast lane before they crash. Some find religion, some find family life. But Elton has found Watford FC. He delights in his team, and also revelled in the anonymity of China, where his music is unknown and he is no more than an exotic curiosity, like a video game or a Beefeater.

As Taylor set about exhausting the China goalkeeper I strolled across the pitch and talked to Shen Xiangfu, the team's number 11 and major star. In what looked like size-2 boots, with his square, vigilant face, Shen answered each question with the same laconic caution.

He was unmarried, like all the China players. He was a student and instructor at the Peking Sports Institute. He earned 75 yuan a month (£25, a fraction above the national average) plust 20 more for dietary expenses (steak, butter). Did he enjoy travelling with the team? Yes, he did. Would he like to play in England one day? Yes, he would. Which British players did he admire? This time the response was immediate: 'Cheega!' The interpreter looked at me helplessly, but I knew who this must be: none other than Keegan Ke-vin. I told Shen how much Keegan earned in a month. He giggled – in embarrassment, as an Englishman might giggle at the sudden mention of sex – and then reassumed his blank and watchful stare.

That night Watford dined at the Great Hall of the People, where their quivering chopsticks negotiated the usual menu of fish stomachs, sea slugs and ancient eggs. Lustrously dinner-jacketed, Elton John was introduced as 'the world's greatest superstar' by the general secretary of the China FA. Elton did his stuff, very nicely, and silver salvers and plastic footballs were exchanged. When it comes to banqueting, the Chinese have something else to teach the West: speeches come first, at which stage sobriety and greed can be relied upon to keep them short.

The star guest at my table was the manager of the Workers' Stadium. (His groundsman was seated at the next table along.) He looked like a handsome Thai pirate out of a documentary about the Boat People. From accounts of the West Bromwich Albion tour of China in 1978, I had gathered that the Peking football crowds were as hushed and respectful as a first-night audience at Covent Garden. No 'Ooooh wanky wanky.' No 'You'll neAGHver walk alone.' I asked the *mao-tei*-quaffing bigwig about this, and his reply was reassuringly serene.

That's right – Chinese crowds do not indulge in partisanship, and why should they? If your team is winning, you're happy. If your team is losing, you're even happier – because a superior team is schooling you for the future. I wondered how this line would go down at the

Anfield Kop, say, as Liverpool trailed 0–4 to an Albanian eleven in the European Cup. How thrilled were the Chinese, I asked, when their team so narrowly failed to qualify for the World Cup in 1982. But my interlocutor's face had closed and hardened. He was as relieved as I was when a voice abruptly announced: 'That's all for the banquet. Goodnight!'

From the outset, the Watford group had been split into three parties, each served by its own coach and guide: Players, Directors and Tourists. This last contingent was made up of businessmen associated with the various club sponsors and included a cadre of epic drinkers (known as the Gang of Four) who were clearly destined to become the true heroes of the long march. Due to some administrative whim – or to Taylor's protectiveness of his players – it was with the Tourists that the small Press corps was initially billeted.

So while Watford repaired to the luxurious mosque of the Fragrant Hill Hotel, I took my chances at the musty Yan Jing on one of the great avenues of downtown Peking. Here, in the bar, the Gang of Four began their nightly skit on the comic Britisher abroad. Soon their table was a float of dead beer bottles. They sang songs and verbally goosed the passing girls. Thus did they strive to convince themselves that they were not in a coffee shop in Fu Xing Street but in the Old Bull and Bush back home.

On the way to the match, through the half-industrialized loops of urban Peking, a Tourist paused in his passionate accompaniment to 'My Way' on the coach Muzak system and said, in a tone of grieved bewilderment, 'Look at the state of that excavator. Where is the maintenance? Where is it?' But there were other things to catch the eye. The crowd, as it approached the Workers' Stadium, resembled an entire ecology on the move: squirming busloads, open lorries from the outlying factories carrying their human freight, the furtive touts at the intersections, and 50,000 bicycles soon to be stacked like cutlery at the stadium gates. (The match would have been a sellout twenty or thirty times over, and was being televised live to an audience of 350 million.) We disembarked on the trampled concourse and writhed through the crush. It was only when I reached my seat that I realized, with another kind of disquiet, how little menace such massed humanity could generate.

But during the game the anthill buzzed. Despite the squawked chidings from Big Sister on the PA system, there were regular cries of 'Suit! Suit' (shoot), '*Shou-qiu*' (hand ball), even a cautious chant (translated for me as 'More grease! More grease!' – more fuel, more work), as well as the ceaseless groundswell of coughed and spluttered comment: Ay! Tsk! Ayuh! *Eehyahah!*

The female voice-over sounded scandalized. 'The Department of Public Security asks the audience on platform 20 to sit down . . . Strive to become a peaceful and civilized audience.' But the applause for the Watford goals, when they came, was immediate, spontaneous, containing a hint of stoic humility. From then on, moments of weird silence punctuated the game, and you could hear Taylor's hoarse bollockings from the bench – 'Hit the goal, Nigel! BE ACCURATE!' – right across the length of the field.

Weakened by the heat, and by the absence of their four key players (still on domestic duty in the Home Internationals), Watford struggled to contain the swift and skilful Chinese – particularly my pal Shen Xiangfu, who ran them ragged on the right. A sun-helmeted Elton quit his throne in the stands and frolicked on to the pitch as Watford plodded off, 3–1 winners. They could have lost 3–4, as Taylor was quick to admit. 'Do not molest or beat up the performers or referees,' cautioned the loudspeaker. As the tame multitude quietly siphoned itself into the night, the advice sounded unnecessary, even sarcastic. It didn't sound unnecessary after the return match, but that was still a week ahead.

The easiest way to get to know the players, I reckoned, was to get to know their nicknames – not for my personal use so much as to shine a light into the dark frat-house which all teams erect around themselves. A footballer's nickname takes any of three forms: a handy diminutive of the surname (as in Greavesy, Mooro, Besty, etc.); a TV tie-in based on some fancied resemblance to a small-screen star; or a third alias of a physical, usually offensive, nature. The players showed a cunning readiness to fill me in, and I was especially indebted to David Johnson, the reserve player whose almost ludicrous charm has long established him as the team mascot.

Goalkeeper Steve Sherwood is called Shirley or Concorde ('because of his nose'). His deputy Eric Steele is called Steeley or Hadley (TV tie-in). Captain and senior player Pat Rice goes under the names of Ricey, Stoneface, Anvil Head and Father Time. Wilf Rostron – Wilfy, The Dwarf. Steve Terry – The Big Man, Frankenstein. Richard

Jobson, or Jobbo, is remorselessly teased about his effeminate good looks: aka Curlers and Boy George (after the hermaphroditic lead singer of Culture Club). Paul Franklin – Gower (after David Gower). Ian Bolton – Webby ('he's got webbed feet'). Jan Lohman, who is Dutch, is called Herman (the German), Adolf and Psycho ('because he's barmy. He is. He's mental'). Nigel Callaghan – Cally, Stump ('his hair') and Beaver ('his teeth'). Les Taylor – Little Legs or Rampant. Ian Richardson – Richo or Shaky (non-existent resemblance to Shakin' Stevens). Steve Sims, Simsy, is called Plug. 'No I'm not,' he said. 'They call me Male Model.' 'No we don't. We call him Plug.'

The nicknames of the four internationals are more respectful, but only marginally so. Kenny Jackett: Jackdaw or Chinaman (because of his sloped eyes – he was guyed about this almost as much as Rice was guyed about rice). Gerry Armstrong: Your Man ('Your what?' I asked. 'Jesus Christ. *Y,E,R M,O,N*'). Luther Blissett: Luth or Black Flash. John Barnes: Barnsey, Digger (TV tie in: Digger Barnes from 'Dallas') and Caramac (a reference to the light-hued chocolate bar). As for David Johnson himself: 'They call me DJ, Or Abdul. Or Gupta – that's G,u,p,t,a. Or Elephant Boy. Anything to do with Africa.'

But were Watford having anything to do with China? The day after the match they tackled the Great Wall. The section open to tourists splays off in two excitingly steep ascents, and the players confronted the challenge as a macho hangover cure. 'Gor. I hope the Boss doesn't use this for pre-season [training],' said a player, from beneath the antennae of his Sony Walkman. Elton puffed his way to the top in his Humpty Dumpty suit, his startling pallor unaffected by the heat. It was left to one of the Gang of Four to leave a distinctive calling-card on the only human artifact visible from space: he vomited down the parapet, as over a ship's side.

After lunch Watford checked out the Ming Tombs. We paced down a lavatorial stone staircase into the arched tunnels and vaults. A Tourist drew a learned comparison between the featureless, rust-coloured casements and the creosote used on truck undercoats. Interest was in danger of flagging entirely until an interpreter weighed in with some salacious accounts of the premature burial of imperial concubines. 'When's the next tram to Cockfosters?' cracked a Director. If there had been a train to Cockfosters, the suggestion was that he would have been on it.

'Fpall?' said the elderly lift-operator, and kicked a leg in the air like a chorus girl: 'PSAIOW!' The scene now briefly shifts to Shanghai, though Watford's points of comparison remain wistfully homebound. The harbourfront embankment 'is like Liverpool'. The near-slums which it conceals 'are like Glasgow'. The yellow and shoreless Yangtze 'is like the Mersey'. The players settle on the deck of Special Class for the three-hour cruise up the Hwangpu. 'Row, row, row your boat,' says one. 'Slow boat to China,' says another. 'Don't rock the boat . . . I am sailing . . . Sailing along . . . Riding along in my automobile. . . .'

From Peking's Yan Jing I check into Shanghai's Jing Jiang, and for the first time I am on the same menu as the players. Bacon and eggs, chicken and chips, steak and chips. At lunch the four internatrionals fly in from their stopover in Hong Kong. England's two black strikers, Blissett and Barnes, glisten with youth, power, muscle-tone. They look like racehorses – in shocking contrast to the Gang of Four.

That night we went to see the Chinese acrobats, and witnessed their otherworldly feats of strength, balance and artistic contortion. Not for the first time since my arrival in China, I felt assailed by the evidence of Earthling variety: the players, the Gang, the Chinese, with their abstract humour, their ritual courtesy disguising unknown restlessness – and all this so fully expressed by the controlled tension of the acrobats . . . Back at the hotel an American party had just arrived. An exhausted twenty-stoner awaited service from the flogged lifts. Shot to pieces gastrically, he looked as though his own weight was about to drive him into the ground like a tent-peg. 'Come on, Duane,' said his friend, 'it's only one floor up. Let's walk it.' But Duane had few options. 'I, uh, believe not,' he said firmly.

Of the three coaches, Players', Directors' and Tourists', the Players' is by far the most restfully taciturn. The Tourists' coach booms with rugby songs, business talk and hangover boasts. The real nerve-frayer, though, is the Directors' coach, a rumpus room of almost psychotic good cheer. It was in this charabanc of Laughing Policemen and Jimmy Tarbuck soundalikes that I made the journey to the Shanghai ground, past lean-tos and godowns, bamboo department stores and buses packed with waving arms and beaming steel-flecked dentition, through streets latticed by plane-tree fronds, tram cables and wet washing.

The stadium was an elegant ruin, a shallow bowl of bleached and flaking stonework. The ballboys sat slumped beneath their sleepy coolie hats. 'Shanghai audiences are good audiences and this is a Shanghai audience,' cackled the loudspeaker. This was a Shanghai audience all right, but it wasn't a good one. When the home team went one up, there were firecrackers and cherry bombs – practically a counter-revolution. When Watford equalized and then took the lead there was an experimental riot in one bank of the stadium – fomented, it turned out, by the Gang of Four, who were feeding Watford souvenirs through the steel netting. Like the crowd, however, the game soon fizzled out in the impossible humidity. At half-time Taylor marched into the dressing room. He drew in breath to denounce his team, then burst out laughing. Several players sat with icepacks on their heads and jets of steam billowing from their ears.

China now toils through her sixth Five-Year Plan, and is rolling up her sleeves for the seventh. There are smiles, handshakes, spurned gratuities; there are the new incentives of the Responsibility System, the crusades of Social Public Morality; there are colour TVs. You also sense a hidden life of impatience and frustration, a resented exclusion from the world of freedom and reward. (Recent attempts at Western marketing show the full gulf of naïveté: a lipstick called 'Fang Fang', a type of battery called 'White Elephant', a range of men's underwear called 'Pansy'.) Football is part of this interchange, and China seeks inclusion here as feelingly as she seeks it elsewhere.

The national side performed well in its first match against Watford, and hopes were high for the second meeting in Peking. Yet China played a spoiling game, and were thrashed 5–1. Towards the end, the climbing anger of the crowd took a surprising form: Watford's black stars were booed whenever they touched the ball. One tried hard to resist this conclusion, since it attacked everything one wanted to believe about China. 'No, no,' said our suavest interpreter. 'They're just trying to put them off because the black players are so good.' But the aggression was selective and unmistakable, an incensed submission to the lowest instincts.

'I wanna go home,' sang the Gang. 'I wanna go home. This is the worst trip/I've ever been on. . .'

The tour now petered out in pleasant anti-climax, with celebrations, sightseeing and some predatory shopping. Elton John spent forty times the local per-capita income in a single spree. His purchases included replicas of the stone lions beneath Mao's portrait which gaze across the square at the Great Hall of the People. That night, with eyes like two lumps of sweet-and-sour pork, Elton mastered his exhaustion and took to the piano to crown the farewell shindig. The high point of his tour, he said, had come at a children's festival when a ten-year-old girl prodigy presented him with a painting of a flock of gambolling kittens. Elton was moved – 'well chuffed'. This would give him more pleasure than anything else he intended to bring back from China. Money isn't everything, he pointed out. And China, however reluctantly, would be forced to agree.

On the flight home the 747 made its first stop in Hong Kong, arrowing in through the genie-clouds above the bay, then past the golden cigarette-lighters of the skyscrapers and sparkling hotels – a Manhattan, a Mammon, a vast duty-free store, perched on the very tip of the East, and destined to be dismantled and flattened out into the Chinese fold. While the Directors sprawled in First and Club, the players dozed with their manager in Economy, their faces set in scowls of discomfort as they slept the sleep of the good. But the team roused itself for the transit lounge (where they have cameras and gadgets, as well as silk and jade) and we all trudged out for one more crack at the loot.

from *The Observer* Colour Magazine, 10 July 1983

Side by Side
JAMES KELMAN

Alison was fine. Much more in control of the world.

Patrick inhaled a lungful of fresh air but did it too quickly and had failed to empty his lungs first so he did a wee exhalation and then a wee inhalation and began again. The idea of not even being able to breathe properly was just a fucking joke really and he smiled, and then chuckled, before exhaling as much breath as he could from his body; and he paused before inhaling, and he inhaled very slowly and calmly, taking in great wads of new air, sending this fresh oxygen flying through his brain. Then he turned away from the windows and strode back to the kitchen, and back out into the lobby, to the bathroom, because he was now having to empty the bladder at once, if not sooner had he been an elderly chap with prostate problems, not something to joke about touch wood touch wood.

And a football match a football match! Holm Park and see the good old fucking Yoker! Who were their opponents for christ sake! Did it matter! Not a whit, not a bloody damn whit! Okay. Fine, that'll do, and let it go, let it go, easy, easy, easy oasy, a nice easy oasiness, scarcely moving at all, like a hibernation, one bit of oxygen lasting ye god knows how long, and just being able to move with as few movements, acting with as few exertions, just biding, biding.

It was a good day, and that was a surprise; and it exemplified much of what was going on. It went side by side with things. There were two things always and just now one of them was this being a good day. Ideally Patrick could have had the two things out in the open so that he could compare them – even just to have seen them side by side, that he could have known he had seen them so that in the future there would be these two things that had happened and he had known and borne witness to them. Perthshire was the opposing team. They came from around the High Possil district and if Patrick minded correctly their own football park had one touchline about 6 feet higher than the other which was great if your team was hitting in corners but rubbish if it was the other mob. Anyway, Holm Park was not like that. The pitch was really muddy today. It was great. The full-backs came sliding in with mammoth upenders of tackles, leaving deep scoops out the ground and one occasion nearby the touchline a big guy came crunching in on this poor other guy and he goes crashing to the deck, a big shower of mud came flying through the air and the spectators had to fucking all duck in case they got spattered. It was fucking marvellous and made everybody laugh. There too was the sound of the guy peching when he finally got himself on to his feet and trotted back down the field. You could see the gash down his shin, the blood and the muddy streaks, that especial whiteness at the bit where the studs had erased the outer skin. He was a lanky big guy and he reminded Patrick of an inside-forward who used to play for Partick Thistle years ago, back when the family lived in Maryhill and the da used to take him and Gavin to some of the home games. It was a teacher he reminded Patrick of. Not any teacher in particular.

It was just something about the way he looked when he got himself back on to his feet and trotted back into the fray. And the way he played the game, an attitude to it, as if the playing was just some strange sort of obligation he had, and that absent determination. Patrick felt the kinship. He had felt an awful pity for him at the same time and dreaded the moment the ball was passed to him. He couldnt watch the game because of it, not being able to look away from this man. And he couldni have been more than ten years of age at the time and yet recognizing that something. It was something important.

But was it something good? Probably it was fucking something bad – a stupid fucking self-consciousness. He was probably just a big self-conscious fellow who felt he was just too skinny and lanky to be playing professional football, he was all knees and fucking elbows. And Patrick felt like greeting. My god. Imagine a ten-year-old boy wanting to greet about something like that! How in the name of fuck had he managed to survive the next fucking twenty years. Christ. He was a poor big guy but. And he was out there doing his best. The sort of player who hears every last shout from the crowd:

Ya big fucking flagpole ya cunt ye! Gone ya big fucking flagpole! Ya big drainpipe! Heh look at the state of that cunt man he's a fucking drainpipe, look!

And the poor guy blushing as he attempts to hit the ball round the full-back and ends up tripping over his own two feet.

Look at the fucking poof! Heh you Hen Broon, ya fucking dickie ye! Your maw's a fucking shagbag, she's a darkie ya cunt! Beautiful cries from the heart. Gone ya fucking dumpling ye ya cunt ye couldni score in a barrel of fannies! A what? A barrel of fannies. A barrel of fannies? What in the name of christ!

It had taken him another couple of years to work that yin out and he would have been best left in ignorance. A barrel of fannies. It was enough to put ye off sex for the rest of your life. A case of the shudders every time he thought about it. What was it like at all? a barrel of fannies – was it actually a nightmare, a form of male nightmare?

A man with a hat and a mournful face was standing a couple of yards from Pat. He looked like the stereotype of a hardbitten football journalist. Or a scout. He could have been a scout for one of the senior clubs. But no, definitely more like a journalist. Unless even here you were getting the fucking CIA or the fucking MI5. Dirty bastard. Here he was infiltrating one of the last bastions of ordinary life. Journalists were a lesser breed than teachers. Or were they? maybe they were on a par. They all sold out. What the fuck difference did it make. At least the MI5 were proud of being fascist rightwing bastards.

He had his hands in his coat pockets, the man, gazing at the play, his head turning to follow the flight of the ball, a cigarette wedged in at the corner of his mouth. And his mouth had a meanness about it. A kind of a crimped look there, in the lips.

Shocking!

To say that about somebody. Just because of the physical characteristics of the face you make snap judgments on personality, how the person makes his or her decisions, how they move in the midst of their fellows. Desperate. It is just not fair. It is not good. It is shocking.

Patrick missed the only goal of the game at this juncture. And serve him right. He was shaking his head and looking in the direction of his shoes, and then the blokes roundabout were cheering and applauding and waving. Yoker had scored. And what a goal as well according to everybody: their winger had cut in from the right and chipped the ball over the heads of the defence and back to the 18–yard line where the striker caught it on the volley and bump, straight into the corner of the net, a fucking beauty. And you aye remember goals. It is a fact one does not hesitate in admitting. There was one Patrick scored when he was playing for the BB and it was a real fucking beauty although painful, a header, but him letting the ball bounce that wee bit instead of actually meeting it on the attack, which is the correct way of using the nut, you have to go and meet it and not let it come and crash against ye. Joe Cairns said that as well, about remembering the goals you scored. He didnt talk about football very much but when he did Pat liked to be in the vicinity. There was that good yarn about when he was with Stirling and they were up for a cup game at Ibrox and holding them to a draw right up till the last couple of minutes and then the jammy bastards got their usual last minute Loyalist handshake of a penalty. So typical. So absolutely typical.

Junior football was much better. Although some of the supporters there were just as bigoted and fascist and some of them were fucking maniacs. Pat was at a game just after Christmas and he was standing down near to the corner flag; up comes a player to take a corner and the entire section of the crowd nearest started clearing their throats at him, dollops of catarrh. They were all men as well, no boys. Frightening. A shower of catarrh. Worse than a storm of hailstones.

There was one goal and I missed it.

That would make some fucking epitaph right enough! Missing the only goal of the game. But who cares. Life just cannot be taken as seriously as that. Otherwise it becomes too much. It becomes a total burden. Pat's life.

Pat's life! Who the fuck cares. In the name of all that is and is not holy, that becomes as holy.

The man with the mournful face was looking at Pat. He was actually looking at him. It was funny. No it wasnt. But just as well paranoia was not a problem. No doubt he was an emissary from the education department of Scotland, sent to keep an eye on the chap Doyle who fails to turn up for headmagisterial appointments on top of everything else, these ghastly rumours, the chap's political beliefs, it seems he's agin the government. How awful. How absolutely fucking awful and incendiary. Dont tell us the bounder dislikes being a teacher! Dashed uncivil! And he has the dem cheek to stand up in front of children! Old Milne should maybe not have been ignored though. Patrick has probably shown him disrespect. But he deserves disrespect. That is the thing he deserves, disrespect. Him and his fucking flapping MA gown. Auld Clootie come to haunt the weans. The wee first yearers going to the big school for the first time and meeting up with that sort of reality. Middle-aged warders. Middle-class warders – policemen; professional wanks on behalf of institutionalized terror. Institutionalized terror Patrick you tell them! Aye I'll tell them, dont worry about that. What happens is you want to punch some bastard in the mouth, him with the mournful face for instance. I'll give him something to be fucking mournful about, him and his crimped fucking lips the bastard.

Poor old bastards. What have they done to deserve all this, this opprobrium. Children whose parents never got married for whatever reason. And right beside the mournful-faced bloke was this younger guy who looked about ages with Pat, or even slightly younger. How come he hadni noticed him earlier. He actually resembled a polis who had come to the school recently to give a talk on public initiatives with third-year tearaways, for the benefit of the teaching staff. Pat attended. It was really interesting. And if he hadnt gone it would have been noted. But if people were being sent to keep watch on him then they would not have sent somebody he'd seen previously; they would have sent somebody anonymous. That was obvious. And yet was it? Christ but it was easy to become paranoiac. And rationally: rationally one had to admit of certain facts, that certain tenets one held to be true, certain activities that one hoped would take place, that would not endear him.

But surely not in a public place. If they were going to do something to him they would surely choose somewhere private – not an actual football ground. What could be more conspicuous than that! And yet, when you thought about it, this was precisely the type of place an assassin would choose to perform the dirty deed; while the crowd roared on the two teams the poisoned umbrella comes out and is quietly inserted between one's shoulderblades. Maybe a crowd was the last place to be if safety was sought. Perthshire was about to take a shy. Patrick stepped to the side, and back a pace, and was on par with the mournful chap in the hat. He smiled at him and nodded. The man looked at him and nodded in reply. And Patrick said, I missed the goal. What d'you make of it? one goal and I missed it!

We'll get another yin, said he. He touched the brim of his hat, glanced at his watch: There's still time yet.

The younger man was not paying any attention to the interchange. He was straining to follow the play now, the Perthshire forwards moving upfield toward Yoker's goal area. They had a small boy out on the wing who was really good with the ball at his feet but was tending to slow things down, if he had been that bit more direct Yoker might have been in trouble. And then Yoker attacking out of defence. Exciting stuff and not at all square. Not bad at all. Patrick nodded. It was good. Football could be a direct game. He closed his eyes and stepped backwards.

from *A Disaffection*, 1989

Liverpool v. Wimbledon: The Cup Final, 1988
DAVE HILL

The Cup Final scene was both depressing and bizarre. Of the 92,000 present, only a small platoon were conspicuously and devoutly Wimbledon fans. Touts had a field day with Wimbledon's ticket allocation, which massively outweighed demand, and the huge preponderance of red that lined Wembley's interior was ample evidence of the number that had found their way up the M6 to Merseyside. The journey to Wembley was the usual grim adventure, despite the big-match atmosphere, this time given a strange twist by the glaring discrepancy in support for the two sides. Wimbledon's supporters took after their team in glorying in their underdog image. At Anfield a few weeks earlier they had delightedly indulged their self-mocking humour, affectionately putting themselves and their own players down. They had a little tune for their marauding centre-forward that was as uncomplicated and as effective as its subject: 'He's big, he's black, he leads the Don's attack, Fashanu, Fashanu.' A tiny minority squeezed in among Liverpudlian interlopers unable to get seats anywhere else, they hissed impertinent insults at Beardsley every time he ventured near their goal: 'Ug-leee! Ug-leee!' To Barnes they sang: 'Hello, Hello, Watford reject!' A gallows mentality and not to be underestimated. At Wembley, the Wimbledon players brought it to bear on Liverpool and sent the banks of Merseyside supporters into seizures as the imperious League champions fizzled, floundered and faded away.

There is a loose consensus among more thoughtful football observers as to why it was that Wimbledon prevailed. Some of it is obvious enough. It was the biggest day in their players' football lives, one which they might never experience again. They were bits and pieces players for the most part, some picked up from lower divisions and honed to fit the Wimbledon mould. Others, though respected, were little more than spirited artisans if assessed individually. But Wimbledon were in their meanest, nastiest frame of mind . . . and how they wanted to win. Their desire could not be doubted. Their bloody-minded doggedness never had been. Psychologically, that adds up to a pretty disturbing prospect for any team to face. Liverpool, on the other hand, were expected to do much more than just win the game. Though some casual sentiment was with the underdogs, Liverpool were now loved for their style. Connoisseurs wanted them to give Wimbledon a lesson, to vaporize them and all they stood for. Liverpool's professional pride insisted that it should be that way as well. The demand was for champagne all the way.

It is known that Wimbledon players' efforts to intimidate Liverpool began in the tunnel even as they readied themselves to say 'hi' to Princess Di. McMahon, Liverpool's most abrasive midfield player, was the target for much of it and also for early punishment from a psyched-up Vinny Jones once the game was under way. Beardsley, in his biography, confirms that 'The Wimbledon team were shouting things in the tunnel before the game,' and you could hear them at it as the TV cameras pried into the darkness. As Barnes walked from the tunnel, you could see him grin uncomfortably as Jones pushed his mug into his face.

Beardsley denies that Wimbledon's verbalizing upset Liverpool's concentration. 'We're experienced enough to cope with that and laugh it off.' He also makes light of the backchat on the field. But if Liverpool were not spooked by Wimbledon's snarls, they played as if they were. And when the run of the ball seemed to go against them, they suddenly ran out of ideas. Beardsley was denied a charming goal thanks to a famous misjudgement of the advantage law by referee Brian Hill. Though he was fouled by full-back Phelan, Beardsley still got through and chipped the ball past Beasant. But the whistle had already gone. Liverpool had barely got over their consternation, when Wimbledon were back down the field. From set pieces they are aggressive, well drilled and blessed with plenty of brawn. Wise, their most subtle performer, chipped in an angled free-kick and Lawrie Sanchez popped an innocuous glancing header into the far corner of the net.

From then on, Wimbledon were in their element. Having tweaked the nose of the aristocracy they were not about to touch their forelocks. They did what they are best at – digging in. Liverpool muddled on, struggling to find a route through a wary, retreating defence which refused to unbutton itself. It was a flawless defensive operation. As Liverpool pushed forward, Wimbledon gave ground just enough to take their momentum away. Attack after attack petered out around the penalty box. Kenny's massive army fell into an eloquent silence as the time slipped away. In goal, Beasant surpassed himself, rising to the occasion the few times Liverpool breached Wimbledon's stout resistance. When Aldridge was awarded a debatable penalty kick, it seemed that the tide must turn. But the man who had seemed infallible from the spot failed to convert. Lurch lunged to his left, saved the kick and lifted the Cup. 'The crazy gang have beaten the culture club,' thrilled John Motson on the BBC.

But there was not much romance in this underdog victory, no matter that TV priorities demanded that some be found. A match-day official who was down on the pitch listened to Wimbledon celebrate: 'We got the bastards. We did them.' As the droves of Liverpool fans slouched, numbly, back down Wembley Way, everybody tried to figure out what went wrong.

It was a result that begged many questions. Tommy Smith says that if anyone had tried winding up the Liverpool teams he was in, there would have been a fight in the tunnel. Others maintain that if it had been Shankly's Liverpool out there, Jones, and one or two others, would have watched the second half from a hospital bed. But, notwithstanding Wimbledon's likely willingness to walk it as nasty as they talked it, it seems glib if not unjust to attribute Liverpool's misfire to fear. Luck played its part. The penalty aside, Liverpool had precious little of it. They had two men short of fitness. Beardsley looked tired and tried too hard. The midfield was battened down and Aldridge walked alone. Barnes, meanwhile, was totally neutralized by a man who looked as if he had baled out of a Sopwith Camel in 1914 and only just found his way home. Clive Goodyear was the full-back detailed to mark the double Footballer of the Year and, with a posse of helpers to hand, he soon began winning battles that more illustrious contemporaries had been losing all year.

Dalglish appeared to try no radical tactical change. It was as if Liverpool, held hostage by their own high expectations, did not believe an entire match could pass without them slipping into gear. They died quietly in the end, with no single player doing himself justice. Barnes's weak showing was grist to the mill of those who insist that truly great players always find a way to impose their will on a game. It didn't happen with Barnes. With the Liverpool system disrupted he didn't know where to plug himself in. As for Wimbledon, they did what they went out there to do. They did what football demands. They won.

From *Out of His Skin*, 1989

Fanzines
PHIL SHAW

It is a wet, windy Friday night on the terracing – no, make that cinder-banking – exclusively reserved for away fans because it has no cover, no crash barriers, no tea bar, no toilets and no future except as the site for another Sainsbury's.

The tiny knot of visiting supporters, one deep, surges forward towards the 6-foot high perimeter fencing as their team's left-winger breaks clear of the defence. He reaches the home penalty area, and squares a perfect pass inside to the unmarked No. 9. Forty-six arms are raised in expectation . . . he can't miss . . .

Once the ball has been retrieved from what will shortly be the hypermarket's yoghurt section, the home side make the most of their escape. They score the only goal – off a knee, from what must have been an offside position, in time mysteriously added on by the referee.

A phalanx of local police escorts the away end to their coach, ignoring requests for the return of the umbrellas confiscated and making sure no one steps out of line on to the pavement, though not before all 3,783 home spectators are either in the pub or by the living-room fire.

The driver won't stop at the motorway café – which anyway has a sign saying 'No Football Coaches' – and 80 miles from home the bus splutters to a halt at the side of the road.

As the stoics shiver and wait for the AA, the team's luxury coach speeds past. The players seem to be cheerful enough, and an odd hand twitches and threatens a half-wave. The rural silence is shattered by a defiant chorus of 'We'll support you evermore,' though the thought occurs to more than one that this time next year half that lot will probably be playing in the obtrusively sponsored pinstripes of the bunch who have just beaten them.

The team, as per manager's orders, is taking each match as it

295

comes, and this one has gone. The board of directors are still in the hospitality suite sounding off about the yobs who aren't real supporters. The yobs, meanwhile, have paid for the privilege of getting the cold shoulder on the hard shoulder. All for the love of the game, *their* game.

THE FANZINE PHENOMENON

Most players hate the fanzines. They tend to be critical of footballers and the way the game is run. Professional players are very wary of anything that makes fun of them – they can be absurdly loyal to the game's good image . . .

If the fanzines have a pet hate, it's the egomaniac in the boardroom. They hate the thought that a game which provokes the loyalty of a community should be run to suit the whims of a rich businessman. (Pat Nevin)[1]

Football is often called 'the People's Game', but the people who run it and indeed own its clubs are not the people invoked in that romantic, almost naive phrase.

The question of to whom the professional game 'belongs' has been asked as long as it has been played. A letter writer to the *Birmingham Mail* in 1892 said: 'I venture to suggest that the turn has come of the public who bring the grist to the mill. Why not covered accommodation for spectators, dry ground to stand on, and a reduced admission if possible? The profits will stand it. Many a wreath has been purchased by standing on wet ground on Saturday afternoons.'

Nearly a century on, the debate has been re-opened with fresh vigour, prompted by a sorry catalogue of disasters – in the literal sense, not as in *Sun*speak for an own goal – and débâcles.

The tragedies at Bradford and Sheffield produced more than 150 wreaths. A Tory government obsessed with hooliganism set about imposing a compulsory membership scheme – in the face of opposition from clubs, police, fans and even some of its own MPs – while ignoring the less vote-worthy issue of spectator safety until it was too late.

The biggest clubs plotted to form a breakaway Super League, without any consultation of their supporters, out of vanity and greed.

Charlton suddenly abandoned The Valley for the alien turf of Crystal Palace's Selhurst Park (although there was to be a happy end to that saga). Tottenham sneered at their supporters, and at the local council when they protested about the decision to build executive

1. Stuart Cosgrove, 'Off the ball, off the wall', *City Limits*, 17–24 March 1988.

boxes on the popular-side 'Shelf' terracing. Spurs then called off the opening game of the 1988–89 season, because of building work, but not before fans had set out for White Hart Lane from all over the country.

In perhaps the most sinister development, Fulham and Queen's Park Rangers were to be merged at Shepherd's Bush, with 'yuppie' flats constructed at Craven Cottage, before public outcry embarrassed the property moguls into retreat. A similar threat hovers over Mill-town, home of Ireland's most famous club, Shamrock Rovers of Dublin.

Aston Villa epitomized the store most clubs set by their traditions when, in the cause of rampant commercialism, they abandoned their claret and blue shirts for a mélange of purple and pink that one reporter described as resembling a summer pudding.

In each instance – and these were the tip of a considerable iceberg – it was clear that the supporters who sustain football through thin and thinner were usually the last to be considered, let alone consulted.

All this happened at a time when executive-boxes, with their colour televisions, and supply of Cabernet Sauvignon, were sprouting every-where. When football's legendary 'missing millions' were being harangued by the Prime Minister and her Minister for Sport into believing they were bound to be attacked by vicious thugs if they gave the national game another go.

And when, as one sagacious peer put it in the House of Lords during a debate on Mr Moynihan's Football Spectators Bill, there was actually more chance of getting beaten up on the streets of Windsor or Bracknell than at a match.

The question of whose game it is has found resounding, positive answers. In the wake of the Heysel disturbances in which another thirty-nine died in 1985, a militant pressure group was formed in Liverpool. The Football Supporters' Association (FSA) began to chal-lenge the age-old perception of the fan as a passive, uncritical, gullible consumer with deep pockets who knew his/her place – which more often than not was on that wet, windy cinder-bank.

This radical upsurge needed a propagandist voice. It has found one in the subcultural and publishing phenomenon of the second half of the 1980s – the football fanzine. Late in 1989, there are around 200 such magazines. Most are club-based but there is a healthy sprinkling covering the game in general. Among the latter is *When Saturday*

Comes (circulation 17,000 and rising – above the average gate for half the First Division), while the majority of teams in Britain have at least one publication devoted to them (Celtic's *The View*, with 11,000-plus sales per issue, is the market leader).

A survey of fanzines by the Sir Norman Chester Centre for Football Research, at Leicester University's Department of Sociology, found that the 'average circulation per issue of each fanzine ranged from forty-five to 11,000, yet the majority (55 per cent) fell between 200 and 1,000 copies per issue'.

The researcher deduced from the findings this staggering statistic: 'When one calculates the number of issues per season and the average circulation per issue, then at a conservative estimate more than *one million* fanzies will be bought this season [1988–89].'

The message from virtually all these magazines, so varied in quality and allegiance, is clear. It is that football belongs not to television, to an elitist clutch of clubs, to rapacious agents or sensation-hungry tabloids, or to the shareholders and sponsors, but to the people whose pounds and partisanship sustain the sport. Fittingly, the FSA's own journal is called *Reclaim The Game*.

But how did it all start? The *Oxford English Dictionary*'s new, twenty-volume edition (a snip at £1,500) traces the usage of the word 'fanzine' back to 1949 and the United States: 'A magazine for fans, especially science fiction.' After it was re-invented in Britain in the mid-1970s, the definition should have changed to 'for *and by* fans'. Anyone who attended a punk-rock or 'new-wave' gig at that time will remember having copies of *Ripped & Torn*, *Sniffin' Glue*, *48 Thrills*, *Temporary Hoarding* and other xeroxed paeans to the Sex Pistols, Clash, Damned, Jam et al. thrust in their face.

Punk came in snarling and spitting at rock's establishment, many of them one-time rebels. The aim, apart from getting smashed, was to reclaim 'their' music from the giant record corporations and the over-produced, over-paid groups they perceived as having 'sold out'.

Time Out's rock editor felt sufficiently threatened to denounce punk as having 'the life expectancy of a scab'. It survived rather longer, but most of its central figures were soon incorporated into the mainstream by major labels. As Stuart Cosgrove, St Johnstone supporter and a particularly perceptive music journalist, has pointed out: 'Not even at the glorious height of punk did fanzines come close to exposing the inner workings of the music industry – let alone incurring the wrath of the company boardrooms.'[2]

Cosgrove was alluding to reports that a number of clubs – from Tottenham, Arsenal, Celtic and Manchester United to Airdrie, Boston United and Wealdstone – had banned fanzines about them from their grounds. It has been remarked that punk changed nothing but the width of a generation's jeans; football fanzines, with their more campaigning approach, appear more capable of striking the relevant raw nerves and rallying support for genuine change.

There can be no denying, however, that this late-1980s publishing boom has taken more than its generic moniker from *Sniffin' Glue* and its ilk. By economic necessity, the felt-tip pen, typewriter, scissors and cow gum are still key production components, although several of the better-selling football fanzines have been able to go in for professional printing.

The links with the 'independent' music scene do not end there. John Peel, its DJ father-figure, regularly extols the virtues of Liverpool FC on his Radio 1 show; Pat Nevin, dubbed 'the first post-punk footballer' by the *New Musical Express* (and 'the first yuppie of football' by the *Chelsea Independent* fanzine) told bemused tabloid hacks of his passion for groups like Crispy Ambulance and Joy Division; a Leeds band, The Wedding Present, called their debut LP 'George Best', and his picture rather than theirs adorned its sleeve; Half Man Half Biscuit, from Birkenhead, eulogized Tranmere Rovers in interviews and Subbuteo in song.

Scottish duo The Proclaimers sang of 'going to Kilmarnock to see Hibernian play', and a Hibs fanzine reciprocated by taking the title *The Proclaimer. Brian Moore's Head*, a Gillingham fanzine, produced a cover parodying the artwork for the Sex Pistols' 'Never Mind The Bollocks' album. Oxford's *Raging Bull* and West Ham's *On The Terraces* gave away flexi-disc pop singles.

And so on . . . even the titles *When Saturday Comes* and *The Absolute Game* (a magazine covering Scottish football in general) were taken from songs by The Undertones and The Skids respectively.

Tim Colliew of the specialist London bookshop Sportspages, pointing out that several football-fanzine editors actually started out with punk publications, said: 'It's a fairly natural association. Most are put

2. Ibid.

out by lads under the age of twenty-five and the most important things in their lives are music and football.'[3]

Yet there was an earlier, seminal influence. *Foul* – the name was a deliberate parody of magazines like *Shoot!* and *Goal* – first appeared in October 1972; its thirty-fourth and last issue hit the newsstands exactly four years later. Issues 1–9 were typewritten; from No. 10 onwards it was typeset and distributed by the firm who handled *Private Eye*.

Concerned with the game as a whole rather than any particular club, *Foul* kicked against the frightening and frightened football of Revie and Ramsey; against reactionary administrators, like the late Football League secretary Alan Hardaker (incidentally, there is a current fanzine called *Hardaker Rises Again . . .*); and against ego-maniac managers.

As Mike Ticher, founder of the *Foul*-influenced *When Saturday Comes*, put it: 'It railed against the whole structure of football and often did fine investigative jobs on individual clubs and their masters. Most importantly, it was very funny.'[4]

'Football's alternative paper', as it styled itself, *Foul* was edited by a group of Cambridge graduates, only one of whom, Steve Tongue, has made a career out of football writing; most of today's fanzine editors have been to Cambridge only to watch Fourth Division or Southern League football. It may have failed to bring down the FA or force Norman Hunter to hang up his studs, but *Foul* did open its pages to the 'ordinary' fan. And its *Private Eye*-style format (the 'rag-outs' of newspaper gaffes, the spoof tabloid letters, the cartoons and 'bubble' captions of photos) left a blueprint for the next generation.

The *bêtes-noires* have changed in the ensuing decade; for Ramsey, Hardaker, Hunter and Leeds read Robson, Maxwell, Souness and Wimbledon (although Brian Clough is still around and more, er, idiosyncratic than ever, while the combination of Vinny Jones and Leeds was a real throwback). And where *Foul* was concerned with exposing foot-up hackers and supine hacks, the 1980s fanzines have had to confront the sport in its post-Heysel, post-Maxwell state and to tackle fundamental issues such as misconceptions about the extent of hooliganism (labelled 'the British disease' by lazy journalists), the

3. Quoted in Lloyd Bradley, 'A right result', *Q* magazine, March 1988.
4. Mike Ticker, *Foul! Best of Football's Alternative Paper, 1972–76*, 1987.

conniving of chairmen and property developers, and scheming between TV moguls and self-styled Super Leaguers.

The first club-oriented fanzines – *Terrace Talk* (York City), *City Gent* (Bradord City), *The Web* (Queen's Park), *Pink 'n' Blue Bushwacker* (Dulwich Hamlet) and *Fingerpost* (West Bromwich Albion) – had no single battle to fight. But their emergence, after two decades in which football fans had become media folk-devils, helped in a greater cause: that of restoring the dignity of the game's followers.

Many of those who started the early fanzines had grown up as readers of *Shoot!* and *Match*, colour magazines for children and adolescents which tend to gloss over the unsavoury aspects of football. Team photos and ghosted personality columns are their staple diet; criticism rarely rears its head.

The case of Gordon Strachan's transfer from Manchester United to Leeds in March 1989 offers a classic example of the puerile approach of such magazines. Strachan chose a Second Division club in preference to two in the First, but there was no mystery as to how he had arrived at his decision. Ron Atkinson, who had hoped to buy him for Sheffield Wednesday, announced ruefully: 'There was no way we could match what Leeds were offering.'

Strachan, understandably for a professional in the later stages of his career, had taken the best offer available. *Shoot!*, meanwhile, asked its readers to believe that 'Wanted man Gordon Strachan declared his passion for Leeds almost before the ink had dried on his £300,000 deadline-busting deal.' The player was pictured in the now-obligatory pose with club scarf, and neither the word 'money' nor its usual stand-in 'personal terms' was mentioned in the accompanying 300-word piece.

For the discerning fan who is disinclined, in the words of a million fathers (including my own), to 'grow out of this football thing' but who nevertheless does not want to be patronized, there is a problem of what to read. Magazines aimed at the older end of the market, such as *Football Monthly*, tend to ape their junior brethren by perpetuating euphemisms like tough-tackling (dirty) or want-away (greedy).

One of its colour competitors, *Football Today*, at least appears to be facing up to issues such as Mr Moynihan's Football Spectators Bill. The magazine handed out thousands of red cards for spectators to brandish at the Tannoy announcer's behest during a televised match between Aston Villa and Manchester United, and its cover bears the street-cred slogan 'Endorsed by the PFA'. But the format, tone and style remain basically old-fashioned, and it is certainly no *When Saturday Comes*.

In short, with the possible exception of promising, fanzine-influenced Scottish newcomer *The Punter*, none of the magazines available in the big retailers demonstrates much sympathy for the way the game is perceived by a significant portion of its audience. They do not appreciate football's place within a broader cultural context, nor understand the football-match experience. They appear, to put it generously, to be out of touch.

That 'experience' often includes having a convivial drink before a game with 'rival' supporters, and exchanging anecdotes and information about police/press/players/programmes/pies and pints. Journals like Bradford's *City Gent* and *The Pie* (Notts County) often fill several pages with details of where to find the best-kept beer or a good curry on away trips. Although *City Gent* adopted the slogan 'The Voice of Bantam Progressivism' and lists among its contributors the militant Labour MP Pat Wall, it sometimes seems closer to *Suppin' Ale* and *Sniffin' Glue*.

The most striking characteristic of *City Gent* is the warmth and concern (summed up by John Dewhirst, one of its editorial team, as 'critical allegiance') its contributors show towards the Bradford club and the game in general. They were quick to produce a 'special' in aid of the Hillsborough Disaster Fund. Unusually, City's players, directors and staff have cooperated with the *Gent*, whose founders prefer to call it an 'independent supporters magazine' rather than a fanzine.

City Gent was typical of the first wave of publications (No. 1 came out in October 1984) in its attempts at bridge-building between supposedly antagonistic followers of different teams. They drew the line at Leeds United (perhaps understandably, in view of a chip-van blaze started by Leeds 'supporters' at City's temporary home, Odsal Stadium, eighteen months after the Valley Parade tragedy) and published a provocative booket sarcastically titled *Leeds United – The Glory Years*, in which every page was blank.

Generally, though, differences were played down and, with the burgeoning FSA playing the leading role, common grievances and shared aspirations magnified.

Off the Ball's arrival in January 1986 – seven months after Brussels and Bradford – marked a significant advance. A national magazine, which was its greatest strength and its main weakness, the highlight of the first issue was a feature based on interviews with Wolves' chief executive and the chairman of the then-outlawed supporters club. (This was pre-Graham Turner and Steve Bull, when Wolves were rapidly sliding down the divisions under dubious ownership.) The writer, Adrian Goldberg, concluded that what remained of the Molineux faithful must 'get radical'.

I was writing the *Guardian*'s 'Soccer Diary' at the time and chose to lead the column with a piece welcoming *Off the Ball*, beginning: 'Libel lawyers are not the only ones who miss *Foul* . . .' I may have been over-anxious to recreate my youth by implying there was a qualitative similarity; in truth the first edition was short of good writing, humour and design awareness. But it was a start.

My concluding remark that 'its grey pages contrast starkly with the vitality of rock fanzines' appeared to have been taken to heart, for in the following two years *Off the Ball* came up with a series of classic covers. The best, for the October/November 1987 issue, grafted Graeme Souness's head on to Michael Jackson's androgynous leather persona. The collage made a 'satirical comment on Souness's psycho-pathic hardman image' according to Stuart Cosgrove.

Another cover, of which *Foul* would have been proud, was headlined 'Salute to Portsmouth' and highlighted the First Division newcomers' staggering litany of indiscipline and even crime. A third depicted the acquisitive millionaire publisher Robert Maxwell, who, remember, had tried to commit merger most foul by uniting Reading and Oxford as 'Thames Valley Royals', only to back down in the face of opposition he condemned as 'parochial' and 'conservative'. Blood was dripping from his mouth, in a pastiche movie poster for 'Mad Max 4'. 'Now showing at Derby, Oxford, Reading and Watford', it said, listing clubs in whom Maxwell had an interest or was, as it were, showing an interest. It added portentously: 'At a ground near you soon'.

Although, like *Foul*, *Off the Ball*'s quality tended to be uneven precisely because it offered a forum for anyone who cared to put pen to paper, former *Foul* contributor/TV scriptwriter Stan Hey was sufficiently impressed by its early progress to call it 'the most radical voice' and praise its 'amusing distaste for local (Midlands) chairmen'.[5]

5. Stan Hey, 'Fanfare for the common supporter', *The Independent*, 18 December 1987.

In March, 1986, *When Saturday Comes* arrived, as an offshoot of a music fanzine named *Snipe!* Mike Ticher, having apparently written, laid out and typed most of the first issue, set out its editorial policy on the front. Ticher, a Chelsea supporter for whom Pat Nevin personified good and Ken Bates evil, was stronger on what his publication would not be about than on what it aimed to achieve.

It's not going to be clichéd, hackneyed, lazy journalism. It's not going to be banal, ghostwritten platitudes. It's not going to be tedious, whitewashing interviews, it's not going to be full of statistics or match reports, and it's certainly not going to indulge in petty rivalries . . . All that stuff is available in abundance elsewhere.

What it might be a bit more like is the sort of thing you talk about in the pub. Gossip, stories, arguments, some serious things that never get discussed anywhere else, like racism at football but mostly not.

If that sounded sanctimonious – a common fanzine failing, often accompanied by blanket dismissiveness about 'the media' or attacks on 'the so-called Minister for Sport' à la *Private Eye*'s revolutionary student columnist 'Dave Spart' – Ticher redeemed himself with a leavening of wit. 'What is it about certain clubs (e.g. Liverpool, Ipswich, Arsenal)', he asked, 'that attracts so many players with big noses? Does anyone in football actually *like* Ron Saunders? These are the sort of questions I've always wanted the answers to, but no publication ever tells me. Maybe *When Saturday Comes* will: it's up to you.'

The response was such that Ticher and his collaborator Andy Lyons were soon producing professionally printed, stylishly laid-out issues. A strong editorial line had been established in No. 1's attack on the ever-changing team strips ('Come on you blue two-tone hoops with red and white trim and a little emblem on the sleeve and the manufacturer's logo and the sponsors' name across the chest'), and many of the readers who contributed as *When Saturday Comes* became the best-seller showed a strong empathy and considerably journalistic flair.

Some of them suitably stimulated, invested in scissors, paste and Letraset and set to work on fanzines about their own clubs. Mike Wilson, writing in *The Observer*, reckoned *When Saturday Comes* and others had 'won legitimacy for fanzines'.[6]

They certainly provided an inspirational example, though legitimacy is unlikely to be high on many lists of editorial priorities, particularly

6. Mike Wilson, 'Putting the boot in from the terraces', *The Observer*, 8 January 1989.

among those who may regard themselves as punk's progeny. Some of the titles speak volumes for their subversive aims: e.g. *Not The View* (an obvious dig at *The Celtic View*, the Glasgow club's tame official newspaper); *Kick Up the R's* (run by Queen's Park Rangers fans who see no contradiction in combining partisanship with the need to kick boardroom backsides); *Tired and Weary* (pointedly plucked by long-suffering Birmingham City supporters from the terrace anthem 'Keep Right On to the End of the Road'); and *Chelsea Independent* (a name clearly intended to distance its publishers, the Independent Supporters' Association, from the more acquiescent official supporters' organization and from the chairman Ken Bates).

Then there are the hard-nosed realists (pessimists), like *The Final Hurdle* (invented by Dundee United fans because, presumably, their team keeps falling at it); Brighton's *And Smith Must Score!* which commemorates the painful moment in which Gordon Smith missed a chance from which Cyril Smith would have expected to score, and the FA Cup slipped from their grasp; *Elm Park Disease*, from Reading, which is self-explanatory; and *NHS*, produced by stalwarts of homeless Vauxall-Opel Leaguers Kingstonian, which stood for No Home Stadium, although the club has now put down new roots at nearby Norbiton.

There are those which draw on the terrace songs and chants: they include my own favourite, the brilliantly titled *Sing When We're Fishing* (Grimsby Town), which works on a number of levels; *One-Nil Down, Two-One Up* (derived from Arsenal's gloating chant about famous recoveries against Spurs and Liverpool); *There's Only One F in Fulham* (geddit?); *One Team in Ulster* and *Follow, Follow* (lifted from the Loyalist – that's with a capital 'L' – songs of the fans of Linfield and Rangers respectively).

Some simply reflect gushing adulation, notably *Brian* (Clough, of course), *King of the Kippax* (after Manchester City's popular side, Kippax Street), and *Flashing Blade* (Sheffield United, nicknamed the Blades).

Other names aim to make a point, like *Marching Altogether* (by Leeds Fans United Against Racism and Fascism) and *From Behind Your Fences* (Boston), which was given a terrible new relevance by Hillsborough; a few come across like applications for a sub-editor's job on the *Guardian*, with punning titles like *Leyton Orientear*, *Abbey Rabbit* (Cambridge United), and *Witton Wisdom* (Aston Villa).

One or two show real wit and imagination, such as *When Sunday Comes* (a Liverpool fanzine's subtle way of pointing out how often their team were selected for ITV's live Sunday show 'The Match'), *The Memoirs of Seth Bottomley* (Port Vale – named after an imaginary ex-player created to humour moaning older Valeites, one of whom, the editor swears, was heard to remark that a present-day midfielder 'couldner owd a candle ter Bottomley'), and *Champion Hill Street Blues* (Dulwich – one of a number of high-quality efforts by non-League followers remarkable for circulations often higher than the team's average crowd).

Others are unashamedly, self-consciously wacky, especially *Brian Moore's Head*, taken from a Half Man Half Biscuit song in honour of the balding ITV commentator and former Gillingham director which originally had the suffix *Looks Uncannily Like The London Planetarium*, Middlesbrough's *Fly Me To The Moon*, Cardiff's *Intifada* (Arabic for 'uprising'), and St Johnstone's *Wendy Who?* (as in 'Oh Wendy Saints go marching in . . .').

Stan Hey, a former *Foul*-mouth, detected 'a commendable sense of fraternity and mutual promotion between all the magazines, as they have realized from the onset that they share common enemies'.[7] In September 1988, there was the sight of Leeds *and* Chelsea supporters joining forces before a match between ostensibly sworn enemies to picket and leaflet Elland Road in the cause of anti-racism.

That magnanimity is not universal, particulary among Scottish fanzines, although the owner of the Edinburgh shop Football Crazy, Alan Cunningham, has spotted 'a lot of cross-loyalties where a fan of one team will buy another club's fanzines'.

For instance, Rangers' *Follow, Follow* called Celtic the 'athletic wing of the IRA' and can not apparently see the contradiction in attacking the barracking of black players and poking fun at the supposed stupidity of their rivals' Irish Catholic supporters, whom they refer to as 'beggars'. Dundee's *Derry Rumba*, a title with sectarian connotations, depicted Dundee United's black striker Raphael Meade with a bone through his nose. *Heartbeat*, produced by Lancashire-based Heart of Midlothian stalwarts, was let down in its debut issue by schoolboy jokes at Hibernian's expense.

In most magazines, fans have found funnier, almost affectionate

7. Stan Hey, op. cit.

ways of expressing traditional antagonisms than saying merely 'We hate the bastards in red/blue/green'. Witness the series run in both *Flashing Blade* and Chesterfield's *Crooked Spireite* entitled 'They Refused To Play For Wednesday'; or the balloon bearing a picture of the Dunfermline manager Jim Leishman given away in the *Falkirk Unofficial Fanzine*, whose editors considered him to be just that – to use the vernacular, a big balloon.

Indeed, the Falkirk publication epitomizes those produced by fans of the middle tier of Scottish clubs, like Kilmarnock, Raith Rovers and Airdrie, which tend to convey greater wit and passion than fanzines devoted to the bigger clubs.

That sense of humour, allied to a cutting edge, is an essential ingredient in the better fanzines. *Brian* ran a series on players' hairstyles alongside critiques of poor facilities at grounds. *Not The View* dealt with the subject of racism in Scottish football and offered a more acceptable object of ridicule, the Rangers player-manager. Taking The Proclaimers' hit song 'Letter from America', it produced a new lyric: 'If you go will you send back/Souness to Sampdoria/Take a look at your full-backs/Two million for absolute crap'. *The Spur* campaigned against ID cards while having fun with Tony Adams's obsession with claiming offside decisions for Arsenal.

Self-mockery is an element in many fanzines. *The Spur* adapted Paul Gascoigne's nickname 'Gazza' to 'Guzzler' in recognition of his eating prowess, and several run 'Best & Worst XI' sections. *When Skies Are Grey* celebrates some of Everton's more embarrassing signings in 'They Gave Us The Blues', *Not The View* has a feature called 'They Embarrassed The Hoops', and *Killie Ken* remembers the 'Chocolate Teapots' (as in 'he's as much use as a . . .') of Kilmarnock.

It is true that many fanzine 'attacks' walk a fine line between irreverence and name-calling. But in the context of the dominant football press – the tabloids' fantasy world of 'now-I-must-tell-all' revelations, verbal sniping, plus fiction masquerading as transfer news, and the sometimes po-faced or pretentious posturing of the broadsheets – they perform the function of a disarmingly blunt antidote.

'Alternative' media are invariably preoccupied with their 'establishment' contemporaries. *Foul* ran some memorable spoofs, of the *Sun*'s shock-horror-probe headline style and of a 'Brian Glanville' report from The Den . . . in Italian. Tabloid pastiches are perhaps overworked in today's fanzines, but *Glenmalure Gazzette* (Shamrock

Rovers) shows that the 'serious' press is still fair game by lampooning a certain controversial pundit as 'Eamon Grumpy'.

The fanzines also help to demystify the notion that 'fans' and 'writers' are, of necessity, breeds apart. (Scottish football journalists, as one of their number noted, are merely fans with typewriters.) There is real merit in many of the contributions herein, though in most cases their authors have neither journalistic training nor experience.

Meanwhile, the fanzine phenomenon shows no sign of burning out. (Its status as such was confirmed in *When Saturday Comes*' 'Your Favourite Over-Used Football Facts' section: alongside 'The Cup is a great leveller' and 'John Barnes never turns it on for England', it told us 'Football fanzines are a phenomenon.') It has even spread to Italy, where *giornali de tifo* have begun to appear.

The bug has bitten other sports, too, and by the Spring of 1989 four Rugby League fanzines were on sale – *The Steam Pig* (Bradford Northern), *Flag Edge Touch* (Hull KR), *The Tangerine Dream* (Chorley Borough) and *The Loiner* (Leeds). The first-named gained instant kudos when the Bradford board banned it from being sold inside their (council-owned) Odsal Stadium.

There is also a self-styled 'alternative' cricket journal, *Sticky Wicket*, which has a full-colour cover and slick design. Rugby Union, as yet, has no fanzines, unless one counts the *Daily Telegraph*.

Andy Lyons, who took over as editor of *When Saturday Comes* when Mike Ticher responded to Chelsea's relegation in 1988 by going to live in Australia, said during the build-up to 1989–90 that he was hearing of new titles each day. His magazine (which curiously never calls itself a 'fanzine') has a full-time staff of four and a word-processor. It has even begun to appear on the shelves of W. H. Smith. So much for street credibility!

When Saturday Comes also demonstrates a marketing awareness which belies its bedsit origins and will probably ensure its survival after some of its rivals and offspring have folded.

It sells T-shirts bearing the magazine's masthead and slogan ('The Half Decent Football Magazine'), produces polished advertising inserts for subscription offers, and organized a trip to watch England in Albania which took the product's name into millions of homes via TV, radio and the press.

Lauded in the quality dailies, doubtless to murmurs of 'sell out' from some provincial scissors-and-paste iconoclasts, it is one of the exceptions to the rule. For every neat, new-tech publication facilitated by the advent of cheap-ish 'desk-top' publishing, like the outstanding *An Imperfect Match* (Arsenal/European football) and *Fortune's Always Hiding* (West Ham), or, from the other end of the football spectrum, Kidderminster's impressive *The Soup*, there are two or three distinctly home-made efforts.

But where do the fanzines go from here? Heading 'upmarket' takes time, money and contacts, so that may not be a viable option for many editors even if they wanted so to do. Most are labours of love anyway, making little or no profit. Those produced by individuals may fall by the wayside as enthusiasm wanes or ideas dry up. Those which involve disparate talents, like the *City Gent*, will surely evolve and, dare one say it, become established.

It may be that saturation point will be reached, both in terms of numbers of publications available and the size of the buying public, after which there would have to be a degree of rationalization.

It is conceivable that regional- rather than club-based fanzines could prosper. The potential audience would, of course, be greater than for productions restricted to one team, although against that must be set the possibility that the inevitable watering down of partisanship might make joint efforts bland.

The success or otherwise of *400 Yards* (Notts County and Nottingham Forest) will be fascinating to observe. Such a format looks a more plausible way forward than the fanzine devoted to two unconnected clubs, of which *UTD United* (West Ham and Dundee United) was an unexpected trailblazer. Incidentally, by issue 2 the latter's co-editors had not even met!

Merger of a different kind would make more sense where more than one fanzine is produced for one club – e.g. Arsenal, Cardiff and Hibernian (four each), West Ham and Charlton (three apiece), or, down the scale, Northwich Victoria (two).

Another possible trend is towards fanzines produced for specific matches, where they can be sold on the terraces, almost as surrogate programmes. *The Memoirs of Seth Bottomley* was shrewdly launched the day Port Vale played host to Wolves before their biggest crowd in a quarter-century. It sent up the phony 'welcome to our visitors' platitudes found in most programmes: 'We thank you for your cash but hope you go home miserable after a good hiding.' There was also a programme-style profile of Steve Bull. *Seth*'s local rival, *The Oatcake*, is produced for every Stoke City home fixture.

City Gent was actually started because of dissatisfaction with the club programme. One cannot help feeling that Bradford City, among others, should now do the decent thing and hand over to their erudite followers. City have made an enlightened start by giving the *Gent*'s editor, Mick Dickinson, a page in the programme in which he plugs fanzines, fraternity and the FSA. How long before the first 'official match-day fanzine'?

A more interesting possibility is that fanzines will evolve into broad-based 'lifestyle' journals taking in music, film, books and other facets of popular culture. *AWOL*, produced by Meadowbank Thistle followers, has built a circulation around twice the club's average gate of 750 with a polished product bristling with record, gig and movie reviews plus pieces on nuclear power and fox-hunting – alongside swipes at Stenhousemuir and Stranraer. It has become essential reading for Edinburgh's renaissance persons, as has *Hull, Hell and Happiness* (Hull City) on north Humberside with a similar cocktail.

AWOL's cartoons are of a particularly high standard, as are those in *Bernard of the Bantams*, an offshoot of *City Gent*. The success of *Viz* suggests there may be a sizeable potential readership for a less parochial football-cartoon magazine.

Talk of music brings us full circle. If 1970s punk fanzines changed little, as Stuart Cosgrove claims, what will historians make of their football successors?

They will record, rightly, that their contribution to punctuation, literacy and the laws of libel was often roughly on a par with Paul Channon's to transport or Mike Channon's to grammar (the latter's gormless TV catchphrase from 1986 is now immortalized in the humour-fanzine *The Lad Done Brilliant*). They will also note, one trusts, that along with the craze for inflatables – notably bananas, rainbow trout, posing as haddock, pink panthers and black puddings – fanzines contributed much towards the game's greater sense of fun and tolerance between the nadir of 1985 and the numbing déjà vu of Hillsborough four years later.

If that were to be their legacy, it would be enough. But there is evidence to suggest that football's new wave really do have the clout to agitate successfully for change. *The Spur* was in the vanguard of a campaign by a group of Tottenham supporters (working under the acronym LOTS – Left On The Shelf) to stop their club, or rather their plc, from destroying the most popular stretch of terracing at White Hart Lane. In March 1989, Tottenham unexpectedly announced concessions which would allow 3,000 supporters to continue to stand on The Shelf. 'Big deal' was a common reaction, but the decision represented a change of heart out of keeping with the club's previous contemptuous attitude.

Later the same day, a packed meeting of Charlton fans heard that after three and a half years' exile at Crystal Palace, their team would soon be going back to the Valley. Lennie Lawrence, the Charlton manager, praised the campaigners' tenacity in classic managerial parlance – 'They got a result' – but perhaps more significantly, the journalist Patrick Collins highlighted the role of 'an excellent alternative magazine [*Voice of the Valley*] dedicated to a return'. Praise indeed from that bastion of 'alternative' values, the *Mail on Sunday*.[8]

It would be facile to suggest, for instance, that Irving Scholar said to his directors: 'Right – *The Spur* has got us by the short and curlies . . . what are we going to offer them?' But the very fact that several top clubs have banned and harassed fanzine-sellers suggests they are aware of the thorn in their sides, and, by implication, of their views. The Leicester University survey found that 34 per cent of fanzine editors described their club's attitude as 'opposed'.

As the 1988–89 season closed amid sadness and anger at the deaths of more 'ordinary supporters' – and, optimistically, implicit recognition by Lord Justice Taylor's Hillsborough inquiry that spectators actually have rights when he gave the FSA equal representation with the FA, clubs and police – it was clear that the fanzine's capacity to get up the appropriate noses was undiminished.

It was not just the big clubs. Grimsby Town officials alerted police to the fact that 'bogus programmes' were being sold (it was *Sing When We're Fishing*); one seller was arrested and detained for twenty minutes while officers muttered about prosecution under the Obscene Publications Act.

And at one leading non-league club, fanzine attacks on the sale of players prompted a rapid response. The editor was instantly banned from the stadium and, he told *The Independent*'s 'Sports Diary', informed that he would be 'buried in the ground' and phoned at

8. Patrick Collins, 'The real identity', *Mail on Sunday*, 26 March 1989.

home when what he describes as 'totally inaccurate allegations about my sexuality' were made! Clearly, the fanzines must be doing something right . . .

Three years after I used the *Guardian*'s 'Soccer Diary' to welcome *Off the Ball*, one of my successors on the column, Stephen Bierley, felt moved to write: 'Fanzines have been one of the delights of football in the past few years, glorious pulsating beacons of irreverence, wit and real information.'[9]

What they prove is that there are people who love the game and see its funny side (and I don't mean the BBC dredging up 'comedian' Stan Boardman every time Liverpool reach Wembley); who are naive enough to believe the clubs in whom they invest emotionally and financially belong to them, and criticize only because they care; who would not sit in an executive-box if they were paid to, because they value the sense of togetherness they feel on the terraces and would not be able to sing their hearts out 'for the lads' behind double glazing; who do not ambush rival fans except with offers of a pint, or make 'monkey' grunts at black players.

If that sounds like you, read on. Better still, write on. If you are wondering when your club will be getting a fanzine, maybe you are missing the point.

Football fanzines are an idea whose time has come. Whose game is it anyway?

from *Whose Game is it, Anyway?*, 1989

World Cup 1990: A Diary
KARL MILLER

An article in *The Independent* of 10 July was headed with these remarkable words: 'Patrick Barclay reflects on a World Cup which was largely lacking in drama, individual dynamism and moments to cherish in the memory.' This is not a description of the World Cup that I have been watching. But it is a good description of the coverage of the football which was offered by Patrick Barclay, by other British journalists, and by experts and commentators who were heard from on television. The

9. Stephen Bierley, 'Mad about the Mariners', *Guardian*, 18 February 1989.

1990 World Cup produced, as it was bound to, its disappointments, patches of dullness and travesties of justice. It was doubtfully regulated and often poorly refereed. But its best stuff was enthralling, and as an occasion in the history of the human race its interest was first-rate. No one team was a match for the Brazilians of 1970 and before, but the Italians were among the most skilful and beautiful sides ever to grace the world game: the true winners of the cup, in my opinion, let down at the last by a lack of aggression and brute force, and of the luck that was so lavishly bestowed elsewhere.

The press and television coverage, pictures apart, measured up to very little of this. At worst, it was meanly patriotic, in a rather twisted sort of way, and even, yes, racist. England was both entitled and unlikely to do well, it could be felt at the outset, and it was a shame and a disgrace when at first they didn't. When matters improved, the tabloids turned their coats and erupted with praise. 'How could our lads play like that?' asked the *Sun* at the beginning. 'They couldn't play, sneered the critics,' said the *Sun* at the end. 'How wrong the world was.' Soccer journalists are different from other critics in that they tend, literally, to know the score, and they are less forthcoming when they don't. Here, in the quality papers I saw, most of the correspondents were unforthcoming both before and after the result. It was a relief to read Hugh McIlvanney in *The Observer* on the Sunday.

Just over a year ago a previous diary of mine had this to say about the young English player Paul Gascoigne, allegedly wayward but already deeply acceptable to the crowd: 'Bobby Robson's team had hardly left the field, after the recent defeat of Albania at Wembley, when he was disparaging the contribution of Paul Gascoigne, who had come on late in the game to score one goal and make another – admittedly, against a beaten side: Gascoigne had been disobedient and had wandered about. Robson seems to like the player, who started out, as he did himself, in the North-East: but there was a wish to put him down . . .' The England manager Bobby Robson was on record as suggesting that Gascoigne was 'daft as a brush'. Those were the days when we were to think that Robson in his maturity was worried about Gascoigne's maturity. The message entered the media in the form of sermons from journalists sympathetic to the manager, as many were not – many were his unscrupulous enemies. For David Lacey of the *Guardian* Gascoigne had a tendency to give away the ball and to be a clown. It was not surprising that his place in the national team remained less than assured. On the eve of the tournament Kenny Dalglish, the Liverpool manager, declared on television that if it was up to him he would not play Gascoigne. Which enables one to say, what with one thing and another, that this World Cup has flashed a light on the psychology of management.

Managers are apt to favour players whom they can control and are sometimes jealous of those with an authority of their own and of those whose claims are pressed. The manager of Italy had not been keen to play Schillaci, soon to be their hero, and the Cameroon manager had wanted, together with the team, to exclude Roger Milla, a subtle player and roasting finisher, now in his thirties, who helped his team to make the first African challenge in the history of the tournament. It was rumoured that the local despot had insisted that the elderly fellow play. Nice one, despot.

England started out in disarray. The news was of big toes needing to be attended to. Bryan Robson had to take his toe home, despite the attentions of a faith healer, flown in from darkest England with the assent of Bobby Robson, who seemed to set himself to give the impression that Bryan was indispensable to the team and that he would have to be dispensed with. 'My heart bleeds for the skipper,' he said. It was as if this individual player mattered more than the team – which was not how he had appeared to feel in the context of Gascoigne's jokes. For the manager the team consisted, as a rule, of 'the lads', whom England expected to do as they were told. I doubt whether there were any lads in the (no less disciplined) Italian team.

As had happened in the past, the team came together when an ailing Bryan Robson was reluctantly removed. England switched to a sweeper system of sorts, long resisted by Bobby Robson, with Wright at the back when he wasn't at inside left, and they played very well for the rest of the tournament. It was possible to feel that it was the players who were playing well, and that Bobby Robson had been left behind to make statements to camera. Gascoigne was more than anyone the secret of their success. By general consent, he was the superlative England player. His detractors in the press did not entirely give up, though: late in the day they were still preoccupied with his development, his potential, his mistakes, his personal shortcomings. Patrick Barclay even managed to jeer at his conduct when he was awarded a yellow card for a legitimate tackle in the semi-final game against West Germany – which England were unlucky to lose, at the penalty shoot-out. The tackled player rolled about in a piece of German theatre that might have earned him a place in Goethe's *Walpurgisnacht*, the German officials sprang to their feet and to the touchline in horror. The card meant that Gascoigne would have been unavailable for the final had England survived, and before the penalties were taken he was seen to weep.

Gascoigne's conduct has exercised a colossal fascination in this country and in others. After the narrow quarter-final victory against Cameroon, he exulted and gave Bobby Robson a kiss. The camera followed the boss as he walked off and was observed to wipe away the kiss. Or he may just have been rubbing his cheek. There was no knowing. But it was difficult not to cherish, at that moment of drama, the thought of the putdowns to which the player had been subjected. His power and invention transfigured England's contribution to the World Cup, and his overflows of feeling were part of it.

He was a highly-charged spectacle on the field of play: fierce and comic, formidable and vulnerable, urchin-like and waif-like, a strong head and torso with comparatively frail-looking breakable legs, strange-eyed, pink-faced, fair-haired, tense and upright, a priapic monolith in the Mediterranean sun – a marvellous equivocal sight. 'A dog of war with the face of a child,' breathed Gianni Agnelli, president of the Italian team Juventus. He can look like god's gift to the Union Jack soccer hooligan, and yet he can look sweet. He neither fouled nor faked; nor did the team, which won the tournament's fair-play award. He is the frog that turns into the prince every move he makes. Many may flinch from his practical jokes and his scuffles outside discos; I'm not sure how well he'd do on *Any Questions* or in the House of Commons; he is sure to suffer from the intensified media build-up and cut-down that awaits him. But at present, in his early twenties, he is magic, and fairy-tale magic at that.

The punishment of his German tackle was one of a number of calamitous misjudgements on the part of referees. The policy on violent play reflected a welcome determination to deter, and it succeeded: this was not a violent World Cup. At the same time, there was gross over-reaction from several referees, too few of whom could tell the difference between a foul and a performance. Too many players were sent off for nothing. Too few of the later games were settled by decent goals. Two episodes stand out: the Rijkaard foul and the Klinsmann fraud. When Holland played Germany, the Dutchman Rijkaard felled Völler and then spat at him, twice. Throughout the episode Völler did nothing except avoid a collision with the Dutch goalkeeper. And yet he was sent off, along with his assailant. In Germany's quarter-final match against Czechoslovakia Klinsmann squeezed between two defenders and tumbled harrowingly, winning a place for his team in the semi-final with the penalty that was awarded. Ron Atkinson, who showed some jolly turns of phrase on television, reported: 'I've just seen Gary shake hands with Klinsmann – it's a wonder Klinsmann hasn't fallen down.' Atkinson, however, was also among the many exponents of the bottle theory, which says that foreigners don't have what it takes, that dusky teams are mentally unsound, dusky goalkeepers suspect on crosses. It was a theory that had to struggle to deal with the evidence presented by Egypt and Cameroon.

Germany were never the team that British scribes made out, and there was some more of their theatre in the miserable final against Argentina, which had its own harrowing diver and roller in Maradona. Argentina finished the final two men down, for disciplinary reasons, but Germany never did manage to beat them. It was fitting that the game should have been decided by a somewhat generous penalty award. The scribes and commentators rarely tired of mentioning Maradona, the 'greatest player in the world', who might or might not be in his cortisoned silver age. He has never, in my view, been the greatest player in the world, and no one else has been either. He still has his tricks, and his broad shoulders, he delivered some inimitable balls, and he badly wanted to win. But he was outclassed in the tournament by a cadre of others, including Hagi of Romania, Baggio of Italy, Milla and Gascoigne.

It was said by an expert that Italy bottled out against Argentina. Their 'temperament' couldn't take the 'pressure', according to Liam Brady – a surprising opinion from an excellent player who had actually played in Italy. The fact is that they *drew* with Argentina, deserved to win, and only lost out at the penalty shenanigan after extra-time. Italy against Uruguay was perhaps the finest game in the Cup. Not for the first time in the history of the game, Uruguay proved a very hard team to beat: this was a tough, intimidating side which contained two or three of the most accomplished players in the tournament and half a dozen of the most cunningly hostile. Italy's victory was a victory for football. But the game gave no joy to the journalist who wrote about it for *The Independent*. The Italians hadn't played, had been anxious and upset. Here, too, they had bottled out. It was just as well that his readers knew the score and might have seen the game for themselves.

from The London Review of Books, 26 July 1990

Taking the City
BILL BUFORD

I knew to follow Sammy. The moment the group broke free, he had handed his bag and camera to someone, telling him to give them back later at the hotel. Sammy then turned and started running backwards. He appeared to be measuring the group, taking in its size.

The energy, he said, still running backwards, speaking to no one in particular, the energy is very high. He was alert, vital, moving constantly, looking in all directions. He had taken to holding out his hands, with his fingers outstretched.

Feel the energy, he said.

There were six or seven younger supporters jogging along beside him, and it would be some time before I realized that there were always six or seven younger supporters jogging along beside him. When he turned in one direction, they turned with him. When he ran backwards, they ran backwards. It verged on the preposterous, and no doubt if Sammy had suddenly become airborne there would be the sight of six or seven younger supporters desperately flapping their arms trying to do the same. The younger supporters were in fact very young. At first I put their age at around sixteen, but they might have been younger. They might have been fourteen. They might have been nine: I take pleasure, even now, in thinking of them as nothing more than overgrown nine-year-olds. They were nasty little nine-year-olds who, in some kind of pre-pubic confusion, regarded Sammy as their dad. The one nearest me had a raw, skinny face with a greasy texture that suggested an order of fish-'n'-chips. He was the one who turned on me.

Who the fuck are you?

I said nothing, and Fish-'n'-chips repeated his question – Who the fuck are you? – and then Sammy said something, and Fish-'n'-chips forgot about me. But it was a warning: the nine-year-old didn't like me.

Sammy had stopped running backwards and had developed a kind of walk-run, which involved moving as quickly as possible without breaking into an outright sprint. Everybody else did the same: the idea, it seemed, was to be inconspicuous – not to be seen to be actually running, thus attracting the attention of the police – but nevertheless to jet along as fast as you could. The effect was ridiculous: 200 English supporters, tattooed torsos tilted slightly forward, arms straight, stiffly hurtling down the pavement, believing that nobody was noticing them.

Everyone crossed the street, decisively, without a word spoken and, as they did, a chant broke out – 'United, United, United' – and Sammy waved his hands up and down, as if trying to bat down flames of a fire, urging people to be quiet. A little later there was another one-word chant: this time, it was 'England' repeated over and over again. They just couldn't help themselves. They wanted so badly to act like normal football supporters – they wanted to sing and behave drunkenly and carry on doing the same rude things that they had been doing all day long – and they had to be reminded that they couldn't. Why this pretence to be invisible? There was Sammy again, whispering, insistent: no singing, no singing, waving his hands up and down. The sixteen-year-olds made a shushing sound to enforce the message.

Sammy said to cross the street again – he had seen something – and his greasy little companions went off in different directions, fanning out, as if to hold the group in place, and then returned to their positions beside him. It was only then that I appreciated fully what I was witnessing: Sammy had taken charge of the group – moment by moment giving it very specific instructions – and was using his obsequious little lads to ensure that his commands were being carried out.

I remember, on my first night with one of the United supporters, hearing that the leaders had their little lieutenants and sergeants. I had heard this and I noted it, but I didn't think much of it: it sounded too much like toy-land, like a military game played by schoolboys. But here, now, I could see that everything Sammy said was being enforced by his entourage of little supporters. Fish-'n'-chips and the other nine-year-olds made sure that no one ran, that no one sang, that no one strayed far from the group, that everyone stayed together.

I trotted along. Everyone was moving at such a speed that, to ensure I didn't miss anything, I concentrated on keeping up with Sammy. I could see that this was starting to irritate him. He kept having to notice me.

What are you doing here? he asked me, after he had turned round again, running backwards, doing a quick head-count after everyone had regrouped.

He knew precisely what I was doing there, and he had made a point of asking his question loudly enough that the others had to hear it as well.

Just the thing, I thought.

Fuck off, one of his runts said suddenly, peering into my face. He had a Stanley knife in his hand. It looked like the one I used at home to chop vegetables.

Didja hear what he said, mate? Fish-'n'-chips had joined the interrogation. He said fuck off. What the fuck are you doing here anyway, eh? Fuck off.

It was not the time or the occasion to explain to Fish-'n'-chips why I was there or what I was hoping to achieve; and, if I had tried, I doubt that the little one would have been interested, even if he had been able to understand it (he didn't convey the strong impression of someone who had yet learned how to read).

I dropped back a bit, just outside of striking range. I looked about me. I didn't recognize anyone. Earlier I had spotted Ricky and Micky and Mark and Guerney, and some others whose names I had never caught or couldn't remember, but at the moment I didn't see any of them. I was surrounded by people I hadn't met. Worse, I was surrounded by people I hadn't met who kept telling me to fuck off. I felt I had understood the drunkenness I had seen earlier in the day. But this was different; the people around me were different. If they were drunk, they were not acting as if they were drunk. They were purposeful and precise, with a very strong quality about them, like some kind of animal scent, of aggression. Nobody was saying a word. There was a muted grunting and the sound of their feet on the pavement and, every now and then, Sammy would whisper one of his commands. In fact the loudest sound had been Sammy's asking me what I was doing there, and the words of the exchange rang round in my head.

What the fuck are you doing here anyway, eh? Fuck off.

What the fuck are you doing here anyway, eh? Fuck off.

I remember thinking in the clearest possible terms: I don't want to get beaten up.

I had no idea where we were, but, thinking about it now, I can see that Sammy must have been leading his group around the stadium, hoping to find Italian supporters along the way. When he turned to run backwards, he must have been watching the effect his group of 200 walk-running Frankensteins was having on the Italian lads, who spotted the English rushing by and started following them, curious, attracted by the prospect of a fight or, more likely, by the charisma of the group itself, unable to resist tagging along to see what might happen.

And then Sammy, having judged the moment to be right, suddenly stopped, and, abandoning all the pretences of invisibility, he shouted: Stop!

Everyone stopped.

Turn!

Everyone turned. They had been waiting for Sammy's commands and knew what to expect. I didn't, however. It was only then that I saw the Italians who had been following behind us. In the half-light, street-light darkness I couldn't tell how many there were, but there were enough for me to realize – holy shit! – that I was now unexpectedly in the middle of a gang fight: having dropped back to get out of the reach of Sammy and his lieutenants I was in the rear, which, as the group turned, had suddenly become the front.

Adrenalin is one of the body's more powerful chemicals, and it must have been the one that coursed through my veins at that moment. Seeing the English on one side of me and the Italians on the other, I remember seeming quickly to take on the properties of a small helicopter, rising several feet in the air and moving out of everybody's way. There was a roar, everybody roaring, and the English supporters charged into the Italians.

And in the next second: I went down. A dark blur and then smack: I got hit on the side of the head by a beer can – a full beer can – thrown powerfully enough to knock me over. As I got up, two policemen, the only two I saw, came rushing past, and one of them clubbed me on the back of the head. Nice touch, I thought, and back down I went. I got up again, and most of the Italians had already run off, scattering in all directions. But many of them had been tripped up before they got away.

Directly in front of me – close enough where I could almost reach out to touch his face – a young Italian, a boy really, had been knocked down. As he was getting up, an English supporter pushed the boy down again, ramming his flat hand against the boy's face. He fell back and his head hit the pavement, the back of it bouncing slightly.

Two other Manchester United supporters appeared. One kicked the boy in the ribs. It was a soft sound, which surprised me. You could hear the impact of the shoe on the fabric of the boy's clothing. He was kicked again – this time very hard – and the sound was still soft, muted. The boy reached down to protect himself, to guard his ribs, and the other English supporter then kicked him in the face. This was a soft sound as well, but it was different: you could tell it was his face that had been kicked and not his body and not something protected by clothing. It sounded gritty. The boy tried to get up and he was pushed back down – sloppily, without much force. Another Manchester United supporter appeared and another and then a third. There were now six of them, and they all started kicking the boy on the ground. The boy covered his face. I was surprised that I could tell, from the sound, when someone's shoe missed or when it struck the fingers and not the forehead or the nose.

I was transfixed. I suppose, thinking about this incident now, I was close enough to have stopped the kicking. Everyone there was off-balance – with one leg swinging back and forth – and it wouldn't have taken much to have saved the boy. But I didn't. I don't think the thought occurred to me. It was as if time had dramatically slowed down, and each second had a distinct beginning and end, like a sequence of images on a roll of film, and I was mesmerized by each image I saw. Two more Manchester United supporters appeared – I think there must have been eight by now. There were so many that it was getting crowded, and it was hard to get at the boy: they were bumping into each other, tussling slightly. It was difficult for me to get a clear view or to say where exactly the boy was now being kicked, but it looked like there were three people kicking him in the head, and the others were kicking him in the body – mainly the rib cage but I couldn't be sure. I am astonished by the detail I can recall. For instance, there was no speech, only that soft, yielding sound – although sometimes it was a gravelly, scraping one – of the blows, one after another. The moments between the kicks seem to increase in duration, to stretch elastically, as each person's leg was retracted and then released again for another blow.

The thought of it: eight people kicking the boy at once. At what point is the job completed?

It went on.

The boy continued to try to cushion the blows, moving his hands around to cover the spot where he had just been struck, but he was being hit in too many places to be able to protect himself. His face was now covered with blood, which came from his nose and from his mouth: it was impossible that he still had all his teeth. His hair was matted and wet, and blood was all over his clothing. The kicking went on. On and on and on, that terrible soft sound, with the boy saying nothing, only wiggling on the ground.

The policeman appeared, but only one. Where were the other police? There had been so many before. Where were they now? The policeman came running hard and knocked over two of the supporters, and the others fled, and then time accelerated, no longer a slow-motion time, but time moving very, very fast.

We ran off. I don't know what happened to the boy – I would like to believe that the policeman's appearance saved him from being seriously disfigured or brain-damaged or whatever else might have resulted from eight lads kicking the boy in the head without a prospect of stopping. As I ran off, I noticed that all around me there were others like that boy, others who had been tripped up and had their faces kicked; I had to side-step a body on the ground to avoid running on top of it.

In the vernacular of the supporters, it had now 'gone off'. With that first violent exchange, some kind of threshold, I would discover, had been crossed, some notional boundary: on the one side of that boundary had been a sense of limits, an ordinary understanding – even among this lot – of what you didn't do; we were now someplace where there would be few limits, where the sense that there were things you didn't do had ceased to exist. It became very violent.

A boy came rushing towards me, holding his head, bleeding pro-fusely from somewhere on his face, watching the ground, not knowing where he was going, and looked up just before he would have run into me. The fact of me frightened him. He thought I was English. He thought I was going to hit him. He screamed, pleading, and spun round backwards to get away. He ran off in a different direction. He had been crying.

I caught up with Sammy. Sammy was transported. He was snapping his fingers and jogging in place, his legs pumping up and down at speed, and repeating the phrase, it's going off, it's going off. Everyone around him was excited. It was an excitement that verged on being a something greater, an emotion more transcendent – joy at the very least, but more like ecstasy. There was an intense energy about it; it was impossible not to feel some of the thrill. Somebody near me said that he was happy. He said that he was very, very happy, that he could not remember ever being so happy, and I looked hard at him, wanting to memorize his face so that I might find him later and ask him what it was that made for this happiness, what was it like. It was a strange thought: here was someone who believed that, at this precise moment, following a street scuffle, he had succeeded in capturing one of life's most elusive qualities. But then he, dazed, babbling away about his happiness, disappeared into the crowd and the darkness.

There was more going on than I could assimilate. There were violent noises constantly – something breaking or crashing – and I could never tell where they were coming from. In every direction something was happening. I have no sense of sequence. The images in my mind are disconnected.

I remember the man with his family. Everyone had regrouped, brought together by the little lieutenants, and was jogging along in that peculiarly styled walk-run, and I noticed directly in front of us was a man with his family, a wife and two sons. He was shooing them along, trying to make them hurry, while looking repeatedly over his shoulder at us. He was anxious, but none of the members of the group seemed to have noticed him: they just carried on, trotting at the same speed, following him not because they wanted to follow him but only because he happened to be running directly in front of us. When the man reached his car, a little off to the side of the path we were following, he threw open the door and shoved the members of his family inside, panicking slightly and badly bumping the head of one of his sons. And then, just as he was about to get inside himself, he looked back over his shoulder – just as the group was catching up to him – and he was struck flatly across the face with a heavy metal bar. He was struck with such force that he was lifted up into the air and carried over his car door on to the ground on the other side.

Why him, I thought? What had he done except make himself conspicuous by trying to get his family out of the way? I turned, as we jogged past him, and the supporters behind me had rammed into the open door, bending it backwards on its hinges. The others followed, running on top of the man on the ground, sometimes slowing down to kick him – the head, the spine, the arse, the ribs, anywhere. I couldn't see his wife and children, but knew they were inside, watching from the back seat.

There was an Italian boy, eleven or twelve years old, alone, who had got confused and ran straight into the middle of the group and past me. I looked behind me and saw that the boy was already on the ground. I couldn't tell who had knocked him down, because by the time I looked back six or seven English supporters had already set upon him, swarming over his body, frenzied.

There was a row of tables where programmes were sold, along with flags, T-shirts, souvenirs, and as the group went by each table was lifted up and overturned. There were scuffles. Two English supporters grabbed an Italian and smashed his face into one of the tables. They grabbed him by the hair on the back of his head and slammed his face into the table again. They lifted his head up a third time, pulling it higher, holding it there – his face was messy and crushed – and slammed it into the table again. Once again the terrible slow motion of it all, the time, not clock-time, that elapsed between one moment of violence and the next one, as they lifted his head up – were they really going to do it again? – and smashed it into the table. The English supporters were methodical and serious; no one spoke.

An ambulance drove past. Its siren made me realize that there were still no police.

The group crossed a street, a major intersection. The group had by now long abandoned the pretences of invisibility and had reverted to the arrogant identity of a mob, walking, without hesitation, straight into the congested traffic, across the bonnets of the cars, knowing that they would stop. At the head of the traffic was a bus, and one of the supporters stepped up to the front of it, and from about 6 feet, hurled something with great exertion and force – it wasn't a rock; it was big and made of metal, like the manifold of a car engine – straight into the driver's windscreen. I was just behind the one who threw this thing. I don't know where he got it from, because it was too heavy to have been carried for any distance, but no one had helped him with it; he had stepped out of the flow of the group and in those moments between throwing his heavy object and turning back to his mates he had a peculiar look on his face. He knew he had done something that no one else had done yet, that it had escalated the violence, that the act had crossed another boundary of what was permissible. He had thrown a missile that was certain to cause serious physical injury. He had done something bad – extremely bad – and his face, while acknowledging the badness of it all, was actually saying something more complex. It was saying that what he had done wasn't all that bad, really; in the context of the day, it wasn't that extreme, was it? What his face expressed, I realized – his eyes seemed to twinkle – was no more than this: I have just been naughty.

He had been naughty and he knew it and he was very pleased about it. He was happy. Another happy one. He was a runt, I thought. He was a little shit, I thought. I wanted to hurt him.

The sensation of this sound, the shattering windscreen – I realize now; I did not realize it at the time – was a powerful stimulant, and it had been the range of sounds, of things breaking and crashing, coming from somewhere in the darkness, unidentifiable, that was steadily increasing the strength of feeling of everyone around me. It was also what was making me so uneasy. The evening had been a series of stimulants, assaults on the senses, that succeeded, each time, in raising the pitch of excitement. And now, crossing this intersection, traffic coming from four directions, supporters trotting on top of cars, the sound of this thing going through the windscreen, the crash following its impact, had the effect of increasing the heat of the feeling: I can't describe it any other way; it was almost literally a matter of temperature. There was another moment of disorientation – the milliseconds between the sensation of the sound and knowing what accounted for it, an adrenalin moment, a chemical moment – and then there was the roar again, and someone came rushing at the bus with a pole (taken from one of the souvenirs tables?) and smashed a passenger's window. A second crashing sound. Others came running over and started throwing rocks and bottles with great ferocity. They were, again, in a frenzy. The rocks bounced off the glass with a shuddering thud, but then a window shattered, and another shattered, and there was screaming from inside. The bus was full, and the passengers were not lads like the ones attacking them but ordinary family supporters, dads and sons and wives heading home after the match, on their way to the suburbs or a village outside the city. Everyone inside must have been covered with glass. They were shielding their faces, ducking in their seats. There were glass splinters everywhere: they would cut across your vision suddenly. All around me people were throwing the rocks and bottles, and I felt afraid for my own eyes.

We moved on.

I felt weightless. I felt nothing would happen to me. I felt that anything might happen to me. I was looking straight ahead, running, trying to keep up, and things were occurring along the dark peripheries of my vision: there would be a bright light and then darkness again and the sound, constantly, of something else breaking, and of movement, of objects being thrown and of people falling.

Is it possible that there were simply no police?

Again we moved on. A bin was thrown through the display-window of a car dealer, and there was another loud crashing sound. A shop: its door was smashed. A clothing shop: its window was smashed, and one or two English supporters lingered behind to loot from the display.

I looked behind me and I saw that a large vehicle had been overturned – was it a lorry? – and that further down the street flames were issuing from a building. I hadn't seen any of that happen: I realized that there had been more destruction than I had been able to take in. There was now the sound of sirens. It was actually many sirens, different kinds, coming from several directions.

The city is ours, Sammy said, and he repeated the possessive, each time with greater intensity: it is ours, ours, ours. He was entranced and wasn't about to notice me or complain about me to his lieutenants, but I was still making a point of not getting too close.

A police car appeared, its siren on – the first police car I had seen since all this began – and it stopped violently in front of the group, trying to cut it off. There was only one car. Where were the others? The police officer threw open his door, but by the time he had got out of his car the group had crossed the street. The police officer shouted after us in Italian, helpless and angry, and then dropped back inside his car, and chased us down, again cutting us off. Once again, the group, in the most civilized manner possible, crossed the street: well-behaved football supporters on their way back to their hotel, flames receding behind us. The policeman returned to his car and drove after us, this time accelerating dangerously, once again cutting off the group, trying, it seemed to me, to knock down one of the supporters, who had to jump out of the way and who was then grabbed by the police officer and hurled against the bonnet, held there by his throat. The police officer was very frustrated. He knew that this group was responsible for the damage he had seen driving from the ground; he knew, beyond all reasonable doubt, that the very lad whose throat was now in his grip had been personally responsible for mayhem of some categorically illegal kind; but the police officer had not personally seen him do it. He hadn't personally seen the group do anything. He had not seen anyone commit a crime. He saw only the results. He kept the supporter pinned there, holding him by the throat, and then in disgust he let him go.

A fire truck passed, an ambulance, and finally the police – and the police in plentitude. They came from two directions. And once they started arriving, they didn't stop arriving. There were vans and cars and motorcycles and paddy wagons. And still they came. The buildings were illuminated by their flashing blue lights. But the group of supporters from Manchester, governed by Sammy's whispered commands, simply kept moving, slipping past the cars, dispersing when needing to disperse, and then regrouping, turning this way, that way, crossing the street again, regrouping, reversing, with Sammy's greasy little lieutenants bringing up the rear, keeping everyone together. They were well-behaved fans of the sport of football. They were once again the law-abiding supporters they had always insisted to me that they were. And, thus, they snaked through the streets of the ancient city of Turin, making their orderly way back to their hotels, the police following behind, trying to keep up.

'We did it,' Sammy declared, as the group, now exhausted, reached the rail station. 'We took the city.'

from *Among the Thugs*, 1991

Match of the Day
MARTIN AMIS

'Are you going to the match?'

Both men supported Queen's Park Rangers, the local team, and for years had been shuffling off to Loftus Road on Saturday afternoons. In fact they might have come across each other earlier, but this had never been likely: Guy stood in the terraces, with his pie and Bovril, whereas Keith was always to be found with his flask in the stands.

'They're away today,' said Keith through his cigarette. 'United, innit. I was there *last* week.'

'West Ham. Any good?'

Some of the light went out in Keith's blue eyes as he said, 'During the first half the Hammers probed down the left flank. Revelling in the space, the speed of Sylvester Drayon was always going to pose problems for the home side's number 2. With scant minutes remaining before the half-time whistle, the black winger cut in on the left back and delivered a searching cross, converted by Lee Fredge, the East London striker, with inch-perfect precision. After the interval Rangers' fortunes revived as they exploited their superiority in the air. Bobby Bondavich's men offered stout resistance and the question remained: could the Blues translate the pressure they were exerting into goals? In the seventy-fourth minute Keith Spare produced a pass that split the visitors' defence, and Dustin Housely rammed the equalizer home. A draw looked the most likely result until a disputed penalty decision broke the deadlock five minutes from the final whistle. Keith Spare made no mistake from the spot. Thus the Shepherd's Bush team ran out surprise 2–1 winners over the . . . over the outfit whose theme tune is "I'm Forever Blowing Bubbles".'

. . . Guy said, 'The new boy in midfield, Neil . . . ? Did he do alright?'

'Noel Frizzle. He justified his selection,' said Keith coldly.

from *London Fields*, 1989

The Same Old Thing
PETE DAVIES

[Interviews with Chris Waddle, Bobby Robson and John Barnes during the World Cup Finals, 1990]

Now Waddle and Barnes sat in the foyer of the Novotel, and complained articulately about 'the same old thing'.

'We aren't being allowed to get in their half enough – so we're playing like full backs. And we've said that, in so many words – and he probably understands now.'

So would they go out and attack?

'Hope so,' said Waddle. 'He's not said the team yet, so I don't know if I'm in it.'

He said, 'We've got to have a licence. They don't say to Baggio or Hagi or Gullit, we want you back defending. They don't say to Völler or Littbarski or Klinsmann or Scifo, you can't run about, stick in your zone. They go where they want, they make options. Even against Holland, we didn't stick at it long enough – after half an hour I'm back cancelling out their right back. So we end up with three centre-halves, two full backs pushed in, and goalie makes six. Two midfield men makes eight; me and Barnesy run back too, that's ten men defending – and then they say we can't attack. Of course we can't, we're 70 yards from goal . . . and they want us to go zip-zip-zip all the time – but with three men on us?

'The trouble is,' he then said about Robson, 'he's not used to it. He's used to thinking 4–4–2, he's used to thinking English English English – and he's worried about people not doing what they're used to doing. But we need the freedom . . . I'll tell you, and Gazza said this – one of the first sensible things he's said – it should start, systems like we want, when you're young. But you go to county trials, you watch (and the way he said this suggested bitter experience), the guy'll name the biggest squad. Always the biggest – not the best.'

Barnes said, 'You look at England Schoolboys, they're bigger than everybody else. And they might win, because they're stronger – but when the little French or Italian kids grow up they're better, aren't they? And where's your advantage then?'

'In the English First Division,' said Waddle, 'you can play 4–4–2 'cos they all do. But this is the world here – and if I was the England manager (a thought that made him laugh) I wouldn't play that. I'd play 3–5–2. And defenders defend, attackers attack – because to be perfectly honest, we've got the players in this squad who can win this thing. Back, middle, front, we've got it all. And everybody can see it, all the players can see it . . . but at the end of the day, there's a man employed to pick the team. Not us. We can have our little point of view – but at the end of the day, he might not have listened to a word I've said. Like, "It's my team, I pick it." And sure, a manager lives by results – but how many games have we won *away*? 0–0 in Sweden – they played 4–4–2 as well, and was that a boring game, or what? And then Poland, they didn't play 4–4–2 – and they played us off the park. And now here – you're not in your home yard here, are you? Take Scotland – sure, they've gone home – but I was pleased to see them try to play continental. The system wasn't quite right, but who did they beat? Sweden – and what do Sweden play? Then their other two games, they were unlucky – but I bet if you talk to a Scottish player he'll tell you, cor, you get some freedom playing this. See, the only effective 4–4–2 is Ireland – and will they win the World Cup? People said Ireland–Holland was class, so I got a video and watched it – and how was that a great game? And people say Ireland played – but first half, Holland played them off the park. It was pure power that got them back, that's all. Romania'll be thinking after twenty minutes this afternoon, *what is this?* Me, against Ireland – I never dreamt in my life I'd end up standing on my own 18-yard line chesting it down, then just booting it upfield – and afterwards I thought, *what am I doing?* At least if we weren't caught between two stools and just played out-and-out 4–4–2 really hard, the ball'd be hefted up and we might get it free upfield like Sheedy does, or like Barnesy did at Watford . . . but us, it's rigid instructions. Look at Brazil – was Alemao sitting? Was Valdo sitting? Dunga sits, Dunga's the anchor, Dunga's the axe-lad – the others go where they want. At Marseilles it's the same – Tigana sits, me, Papin, Francescoli, we move. But us, we get shown on a bit of paper, more or less – "this is where I want you to play, this position, this role." He'll never say, "You're here, run there, run back and get it, go left, go right, come in, go wide." And the

Belgians – they're a good attacking side. There's so much movement, so many options. Scifo's centre-mid, left, right, forward . . .'

Then he stopped, run right out of his steam and tension. He said, 'But who's to say I'm right? Every system's there to be beat – and it's all opinions, isn't it? That's why it's such a great game . . . anyway, people might say I'm making excuses. I mean, your book'll end up making like I'm knocking the English game – but it's effective, club level. It's just, at world level . . .'

He said, 'I always like watching Ireland, 'cos it's always interesting to see how the other side cope. I wonder if Jack'd play like that if he was the England manager – be interesting, wouldn't it? Though God knows what the crowd'd think.'

We went back to talking about the time we'd been away now; he was missing his daughter, who'd turned two in May – I was missing my son, Joe, who'd been six months on the day I left home.

'He says, what's six weeks away? People were away five years in the war.' Then Waddle grinned and said, 'But they didn't have to play 4–4–2 in the war, did they?'

Robson took Waddle outside, and asked him how he felt. Was he tired? Could he play like he had against, say, the Italians in November? Waddle said he could.

So Robson said, well, do, 'cos I'm playing you. 'Cos people like you and Barnes can win this game . . .

When they came back in Robson called me over, and we went up to his room to watch the first half of Ireland–Romania. He said of the Romanians, 'Bet they pick up a lot of injuries, these lot. The Irish don't half get into you.'

He had injury worries of his own; Lineker's toe was still painful, but improving – and Des Walker, who'd had his leg clattered again by an Egyptian, would worry him right up to the moment he announced his team.

What had it been like, I asked, to leave out Butcher against Egypt?

'Very, very tough. But it had to be done, there's no sentiment – I know what it meant to him, what he's done for us – but sentiment, that can get you unstuck, I couldn't afford it. And he took it so brilliant, he's such a good man – he took it on the chin. He's an example to others. He said, that's fine, it's your decision. I asked him how many caps he'd got – seventy-four. So I said, we must get you the seventy-fifth. Oh, don't worry about that, he says – I'm grateful to get seventy-four.'

About his reasons for dropping him he said, 'We played against Holland with three centre-halves. But against Egypt we'd be over-loaded doing that, it'd be three on one, so we went back to 4–4–2. And some people have this stupid opinion it's outdated – but AC Milan play it, Belgium play it – it's a very good system. Is Liverpool Football Club outdated? In Europe next season, how would they play. Some clever concoction? When people talk to me, it's outdated – are they talking about Liverpool?'

He talked fast, with his mouth tight and angry. If Barnes and Waddle, I suggested, had a little more freedom . . .

'It's down to the player, it's not down to the system. It's tougher here, it's harder, there are no loopholes, there are no bad players on the pitch. There are bad players in the First Division, there are bad players in France – but these are the best out here. Take Egypt – those are the best eleven players in Egypt. And I tell them to play like they play for their clubs – but sometimes better players don't let them. And yes, they've got jobs to do, to get past people and put crosses in, to get in scoring positions – but they've got a duty to the team too. They've got to make defensive runs. So these free roles . . . free to do what? Free to disappear from the game? Free to always be in space? If you're a good player and you go free, they'll mark you. Look, I can demand, encourage, motivate – and if that doesn't work, I can leave 'em out. Drop 'em. People expect the manager . . . but at the end of the day it's up to the players, isn't it? What d'you fuckin' pay them for? You can't control them by remote control, can you? You can't sit there with the little buttons saying go there, tackle, go there, press, drop back, pass him . . .'

John Barnes wasn't a happy man either.

The *Mirror*'d run a groundless and hurtful piece of cod psychologi-cal claptrap about him, that suggested he didn't turn it on for England because his mum used to whack him when he was a kid.

So, I asked, was John Barnes disturbed?

'Disturbed by the fucking press, I tell you.'

He'd done an interview for some offbeat Channel 4 programme a while back, and they'd tried to speculate in it that because of the way he was brought up, he was spoilt. He'd said no – if he was naughty, his mum used to slap him like any other kid. So the *Mirror*'d got hold of this, and turned it into, 'MUM'S BEATINGS STILL HAUNT JOHN'.

'They call it a secret video, I mean, really – if you'd have watched Channel 4 you'd have seen it. But that's how ridiculous the whole thing's got. You know that stupid story about the girl – I don't even know what she looks like. Most of the players don't. And they talk about, "at an official disco players mingled with the hostesses" – there's been no official disco bloody anywhere, we've just stayed right here. But it's been dominating our World Cup, this stuff, unfortunately – and it's a stupid situation. Just stupid.'

So I said, let's talk about football. Did he enjoy the Dutch game?

'I enjoyed the first sixty minutes. After that they took Chris off. For the first half-hour Chris had a free role, inside right, right wing, wherever he wanted, and I was playing down the middle – and we were causing them a lot of problems. But since we didn't have a left winger, their right back was going forward a lot, unmarked. Now he wasn't causing us that much trouble – but they thought he was, so they moved Chris out left to stop his runs, which was ridiculous. To put Chris out there just to run up and down with this right back and stop him playing, rather than thinking, we're causing them more problems than they are us. Chris's threat was nullified. Then when they took Chris off they put me out there, and my threat was nullified, then it's me just running up and down – and that's not my game. But it's the same old thing. For the first half-hour it was brilliant, I was in a position where I could get involved, and run around, and Chris was free – but rather than being positive and saying, OK, if we're going to have a man free, then they're going to have someone free too, so be it – I mean, you can't have it all ways, you can't have men free, and have all their men marked too . . .'

The manager's too cautious?

'He was in that instance. I think so, anyway, definitely. We could have done more going forward. We still had a spare man at the back, so even if the right back did go forward, there was someone there to deal with it. He was running into a position where all he was going to do was cross, he wasn't going to score. And you've got to realize that teams are going to get crosses in against you, they're going to get free men – but we should have free men too, rather than saying, because he's free you've got to mark him.'

The manager holds you back?

Barnes stumbled for a moment. 'No, not necess . . . it's just, not . . . not physically. Not . . . I don't think he means to. But I just feel . . . I feel the way we're asked to play definitely does. Like Ireland, for example, me and Chris were coming back on Ray Houghton and Kevin Sheedy – and a few instances I was looking at us when we're under pressure and I'm thinking, we've got the goalkeeper and nine players defending here – and Gary Lineker isolated up front. And you don't help yourself like that, do you?'

I asked one more time about the trouble with Barnesy – did he play less well for his country than his club?

'What I said still stands – even more so now. Look at the Holland game. We're causing problems, and all of a sudden . . . see, had it been the other way round, after thirty minutes I'd have gone to mark the right back. And the rest of the match I'd have been running up and down. But Chris had to do it – so at least I enjoyed sixty, seventy minutes of it. But after that I was just marking, basically.'

He said, 'Take Gary Lineker. His game's about scoring goals. So if he doesn't get a chance to score, you can't criticize him – because whatever else he might be doing, he's not in the team to do that, he's not in the team to be beating three players, or to be tackling back and chasing. He's in the team to score goals. Give him a chance, and he'll score. But me, I'm in the team to create chances, and to do things going forward. And if I'm not given the opportunity to do that, I'm not going to be effective. I'm not in the team to . . . well, as it turns out, that's what I have been doing, tracking back with the right back. But if that's the way the games are going to go . . .'

And the trouble with Barnesy came down to the crunch.

He said, if that was the way it was going to go, 'I think we'd be better off to play someone else in that position, if he's going to run up and down with the full back. It's like asking Gary Lineker to do it. You might as well not have him in the side. And you might as well not have me in the side, if that's all that's going to happen. Like I've said, if a cross comes in, or a ball comes through, there's only one person can clear it out. So how many defenders do we need?'

And how clear can it get? He was, I said, unhappy.

'Yes.' Long pause. 'I'm unhappy with the job I'm asked to do.'

from *All Played Out*, 1990

Acknowledgements

For permission to reprint copyright material the publishers gratefully acknowledge the following:

A. J. AYER: 'Cock a Double Do' from *New Statesman*, May 12, 1961 © New
Statesman, 1961, by permission of *New Statesman & Society*; MARTIN AMIS:
'Match of The Day' from *London Fields* (Cape, 1989) by permission of
Random Century Ltd; DON DAVIES: 'The Off-sider' and 'Chapman's
Arsenal' from *Don Davies – 'An Old International'* by Jack Cox (Stanley Paul,
1962) by permission of Random Century Ltd; PETE DAVIES: 'The Same Old
Thing' from *All Played Out* (Heinemann, 1990) by permission of Octopus
Publishing Group plc; HUNTER DAVIES: 'A Present for the Wife' from *The
Glory Game* (Weidenfeld & Nicolson, 1972) Copyright © Hunter Davies,
1972, by permission of Sheil Land Associates Ltd; SEBASTIAN FAULKS:
'Pretty Bubbles' from 'Upton and Other Parks' in *Saturday's Boys* (Willow
Books/Harper Collins, 1990) by permission of Harper Collins Publishing
Ltd; PAUL GARDNER: 'Blackpool v. Bolton Wanderers: The Cup Final, 1953'
from *The Simplest Game* (Little, Brown & Co/Sportsman's Library, 1976) by
permission of Little, Brown & Co; GEOFFREY GREEN: 'The Match of the
Century' (I), from *The Times*, November 26, 1963 © Times Newspapers Ltd,
1963, by permission of Times Newspapers Limited; 'The Munich Disaster,
1958' from *There's Only One United* (Hodder & Stoughton, 1978) by per-
mission of David Higham Associates Ltd; 'George Best' from *Pardon Me For
Living* (Allen & Unwin, 1985) by permission of Harper Collins Publishers
Ltd; DAVE HILL: 'The White Nigger' and 'The Cup Final, 1988' from *Out
of his Skin: The John Barnes Phenomenon* (1989), by permission of Faber and
Faber Limited; BARRY HINES: 'Mr Sugden' from *A Kestrel for a Knave*
(Michael Joseph, 1968) © 1968 by Barry Hines, by permission of
Michael Joseph Ltd; ARTHUR HOPCRAFT: 'Bobby Charlton' and 'The
Soccer Conspiracy Case' from *The Football Man: People and Passion in Soccer*
(Collins, 1968) by permission of Harper Collins Publishers Ltd; HANS
KELLER: 'The Brazilians, 1970', from *The Listener*, June 11 and 18, 1970, by
permission of Listener Publications Limited; FRANK KEATING: 'Goalies'
from *Long Days, Late Nights* (Robson, 1984), by permission of Robson Books
Ltd; JAMES KELMAN: 'Side by Side' from *A Disaffection* (Secker & Warburg,
1989) by permission of Octopus Publishing Group plc and Farrar, Strauss &
Giroux Inc; HUGH MCILVANNEY: 'The World Cup Final, 1966' from *The
Observer*, July 31, 1966, 'Even Scots Had Tears in their Eyes' from *The
Observer*, June 21, 1970, 'Jock Stein: a Hero Worshipped by His People' from
The Observer, September 15 1985 © *The Observer*, 1966, 1970 and 1985 by

permission of The Observer Ltd; KARL MILLER: 'World Cup 1990: A Diary' from *The London Review of Books* Vol 12, No 14, July 26, 1990, by permission of *The London Review of Books*; BARRY NORMAN: 'Three Managers' from *The Observer*, October 1, 1972, October 15, 1972 and October 29, 1972, © *The Observer*, 1972 by permission of The Observer Ltd; FRANK NORMAN: 'Inside Forwards' from *Bang to Rights* (Secker & Warburg, 1958) by permission of Aitken & Stone Ltd; GEORGE ORWELL: 'The Sporting Spirit' from *Tribune*, December 14, 1945, by permission of Tribune Publications Ltd; HAROLD PINTER: 'Away' from *The Dumb Waiter: A Play in One Act* (Faber, 1991) by permission of Faber and Faber Limited; J. B. PRIESTLEY: 'Saturday in Bruddersford' from *The Good Companions* (Heinemann, 1929) by permission of Octopus Publishing Group plc, and The Peters, Fraser & Dunlop Group; ALAN ROSS: 'Stanley Matthews' Copyright © by Alan Ross, 1958, by permission of the author; COLIN WELLAND: 'How We Taught the Turks the Meaning of Worship' from *The Observer*, September 17, 1972 © *The Observer*, 1972, by permission of The Observer Ltd; GORDON WILLIAMS: 'Stuck in' from *From Scenes Like These* (Secker & Warburg, 1968), by permission of Curtis Brown & John Farquharson, London.

Faber and Faber Limited apologize for any errors or omissions in the above list and would be grateful to be notified of any corrections that should be incorporated in the next edition or reprint of this volume.